Of human bondage and divine grace : a global testimony

12/8

10

OF HUMAN BONDAGE AND DIVINE GRACE

A Global Testimony

Edited by
JOHN ROSS CARTER

Open Court
La Salle, Illinois 61301

First printing 1992

Printed and bound in the United States of America.

Library of Congress Cataloging-in-Publication Data

Of human bondage and divine grace : a global testimony / John Ross Carter, editor.
p. cm.
Includes bibliographical references and index.
ISBN 0-8126-9170-9 (cloth). — ISBN 0-8126-9171-7 (paper)
1. Salvation—Comparative studies. 2. Man (Theology)—Comparative studies. I. Carter, John Ross.
BL476.03 1992
291.2'2—dc20 92-38704
CIP

For
V. A. DEVASENAPATHI
MARIE A. KOCH
KENNETH W. MORGAN
and in memory of
M. HOLMES HARTSHORNE

Contents

Contributors xi

Preface xiii

1. Our Human Setting according to Śaiva Siddhānta 1
Maheswari M. Arulchelvam

2. The Impurities 11
Maheswari M. Arulchelvam

3. Spiritual Ignorance 23
Maheswari M. Arulchelvam

4. The Liberated One and God 37
Maheswari M. Arulchelvam

5. The Gift Immutable 47
Maheswari M. Arulchelvam

6. *Karma, Bhaktiyoga,* and Grace in the Śrīvaiṣṇava Tradition: Rāmānuja and Kūraṭṭāḻvāṉ 57
Vasudha Narayanan

7. BONDAGE AND GRACE IN THE ŚRĪVAIṢṆAVA TRADITION: PIḶḶAI LŌKĀCĀRYA AND VEDĀNTA DEŚIKA 75
Vasudha Narayanan

8. THE PATH IS NOT *MY* WAY 95
John Ross Carter

9. EMPTINESS ABOUNDING 107
John Ross Carter

10. WHEN BROKEN TILES BECOME GOLD 123
Taitetsu Unno

11. INTERLUDE: THE WAY OF THE *KAMI* 145
John Ross Carter

12. ANCIENT GREEK RELIGION AND THE GOD OF HUMANITY 155
John Efstratios Rexine

13. A JEWISH VIEW OF BLESSING 171
Peter Ochs

14. OUR RELATIONSHIP WITH GOD, THE MERCIFUL 187
Muhammad Abdul-Rauf

15. GRACE IN THE GREEK ORTHODOX CHURCH 207
John Efstratios Rexine

16. GRACE AND SALVATION IN THE PROTESTANT TRADITION 227
Joyce Irwin

17. THE SACRAMENTAL LIFE OF CHRIST IN US 241
Leonard Kotzbauer

18. INCARNATION: INTERACTION AS A MEANS OF GRACE 251
Patricia Dutcher-Walls

19. GRACE IN THE PASTORAL MINISTRY 265
Vernon H. Ross

20. OF HUMAN BONDAGE AND DIVINE GRACE 275
M. Holmes Hartshorne

A POSTSCRIPT 291
John Ross Carter

GLOSSARY 295
INDEX 317

Contributors

Since the January Special Studies Program at Colgate University in 1981, some of the contributors have changed institutional contexts in which they have carried on their lives of scholarship and of service; in those cases, we list their positions formerly, at the time of the Special Studies Program, and their current positions.

Dr. Muhammad Abdul-Rauf

Formerly Director of the Islamic Center, Washington, D. C.; currently President, American Islamic Research Institute

Maheswari Manonmanie Arulchelvam

Formerly a post-doctoral visiting fellow at the Center for the Study of World Religions, Harvard University; currently Senior Lecturer in Sanskrit in the Department of Classical Languages, University of Peradeniya, Sri Lanka

John Ross Carter

Professor of Philosophy and Religion, Director of Chapel House, Director of the Fund for the Study of the Great Religions, Colgate University

Rev. Ms. Patricia Dutcher-Walls

Formerly Instructor in Philosophy and Religion, Assistant Chaplain, Colgate University; currently Th.D. Candidate, Graduate Theological Union, minister of the Presbyterian Church (USA)

M. Holmes Hartshorne

Formerly Harry Emerson Fosdick Professor of Philosophy and Religion Emeritus, Colgate University

JOYCE IRWIN

Research Assistant, Department of Philosophy and Religion, Colgate University

REV. LEONARD KOTZBAUER

Formerly Catholic Chaplain to the Newman Community at Colgate University; currently Pastor, St. John's Church, Liverpool, New York

VASUDHA NARAYANAN

Formerly a post-doctoral visiting fellow at the Center for the Study of World Religions, Harvard University; currently Professor of Religion, University of Florida, Gainesville

PETER OCHS

Formerly Assistant Professor of Philosophy and Religion, Counselor to Jewish Students, Colgate University; currently Wallerstein Associate Professor of Jewish Studies, Drew University

JOHN EFSTRATIOS REXINE

Charles A. Dana Professor of the Classics Emeritus, Colgate University

REV. VERNON H. ROSS

Pastor Emeritus, First Baptist Church, Hamilton, New York

TAITETSU UNNO

Jill Ker Conway Professor of Religion, Smith College

Preface

This volume is the result of a January Study Program held at Colgate University, Hamilton, New York in 1981. The course was designed to lead persons to begin a process of reflecting upon the testimony of humankind, globally considered, about an interpretation of life as it is experienced in its present existential context, both in an awareness of bondage and of grace. The subject is hardly exhausted within the scope of the lectures presented here.

No attempt has been made to do exhaustive comparative lexical studies on the historical development of terms in the several languages involved and whether those terms carry an exact equivalence with the English words "bondage" and "grace." Nor have there been sustained theological investigations in an historical rubric. Our contributors were given the title of the course, "Of Human Bondage and Divine Grace," and were asked to address it from within their particular perspectives. Those of us who are Jews or Muslims and those of us who are at home with Shinto will find that "bondage" and "divine grace" are not automatically part of one's working vocabulary as one attempts to speak about central dimensions of meaning in one's life.

Obviously, not every major intellectual movement or theological development could be addressed in this study: one should not fail to note the absence of a consideration of our theme from the point of view of the most noble strand of the humanistic tradition of the West or the absence of lectures focusing carefully on current interpretations of what constitutes "liberation theology" and "feminist theology." At the same time, humanists of the grand mold will find companions within these pages, and liberation theologians will recognize the foundational nature of the considerations here presented.

All of our contributors prepared their presentations for the undergraduate classroom. The lectures were first recorded, then transcribed, then sent to each contributor for revision. The request was made, however, that each contributor try to maintain the structure of the presentation as it was originally given to college-age young men and women.

Bondage is not a subject frequently addressed today in the United States, nor is grace, for that matter. Somewhere between a current theological preoccupation with hermeneutics—how one can really interpret anything—and a continuing philosophical praxis of analyses of propositions—how one can really say something—an intellectual paralysis has arisen. It is possible, yet, that comparative studies and developmental depth psychology might contribute to turning our attention once again to the great considerations that have permeated our human experience and have graced our human existence.

We turned to the theme "Of Human Bondage and Divine Grace" and chose to introduce this by beginning with an Indian testimony shared by men and women who participate in a religious tradition known as Śaiva Siddhānta. Diligent students would not miss the overwhelming celebration of grace that forms the core of the witness that in turn has formed the Śaiva Siddhānta tradition. Those same students would quickly understand the context of the notion of bondage that is remembered in the Śaiva Siddhānta heritage. Having come to understand the theme in that setting, one can readily see the point of those in the Śrívaiṣṇava tradition and the affirmation of others, including Protestant reformers. Hence, students in a classroom in upstate New York sought first to understand persons living on the other side of the globe in order to become prepared to understand their closer neighbors, with the subsequent realization that we are all participants in one global religious history, becoming ever increasingly neighbors all.

We had planned on having Professor V. A. Devasenapathi, former Director of the Sarvepalli Radhakrishnan Institute for the Advanced Study of Philosophy, University of Madras and among whose works is *Of Human Bondage and Divine Grace* (Tirupapuliyur, India: Saraswathi Press for Annamalai University, 1963),[1] join us for the course, to launch us into our theme. So intense was his loving concern for the health of two members of his family that his own failing health, at the last moment, made it necessary for us to cancel plans to have him with us. We are especially grateful to Dr. M. M. Arulchelvam, who was then a post-doctoral visiting fellow at the Center for the Study of World Religions, Harvard University, a scholar well-versed in the work of Professor Devasenapathi, and a specialist in Śaiva Siddhānta, for responding to our invitation and for her important role in working with Colgate students.

It was not possible for our contributors to attend all lectures during the month. For the most part, they were able to find only enough time to prepare their lectures and to give them. The editor here expresses his thanks and admiration for these kind persons and good colleagues who took on that additional load, somehow to find the time, somehow to commit their minds in the patient act of teaching. Although this volume is not the result of a workshop, where each contributor has heard the work of the others and has revised his or her work subsequently, or of a symposium in which each contributor is aware of the presentations offered by the others, the degree of coherence is striking.

The editor wishes to thank Maxine Campbell, Elizabeth H. Davey, and Joan Kokoska who, with remarkable patience, have transcribed these lectures into chapters and, in their customary scrupulous work, contributed significantly to the appearance of this volume. Many thanks also go to Marie A. Nardi for help in the preparation of the index for this volume.

This volume is dedicated to four persons, without whom the lectures, the classroom experiences, and now the published copy would not have fallen into place:

Professor V. A. Devasenapathi did not so much give us the theme of the course, which is hardly new, as he has made it patently clear, in his scholarship and in his life, that testimonies of lives of grace are eminently worth studying and worth sharing;

Professor Kenneth W. Morgan, Professor of Religion emeritus, Colgate University, sterling interpreter of the religious traditions of humankind, who had the vision over three decades ago to provide a means for Hindus, Buddhists, and Muslims also to present their views and interpretations of life to English readers,[2] made it possible for the Fund for the Study of the Great Religions of the World and the endowment for Chapel House to be established at Colgate. He served as the first director of the Fund and as the first director of Chapel House from 1959–1974. Professor Morgan also made it possible for Professor Devasenapathi to visit Colgate in the spring of 1973, when he and the editor first met. The Special Studies Program was sponsored by the Fund for the Study of the Great Religions of the World, Colgate University;

Marie A. Koch, who was Resident Supervisor at Chapel House on the campus of Colgate University, had through seventeen years served as hostess to Chapel House guests from all over the world. In her quiet way of attending to the needs of guests, of being a support for students, she was an important part of the Special Studies Program of which this volume is one expression;

Professor M. Holmes ("Steve") Hartshorne, Harry Emerson Fosdick Professor of Philosophy and Religion emeritus, Colgate University, is no longer with us to see his chapter appear in published form. An insightful author[3] and master teacher who left the healing imprint of his thinking on the hearts of generations of men and women, Professor Hartshorne cheerfully accepted the editor's invitation and found the time and summoned the energy, while writing on several other subjects and working on other projects during his retirement, to return once again to the classroom and to provide the last chapter of this book.

JOHN ROSS CARTER

NOTES

[1]This book by Professor Devasenapathi was required reading for the first part of the course. Professor Devasenapathi is aware of our indebtedness for the first part of the title of his book, of our course, and of this book, to W. Somerset Maugham. Maugham himself acknowledged his own indebtedness for this well-known title to Spinoza when he wrote, "I chose finally the name of one of the books in Spinoza's *Ethics* and called it *Of Human Bondage*" ("Foreword" to *Of Human Bondage* in *Mr. Maugham Himself* by W. Somerset Maugham, selected by John Beecroft [Garden City, New York: Doubleday & Company, Inc., 1954], p. 2). Reference is to the fourth part of Spinoza's work, variously rendered as "Of Human Bondage or of the Strength of the Affects, " as in *Ethic: Demonstrated in Geometrical Order*, translated from the Latin of Benedict de Spinoza by W. Hale White and revised by Amelia Hutchinson Stirling, 2nd edition (London: T. Fisher Unwin, 1894), p. 176, and as "Of Human Bondage; or of the Strength of the Emotions," in *Ethics* by Benedict de Spinoza, translated and edited, with an Introduction, by James Gutmann (New York: Hafner Publishing Co., 1949), p. 187.

[2]Professor Morgan edited the following companion volumes: *The Religion of the Hindus* (New York: The Ronald Press Company, 1953), *The Path of the Buddha* (New York: The Ronald Press Company, 1956), and *Islam the Straight Path—Islam Interpreted by Muslims* (New York: The Ronald Press Company, 1958). All three of these titles have now been reissued by Motilal Banarsidass, New Delhi, India.

[3]*The Promise of Science and the Power of Faith* (Philadelphia: Westminster Press, 1958); *The Faith to Doubt: A Protestant Response to Criticisms of Religion* (Englewood Cliffs, New Jersey: Prentice-Hall, Inc., 1963); and his last volume, published posthumously, *Kierkegaard: Godly Deceiver—The Nature and Meaning of His Pseudonymous Writings* (New York: Columbia University Press, 1990).

1

Our human setting according to Śaiva Siddhānta

M. M. Arulchelvam

Śaiva Siddhānta is one of the many religious strands that has been differentiated and preserved by men and women living in India. Focusing on Śiva as loving Lord, one seeks to prostrate oneself at his feet. Śaiva Siddhānta means, roughly and very generally, "the culmination or finality in perfection that pertains to Śiva" and carries the extended meaning of "the ideal, final, and well-established culmination of human existence that is pervasively qualified by the agency of Śiva."

This tradition has flourished in South India, particularly among those whose mother tongue was and is Tamil. Persons living within this tradition have tended to be introduced to the initial perspective through the moving, poetic hymns left to us by the saintly *nāyaṉmārs* ("precursors" or "leaders"). These Śaivite Tamil hymns, collected as early as the tenth century, have attained a great significance in Śaiva Siddhānta, which, as a separate movement, dates roughly from the thirteenth century.

In beginning our study of human bondage and divine grace, it will be necessary for us to attempt to define the subject. The phrase "human bondage" implies that we, as we are, are less free than we should have been. It could also imply that there was a time when we were free. It certainly means, religiously, that we could be free, that a state of freedom, of liberation, is possible for human beings. So existence in this world seems to be an intermediate or temporary period between a state when we were free and a state when we will be free.

The subject raises the questions: What was it that brought about this bondage? Whence came this bondage? To what extent is the human will involved in this bondage? Was it of choice? Was it of necessity? What does being in bondage mean to a human being? How does it affect us? How does it circumscribe us? And, granted that one is in bondage, the subject poses the further questions: Does one know that one is in bondage? Is one aware of it? Or is one ignorant of it? And if one is ignorant, how does one come to a knowledge of it? What is it that can liberate us? Can we by our own efforts find liberation? Or do we need help? Are we totally dependent on outside help? What does liberation mean? How will it alter this present condition?

The subject of human bondage and divine grace takes us even further back to inquire what humankind is, who we are. What is our make-up? And how do we relate to the world around us? And if, as is implied in the phrase "divine grace," we posit the existence of a God, we need to inquire how one relates to this God. Did God create men and women? And what purpose was there in this creation? As I pondered these questions I realized that this is precisely what Śaiva Siddhānta speaks about.

Śaiva Siddhānta is not a philosophy that presents ontological categories or metaphysical truths that have no bearing on life. Its whole theme is this—that men and women are in bondage and that they can find liberation in divine grace. It shows men and women how to find this liberation. If it speaks of the existence and nature of God or of humankind or of material creation, it is all in relation to this central theme—the fact of humankind's bondage and the liberation that is available through divine grace.

Śaiva Siddhānta starts from certain basic postulates about the meaning of freedom. Freedom, according to Śaiva Siddhānta, implies certain conditions. To be free is not to be fettered by association with matter. To be free is not to be perceptible to the senses. It is not to be subject to the limitations of time and place. It is not capable of being analyzed into parts. It is to have knowledge without being dependent on organs of perception. It is not to be dependent on another, and it is not to be bound by action by the law of cause and effect. Judged by these criteria, the human being is not free.

The human being, by being in association with matter, is

subject to change. We are born; we live and we die. Not only human beings but all else that is seen in the material world is subject to this threefold process—birth, existence, and decay.[1] Plants sprout and grow and die. Life goes on. Men and women are caught in this never-ceasing rhythm of birth, living, and death and are powerless to alter it. They are caught in a cycle from which they need to be free.

Secondly, to be free is not to be perceptible to the senses. Śaiva Siddhānta texts say that that which can be pointed out as he, she, or it, is subject to the threefold process of birth, existence, and decay.[2] And again they say that that which is perceptible to the senses is changeable. So to be perceptible to the senses, to have a body that can be seen and touched, is to be subject to birth and decay.[3] It is to be changeable. And, conversely, to be imperceptible to the senses, not to be possessed of a body that can be seen or felt, is to be free. It is said in Śaiva Siddhānta texts that the essential nature of the soul is to be without form (*arūpi*).[4] Existence in human form would then mean a state of bondage, bondage to a body that is perceptible and subject to change.

Thirdly, to be free means to be beyond the limitations of place and time. The soul is said to be pervasive (*vyāpi*), something that can escape, like air, like gas; something that can spread, not subject to a limit or place. So the soul as it is caught in the human body cannot be all pervasive; it is limited to where the body is, it cannot be everywhere. In life, it is circumscribed by time.[5] It has a past, a present, and a future. It is as if it had stepped out of the eternity to which it belonged, had escaped when there was neither a beginning nor an end, to the human state that is limited. So to be free is to be beyond the shackles of place and time, to belong to this eternity, to be all-pervasive.

Fourthly, to be free means not to be capable of being analyzed into parts. When the human body dies, the body decays, disintegrates. What then happens to the body that was? It is believed to dissolve into its component parts and then to become one with the primordial matter from which it evolved. In Śaiva Siddhānta the human being, made up of thirty-six elements (*tattvas*) which have evolved in a certain order from primordial matter (*māyā*), is regarded as the end product of the process of evolution.[6] All of the human being, with the exception of the immortal soul, is matter.

Matter, in this context, is that which has no spirit or life of its own (*asat*) or that which is inanimate (*jaḍa*).[7]

All matter is referred to as *asat* or *jaḍa*. Not only is one's physical body a product of matter but even one's internal organs (*antaḥ-karaṇa*): mind (*manas*), will (*buddhi*), individuality (*ahaṅkāra*), heart (*citta*). *Antar* means "internal" and *karaṇa* means "organ," distinguishing from the external organs, the eye, the ear, the hand, and so forth. So *antaḥkaraṇas* constitute *citta, buddhi, ahaṅkāra,* and *manas,* and these are really a little difficult to define. We can say intellect, discrimination, mind, will—all these are implied in the foregoing four words. These together make up the discriminating, evaluating, thinking part of us. Not only is one's physical body a product of matter, but also these four organs (*antaḥkaraṇas*) are considered to be material.[8] All that one would consider as part of one's personality, what makes one different from another human being, is looked upon as matter. The core of the human being, encased in some of the elements (*tattvas*), is the immortal soul saddled with an impurity (*mala*). So the soul with its impurity (*mala*), the inherent *mala,* the defect of the soul, is central, the core. And this soul is accompanied by some of the elements (*tattvas*). This constitutes the transmigrating self, the transmigrating ego; it goes from birth to birth. And further there is the gross body, with the sensory and motor organs: the eye, the ear, the nose, skin, tongue, hands, feet, the organ of speech, anus, and the generative organ. All these, in all thirty-six elements, make up the human being.[9]

So the human being is not an entity. It is not a unit that cannot be analyzed and so it is finite, subject to birth and decay as all evolutes are. It is from the primordial matter (*māyā*) that this human being has evolved. And the final human being with the thirty-six elements is the end product of this scheme of evolution. When one goes to analyze this human being when it decays, when the body ceases to exist, what happens? All these elements fall away. The human being is something that can be analyzed, something that did not exist as it is from eternity. It is saddled with a body that is subject to disintegration.

The fifth point that we mentioned—to be free is to have knowledge without being dependent on organs of perception. The soul in its embodied state is limited. The soul in Śaiva Siddhānta has no independent means of knowledge; it cannot know by itself. It depends on something else or someone else for its knowledge. The soul, being spirit, eternal like God, is capable of understanding;

it cannot understand by itself, but it is capable of being taught, it is able to think and to understand (*cit*). God is *cit,* and the human soul is also *cit.*[10] God knows; and the human soul can know, but it cannot, like God, know by itself. It can derive its knowledge from two sources: through the instrumentality of its body and from the indwelling spirit of God in it.[11] The soul by itself cannot understand. Encased in the human body, the soul derives its knowledge through the senses, the bodily organs; the eye brings in the sight, the ear brings the sound, so the soul inside has no direct contact with the world outside. The contact is all through the senses. What information the senses gather is presented to the internal organs, *citta, buddhi, ahaṅkāra,* and *manas.* It is a process. The senses gather the information, they present it to the mind, the will, the discriminating, deciding factor in the human being. The *citta, buddhi, ahaṅkāra,* and *manas* decide, evaluate, coordinate the information, which then comes to the soul, and through them the soul knows.

So long as the soul leans on these material instruments of knowledge, its knowledge is of the world, and when it leans on God, it is illumined by God. The soul either depends on the world for its knowledge or receives knowledge from God. If it depends on the world for its knowledge, the knowledge that the senses bring is the knowledge of the world outside, of all the manifold attractions of the world. When it learns to lean on God, it is illuminated by God. So whether it leans on the world or on God, its knowledge is dependent knowledge.

Sixthly, to be free is not to be dependent on another. It is to be self-dependent. The human state, as we see it in this world, is not a state of self-dependence.[12] The human being has no source of knowledge of its own but is dependent on something or someone else for its knowledge. It cannot choose its pains and pleasures. These are given to the human being by forces seemingly beyond its control. One comes into the world without asking for it. One is subject to experiences that are not of one's own choosing. One is not able to liberate oneself from this embodied state solely by one's own efforts. So the human state is a state of bondage in that it is a state of dependence.

And lastly, to be free is to be untouched by the law of cause and effect. Every cause has its own effect. And every action brings its own reward or consequence. So to be human is to be constrained, to act, and to be caught in the web of action and consequence.[13] To be free one must escape the fetters of action and reaction.

In general, these constraints are of two types. Firstly, the soul's state of dependence and the soul's limited intelligence are part of its status as soul, as less than God. The intrinsic nature of the soul is to be dependent for knowledge on something or someone else. Secondly, the soul is limited by, or is in bondage to, matter, time, place, and action; and these limitations constitute the limitations imposed on it by its embodied state. In its embodied state as a human being, the soul is limited by, encased in, matter. It is affected by the decay that the body undergoes, and it is subject to time and to place. It cannot move around as it pleases, and it is subject to action and consequence.

These four factors—matter, the association with matter, the limitations of time and place, and bondage to the law of action and reaction—are the limitations imposed on the human being by its human state. The human being is like a sacrificial animal that is tied to a post and is referred to as *paśu,* as animal.[14] In the old Indian sacrificial system, there was a custom of having a post to which the sacrificial animal was tied at the place of sacrifice. And the human situation, according to Śaiva Siddhānta, is like that of the animal that is tied to such a post. The animal, being tied with a rope, cannot free itself. That is the way the human being is in life, in this world. And so the term used for the soul in Śaiva Siddhānta is the word *paśu,* which means "animal."

Now in contrast to this limited, finite human being, God is eternally free.[15] God is not restricted to time and place. He is all pervasive, existing everywhere at the same time.[16] God is spirit who has no body of matter (*māyā*), who is not tied down to a form and place. And so God as spirit can exist everywhere, all pervasively, at any time. Time and place do not tie down God. He has no beginning, no end. The human being has a birth, exists, and decays; so there is a beginning and an end to human existence. But God, in contrast, has neither a beginning nor an end. God is the only one who exists as he is at the end of the aeon when all beings and things created return to their original state. He it is who orders the unfolding of creation again.[17] He is beyond creation, destruction, birth, and decay. There is a time when creation comes and a time when it is dissolved. Then again it comes, and again it dissolves. This happens to everything; everything that is created undergoes this process of periodic creation and destruction—all except God. God is the one who is beyond this creation and destruction, who is not subject to this coming into birth and going out. God is the one who remains, who is left at the end of the aeon when all creation goes back into primordial *māyā,* the matter from which it came. God alone is there, and then God wills that creation comes back unfolding like a flower. He is beyond creation and destruction, birth and decay. God is not associated with matter. He is not capable of being analyzed into parts, into elements.[18] He is just as he is. He knows by himself; his knowledge is not dependent on anything or anyone else. He does not need organs of knowledge or perception. He does not need to come into contact with matter or anything else. He just knows. He is omniscient.[19] He does not need to depend on anyone or anything else as does the human being. He is self-dependent (*svatantra*). God does not need anyone or anything to complete his happiness.[20] He is complete. God acts, but not within the realm of action and consequence. He activates action and so keeps himself unfettered by action and consequence.[21]

God exists, the soul exists, and there is matter. These three are eternal. Since all things perceptible, male, female, and neuter, undergo appearance, existence, and dissolution, the material world must have been created and would sink back from whence it came. In the same manner as it was dissolved it would evolve again. Do we not see this in nature? Every species of plant grows, matures, and decays and then from the seed again the shoots come forth, a periodic creation and dissolution of the world.[22] All things that one can see in nature undergo birth, existence, and decay; this is the pattern of life. The world, once it is created, would last for a number of aeons, and at a certain point God wills that the souls should have a period of rest from embodied existence, and so he orders that there be an involution, a drawing in, an absorption, into the primordial stuff from whence it evolved. And then God orders that creation should unfold, and so it goes on in never-ending succession.

The inference that is drawn is that the world is an existing thing. It is not an illusion, a mirage. It is something that truly exists. Why? Because only an existing thing can come into appearance.[23] Something that does not exist can never appear or become perceptible. It comes as nature, as things; it makes an appearance. Why? Because it was there in *māyā,* in primordial matter. It was imperceptible. It was there and unfolds in creation.

What exists cannot come into being without a producer. Someone has to be the agent of the production. Just as pots do not emerge from clay without the potter—the clay is here, the pots are here, but unless the clay is made into pots, clay cannot become pots. And in like manner, we have matter (*māyā*), and we have the world in the form that we have, but matter cannot become the world unless there is someone who is the agent for creation, someone who is like the potter, the efficient cause of creation.[24] There is a God who is the agent, the person who brings creation into being.

NOTES

Śiva-ñāna-bōdham: A Manual of Śaiva Religious Doctrine, translated from the Tamil by Gordon Matthews, Oxford, 1948 (*SJB*)

Nallaswami Pillai, *Śivagñāna Siddhiyar,* Madras, 1913 (*SS*)

Hoisington, H. R. *Śiva Pirakāśam, Journal of the American Oriental Society,* iv (1853–4), pp. 127–244 (*Siva*)

Tiru-aruḷ-payan, translated by G. U. Pope in his translation of Māṇikkavāçagar's *The Tiruvāçagam,* Oxford, 1900 (*Tiru*)

1 *SS,* I.1,2; *Siva* 16.

2 *SJB,* i.

3 *SJB,* vi.1; *SS,* VI.2,3.

4 *SS* IV.20, 38.

5 *SS* II.54. Time is also an evolute of *māyā.*

6 *SS* II.52–72.

7 *SS* VI.2.

8 *SS* II.58, 59.

[9] *SS*.II.58–60. *EVOLUTES OF MAYA*

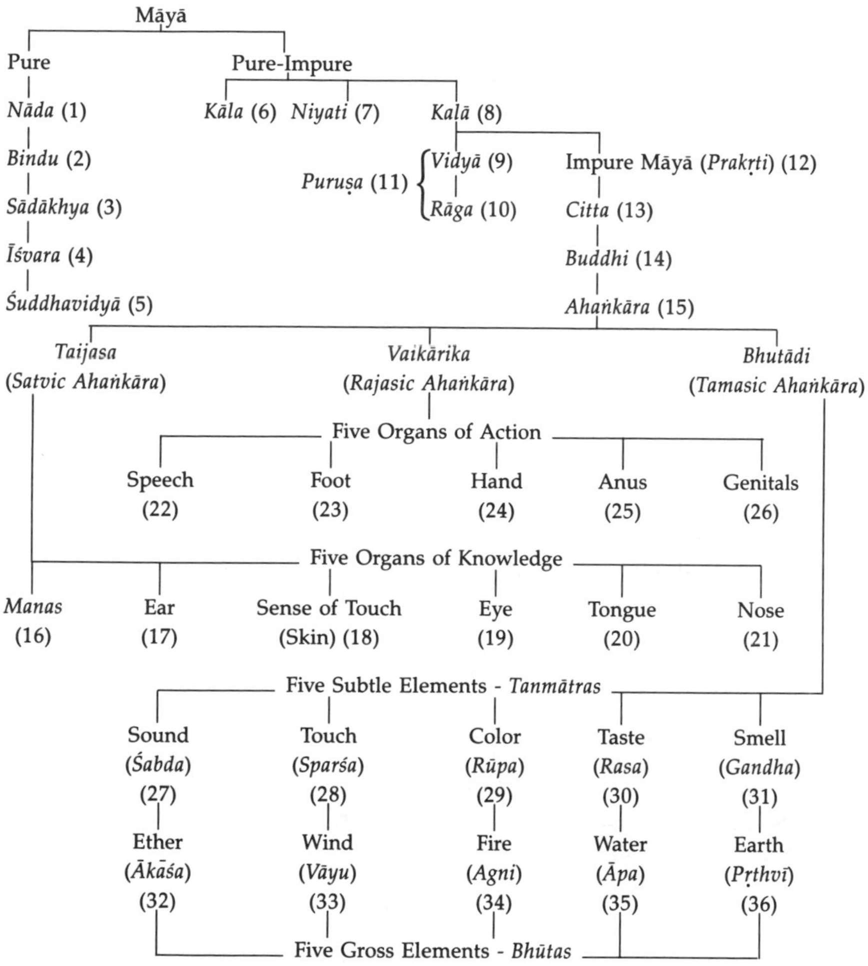

1–5 *Śiva tattvas*
6–11 *Vidyā tattvas*
12–36 *Ātma tattvas*

Māyā is of three kinds: pure, pure-impure, and impure.

Of the 36 *tattvas,*

1–5 *tattvas* (called *Śiva-tattvas*) are of pure *māyā*. Also called *preraka* (literally, "setting in motion").

6–12 *tattvas* (called *Vidyā-tattvas*) are of pure-impure *māyā*. Also called *bhoktṛ*, (literally, "enjoyer"). These form the *puruṣa tattva* or the karmic ego.

13–36 *tattvas* (called *ātma-tattva*) are of impure *māyā*. Also called *bhogya* (literally, "enjoyed").

God works through the *Śivatattvas* and the *Vidyātattvas* to evoke the cognitive, conative, and affective powers of the soul.

Of the *Ātma-tattvas* eight (*buddhi, manas, ahaṅkāra,* and the five *tanmātras* or "subtle elements"), together referred to as the *puriyaṣṭaka,* with the soul form the transmigrating ego, the *sūkṣma śarīra.* This aggregate goes from birth to birth during the *yuga* ("aeon") but disintegrates at the time of dissolution. It will form again at the beginning of the next aeon. See *SJB,* pp. 36–37.

The gross body or *sthūla śarīra* is constituted of the above mentioned eight *tattvas* and of sixteen others: the *citta,* five sensory organs, five motor organs, and the five gross elements.

See *SS* II.64, 69–70, 55–56n.

[10] *SS* VII.4.

[11] *SJB* i.3; *SS* I.17; V.3,4,5.

[12] *SJB* i.3; *SS* XI.7.

[13] *SS* I.64; II.10–12, 39–40.

[14] *SS* IV.20.

[15] *SS* I.1.

[16] *SS* VI.1; VII.4.

[17] *SJB* i.2,3; *SS* I.34–35.

[18] *SS* I.41; V.6; VI.1.

[19] *SS* I.41; VII.3; VIII.17.

[20] *SS* II.27; *SJB* viii.2b.

[21] *SJB* i.2c; *SS* II.33. Creatorship is distinguished into two types, directing creatorship and directed creatorship. Śiva is the directing creator while the other gods engaged in creation are directed creators. See V.A. Devasenapathi *Śaiva Siddhānta* (Madras, India: University of Madras, 1974), p. 72.

[22] *SJB* i.1a, p. 30; *SS* I.1,8,9.

[23] *SJB* i.2, p. 31. Śaiva Siddhānta believes in *satkāryavāda,* the theory that says that the effect exists in the cause. It implies that only what exists in subtle form in the cause can manifest itself in gross form as the effect.

[24] *SJB* i.2, p. 31.

2

The Impurities

M. M. Arulchelvam

Hindus often speak of three Gods—Brahma, who is the creator; Viṣṇu, who is the preserver; and Śiva or Rudra, who is the destroyer. Śaiva Siddhānta regards Śiva as the highest God, and stresses that he who is the destroyer is he who can create, that the destroyer is more powerful than the others. So the world comes out, out of whatever it goes into; the person who destroys is the person who can create. Lord Śiva, who is himself beyond destruction and is the author of the dissolution of the world, is also the author of the creation of the world.[1]

Śiva, who is the efficient cause, activates creation, not out of himself nor out of nothing but out of primordial matter, *māyā*. God is not bound by the action of participating in the evolution, maintenance, and dissolution of the world. God is not bound by action. He is beyond this law of action and consequence; he is transcendent; he is apart from these activities. An analogy given is that he is like a person who remembers when awake the things that he has dreamt.[2] You sleep, you dream; when you are awake you are apart from the dream. It is something like that. God is also compared to time which, though differentiated by us into past, present, and future, does not itself undergo change.

God acts, not because he needs to but because he feels sorry for human beings who are in bondage. There are eternal souls fettered from eternity by an impurity, and God creates, God activates, this creation for only one purpose: to liberate souls that are fettered by an impurity.[3] God is eternally existing and souls are eternally existing. God is the primal cause, the creator. Human beings are dependent on God who is also the cause of the dissolution of the world and whose knowledge is not sense-conditioned.

How do we conclude that there are souls? Because there is something that denies the proposition that there is a soul. When you say there is no soul, that something which denies the proposition that there is a soul is itself the soul.[4] We also know that there is something in us that is apart from our body, apart from our senses, that is different from our respiration, from our dreams, that can know when it is taught. There are, therefore, three eternal verities. Firstly, there is a God who is omniscient, all-pervasive spirit, without any touch of matter. Secondly, there is a primordial material stuff, *māyā,* which is the source of all perishable creation. And thirdly, there are innumerable souls which are spirit, like God, capable of knowledge and yet in the human state, limited and in bondage. To grant that souls and matter (*māyā*) are also eternal like God is not considered derogatory to God because he is all-pervasive; he pervades souls and matter. He does not know them objectively as something apart from himself, but intuitively in his pervasiveness.

God who is existent and knowing is said to be *sat.* The word *sat* means "being, something that exists." It has been translated in various ways as "existent," as "spirit," as "something that is unchangeable." And God is also knowing, someone who knows. He is *cit.* He has knowledge and so is *cit.*[5] In contrast, the material stuff (*māyā*) is referred to as *asat,* "not existing," "changeable," "non-spirit," because it is subject to change, because it is not spirit, and also because it is *acit,*[6] "something that cannot know." It is material. *Māyā* cannot exist in the presence of God who is *sat,* as darkness disappears when light, "the all-pervasive God," comes. Darkness just vanishes; it cannot stand in the presence of light.[7] In the same way, in the presence of God who is *sat,* the *asat māyā* just ceases to exist or is not a reality any longer.

Now human beings are *cit* and *sat* also. They are *cit* like God because they can know, not that they know by themselves but that they are capable of knowledge, they can be taught. The human soul is also *sat,* being spirit like God. But the soul is also encased in a human body which is *asat,* which is *māyā.* You see, the human being has two parts. It is a *sat* and an *asat.* It has a soul that is *sat* and it has a body that is *asat,* and therefore the human being is called *sat-asat,*[8] spirit and non-spirit. The human being is thus a citizen of two worlds, both spirit and matter, and it is captivity to matter that constitutes one's bondage. One has an eternal, undying soul akin to God, and one is encased in a perishable body.

In Śaiva Siddhānta the human soul is said to be fettered by three impurities (*mala:* impurity, dirt). The soul in its embodied state, possessed of a body that is a product of matter, subject to birth and decay, is said to be fettered by the impurity of *māyā,* matter. *Māyā* is what we see in nature. The body that fetters the human soul is *māyā.* There are four things that the soul gets from *māyā:* (1) the body; (2) the organs, that is, one's sensory and motor organs and the organs of the body, the internal organs; (3) the world in which the body is placed; and (4) the enjoyments that the world offers.[9] The association with *māyā* is a fetter (*pāśa:* rope or fetter). *Māyā* becomes a rope, a fetter on the soul because it deludes the soul. The soul forgets itself. *Māyā* makes the soul long for and seek the pleasures of the world. The soul, because it is associated with the body, wants pleasures. The senses of the human body are by nature reaching out. The eye looks out, the ears hear something from outside. All these organs are just reaching out, as it were, going out. They get the impressions, receive the information of the world outside. They bring in the experience and the information of the world outside, and this taste of worldly pleasures creates an ever greater longing for enjoyments. Once something sweet is tasted, one wants more of it.

More and more the senses drag one into involvement with the world. The tastes of worldly pleasures create a great longing for the same pleasures and one works towards securing an ever greater enjoyment of them. One is drawn towards the world and one forgets that one is intrinsically a spiritual being, that one is akin to God. This attraction to the world is understandable because the body is of the same material stock as *māyā,* as the world. This attraction of the senses for the world has long been recognized in India. We hear of Hindu saints and mystics who have sought to draw away from the world, from involvement in it, to withdraw their senses from contact with it. Hindu saints, in many of their hymns, have likened their senses to demons, to elephants, to horses, that drag one in whatever direction they please. A horse, if you cannot control it, will drag you where you do not want to go. And the saints have emphasized repeatedly the necessity to withdraw one's senses from contact with the world, like a tortoise that draws its legs under its shell and lies still like a little stone. One is advised to draw one's senses inward, to integrate, to turn the senses inward and to bring them under the control of the mind and the will and then to turn to God.

The association with *māyā,* matter, has very much more serious effect on the soul than merely distracting it. *Māyā* deludes the soul. It makes the soul identify itself with the world. The soul forgets spirit. This association with *māyā,* this fetter of *māyā,* makes the soul identify itself with matter, with these senses, with the world. It almost transforms the soul's nature. As mentioned previously, the soul is not self-dependent; it needs to depend on something, and as it leans on the world, as it turns to the world, its very nature becomes obscured, changed. The four internal organs, *citta, buddhi, ahaṅkāra,* and *manas,* which constitute the mind, the will, the discrimination, and the desire of human beings respectively, receive the information that the senses bring. They help the soul receive sense impressions, to question and to decide. And these are mere channels of knowledge. They have no knowledge of their own. Just as a king transacts his business in conjunction with ministers who assist him by their counsel, because he has not precise knowledge himself, so the soul, devoid of knowledge because of "innate impurity," is associated with the inner faculties which assist it with their counsel so that it may have reasoned knowledge.[10] These material organs are as different from the soul "as lamplight is different from eyesight." But they seem so intelligent. They seem able to decide. They seem able to think. And what does the soul do? The soul identifies itself with these material internal organs, these products of *māyā.* It forgets that it is not self-dependent and imagines that it is capable of knowledge and decisions on its own, in its own right.

This is the first stage of the soul's association with matter. The soul, enamored of the delights of the world, is first distracted and deluded into thinking itself the agent of action. Soon the glamour of the world wears off. The experiences of repeated births, the pleasures and pains suffered by right and wrong actions, prove to the soul that there is no final satisfaction in the pleasures of the world, and then the soul is ready to turn to God. The association with matter has two effects on the soul. First, like little children running after things, the soul also runs after sense pleasures, but soon it realizes that these sense pleasures have no final lasting satisfaction. It becomes tired; it goes through so many births, it undergoes so much pain and pleasure as a result of its right and wrong choices, that it finally comes to the realization that there is no final satisfaction to be had from these things, the pleasures of the world.

Then the soul is mature. It is ready to turn to God, to be detached from actions, to withdraw from the world. The soul comes to a realization about the truth of the nature of this world. It is compared to a crystal. Like the crystal which reflects the color of the object placed adjacent to it, the soul identifies itself with that which it depends on. When one looks at a crystal, it displays various colors and one might think that those colors are the nature of the crystal. But when one sees that these are not actually the nature of the crystal, but a reflection of the object placed adjacent to it, that the crystal is something apart from the colors, then one knows the true nature of the crystal. The soul first thinks that the body is itself, the eye, the mind, all these pleasures are itself. Soon the soul realizes that these sense organs are a thing apart, that this body is a thing apart, that the soul is something quite apart from these senses, from the body and the organs, from the world outside. It knows that it is different, that there is something that is in it that is different from all these material things that it is associated with. And then perceiving that all these are different, the soul rejects the false and turns to the truth.

The fetter of *māyā,* the first of three fetters (*pāśas*) mentioned, does two things as far as the soul is concerned. It first obscures the soul. It hides the true nature of the world, makes the world seem attractive, and drags the soul into involvement with the world. It entices the soul into identifying itself with the internal organs, to imagine itself the agent of actions, and then in the second stage, when the soul is wise to the nature of the world, *māyā* helps the process of enlightenment. The same bodily organs that proved a snare to the soul are now channels of knowledge. They bring knowledge of the true nature of the world and of the body as different from the soul. *Māyā* helps the soul to see and thereby disentangle itself from the world. *Māyā* is therefore compared to a lamp, a lamp that one would have till the break of dawn.[11] *Māyā* is also compared to spectacles that help the eye to see.

There is another fact about this association with *māyā* or this fetter of *māyā*, this material matter, that is important. *Māyā* is said to be of three kinds. There is a pure *māyā*, a pure-impure *māyā*, and an impure *māyā*, and the human being, with its thirty-six elements (*tattvas*), is made up of all three kinds of *māyā*. Of course, the last kind predominates; the major component of the human being is the impure *māyā*. Through these others, the pure and the pure-impure, the power of God works in humankind. God's power is able to work through the pure *māyā* and also through the impure-pure because through those God awakens the cognitive, conative, and affective powers of the soul—the thinking, desiring, acting powers of the soul. Embodied existence is a necessary bondage, not an unnecessary one, because God's power cannot reach the human soul except in its embodied state, and the human soul cannot receive God's power except in its embodied state. It is only as the human being, as the human soul in this encasement of thirty-six elements (*tattvas*), that God's power can come. The soul cannot be receptive to the influence of God except in the human state. It is said that wise ones wish for human existence as an opportunity to rid themselves of birth and to go into liberation.[12]

Māyā that we called the fetter is both a fetter and a help. It is a fetter because it binds one to the world. It is a help because it allows the knowledge of God and of the world to come in such a way that the human soul can break away from this bondage.

The second impurity is *karma*. *Karma* refers to the results of good and bad deeds that accompany the soul. The word *karma* means "action." It can connote a physical act or an act of mind or tongue. One's thoughts, one's word, one's action—these are *karma*. An act can be good or bad as it helps or injures other sentient creatures. A fundamental postulate of Hinduism, Buddhism, and Jainism is that no action is ever lost. Nothing that one does is ever lost. Every act will bring, at some future date, its own reward or punishment. The diversity in human life, the alternation of prosperity, adversity, happiness, and pain enjoyed and suffered by human beings, is seen as the result of good and bad deeds done in previous births.

> Gain, loss, pain, pleasure, honor and disgrace, all these become attached in the womb. They manifest themselves as the result of one's

> endeavor. They are the result of the endeavor made in a previous birth. Results of present endeavor will be manifest in a future birth.[13]

So a text says. The body that one is equipped with, the experiences one undergoes, are all in accordance with one's deeds in a previous birth. And what one suffers, the experiences one has, are all in accordance and are commensurate with what one has done in a previous birth.

One goes from birth to birth, reaping in a future birth what one has done in a previous birth. And as one reaps these fruits, one is still involved in actions, and these actions will lead one into another birth. And so it goes on.

These actions really have an educative value. God uses them as a deterrent. As one suffers, one realizes that bad deeds make one suffer. One turns to good. And if one reaps the good, still one realizes that even good will bind one to the world, and one learns to detach oneself from the good. Good deeds and bad deeds are compared to chains of gold and chains of silver.[14] The good deed is like a chain of gold and the bad deed is like a chain of silver. Either way a deed is a chain. So one is advised to get away from both good and bad, not that one should not engage in action but that one should be detached from the action.

This body and *karma* are like cause and effect. They are compared to the seed and the tree.[15] The tree causes the seed and the seed causes the tree. The results of action recoil on the doer because he or she is concerned about its outcome, because he or she has a selfish interest in it. One engages in action because one has a motive or a purpose, an end in view. It is this involvement that makes the effect come back to one. How can one get away from this *karma?* How does one break away from this endless chain? By detachment, disinterested action. One must not be interested in the effects of what one is doing. One acts because it is one's duty but one is to keep one's interest, one's mind, one's attachment away from it. If one can keep detached from the action, if one can be free from attachment or attraction for it, then one will be untouched by the results of one's action.

There are different planes of existence. The human plane is not the only plane we are talking about. One can be born a god, then one can be born a human being, one can be born in hell, one can be born an animal, bird, plant, anything; it can go down right to a worm.[16] As one's act is good, one ascends in the scale. As one's act is bad, one descends in the scale. As one lives well, as one does good, one reaps the reward of it but at the same time one's soul is maturing and one is purified. It is not a useless process that is going on. All these births are not purposeless. The purpose is that as one goes through these births one gets more and more spiritually mature. It does something to one's soul. Wherever one finds oneself, whether in affluence or not, it does not affect one. It is said that the souls could be born in low forms or as birds and animals or in higher forms, that there could be as many a eighty-four hundred thousand births. It is a fantastic figure. Eighty-four hundred thousand births one could go through before one could reach God's feet.

These acts-consequences are of three types. *Sañcita* is something that is accumulated, something that is kept in abeyance like a bank balance of acts, in abeyance till the time is ready for their fruition. *Prārabdha* refers to those acts-consequences that have landed one in this current birth. *Āgāmya* refers to what is going to come following upon the actions one is presently doing.[17] All of this is compared to what the farmer does: when he reaps, he stores some grain (*sañcita*), he uses some (*prārabdha*), and he has some grain as seed grain for the next crop (*āgāmya*).[18] Each karmic effect will cease to be only as it has been endured or "eaten" by the soul. When does the karmic effect cease to be? When one has suffered it, endured it and has finished it, then it is cancelled. Each karmic effect will cease to be as one eats the fruit of it. But by then what happens? One has done more things and so it goes on. The soul is never free from *karma* till it is near liberation. *Karma* is a fetter in that it places the soul in bondage to a series of finite existences.

God can reach humankind through the embodied state. God makes men and women good through this embodied existence because it is good for them. God and the human soul are inseparably united. They are two but yet they are inseparably united. God is one with the soul, but one does not know it because one is blinded by that impurity that blinds one's eyes from seeing God (*āṇava*). One cannot realize that there is God within one, that there is this divine element in one. God is there but God will not force his way. God waits for one to choose to go to God.

There are three states of the soul: the state before birth (*kevala*), the embodied state (*sakala*), and the state after liberation (*śuddha*).

Considering only the first two at this point, one notes that the first state (*kevala*) is before the soul comes into embodied existence, when the soul is alone with its impurity. (Of course, God is always with the soul but God does not reveal his presence.) The soul, as it is, is with the impurity. The second state is the embodied state (*sakala*), where the soul is fitted with a body, with organs, with the world, with enjoyments and so forth, and the chance to receive knowledge of the world outside, the elements through which God acts on the soul. God does not reveal himself, but God makes it possible for one to get this knowledge of the world and of one's body and to know that one is different from the world and the body. God does not reveal himself straightaway as he is. What he does is to make the human being capable of thinking, of desiring, of acting, of knowing. What happens when the soul gets the knowledge of the world outside? It realizes that its body is something different from it. And that realization, that all this is apart from the soul, makes one lean towards God. Turning to God is a voluntary choice on the part of persons and comes because God allows them to go into embodied existence, to get involved, suffer, endure, and be wise.

The impurities are almost intrinsically a part of the soul, a defect of the soul. There are two explanations given. One is that the soul can get rid of its impurity. An example used is rice. Rice or any grain has its coating of bran. It is there as the grain is formed, the bran is part of it. But yet the bran can be polished off. Another example is copper. Copper has this coating of verdigris, the colored matter that forms on it. It forms on the copper but it is possible to polish it off. So according to this view, this impurity can be got rid of. The other explanation says that the impurity becomes impotent. It is rendered ineffective. In other words, when somebody takes a poison, one gives an antidote. The poison is in the body, the antidote is also in the body so much so that the poison does not act on the body. And then as one gets rid of the body, as one gets out of this embodied existence, this impurity (*mala*) also passes away with one. The impurities are either rendered ineffective or destroyed.

God does not go through this process. He is referred to as eternally free. He has no impurities (*malas*). He is referred to as "beginningless, free, and knowing" (*ānādi, mukta, cit*). One wants to be near God, and the goal of human life is to realize this inseparable reunion with God. It is quite clear that one does not become God.

One gets near God, but God is the creator. We are the ones who are created. God is self-sufficient. We are dependent. God knows; we need to be told. Even though one becomes like God, one does not become God.

We have referred to the first of the three fetters (*pāśas*), association with the material (*māyā*), and the second fetter, the association with action (*karma*). The third fetter is *āṇava,* which is blindness, darkness, egoism, self-elevation, delusion, and all which is part of the human soul. That is the reason the human being comes into this world. The human being is brought into this world not for the fun of it but because of this intrinsic defect, this impurity of the soul. And God gives this *karma* and this world to men and women because he wants to liberate them from the final impurity of *āṇava.* It is a slow perfection, but a sure end is there.

God has no damnation. There is no hell. God acts by giving us this *māyā. Māyā* is God's act of grace. God brings us into this world so that we might be purified by this suffering and these experiences. And also God gives us the experiences, the right *karma.* He is like a king who is meting out punishment and reward. He chooses the right thing for each person at the right time and does so for our souls. God acts out of love. It is God's grace that brings us into this life. It is God's grace that makes us suffer. It is all part of God's act of grace.

One's destiny is to acknowledge Śiva as the Supreme God and oneself (that is, the soul) as his servant in devotion and love.

Notes

[1] *SJB* i.3.

[2] *SJB* i.2c. See chapter 1, note 21 above.

[3] *SJB* i; iv.2.

[4] *SJB* iii.1.

[5] *SJB* vi.2; *SS* I.1;VI.1,5; VII.3.

[6] *SS* VI.1–3; II.53.

[7] *SJB* vii.1.

[8] *SS* VII.2. The soul, while related to both *sat* and *asat,* does not arise from either as cause and effect. It is a unique relationship. It is produced from them as the fragrance comes out of the flower.

[9] *SS* II.81; VI.2. Referred to as *tanu, karaṇa, bhuvana, bhoga*—body, senses, worlds, and enjoyments, respectively.

[10] *SJB* viii.3a; *SS* IV.21, 25–27.

[11] *Tiru* 3.10; *SS* II.84; *Siva,* p. 166; *SJB,* p. 38.

[12] *SS* IV.35.

[13] *SS* II.9.

[14] *SJB* viii.1b, p. 57.

[15] *SS* II.10.

[16] Saint Maṇikkavaçakar says in his *Tiruvāçagam* that he was wearied by traversing through many births as grass, herb, tree, animal, bird, snake, stone, man, demon, sage, and god. See also *SS* II.33, 89.

[17] *SJB* ii.2a, p. 35.

[18] *SS* II.12.

[19] It is said that *āṇava* is a defect of the soul like a cataract of the eye, the removal of which does not kill the person. If *āṇava* were considered a quality of the soul, with the destruction of *āṇava* the soul which possessed it would also be destroyed. In the *kevala* state, that is the state before embodiment, the soul appears saddled with *āṇava.* But even this is a phenomenal state and not the pure ontological state of the soul. See *Tiru* 3.7; *SJB* p. 75; Dhavamoney, Mariasusai, *Love of God According to Śaiva Siddhānta* (Oxford: Clarendon Press, 1971) p. 279.

3

Spiritual ignorance

M. M. Arulchelvam

In the previous chapter, we discussed the two fetters (a) of the material world and the body that envelops us (*māyā*) and (b) the result of our acts which follow us from birth to birth (*karma*). These two fetters, *māyā* and *karma,* are referred to as subsequently adventitious or as visitors, things that come for a time (*āgantuka*).[1] *Māyā* and *karma* come to the soul only for a time, in association with the embodied state. *Karma* must have had a beginning because it starts with acts performed by men and women in time. It must have started in time, at some point. And at the period of world dissolution when the world dissolves, and everything goes back into primordial *māyā, karma* also goes back into primordial *māyā. Karma* does not stick to the soul; it goes back into *māyā.*[2] There it remains till it is time for creation to unfold again. These two, that is *karma* and *māyā,* do not bind the soul with the same relentlessness with which the third fetter, *āṇava,* accompanies the soul.

Āṇava is the third fetter. This is "born with" (*sahaja*) the soul. *Āṇava* goes with the soul from birth to birth; it does not let the soul go. *Māyā* and *karma* come for a period in embodied existence. They let the soul be when it is a period of dissolution. Then again when creation unfolds, the soul gets its *māyā* and *karma. Āṇava,* however, goes with the soul from birth to birth right from eternity till liberation. There was no time when the soul was not thus fettered by *āṇava.* In the first chapter, I remarked that the phrase "human bondage" could imply that there was a time when the soul was not in bondage. But a state when the soul was free from this fetter of *āṇava* cannot be imagined.[3] There is no reason that would explain why the soul that was free earlier has subsequently got into a state of bondage. If the soul did get into bondage of its own free will, it could get out in the same manner. But the soul from eternity is under the bondage of *āṇava.*

Now this word *āṇava* is derived from the word *aṇu. Aṇu* is the word that is used commonly in Tamil for "atom, the smallest particle." And so *āṇava* is explained as that which fragments or atomizes the capacity that the soul has for knowledge. It fragments the powers of the soul. *Āṇava* is that defect of the soul that causes spiritual ignorance, blindness, self-elevation, and delusion. *Āṇava* blinds the soul to the truth of its own nature and the fact of its dependence on God. The soul blinded by *āṇava* does not realize the presence of the all-pervasive God in its own being—it cannot see. The soul does not realize its own spiritual nature and destiny. Instead the soul is deluded by the attractions of the world, identifies itself with the psycho-physical body that it has, and imagines egotistically that it is the agent of action, forgetting its dependence on God.

The bondage of *āṇava* is not a negative state. It is not a state of being without knowledge or light. It is not the non-existence of knowledge. It is a positive state of spiritual blindness and ignorance. The analogy often given is that of the owl. The owl does not see during the day, not because daylight does not exist but because the owl is blinded by that light.[4] So it is with the soul. God is there always present with the soul but the soul cannot realize it because there is a defect in the soul that blinds it to this fact. *Āṇava* is said to be worse than darkness. The darkness, though it hides everything else, at least reveals its own presence. But when *āṇava* is there, the soul does not realize it.[5] *Āṇava* does not reveal its presence. *Āṇava* is also compared to a woman who plays the harlot with a lot of men but who is too bashful to show herself to her own husband.[6] *Āṇava* is so subtle that the soul is not aware of its existence. The soul does not know its own spiritual defect, does not know to try to get rid of it. The soul that has this *āṇava* does not know it has *āṇava.*

Āṇava is not an attribute of the soul. For if the "attribute" *āṇava* is destroyed, the soul to which it belongs would also be destroyed.[7] *Āṇava* is regarded as a defect of the soul on analogy with the eye. Blindness would be a defect of the eye whereas sight or light would be its quality. One would not speak of blindness as a quality of the eye. In the same way *āṇava* is not a quality of the soul. It is regarded as a defect.

That the human state is a condition of darkness, blindness, and delusion is commonplace in Hindu literature. Throughout Hindu literature this is the prevailing theme, that the human state, that humankind, is in darkness, is blinded, is deluded. That *āṇava* is a state of darkness, of blindness, and of delusion is particularly stressed in Śaiva Siddhānta. Śaiva saints often pray for light that would remove this veil of darkness, blindness, and delusion. Darkness, blindness, and delusion are literally called a veil, something that obscures one's vision. Light is equated to knowledge, to enlightenment and the realization of God.

Whenever texts speak of impurity (*mala*) in the singular, it is to *āṇava* that they refer. This is the fundamental impurity of the soul. It is referred to as the root (*mūla*) impurity or defect (*mala*). The fundamental impurity of the soul is *āṇava,* and this is what Śaiva Siddhānta is all about—the liberation of the soul from this fundamental impurity of *āṇava.*

The three *malas*—*āṇava, karma,* and *māyā*—have been likened to the husk, the bran, and the seed of a grain of rice.[8] *Māyā* is like the husk that helps in the removal of the bran that is *āṇava,* and the seed that is *karma* is the cause of new life. Further, these *malas* are referred to as inanimate material, as *jaḍa.* We distinguished between what is spiritual and unchangeable (*sat*) and what is material and changeable (*asat*). These *malas* are not *sat,* they are not spirit. They cannot, of themselves, find the soul to which they must go. They need to be associated with a soul by someone who is spirit, who is *sat. Māyā* and *karma,* being *jaḍa,* being inanimate material, do not have the capacity to seek out a soul and stick to it. The soul, though it is spirit, is blinded by *āṇava* and is not aware of its own state of bondage, and turns away from God, the only one who can work towards the removal of *āṇava* by bringing the soul into contact with *māyā* and *karma.* Whether *āṇava* exists eternally or is created by God is not answered. It is the state of the soul as it is.

The soul is blinded by *āṇava.* It is blinded, but God gives it the body so that it would have a chance to get to know the truth about its own self and so dissociate itself from all this. This leaves only God as the one and the only one who can work toward the removal of this *āṇava* by bringing the soul into contact with *māyā* and *karma.*

We noted briefly in Chapter 2 that Śaiva Siddhānta speaks of three states of the soul: the state before birth (*kevala*), the embodied state (*sakala*), and the state after liberation (*śuddha*). The first state is the condition before the soul takes on a body, that is, before it comes into the world arena. It is the state when the soul is fettered only by the impurity of *āṇava*. This is the worst of the three states in that the soul has neither a body nor the world which could help it to work out its *karma* and to receive the knowledge that would lead to liberation. This is the worst state also because the soul does not know it is in bondage. It has no way of getting knowledge. It is just inert, actionless, motionless.[9] It cannot do anything for itself. It just cannot, of itself, get out of that state.

The second state is when the soul is in the embodied state. The soul is now fettered by all three *malas*. There is a body that is *māyā* and it has the *karma* that has got to be endured and, of course, the *āṇava* that came along with it. But this stage is preferable in that the soul has a chance to work towards liberation; there is knowledge of the world coming in, there is also the action of God through the elements (*tattvas*). Among the elements that constitute the human being there are elements that give it the amount of light it needs to work towards its liberation. So this state is to be preferred.

The third state, of course, is the pure state (*śuddha*), when the soul is rid of all the *malas*, when the bonds of *māyā* and *karma* are destroyed altogether and *āṇava* is rendered ineffective, powerless to blind the soul.

Another analogy of these three states is drawn. *Āṇava* is like the sun in early morning when the sun is hidden altogether by the clouds. This is like the soul being in *āṇava*.[10] Absolutely no light is filtering through. And when the sun has dispelled those clouds, when the clouds have ceased, a little of the light comes through. This is like the embodied state when the soul is able to get a limited amount of knowledge. When all the clouds have been blown away and the sun shines in its full glory, it is like the soul in the free state, in the liberated state.

Now we notice that the soul is in bondage to matter, to time, to place, and to *karma,* and these are limitations that are brought on by its human state. But we also notice that the soul as it comes on the world arena, on the world stage, has a defect that is part of its make-up, and this is the reason for its association with *karma, māyā,* and all else that follows. *Āṇava* is the reason for the soul coming into embodiment, into this embodied state. It is because of *āṇava* that the soul is brought into the world and because of *āṇava* that it is associated with *karma* and *māyā*. Śaiva Siddhānta starts from this point, the existential situation of the soul. The soul is in bondage and the goal is for the soul to reach the feet of God, to find liberation. We have a soul that is in bondage and is ignorant of its state of bondage. We have primordial matter that has no knowledge and has no capacity to act. So the task of liberating the soul from bondage falls on God, and he must take the initiative in the matter.

God, being eternally free, not subject to the limitations and fetters, as is the soul, is the only one who can activate this process of liberation. God is not bound by the same limitations or fetters as is the soul, and so God is able to act. Unlike the soul with its dependent knowledge, God knows, and God can make known. God's knowledge is not dependent on organs of perception and, as the in-dwelling power in us, he knows the soul's predicament. God alone knows the state of the soul. The soul does not know itself. God alone is aware of the soul's state of bondage, and it is said that even as an inmate of the house knows that disease is in the house, so God, who is intimately linked up with the soul, is the only one who is aware of the soul's state of bondage.[11]

It would have been easy for God to destroy *āṇava* and bring the soul into union with him, but not so God as known by Śaiva Siddhāntins. God decides to bring the soul into contact with matter, to subject it to the attraction and delusion of the world, to implicate it in action and consequence till at last the soul realizes its true nature and the nature of the world and turns in disgust from that world to God. This is all deliberate on the part of God. It is a long process of edification for the soul. The soul has to undergo many births in different planes of existences and suffer the consequences of its *karma* till it will willingly let go of the world and yearn for God.[12] The first requisite for liberating the soul from *āṇava* would be a plane of enjoyment and activity, the world and an apparatus or instrument for enjoyment, the body and organs. The world and the body are evolved from *māyā,* that is, the primordial *māyā,* matter. Śiva, for Śaiva Siddhāntins, is all *sat,* all spirit, without a touch of matter. It is as if matter is non-existent because it loses all reality in his presence. And he does not come into contact with matter. If he were to act he would be implicated in the law of action and consequence. Therefore God keeps himself aloof from matter and wills his *śakti,* his power to activate the process of evolution. God must create the world but he cannot act. He cannot act the way we know a person acts; so there are his deputies who act for him. His *śakti,* his power, his grace, is part of him, yet that power acts. God keeps himself transcendent, aloof, but he makes his power or grace or *śakti,* as it is called, act for him. It is God's *śakti,* his power, which is also personified as his grace, that starts this process of evolution, that starts the flowering of creation. God and his *śakti,* his power, are compared to the sun and its light; just as the sunlight is not separated from the sun, in the same way his *śakti* is not anything apart from him.[13] God and his *śakti* are the same, but yet God keeps himself aloof and lets his power act. *Śakti* means "power," God's power and his grace.

The function of *śakti,* the power of God, is fivefold: (1) it is the desire of God to liberate the souls from the bondage of *āṇava;* (2) it is the knowledge of what complex of actions (*karma*) and consequences are to be worked out by the soul; (3) it is the act that provides the soul with the body necessary for the soul's enjoyment; (4) it is the power that activates the evolution of the world to delude the soul at the outset and to provide the arena of activity; (5) finally, it is the grace that opens the way to liberation when the soul is ready for it.

Śaiva Siddhānta speaks of five functions of God which are referred to as creation, preservation, dissolution, obscuration, and the bestowal of grace.[14] The first three functions need little comment. We have already referred to the cyclical view of the world and that it undergoes creation, preservation, and dissolution periodically. This view is common to all Hindu philosophies, not only Śaiva Siddhānta. It is notable in Śaiva Siddhānta in that it is here made part of the overall purpose of the liberation of the soul. It is not a meaningless act on the part of God. The world is evolved to provide the arena of experience for the soul to act, and it is withdrawn so that the soul, wearied by traversing from birth to birth, would have a period of rest.

The fourth task of God, obscuration, is peculiar to Śaiva Siddhānta. The path from bondage to liberation is not made easy. God deliberately ensnares the soul by making the attractions of the world manifold. The soul is exposed to the temptations of the world, the experiences of the world being seen as the necessary period of edification to wean the soul from bondage to matter. God obscures, he blinds the soul, as it were, by making the world attractive. The soul runs after the attractions of the world, which is regarded as a necessary period of edification to wean the soul from this bondage to matter (*māyā*) and bondage to *āṇava.* This is God's function of obscuration. He obscures the reality of the world. He obscures the reality of the nature of the soul. Why? Because the soul must learn through suffering. When the soul is matured by this experience in the world God is ready to show his grace and lead the soul on the last lap of the journey to liberation.

This is his fifth function, the function of grace. At the last moment when the soul is absolutely ready for liberation, God, through his grace, steps in to lead the soul to liberation.

In these tasks of creation, preservation, dissolution, obscuration, and bestowal of grace, God's *śakti* is assisted by other lesser gods or manifestations of God whom Śiva has deputized to act on his behalf, one for each task.[15] God is regarded as transcendent, the one without form (*arūpa*). And when God is seen in his forms, in his manifestations, as he is seen in abstract form (*rūpa-arūpa*), or in figures, with various distinctive characteristics (*rūpa*), God reveals himself. God is in two forms—the transcendent (*arūpa*) and the manifest (*rūpa-arūpa* and *rūpa*). The transcendent is the formless God, the one who is apart from activity, the one who is apart from creation and all this involvement. But his manifestations, his deputies, are these other gods who act on his behalf. So Śaiva Siddhānta has five gods who participate in each one of these five acts of God. These gods are: Brahmā, the God of creation; Viṣṇu, for preservation; Rudra, for dissolution; Maheśvara, for obscuration; and Sadāśiva, for grace. They assist God's *śakti,* and each one of these gods cooperate in the evolution of the world.[16] God remains transcendent but his deputies act on his behalf, as a king orders his ministers to do the work on his behalf. The king himself does not do the work, which is done by his deputies or officers.[17] These Gods perform with *śakti* each of the five functions, and Śiva remains untouched in his transcendence.

Śiva is like the potter who uses the potter's wheel to fashion pots. We speak of three causes: the efficient cause, the instrumental cause, and the material cause. There is the potter who is the efficient cause, there is the wheel that is the instrumental cause, and there is the clay that is the material cause. In the same manner, God is the efficient cause, the five gods activated by *śakti* are the instrumental cause, and *māyā* is the material cause of the world creation.[18]

Now the soul is shrouded in *āṇava* and does not have the capacity to get enlightenment for itself. So it must be equipped with a body and organs, powers that would bring in the knowledge necessary to lead it from bondage into liberation. These organs bring to the soul the knowledge of the world outside, and it is through all these organs, these elements of the body, that the power of God can act. So we see that the whole psycho-physical apparatus of the human being is designed with one purpose and that is to bring it knowledge and experience; the body that God gives to the human being has only one purpose, to bring it the knowledge and experience that is needed to lead to liberation. All these thirty-six elements (*tattvas*) bring in information from the world outside. The internal organs (*antaḥkaraṇa*) help the soul evaluate that information. The body is a necessary thing. It is given to us by God as an act of grace because we need to have the knowledge that will lead us to liberation.

The physical world of nature, likewise, is evolved from *māyā* for one purpose, and that is to provide the plane of enjoyment and experience for the soul to lead it from bondage to liberation. The world itself has no other purpose.

The soul that is ready to enter upon the world's arena must be given the right *karma,* the right body, and the right experiences. Out of the mass of actions must be chosen those that are ready for fruition, to bear fruit in that particular birth. There is a lot of *karma* that has been accumulated, and out of that has to be chosen whatever is necessary in that birth for that soul—the right body, the right experiences for the soul in that particular birth. And *karma,* as I said, is *jaḍa;* it is material. *Karma* cannot of itself attach itself to the soul.[19] And so God, the knowing spirit, takes on the responsibility of associating the right *karma* with the soul in that birth. And here again an analogy is made; it is like a person (God) placing iron filings (*karma*-consequences) near a magnet (the soul).[20] The iron filings attach themselves to the magnet, but they are placed within the attraction of the magnet by someone, namely God. In the same manner God chooses the right *karma* and the *karma* attaches itself to the soul; God places *karma* in the right place or brings it near so that the *karma* would attach itself to the soul. God's participation in associating the right *karma* with the soul has a further purpose beyond mere reward and punishment. The punishment suffered for evil deeds makes the soul seek to do what is good. The soul realizes that the reward of a good deed is equally binding and would involve it in further birth, so it learns to be indifferent. So the good and bad consequences which follow as reward and punishment are not without purpose. When the soul does something bad it suffers bad results and the soul realizes, "Oh, I shouldn't do that, I should do good." The soul will go on to do good and then realize that even good deeds mean further and further involvement in life. Then the soul realizes that it should not be involved in good or bad. The soul realizes that it should be indifferent to action, be without involvement in action. So this act of God of associating *karma* and giving reward and punishment is not without a purpose. It is part of his process of leading the soul from bondage to liberation. The God who oversees this task is like a physician giving both sweet and bitter medicine to a sick person for his or her own good. Even bitter medicine can be for one's own good. God is referred to as the good physician, the one who gives the right medicine. And it is also said that God is like a parent who chastises and punishes the child. He punishes the child so that the child may mend his or her ways and do what is right. In the same manner God uses this *karma*-complex as a parent who punishes the child or a physician who gives bitter medicine to a sick person.[21]

The participation of God in the association of *karma* with the soul occurs at every rebirth. *Karma* cannot, of itself, attach itself to the soul. The doer and the deed all go, they perish, literally they perish, but God knows what to choose and give to the soul.[22] It is God who makes the selection.

So the experiences of the soul in its association with the world and with the body and its *karma* serve at last to make the soul realize that it is different from all this. It sees its relationship to its bodily organs as that of a showman to his puppets or a charioteer to his chariot.[23] The soul sees that it is different from the body, from the world. It realizes that the world is like a mirage, that it is a perishable thing, being perceptible. It realizes that the knowledge that it has gained of the world through the senses is of no avail, being obtained through perishable means.

Now this knowledge that it has so far gained is the knowledge of the world (*pāśajñāna*) and the knowledge of itself (*paśujñāna*) as different from its body. *Pāśa* means "fetter" and *jñāna* means "knowledge"; *pāśajñāna* thus means "knowledge of the fetters, the bonds." In *pāśajñāna* the soul identifies itself with the products of *māyā* and takes the experience of empirical reality as the true one. On the other hand, *paśu* means "the soul," and *paśujñāna* is "knowledge of the soul itself," as different from the body and organs. But there is yet another knowledge, the knowledge of the

Lord, *patijñāna.*[24] *Pati* means "Lord, master, husband." The soul has yet to get this *patijñāna,* knowledge of the Lord, with whom it is inseparably united. This knowledge is beyond the reach of the senses. The soul cannot by itself see the Lord who makes it see.[25] The soul must discover by spiritual vision the God who cannot be known by defective human vision.[26] That revelation, the *patijñāna,* the revelation of God, must come from God.

When the time is right for God to reveal himself God comes in the form of a *guru,* a preceptor, a master, a teacher, who imparts this knowledge of God. God reveals himself through a preceptor to the soul that is ready for this knowledge. God is not born a human, does not come into the world as God incarnate in one human life. However, God on occasion takes human form for a temporary period to help souls. This revelation is through a human *guru,* for the *guru* is one with his devotees and his devotees are one with him.[27] When a person becomes a devotee of God, when a person becomes a liberated soul, that person is one with God, that person does not become God but is one with God. The *guru* is one such liberated soul, a person who has realized the oneness of God with him, who through his experience can reveal God to the person who is ready to receive that knowledge. It is said that one should regard the *guru* as the great Śiva himself, as the highest knowledge, as identical with all the manifestations of God, and then the *guru* becoming the Lord himself will convert the disciple by his touch, thought, and sight.[28] It is said that as one would use a tame animal to catch other animals, God uses one of his devotees to lead others to him.[29] It is said that as tears and a mother's milk, which first were not seen, appear as visible forms of an indwelling love, so God who is formless reveals himself as *guru.*[30]

The initiation through a *guru* into this knowledge of God is done in many ways: by a look of grace, by a touch, by a teaching of the *mantras* of the sacred formula, by identifying oneself with the ready soul, by imparting instruction, by becoming one with the soul, by *yoga;* in many ways this initiation can be done. The *guru* can, just by a look, make the soul realize God. He can teach the *mantras;* he can teach the scriptures; he can identify himself with the soul by *yoga.* In some way, the soul is initiated into this knowledge of God, "Just as the crystal emits fire when brought before the sun, so when the Divine *Guru,* out of the fullness of His Grace, appears before one, there will arise *Śivajñāna* in him. . . ."[31]

At this stage God's *śakti,* which had worked thus far to entangle the soul in the world's attraction, shows its true nature as grace and floods the soul with light. The stage when the soul's eyes are opened, as if its heart becomes receptive to the revelation through the *guru* who has come, is called "the descent of *śakti,*"[32] "the descent of grace," "the coming of *śakti.*" It is as though a flood of light bathes the soul and the soul sees itself and knows that it is not different from God. The soul, which hitherto could not fully comprehend its own self, now in the knowledge of Śiva (*Śivajñāna*) realizes not only God but its own self, too. This knowledge comes as the *guru* imparts this knowledge of God to the soul. The soul comes to a realization that is God-given. And in this knowledge, there is no distinction of knower, knowledge, or known. In ordinary knowledge we have these three categories: the person who knows, the act of knowing, and the thing that is known. But this knowledge of God is something in which all these categories just cease to be. The soul does not see itself as the knower. It does not even realize that it knows. It only sees that it is one with God. It is not a mental affirmation. It is a spiritual experience of union with God, of inseparable union with God.

The path from bondage to liberation is said to be a long one, but it is possible for a soul to reach liberation in one birth. If the soul is ready, God is willing to reveal himself. But the world is so mad that it does not see this straightway. Everyone tries different ways to reach God. It is said that there are those who perform sacrifice, penance, meditation, mutter sacred formulae, go on pilgrimages, perform charity, observe fasts, study the sacred texts, and so on. These are all various ways in which one attempts to reach God, to advance in the spiritual life. All these acts of worship are not without reward. One reaps the reward of these meritorious acts, perhaps in heavenly places, although one must be reborn on earth because these virtuous acts do not lead to final liberation.

Śaiva Siddhānta highlights particularly four modes of worship in reaching God.[33] The first is the path of service (*caryā*). The person who performs *caryā* is the person who helps sweep, wash, or clean the temple, who gathers flowers for worship. All these acts are service (*caryā*), and this service is referred to as the path of a slave. Like a slave one does the menial acts associated with the temple, and that is also worship. That is the path of *caryā,* the very lowest stage. The second mode of worship is through religious ritual or ceremony (*kriyā*). Both physically and mentally one participates in the ritual and advances to a higher state. The third is *yoga. Yoga* is control of body and mind. One concentrates and meditates on God by withdrawing all the senses, controlling the breath, the posture, even diet, thus the whole body and mind are brought under control. The soul meditates undisturbed on God, God without form, the transcendent God, through *yoga.* This is another way of reaching God. The final is *jñāna,* the path of knowledge, the highest path. And in this path, the last path, the human being studies all the sacred texts, sciences, and arts and rates all these as inferior to the truth of the three eternal verities: God (*pati*), the soul (*paśu*), and the fetter (*pāśa*). Also realizing that there is no distinction of knower, knowledge, and known, the soul reaches oneness with God. It realizes its oneness with God and that is the knowledge, the knowledge that comes by the realization that all else is worthless, that this experience of the inseparable union with God is the one thing that matters. This is the final stage leading to liberation, the soul's coming to the realization of its inseparable oneness with God.

The first three of these modes would give but temporary liberation, a limited period in the presence of God. It is said that each one of these three modes, *caryā, kriyā,* and *yoga,* can lead to a reward, a temporary liberation as the soul reaches the presence of God but cannot stay eternally with God. It is said that those who thus attain temporary states of liberation, if found deserving of God's grace, would attain to God's feet at the time of world dissolution. If not, they would be reborn and reach God through the path of *jñāna.*[34] These, the four modes, are like the steps in a ladder, and this way of the steps (*sopāna-mārga*) is a way of ascent towards God. The soul can start with the first and go step by step, or start in the middle, with ceremonies, and finally get to *jñāna* or straightway go into *jñāna.* These are all steps by which one can ascend.

God in his final act in the process of liberation strikes at the root of the impurity (*āṇava*).[35] This is another milestone on the soul's spiritual journey. Referred to as "maturity of the fetter" (*malaparipākan*), it implies that *āṇava* is now ready for removal like a cataract of the eye which can be removed only when it is mature, or a fruit which breaks off from the stalk when it is ripe. *Āṇava* manifests itself as ignorance, blindness, egoism, and delusion, which are but the efflorescence of the plant that is *āṇava.* Only God as *guru* can destroy the root. One might try to get rid of this manifestation but until the root cause of *āṇava* is destroyed one cannot be free. And the destruction of *āṇava* is God's supreme act of grace. *Āṇava* is the cause of the delusion, the egoism, the blindness, the ignorance; everything detrimental springs from this one fundamental root defect of the human soul. God makes *āṇava* ineffective. It is this revelation of the *guru* that can destroy this *āṇava,* and when *āṇava* is destroyed everything else that stems from it, everything else that is a result of it, will vanish. One can just try to pick away these little faults but unless one gets to the root cause of this estrangement from God, one cannot find freedom. God's act of grace, therefore, is that he strikes at the root of this *āṇava.*

NOTES

1 *SJB* p. 44.

2 *SS* II.40. It appears that the *karma* to be endured by the soul during the many rebirths in an aeon is determined by God at the beginning of the aeon and abides in *buddhi,* one of the elements that make up the subtle body. See *Śiva* pp. 159–160. The gross body, it is said, arises from the subtle body like a tree from its stump. *SS* II.36, 48–49.

3 *SS* IV.19.

4 *Tiru* 2.9.

5 *Tiru* 3.3.

6 *Tiru* 3.5.

7 *Siva* p. 150; *SS* II.85; *Tiru* 3.7.

8 *SS* II.86; XI.6.

9 *SS* IV.37–40; V.4.

10 *SJB* xi.2d, p. 75.

11 *Tiru* 5.2.

12 *SS* V.8.

13 *SJB* v.2c, pp. 47–48; *SS* V.9.

14 *SS* I.37.

15 *SS* I.34,54,60.

16 *SS* I.38;II.74. Śaiva Siddhānta speaks of God as *arūpa* ("formless"), *rūpārūpa* ("with and without form"), and *rūpa* ("with form"). Śiva, Śakti, Nāda, and Bindu are "formless"; Sadāśiva represented by the *liṅga* is "with and without form"; Maheśvara, Rudra, Viṣṇu, and

Brahmā are "with form." Rudra, the destroyer god who causes the involution of only the elements (*tattvas*) derived from impure *māyā*, is distinguished from Śiva, the Supreme God, the "formless" form.

[17] *SS* I.61.

[18] *SS* I.18. In the case of human beings, *śakti* appears to be the efficient cause, *karma* the instrumental cause, and *māyā* the material cause. See *SJB* ii.2, p. 35.

[19] *SS* I.11; II.46.

[20] *SJB* ii.2b.

[21] *SS* II.4, 15–16, 33–35.

[22] *SS* II.21. See note 2 above.

[23] *SS* IV.24.

[24] *SS* IV.2; IX.1–3. See Nallaswamy Pillai, *SS* p. 190, footnote 2; Dhavamoney, *op. cit.*, pp. 233–234.

[25] *SJB* ix.1b; *SS* IX.5.

[26] *SJB* ix.

[27] *SS* XII.3; *SJB* viii.w,pp. 58–59. The Siddhānta position is that God is present in the *guru* by possession (*avesa*).

[28] *SS* XII.7.

[29] *Tiru* 5.5; *Siva* p. 136.

[30] *SJB* p. 59.

[31] *SS* VIII.28.

[32] *SJB* p. 58; *SS* VIII.29; *Siva* p. 179ff.

[33] *SJB* viii.1a, p. 57; *SS* VIII.18–22.

[34] *SS* VIII.25.

[35] *SJB* x; *SS* VIII.10; IX.12.

4

THE LIBERATED ONE AND GOD

M. M. Arulchelvam

In the third chapter, we noted the revelation that the soul must receive from a *guru*, a teacher. This is fundamental to Śaiva Siddhānta. The final revelation, the revelation of God, must come through a *guru*. The question is raised whether everybody who sees the *guru* would receive the same revelation, even as the sunlight that is visible to one is visible to everybody who is nearby. The answer given is that the sun causes only the mature lotus to bloom.[1] So it is only to the mature soul that is matured by all the experiences that it has had in the world, that has turned away from the world and is ready for God, that the contact with the *guru* becomes a revelation. The soul that is not ready to receive this revelation will not see it as a revelation, just as when the sun comes up not every lotus bud will bloom.

Now the human soul who has received *patijñāna* or knowledge of God from the *guru* is still in its human body. It has not yet attained the final liberation from embodied existence. Such a person is liberated in life, is a liberated being (*mukta*) who is still living (*jīvan*) and is referred to as a *jīvanmukta*. The *guru* who enlightens this person is another such *jīvanmukta*. A person who is liberated in life, in this embodied state with this body, who has come to an experience of God is called a *jīvanmukta*.

In this preliminary stage when one continues to be in the embodied state, still associated with the body and organs, one is not altogether free from the attraction of *māyā*, of matter. It is said that, just as when one drops a stone into a pond that is covered by moss, the waters get cleared for a while but then they become covered over again, so in the same manner *āṇava, karma,* and *māyā,* which become detached from one when one is attached to God, can again become attached to one.[2] The realization of God that arises with a relationship with a *guru* helps loosen the grip of the three fetters, *āṇava, karma, māyā.* They are destroyed in a way. These fetters would again bind the soul unless it is careful. Such a liberated being, a *jīvanmukta,* could on occasion yield to the world's temptations as a caterpillar that had fed on bitter neem leaves could return to them even after feeding on sugar cane.[3] The soul that has been in bondage even after tasting of this revelation of God, even after coming to this experience of God, could backslide and be fettered again like this caterpillar that goes back to something bitter.

So to guard against a relapse or a return to a state of bondage, to old habits and attractions, the enlightened human being is urged to practice *sohambhāvana,*[4] to practice meditation (*bhāvana*) on the thought that he (*so,* that is, God) is one with me and I (*aham*) am one with him, that "I am He," "I am God," "I am one with God." *Sohambhāvana* is meditation on the thought that the soul is one with God, that the soul is God.

It is said that just as poison leaves one's body as one meditates on the *garuda mantra,* so meditation on the oneness with God would destroy sins, and purity would be attained. In Indian literature we often hear of the enmity of the *garuda*-bird and the snake. The *garuda* is a natural enemy of the snake, so when one has been bitten by a snake one is to meditate on the *garuda mantra.* It is a formula. One meditates on the fact that one is the *garuda* and so the venom, the poison, the power of the poison, is destroyed. In the same manner, as one meditates on the fact of oneness with God, these fetters naturally fall off. The meditation on the oneness with God transforms and purifies the soul's nature and the soul becomes like God.

The uttering of the sacred five-syllabic formula is another practice that is recommended for the spiritual neophyte.[5] This formula is still recited. It is called the *śivāyanama,* or *namaśivāya,* the five-letter formula. The phrase means "salutations to Śiva." The five letters stand for Śiva, *śakti,* soul, the fetter, and obscuring *śakti.*[6] It is ordinarily recited in the form *na-ma-śi-vā-ya. Na* and *ma* stand for the fetter and its obscuring quality. *Śi* stands for Śiva. *Vā* stands for *śakti,* Śiva's power, Śiva's grace, and *ya* stands for the soul. *Śi-vā-ya-na-ma* is a different way of recitation. In this case the soul (*ya*) comes in the middle. *Śiva* (*śi*) and gracious *śakti* (*vā*) are at the front, the soul (*ya*) stands in the middle, and the power of the fetter (*nama*) is behind, so the liberated soul is told that the better way to recite it is with *śakti* in front. The grace of God goes before the soul. So one puts Śiva and *śakti* before one, and the soul stands in between and puts the power of the fetter behind. This is a way of reciting the five-syllabic mantra (*pañcākṣara-mantra*). The recitation of the five-syllabic mantra will help the soul keep clear of future entanglements with the world.

Association with the devotees of God also helps the *jīvanmukta* to remain untainted by the world.[7] One is to associate with people who have known and love God. It is said that those who do not love God cause other *jīvanmuktas* to lose their spiritual illumination, lead one to forget their inseparable union with God, and to fall into the misery of rebirth. If one keeps company with those who do not know God they will drag one down, make one lose spiritual illumination, cause one to forget one's inseparable union with God, and drag one again into the misery of rebirth. And so *jīvanmuktas,* the liberated ones, should be great lovers of the company of Śiva's devotees and seek to assist them through knowledge, to lead them in the good way, and to make them blessed. They would also worship God in his temple for there he is manifest in visible form.[8] These, then, are three things they have been asked to do: to keep company with the devotees of Śiva, to keep company with other liberated people who would uphold them in the spiritual life, and to worship in temples where God is visible, seen in manifest form, in beautiful images.

One of the first results of the realization of the soul's oneness with God is freedom from the bondage of the three fetters. It is said that when the soul, having become one with the Lord even as the Lord is one with the soul, abides in his service, powerful *karma,* the impurity (*mala*) that is *āṇava,* and *māyā* all pass away.[9] It is only the knowledge of the Lord (*patijñāna*) that can help the soul to dissociate itself completely from the self-conceit that speaks of "I" and "mine." It is only when the soul comes to a knowledge of God that it forgets its own self, that it thinks only of God.[10]

Āṇava, we saw, was the root defect of the soul that causes self-elevation, delusion, spiritual blindness. The question again arises whether *āṇava* is really destroyed or whether it merely loses its potency to obscure. One view holds that *āṇava,* being an intrinsic defect of the soul, can never be destroyed. Like the poison that is counteracted by medicine and the darkness that is subdued by light, *āṇava* will lose its power to obscure but will remain with the soul until the soul passes from this body into final liberation; then *āṇava* will cease to exist.[11] The other view that is expressed is that as verdigris is removed from copper, and bran from rice, so the realization of God would destroy *āṇava* completely. Just as one removes the verdigris by polishing it off, or one polishes the bran from the rice, so in the same manner this *āṇava* could be removed, could be destroyed.

The destruction of *āṇava* and the purity gained by the soul do not amount to liberation. We must not assume that just because *āṇava* is destroyed and the person thereby becomes pure, that it is tantamount to liberation. *Āṇava* will truly and finally disappear only as the soul attains this inseparable union with God. In this state of God-realization the fetter of *karma* drops off from the soul. The mature *karma* that brought on the current birth would have to work itself out, like the potter's wheel that turns for a time even after the potter's hands are removed.[12] Whatever *karma* gave one this current birth will have to be endured and finished. But the accumulated *karma,* the bank balance of *karma,* will perish by the look of the *guru* just as seeds put into the fire lose their germinating power.[13] In the same manner all the *karma* that has not been endured, that has not been used up, that has been accumulated, could be destroyed by the grace of God. At the present time actions (*karma*) that are being done would have no binding effect on the *jīvanmukta,* the liberated soul, which has now reached a state of mind indifferent to action.[14] Being indifferent to the results of action, the results of action do not come back to the *jīvanmukta.* It is said that the *jīvanmukta* has no likes and dislikes: gold and a potsherd are alike. The *jīvanmukta* would dedicate all acts to God and, saying it is God who acts through one, become indifferent to the consequences. The *jīvanmukta* could not think or act without God's grace and God, entering the heart, would activate thought and action. And God would guide such a person from the contact with *karma.*[15] And so *karma* ceases to bind the liberated soul.

To be a *jīvanmukta* is to be in a state of God dependence. The soul which was egocentric has now become theocentric. As it cuts off its dependence on the world, it falls into the lap of God like a person who falls on the ground when a swing breaks.[16] When the swing or fetter that holds one to the ego and a dependence on the world gives way, one falls into the lap of God.

The knowledge of the soul's oneness with God is a realization of what has always been the relation of the soul to God. Oneness with God is not a state newly created or attained. It is an awakening to what has always been the truth, that God and the soul are one. They are in an inseparable union always, from eternity. The analogy is that of a child who is born a prince. For some reason he has fallen into the company of savages. He grows up with them. He forgets he is a prince. Suddenly his true father, the king, comes and claims this prince as his own and tells him that he is truly a prince and takes him away.[17] The soul has fallen among these savages that are the senses. The senses drag the soul in all directions into a variety of desires. The soul is redeemed from this situation by God in the form of a *guru.*

God has been described as being one with the soul, as different from the soul, and as prime mover and indweller of all souls. But the soul blinded by the fetters does not realize this indwelling God. Thus the revelation of the *guru* opens the soul's eyes to the truth of the relationship with God. What liberation does is to destroy the cause of the soul's estrangement from God and to open its eyes to the harmony that is the truth of this relationship with God. This inseparable oneness (*advaita*) with God is the truth of the soul's relationship with God from eternity.[18] To the Śaiva Siddhāntins *advaita* means "not (*a*) two (*dvaita*)," not another (*ananya*). *Advaita* does not mean "one." God and the soul do not become one so as to lose their identity. But they are not two, either. The two, God and the soul, are inseparably united. This *advaita* relationship, as Śaiva Siddhānta expounds it, is a unique one. It partakes of "difference" (*bheda*), "non-difference" (*abheda*), and also "difference and non-difference" (*bhedābheda*). It is said that "God is one with souls by association, as soul with body; He is different from souls by nature, as sun and eye; He is in union with souls, being the soul of the soul, as the consciousness of the soul unites with the eyes seeing."[19] Yet they do not become one as to lose their identity. The goal is a union with God in which the soul retains its status as soul and does not become God. There are many analogies used to describe this relationship.[20] It is said to be like a fruit and its juice. Fruit and its juice are one and yet the juice is something apart from the fruit. Or take salt and water; crystal salt can be dissolved to become one with the water, but salt and water are two things that are inseparably united in a solution. Or it is like sand that unites with wax: the wax hardens and the sand becomes firmly set in the wax, yet one sees that the sand is different from the wax. Another example that is cited is that of an iron when heated in fire. A bar of iron in the fire glows red, it become like fire, yet it is not fire. It glows red in the fire but does not become fire. It is that type of relationship; the two are separate and yet are inseparably united in a oneness. So it is with the soul that realizes its *advaita* relationship with God—it is inseparably united with God.

In the face of the many interpretations of *advaita* on the Indian scene, Śaiva Siddhāntins are at pains to explain their definition of *advaita*. Firstly, it is asserted that it is a state of union. It is said that the soul that meditates on the oneness with God becomes one with God. One following the direction of the *guru* reaches God in one's heart, one is God himself. "The seer of such truth will unite with the Lord and will never thereafter leave Him, like the rushing waters of the river breaking its banks, reaching the ocean, become one with it and can never more return."[21] So the soul is one with God and yet it is a state in which the soul is not destroyed or loses its separateness. For if it is a state in which the soul is destroyed, in which the soul ceases to exist, then it is not a union. A union with what is destroyed is not a union. If one says that the soul remains utterly separate, it is not a union either. Or if the soul is destroyed after union, what is it that experiences this liberation? Or if one holds that the destruction of the self is liberation, then it conflicts with the truth that the soul is eternal.[22] The point is that the soul is not lost in this union. Although the soul becomes one with God, yet it is not God; it does not have equal status with God. The soul is still the servant and God its master.[23] It cannot perform the five tasks of creation, preservation, dissolution, obscuration, and bestowal of grace. The soul is still soul. Then God is gracious intelligence, and the soul is that which partakes of this grace. God is the intelligence that causes the soul to go through births and leads it to liberation. The soul is that which is subjected to these births. God is the intelligence that is self-luminous and it illumines others, and the soul is that which receives this light and knowledge. So God and the soul, though in union inseparably, are not of equal status.

This *advaita* relationship is one that we, by our efforts, cannot attain. "God hides like a thief in the heart and man cannot see Him with his usual organs of sight."[24] God is beyond the reach of mind and speech. To say that one perceives God by ordinary senses is a delusion. Yet God is not unknowable. If God is unknowable then there can be no benefits from him.[25] He could never pervade us nor could we unite with him in liberation. He would be like the flowers of the sky or a rope formed of the hairs of the tortoise.

God is knowable but he cannot be known by human faculties of knowledge. He can only be known when our human faculties are transformed into divine faculties,[26] when our "defective human vision" is replaced by "divine vision." It is a perception which is unlike ordinary perception, a perception in which the ordinary distinctions of knower, knowledge, and known are lost.[27] The soul does not see itself as the knower nor is it conscious that it knows. It merely sees Him who is Lord. It is just conscious of one thing, God. It does not see that it knows, it only sees that which is known. God can never become an object of perception, something that one can point to as "that."[28] God is both the knower, the one who activates our understanding, and the one that is to be known. In this perception all these ordinary distinctions merge and the soul has an experience that cannot be analyzed. It is an experience in which the soul melts itself, melts into and loses itself in God. It is the joy like that of lovers in marriage, an indescribable experience that an unmarried man or woman would not know. It is the joy like a cool shelter for one suffering from the heat, the misery of births. It is like the joy of sight to a blind man.[29] It is an indescribable experience. It is an experience that is to be had in receptivity, in being still. It is said that the soul's efforts to reach God must now be still. One has reached the point beyond which one cannot go and so one has to be still, receptive to the revelation that must come.

In self-forgetfulness one can be receptive to the liberation that must come from God. It is not a sight. It is not a mental exercise. This is a transforming experience so it is called an *anubhava* or *anubhūti* (from the same base *anubhū*, meaning "experience"), which we can see from the lives of the Śaiva saints. What is this experience like? Here we have to look at the lives of the Śaiva saints.[30] They forget propriety. They sing, they dance. They behave like men possessed or mad. Their whole being melts in this experience of God and gushes forth as hymns of praise, adoration, and longing. They cannot wait to consummate this union with God, truly to become one with God. They see themselves as a slave, son, friend, and the beloved of God; God is their master, parent, friend, and lover. They are not fearful or reticent about the experience. They are bold, undaunted, proclaiming to all and sundry this experience of God. One of the saints, Apparswāmi, writes:

No man holds sway o'er us,
Nor death nor hell fear we;
No tremblings, griefs of mind,
No pains nor cringings see.
Joy, day by day, unchanged
Is ours, for we are His,
His ever, who doth reign,
Our Śankara, in bliss.
Here to His feet we've come,
Feet as plucked flow'rets fair;
See how His ears divine
Ring and white conch-shell wear.[31]

And there's another one from the *Tiruvāçagan.* This is Saint Māṇikkavāçagar speaking about his conversion:

Lest I should go astray, He laid His hand on me!
As wax before the unwearied fire
With melting soul I worshipt, wept, and bent myself,
Danced, cried aloud, and sang, and prayed.
They say: "The tooth of elephant and woman's grasp relax not,"
So I with love, real, intermitting never,
Was pierced, as wedge driven into soft young tree.
All tears, I like the refluent sea was tossed;
Soul was subdued, and body quivered with delight.
While the world called me demon, mocking me,
False shame I threw aside; the folk's abusive word
I took as ornament; nor did I swerve.
My mind was rapt;—a fool, but in my folly wise,—
The goal I sought to reach infinity! All wondering desire,
As cow yearns for its calf, I moaning, hurried to and fro.
Not ev'n in dreams thought I of other gods.
The One most precious Infinite to earth came down;
Nor did I greatness of the Sage superne contemn,
Who came in grace. Thus from the pair of sacred feet
Like shadow from its substance parting not,
Before, behind, at every point, to it I clung.
My inmost self in strong desire dissolved, I yearned;
Love's river overflowed its banks;
My senses all in Him were centred; 'Lord!' I cried.
With stammering speech, and quivering frame
I clasped adoring hands; my heart expanding like a flower.
Eyes gleamed with joy and tears distilled.
His love that fails not day by day still burgeons forth![32]

NOTES

[1] *SJB* pp. 73–74.

[2] *SJB* viii.4c; *SS* VIII.39.

[3] *SJB* ix.3. *Neem* is *azedirechta indica,* called *nimba* in Sanskrit and *vēmpu* in Tamil.

[4] *SS* IX.7; X.1; XII.3.

[5] *SJB* ix.3a,3b; *SS* IX.1,8; *Śiva* p. 236; *Tiru* 9.

[6] The *Śakti* that implicates the soul in embodied existence and makes it savor the world is called the "obscuring" *Śakti* (*tirodhāna śakti*). When the soul is spiritually mature and ready for God's revelation, *Śakti* becomes the "gracious" power or *aruḷ śakti.* The formula is now to be recited with *Śiva* and the "gracious" *Śakti* going in front of the soul. See *Tiru* 7.8.

[7] *SJB* xii.2, p. 76; *SS* XII.1–3.

[8] *SJB* xii.3; *SS* XII.4.

[9] *SJB* x.

[10] *SJB* x.1; *SS* X.2.

[11] *SS* XI.4–6; *Śiva* p. 228.

[12] *SS* X.6. The analogy is also used of a pot that retains for some time the smell of asafoetida even after it has been taken out of the pot. *SJB* x.2c.

[13] *SS* X.; *Śiva* p. 229.

[14] *SS* VIII.29, 30–31. This state of spiritual maturity (called *iruviṇaiyoppu,* "equal regard for good and bad actions") implies that the soul is no longer concerned to avoid demerit and to accumulate merit. *SJB* p. 58.

[15] *SJB* viii.4; p. 60.

[16] *SJB* viii.

[17] *SJB* p. 33.

[18] *SJB* p. 33.

[19] *SJB* ii.1c,d; vi.2e (p. 530); ix.3b (p. 67).

[20] *SS* IX.7; X.1; XII12; *SJB* viii.4a.

[21] *SJB* xi.2c, p. 75; *SS* XI.9.

[22] *SJB* i.e; ii.4; xii.4; *SS* XI. 10,11.

[23] *SJB* ix.1b; *SS* VI.5,7; VII.36; IX.4–5.

[24] *SS* VI.4.

[25] *SJB* ix.

[26] *SJB* x.1; *SS* VIII.22; XI.2; *Tiru* 8.9.

[27] *SS* VI.5–7.

[28] *SJB* ix, p. 63; *SS* VIII. 36, 38.

[29] *SS* X.3; *Śiva* p. 234; *Tiru* 8.9.

[30] Some of the great Śaiva saints belong to the period between the sixth and the ninth century A.D. This was an important time in the religious history of South India. The Śaiva saints went throughout the length and breadth of South India singing these praises of God in every shrine. They sang to music and would have a great company of devotees and interested people follow them. This religious revival resulted in a great amount of temple building. Most of the temples of South India were built after the sixth century A.D., up to the fourteenth century A.D. The songs and praises of these Śaiva saints have been collected. Māṇikkavāçagar was one of these saints, and his songs form part of this great collection of hymns that we have in Śaivism. The stories of the Śaiva saints portray such a personal communion with God that one would not imagine that that personal relationship would be lost. See V.A. Devasenapathi, *Of Human Bondage and Divine Grace* (Tirupapuliyur, India: Saraswathi Press for Annamalai University: 1963), pp. 47, 52.

[31] Translation from F. Kingsbury and G. E. Phillips, *Hymns of the Tamil Śaivite Saints* (Calcutta: Association Press, 1921), p. 51.

[32] *Tiruvāçagam* 4.59–86, in *The Tiruvāçagam: The Tamil Text of the Fifty-one Poems,* translated by Rev. G. U. Pope (Oxford: Clarendon Press, 1900), pp. 34–35.

5

THE GIFT IMMUTABLE

M. M. Arulchelvam

In liberation, in the inseparable union with God when the soul leaves behind this mortal body, the soul is free from the three fetters of *āṇava, karma,* and *māyā* and the limitations of time and place in the embodied state. When the soul is free from *āṇava, karma,* and *māyā,* the soul becomes spirit like God. It goes back to the formless (*arūpi*) state where it does not have a shape or a form. It becomes like God, spirit (*arūpi*), and it becomes pervasive (*vyāpi*), like God. It is not limited by two limitations: (1) the particularity of place or (2) the particularity of time. However, two other limitations—(3) dependence and (4) dependent knowledge—are part of the soul's status as soul. The soul was destined from eternity to a dependent existence, never for equality or identity with God. In the embodied state, the soul is dependent on and identifies itself with its material organs of knowledge, the internal organs and the senses, and receives the knowledge of the world that they bring. In like manner, in liberation the soul identifies itself with God and is illumined by him.[1] Its knowledge, which was clouded earlier by *āṇava,* is now a cleaver to the fetters, and the soul sees as the indwelling Lord makes it see.

In this state when the soul turns in total self-surrender and self-forgetfulness to the Lord, its focus is not on itself but on the Lord, seeking to reach the feet of God. One particularly expressive analogy for this state of inseparable union is contained in the phrase *tatalai.*[2] This phrase is composed of two words, *tāḷ* and *talai. Tāḷ,* an ordinary Tamil word, means "foot." And *talai* means "head." According to the usual rules of euphonic combination of words, when *-ḷ,* the final letter of *tāḷ* and *t-,* the initial letter of *talai* combine, they are not separated but coalesce to form *d.* So *tatalai* is composed of two separate words but in the combined form, it is one. It is like the inseparable union of God and soul and is particularly expressive because it implies that the soul places its head at the feet of God. It is a common sight in the temples of India to find devotees falling down prostrate on the floor before the statue of the deity, the head touching the floor. One sees even students falling at the feet of the teacher, bowing when they take their leave. Sometimes when a young bride goes to the house of her parents-in-law for the very first time as a bride, she falls at the feet of her parents-in-law. The practice is one of bowing down to place one's head at the feet of the person whom one reveres.

We have been surveying the progression of the soul from bondage to liberation, and we are now faced with the task of assessing to what extent we could consider this progression to be the result of grace on the part of God. Śaiva Siddhāntins insist that it is God's grace that makes this possible. We have in Tamil different words to connote different types of love. Romantic love, the love of a man and woman, is one type of love. And we have another word which is used to denote a more general type of love. And that is the very common word *aṉpu.* The love of parent for child, the love between friends, even the love of God can be *aṉpu.*

But we have a special word, the word *aruḷ,* for God's grace. Generally, English dictionaries tend to define grace as "the unmerited favor of God." Grace is favor which the soul does not deserve but which God gives. God does not have to give, but God gives favor and love to a soul that does not merit it. This type of love is *aruḷ,* a love that is not merited, that is not deserved in any way. So grace becomes grace because one has no claim to it. One does not deserve it. There is no equal transaction between God and man. One would never be able to repay or thank God enough for his grace. God's grace is priceless because one is helpless without it. If there were a way to help oneself, then God's grace would not be so inestimable. There is another dimension to this grace of God who is a perfect, complete, self-dependent being. He needs nothing. He has no desires for himself. If he acts to liberate the soul from bondage it is solely out of his love for it.[3] God acts to liberate souls in bondage to *āṇava,*[4] not for his own benefit, but solely out of his pity for them. The soul would remain until eternity in this inert, blind state if God did not act. It is only in the embodied state that the soul has the chance to rid itself of *āṇava* and to work out its *karma.* It is said that the Supreme One induces the souls to unite in bodies with five senses to undergo pains and pleasures, makes them gather experience by suffering many births, pities their fallen condition, graciously grants the higher knowledge as *guru,* and grants the supreme seat.[5] So God in his grace acts to equip the soul with the body that would bring it the knowledge of the world as well as activate its other powers, its cognitive, conative, and emotive powers. It is God's act of grace that gives the soul the body so that it can get the knowledge necessary to lead it to liberation.

Further, God activates the evolution of the material world. The evolution of the material world has no other purpose than to provide the arena for the activities of the embodied soul. There is no other purpose seen in the creation of the world except this purpose of liberating the soul. The world is provided for the soul to work out its *karma* and to work itself free from this *āṇava.* The soul's association with the body and the material world, with the impurity of *māyā,* though at first deluding, has ultimately a benign purpose. At first the soul is deluded, attracted by the world, and immerses itself in the attractions of the world. God has a good purpose in that. It is said that God uses *māyā* as the washerman uses fuller's earth to make the garment clean.[6] It seems to dirty the garment at the start but it eventually makes the garment whiter. So God uses *māyā* like fuller's earth to make the soul free of its *āṇava.*

Karma, likewise, is used by God to further the purpose of liberating the soul. It is said "that it is out of His love that He punishes the wicked to make them mend their ways. All his acts, therefore, flow out of his love. Parents punish their refractory children, is this not out of love? God's anger is also similarly manifested."[7] Again, it is said "God's acts are determined by love. . . . Making the souls eat the fruit of their *karma* in the different worlds, giving each suitable bodies, God removes *mala,* that is *āṇava,* by means of these medicines and gives the soul the highest bliss and crowns them with his own lotus feet."[8] God's acts are determined by love. So he uses *karma* as a deterrent to teach the soul to act rightly, to wean it from the thought that it is an agent, to get it into an attitude of indifference to actions. So this second fetter, *karma,* is also God's act of grace.

God uses *karma* to liberate the soul from *āṇava.* When the soul is getting ready for liberation, God gives it the knowledge that it needs. He illumines the soul. He gives it knowledge of the Lord (*patijñāna*). It is said that even the greatest sins performed by a *jīvanmukta,* a person liberated in life, will be counted good service. It is said that the sins of God's devotees become virtues and the virtues of loveless men are sinful.[9] In this stage of enlightenment, we find that the nature of deeds that one does matters not. What matters is the state of mind or rather the devotion to God with which one does the deed. So God, in his grace, liberates the soul from bondage to *karma.*

God's participation in the five tasks or acts of creation, preservation, dissolution, obscuration, and the bestowal of grace, through his five forms (Brahmā, creation; Viṣṇu, preservation; Rudra, dissolution; Maheśvara, obscuration; and Sadāśiva, bestowal of grace), are seen as acts and forms of grace. It is because of his concern for the soul's toiling through many births that he wills a period of dissolution so that the soul could rest and then when the soul is ready, he comes in grace to enlighten. It is repeatedly asserted that his various forms are manifestations of his grace. It is said that his form is love. His attributes and knowledge are love. His five functions are love. His arms, feet, and ornaments are love. These things are assumed by the pure God, not for his own benefit but for that of humankind.[10]

It is asserted that "unless the Supreme assumes forms, we cannot have manifestations of his five functions, of his grace to his loving devotees (*bhaktas*). We cannot receive sacred revelation. We cannot eat the fruit of our own *karma* and seek relief."[11] It is out of his grace that the transcendent God assumes form, performs the five functions, reveals the scriptures, and comes as *guru.* When it is time for creation to unfold, Śakti, God's grace, separates herself, but not entirely, in order to assume form, and begins to act. It is said that God's grace is his Śakti. Without this supreme love and grace, there is no Śiva. Without Śiva, there is no Śakti.[12] They are inseparable. It is interesting that God's love and grace are spoken of in the feminine as Śakti (the word *śakti* itself is the feminine form) and personified as his wife. The inseparable oneness of God and his grace is portrayed in that form of Śiva which is half-man and half-woman (the *Ardhanārīśvara* form [*ardha* means "half," *nārī* means "woman," *īśvara* means "Lord"]). The right side is male and the left side is female, both comprising one form. This form personifies or rather embodies this concept that God is one with his Śakti. God and his grace are one.

In Māṇikkavāçagar's *Tiruvāçagam,* one reads that God is addressed as father and as mother. His love is said to be like a mother's love for her child and greater than a mother's love. God is approached as one would approach a mother because a mother is gracious, is loving. The greatest love most human beings experience is their mother's love, and God's love is compared to that.

God's coming as *guru* is the last and most important of his revelations as far as the human being is concerned. The human being has come to the end of self-effort to know God. The knowledge of God, *patijñāna,* must come from God himself and God, in his graciousness, comes as *guru* to initiate the seeking soul. So it is God's final act of grace. He comes as *guru* to take the soul over the last lap of the journey to liberation. The soul reaches a certain point, beyond which the soul cannot do anything; there and then God comes to lift the soul from that state to liberation.

All souls are meant to reach liberation sooner or later. There is no damnation or hell reserved for sinful souls. *Karma* and repeated births provide for a long period of edification and purification for the souls until they are mature for liberation. The souls, after one birth, are not condemned to hell nor are they damned; they have infinite opportunity in repeated births for edification and purification until at last they are ready for liberation.

All souls do not have to take the same path to liberation. There are varying temperaments: those who prefer to do the work in a temple (*caryā*), those who like to help in the ritual (*kriyā*), those who like meditation and *yoga,* and those who prefer the final path of *jñāna.* Souls can advance from various "directions" or ways. They can tread the path of *caryā;* they can come along *kriyā;* they can follow the path of *yoga;* but finally it is through *jñāna,* through this door of enlightenment, that the souls get to liberation. This progressive path to liberation is the way of the staircase (*sopānamārga*), a way of gradual ascent.

It will be noticed in this survey of the ascent to liberation that human participation in the process is also required. In this there is seen God's response to human effort. "The Lord enlightens the soul as *guru* because of the soul's meritorious practices."[13] Further, it is said, that "if a man leaving the alien religions plods the path laid down, observes the duties in the various stages of life, practices penance, masters the holy text, and steps beyond, he will reach the height of Śaiva Siddhānta." And there again, he will tread the path of *caryā, kriyā,* and *yoga,* and then finally reach the path of *jñāna.*[14] So one has to engage in all these meritorious acts, perform penances, and slowly, but surely, one advances. It is obvious, therefore, that one does not advance in the spiritual life without effort on one's part, but the initiative comes from God. He sees our state of bondage and acts to liberate us. He sets the stage for the soul, gives it the world and the body necessary for the task, gives it the desire and the will to act. It is up to the soul to decide whether to accept this opportunity that God offers or to postpone the quest for liberation. The soul is often wayward and will not soon let go of the world's pleasures. But God is gracious and patient and goes on offering infinite chances to the soul until at last it reaches liberation. The soul has the freedom to go on rejecting God's grace any number of times. Yet God is gracious enough to wait, until finally the soul decides to come to God, to reach liberation.

In evaluating this problem, whether it is grace alone or whether one's effort is needed also, we would do well to turn to the Śaiva saints. For them, first and last, it is a matter of a living experience of God's infinite grace. Māṇikkavaçagar says, "It is by this grace that we worship his feet." And another saint says, "Unless we see God with his grace as our eye, we cannot know him, we cannot describe him." We cannot describe God unless God in his grace reveals himself to us. There is no question in the hymns of these saints of one's worth or of one's deserving such grace.

There are certain recurring motifs in these hymns which underline this fact. Firstly, God is an embodiment of all perfection. There is no epithet of perfection that is wanting in descriptions of him. God is the best, the highest, the most gracious, the most wonderful. He is both the transcendent God, the source of all life and yet, at the same time, he is very dear and close to his devotees, a God who dwells in the many holy temples all over the land. He is formless, beyond reach of mind and eye, and yet he is God who is worshipped in visible form in his images possessed of distinctive form and feature. The hymns of the saints are rapturous outpourings of praise, of the power and majesty of God. Words are inadequate to convey all his greatness and his goodness. The devotee often recalls the many gracious acts God has done in times past, giving his love and grace to those who seek him. In the presence of this majestic God the devotee is struck with the feeling of great unworthiness. Māṇikkavāçagar compares himself to a dog, unworthy, like a dog, in bondage to birth and decay. Māṇikkavāçagar says that he was forgetful of God's love, that his heart would not melt, that it was as hard as iron, that he was a slave to the pleasure of the senses, carried away by the pleasure of the world and led astray by women of ruby-red lips. He often regrets this. And God, out of his great love and grace, has deigned to accept as his own such an unworthy creature. He has accepted a creature so unworthy of him. And what happens? One is filled with ecstasy, with unspeakable joy at God's graciousness. One cannot thank God enough for his graciousness because God has accepted someone so utterly unworthy of him, and one is filled with longing to throw off one's mortal coils, to be one with God.

Māṇikkavāçagar says:

Him none by hearing know; He knoweth no decay;
He hath no kin; naught asking, heareth all!
While people of the land beheld, here on this earth to me a cur,
He gave a royal seat;
To me, a dog, all things not shown before, He showed;
all things not heard before, He caused to hear;
And guarding me from future "birth," He made me His.
Such is the wondrous work our Lord hath wrought for me![15]

And another saint, Sundaramūrti Swāmi, sings:

I roamed, a cur, for many days
Without a single thought of Thee,
Roamed and grew weary, then such grace
As none could win Thou gavest me.
. . . . .
My Shepherd, I became all thine;
How could I now myself forswear?[16]

To the extent to which the Śaiva saints conceived of God in superlatives as the highest, most powerful, most majestic, to that extent did they seem unworthy of this love and acceptance. In proportion to one's unworthiness did seem the greatness of God's love, and in proportion to God's unbounded grace was one's unspeakable joy at being accepted by God. So all these factors are present: God's greatness, one's unworthiness, God's unbounded grace, and one's unspeakable joy, the latter three commensurate with the first.

God's participation in the creation, preservation, and destruction of the world is often referred to as *līlā,* as sport, as play.[17] God's five functions of creation, preservation, dissolution, obscuration, and bestowal of grace are symbolized in the form of God as the dancing Śiva (*Naṭarājan,* literally, "king [*rājan*] of dance [*naṭa*]").

Creation is characterized as sport, not because it is purposeless, but because God has no need or purpose of his own to be fulfilled by the creation of the world. These are all acts of grace. God participates in these five acts for one purpose, so that the souls may eat their *karma,* and get rid of their impurities (*mala*), and attain liberation. The starting point is the existential situation of humankind in bondage, to time, place, birth, decay, *māyā, karma,* and above all to the basic impurity of *āṇava.* It is God alone who can act to initiate the process of liberation. He sets the stage for the soul's activity, equips it with a body and organs for this purpose, and when the soul is mature for liberation, God acts to destroy the impurity of *āṇava* that was the ultimate cause of bondage.

And so, every human being, every human soul, echoes the prayer of a Śaiva saint who prays thus: "Oh, for the day when I shall be in inseparable union with the wise, ever-stable One, even as now I am in inseparable union with *āṇava.* Even as I am in inseparable union with *āṇava,* when can I ever be in inseparable union with God?" And God's act in creation, God's grace in creation, is the answer to this prayer.

NOTES

[1] *SJB* iv.2; *SS* IV.20, 31, 40.

[2] *Tiru* 8.4.

[3] *SS* II.27.

[4] *SS* IV.38; V.4.

[5] *SS* V.8.

[6] *SS* II.52.

[7] *SS* II.15,16.

[8] *SS* I.36; II.51.

[9] *SS* II.29.

[10] *SS* I.47.

[11] *SS* I.54.

[12] *SS* I.46.

[13] *SS* V.9.

[14] *SJB* viii.

[15] *SS* viii.11. Śaiva Siddhānta distinguishes between the merits of following the paths of *caryā, kriyā,* and *yoga* and the merit one acquires

by observing the prescriptions of the *dharmaśāstras.* The latter merit referred to as *paśu-puṇya* brings only temporary felicity. Like a person who has eaten becoming hungry again, one realizes that a life of ritual rectitude would not bring final liberation and that one would have to follow the path of *jñāna.* The merit one acquires through *caryā, kriyā,* and *yoga,* however, is never lost. This merit, called *Śiva-puṇya,* would take the soul onward on its spiritual quest. *SJB* viii. See also *Śivajñāna-pādiyam* (Śivajñāna Yogi's commentary on the *Śivajñānabodham*), viii.1.

[16] *Tiru,* xv. 28, p. 56.

[17] F. Kingsbury and G. E. Philips, *Hymns of the Tamil Śavite Saints,* The Heritage of India Series (Calcutta: Association Press and London: Oxford University Press, 1921), p. 77.

[18] *SS* I.36.

KARMA, BHAKTIYOGA, AND GRACE IN THE ŚRĪVAIṢṆAVA TRADITION: RĀMĀNUJA AND KĀRAṬṬĀḶVĀṆ

Vasudha Narayanan

Another major theistic devotional movement that developed in India has come to be called the Śrīvaiṣṇava tradition. Like the Śaiva Siddhānta, the Śrīvaiṣṇava tradition has provided one of the major statements in our human history about God's grace and human responses.

In the chapters dealing with Śaiva Siddhānta, Dr. Arulchelvam gave us a general view of a comprehensive doctrinal complex that enables one to see the centrality of our theme, human bondage and divine grace, as some of us on this globe have discerned it. Now, in this chapter and the one following, Dr. Vasudha Narayanan will turn our attention to the Śrīvaiṣṇava heritage and demonstrate another approach, considering the thought of a few leading thinkers on the relevant issues of human action and religious discipline in the presence of God's grace.

The Śrīvaiṣṇava tradition of South India worships the Lord Viṣṇu and his consort Śrî and considers the theologian Rāmānuja (traditional dates: A.D. 1017–1137) as its most important teacher and interpreter of scripture. The community, like other Hindus, accepts the validity of Sanskrit scripture, that is, the *Vedas,* the epics, *Rāmāyaṇa* and the *Mahābhārata,* the *Purāṇas* and the books on *dharma*/ethics and law, but in addition to these accepts some Sanskrit works known as the *Pāñcarātra* texts as authoritative. This

Sanskrit canon is just one set of scripture for the Śrīvaiṣṇavas who pride themselves on having a dual heritage in two languages: in addition to Sanskrit, they have sacred texts in Tamil. The Tamil literature that the community considers as "revealed," and equal to the *Vedas* (a self-consciously bold claim) consists of 4,000 verses, composed by poet/saints who lived between the seventh and tenth centuries A.D. The Śrīvaiṣṇavas consider that God revealed himself through two languages, and Śrīvaiṣṇava men traditionally have the honorific prefix *ubhayavedāntācārya* ("teachers of the dual-vedanta or philosophy") before their names.

The Tamil poems considered to be scripture were composed by mystics called *āḻvārs,* those who were "immersed" in the love of Lord Viṣṇu. They were contemporaries of devotee poets of Śiva known as the *nāyaṉmārs,* some of whom were mentioned in the previous chapters. The *āḻvārs'* poems are filled with intense emotional and intellectual devotion (*bhakti*). The word *bhakti* is derived from the root *bhaj,* which means "to divide and distribute"; *bhakti* means "belonging to, attachment, devotion, trust, homage, worship, piety, faith or love."[1] The wave of devotion that began in South India around the seventh century A.D. continued in its intensity and influenced the religious patterns that emerged in medieval Northern India. The *bhakti* of the *āḻvārs* was manifested in ecstatic and ritual surrender to the Lord, singing the glory and majesty of the divine name, a sustained meditation on the divine attributes and service to the deity and other devotees.

The Śrīvaiṣṇava community split into two major sub-groups, the Vaṭakalais ("Northern Culture") and the Teṅkalais ("Southern Culture"); the origin of these words is obscure. While the names are fairly late (probably two or three centuries old), the two groups look back to the thirteenth century for the source of their theological disagreements and identify Vedānta Deśika (1268–1368) and Piḷḷai Lōkācārya (born A.D. 1264) as the "correct" interpreters, respectively, of the vision of Rāmānuja. Vedānta Deśika and Piḷḷai Lōkācārya differed primarily in their understanding of divine grace and the human being's role in the scheme of salvation. Like Rāmānuja (and many other Hindus), the two leaders in the thirteenth century accept that human beings are bound to a cycle of life and death because of the consequences of their deeds in past lives which affect the quality of future lives (*karma*) and salvation. The question that Śrīvaiṣṇava theologians find problematic is this: how does the Lord elect or select people for salvation, and what is the human being's role in this scheme? While it is accepted that it is only the grace of the Lord that puts an end to one's *karma* and effects salvation, the issue of a human being's participation (or lack of participation) in this scheme is discussed by the Śrīvaiṣṇava theologians, and the differences in opinion crystallized in the thirteenth century. The theological differences eventually led to a social split of the community and, till the first half of the twentieth century, marriages and even dining with members of the other sub-group was, if not taboo, at least considered to be undesirable in the Śrīvaiṣṇava tradition.

We shall discuss the Śrīvaiṣṇava views on human bondage and divine grace in two stages: in this chapter I shall present the views of Rāmānuja and his disciple the scribe Kūraṭṭāḷvāṇ (eleventh century A.D.). All Śrīvaiṣṇavas accept the views of Rāmānuja. In the next chapter, we shall consider the interpretations of Vedānta Deśika and Piḷḷai Lōkācārya in the thirteenth century; their views are upheld by the Vaṭakalai and Teṅkalai Śrīvaiṣṇavas today, respectively.

RĀMĀNUJA ON *BHAKTIYOGA*

Rāmānuja was one of the greatest Hindu theologians. He differed from the teachings of Śaṅkara, who, in the eighth century A.D., preached a non-dualistic interpretation of scripture. Rāmānuja presented a theistic interpretation of scripture and extolled the importance of devotion to the Lord.

Rāmānuja accepted that a person's *karma* bound that person to a cycle of repeated birth and death and that liberation from this cycle led to eternal happiness with the Lord Viṣṇu in the transcendental abode of *vaikuṇṭha.* In the state of "liberation" a human soul served the Lord with love. Rāmānuja wrote only in Sanskrit to a pan-Indian audience; and in his longer writings, the *Commentary on the Brahma Sūtras* (*Śrībhāsya*), the *Commentary on the Bhagavad Gīta* (*Gītābhāsya*), and the *Essence of the Meaning of the Veda* (*Vedārtha Saṃgraha*), he speaks of the discipline of *bhakti* (*bhaktiyoga*) as the way to attract the grace of the Lord. In other words, it is to a devotee who practices *bhaktiyoga* that the Lord is compassionate. This path of *bhaktiyoga* is restricted to men of the upper three classes of Hindu society, because it entailed knowledge of the Sanskrit scripture; women and the fourth class of society (*śudras*) were prohibited from learning the Sanskrit *Vedas.* We shall first understand Rāmānuja's notion of *bhaktiyoga* as seen in his larger writings, and then turn our attention to what he has to say in his other works—the *Hymn of Surrender* (*Śaraṇāgati gadya*), the *Hymn to the Lord Raṅganātha* (*Śrīraṅga gadya*), and the *Hymn on Vaikuṇṭha* (*Vaikuṇṭha gadya*). In the hymns, he confesses that he does not have the qualification of *bhaktiyoga* and is therefore throwing himself at the mercy of the Lord.

In the *Gītābhāṣya,* Rāmānuja defines *bhaktiyoga* as continuous meditation accompanied by love.[2] In his *Śrībhāṣya* he elucidates this notion of meditation (*dhyāna*):

> "Meditation" means steady remembrance, that is, a continuity of steady remembrance, uninterrupted like the flow of oil. . . . "Meditation" has the character of "seeing" or "intuition." And that remembrance has the character of "seeing" is due to the element of imagination (representation) which prevails in it. . . . Such remembrance has been declared to be of the character of "seeing" and this character of seeing consists in its possessing the character of immediate presentation (*pratyakṣata*). . . . He who possesses remembrance, marked by the character of immediate presentation (*sākṣātkāra*) and which itself is dear above all things since the object remembered is such; he, we say, is chosen by the highest Self, and by him the highest Self is gained. Steady remembrance of this kind is designated by the word "devotion," *bhakti;* for this term has the same meaning as *upāsana* (meditation). . . .[3]

This steady remembrance only results from a strict discipline:

> Steady remembrance results only from abstention, and so on; his words being "This (namely, steady remembrance, meditation) is obtained through abstention, freeness of mind, repetition, works, virtuous conduct, freedom from dejection, absence of exultation according to feasibility, and scriptural statement. . . ."[4]

Bhakti is attained by intense love (*Gītābhāsya* [hereafter abbreviated *GB*] 9-2). The devotee always remembers the divine names and seeks to worship and serve the Lord with joy. This loving activity is combined with a meditation on the Lord, a meditation filled with love and a realization of the knowledge that one is the slave or the "owned-one" (*śeṣa*)[5] of the Lord. Love of the Lord and a knowledge that the human being is his *śeṣa* constitute the matrix of *bhakti.*

> Thus the supreme Brahman is the ocean of infinite and unsurpassed excellences of attributes. He transcends all evil. The expanse of his glory is boundless. He abounds in surpassing condescension, maternal compassion, and supreme beauty. He is the principal entity (*śeṣin*). The individual self is subservient to him. If a seeker meditates on the supreme with a full consciousness of this relationship (between the Lord and himself) as the principal entity and subsidiary entity, and if the supreme Brahman so meditated upon becomes an object of supreme love (*prīti*) to the devotee, *then* he himself effectuates the devotee's god realization.[6]

This *bhaktiyoga* is attained by a synthesis of *karmayoga* and *jñānayoga,*[7] in other words, in the performance of all rituals and actions that are incumbent on one by virtue of one's caste and station in life and a systematic knowledge of scripture.

Bhakti is engendered and nourished by a knowledge of the omnipotence of God. A knowledge of his complete supremacy removes obstacles in the way of *bhakti.*[8] Since this knowledge is stressed, it seems to imply that a knowledge of God's sovereignty is so powerful that it overwhelms and convinces one of one's own finitude on the one hand and the power of God on the other; assured of the omnipotency of God, human beings may turn to him—with humility, love, service, and faith.

But it is not merely with humility and worshipful reverence that one turns to the divine power; a strong element of love is overwhelmingly discernible. There is a basic commitment on the part of Rāmānuja to look upon the Lord as the powerful sovereign on the one hand and as a loving, merciful father on the other. He is the sovereign, the support, the king, and an exalted person who has a right to be served; on the other hand, he inspires it, being a gracious person, to whom "all creatures, existing in all three states of time (past, present, and future) are objects of loving concern" (*GB* 7-26). In the eleventh chapter of the *Bhagavadgīta,* Arjuna is given a vision of the Lord's supreme and awesome form, which precipitates Arjuna's humility; but it is to the father, the accessible friend and lover, that the appeal for grace is made.[9] The Lord makes himself accessible, so as to give rise to this humility, confidence, love, worship, devotion, and faith and does so as a "refuge."[10]

The Lord is conceived as the *nidhānam* (rest, repository) several times. He is the refuge (*śaraṇam*), and Rāmānuja paraphrases this as "the refuge or the Intelligent Being to whom one resorts to fulfil hopes and avoid evil. The only way to cross the ocean of births and deaths is to seek the Lord as a refuge" (*GB* 7-14). All actions are to be dedicated to him, for he is the absolute Lord, the owner (*śeṣi, GB* 9-27). One's heart is to be fixed on him; one is to worship him, bow before and give oneself up to him, for, again, he is both the sole cause, the Supreme Brahman, *and* an ocean of compassion and affection (*GB* 9-34).

A knowledge of the Lord's sovereignty gives rise to *bhakti,* and Rāmānuja's understanding of the Lord as the Supreme Sovereign and as beloved father makes him say that the Lord inspires both service and love in the devotee (*bhakta*). One surrenders oneself to him because he is both mighty and compassionate (*Gīta* 9-34), and these two aspects precipitate the faith, the confidence, the trust of the human being in the saving power of God and accelerate one's complete surrender.

Prapatti—a resorting to the Lord and seeking him as a refuge—is seen as an integral part of *bhaktiyoga.* The Sanskrit root *prapad,* from which the word *prapatti* is derived, essentially means "to drop down," "to go forward," and "to take refuge with," and is used as a synonym of *śaraṇāgati,* which means "to approach for protection." The Lord is sought as a refuge (*āśraya*) out of intense love (*GB* 7-1); and this self-surrender is necessary for *bhaktiyoga* (*GB* 7-15).

Rāmānuja attributes the difference in the types of people who resort to the Lord to the differences in their *karma* (*GB* 7-16). He explains that the evil deeds of a human being are the reason why that human being may not seek the Lord as a refuge earlier (*GB* 7-15). Elsewhere (*GB* 16-19 and 20), while describing the people of the demoniacal nature who hate God, the Lord is paraphrased as saying that he throws them into those bodies which are opposed to being friendly with him.[11]

It is only through *prapatti* that ignorance is cut, that one's access to the clear grace (*prasāda*) of the Lord is obtained (*GB* 18-6). In the *Vedārtha Saṃgraha,* Rāmānuja says that from a surrender at the feet of the Lord one gets an inclination to turn towards him[12], and surrendering to the Lord for his own sake is the very best goal.[13]

Such a devotee is extremely dear to the Lord, and the Lord cannot stand to be separated from such a person and favors that devotee so that the devotee can attain him quickly.[14] To his devotee, who has become dedicated entirely to the Lord, the Lord is an ocean of motherly affection (*āśritavātsalya*). We repeatedly see Rāmānuja asserting that the Lord will shower grace on those who have devotion towards him.

Through incessant devotion to God and singleness of love, the devotee (*bhakta*) becomes the object of God's love (*GB* ch. 8, introduction). The Lord is accessible to those who constantly and lovingly meditate on him (*GB* 8-14); to one who devoutly meditates on him, desiring union, he himself precipitates it (*GB* 9-22). To those who thirst for union, the Lord, out of "loving grace," gives the understanding with which they can join him. Out of compassion alone he dispels the *karma* which is antagonistic to the *bhakta's* wisdom (*GB* 10-10, 11); for those whose thoughts are centered around him, for those who consign all their acts to him and contemplate him with devotion and worship, he becomes the savior and delivers them from the ocean of life and death (*GB* 13-6, 7). The *bhakta,* knowing the truths of the knower (the human soul), the known (that is, God) and the way, becomes competent to attain liberation (*GB* 13-18); the one who serves the Lord with *bhaktiyoga* becomes eligible for union (*GB* 14-26, 27). In fact, the Lord pledges liberation to the *bhaktas.* The Lord pledges that he will destroy the sins that a *bhakta* may have if the *bhakta* would only surrender to him:

> Giving up all *dharmas* take refuge in me alone; I shall save you from all sins, do not grieve. (*Bhagavadgīta* 18-66)

Rāmānuja interprets this verse in two ways. By *dharma,* he suggests first that one ought to renounce the fruit of *jñānayoga, karmayoga,* and *bhaktiyoga,* and by this one's sins will be destroyed. The alternative interpretation is that if an aspirant renounced expiatory activities and penances which are difficult to perform and took refuge with the Lord alone, that aspirant would be rescued from sins. Thus Rāmānuja's understanding of *bhakti* in the *Gītābhāsya* includes *prapatti* or committing oneself completely to the Lord.

The overall impact of this explicit emphasis on one's having to *deserve* salvation is strong. And yet, there is an implicit understanding of the fact that the Lord is not only a father and companion whom one loves, but the owner, the master (*śeṣī*), to whom one owes one's very existence. The Lord is the generator of all activity. He is the inner controller and is omnipotent. Human actions and even the capacity to act are dependent on the Lord, says Rāmānuja, quoting scripture (*Brahma Sūtra* 2-3-33) in support (*GB* 18-15).

A deep commitment to scripture necessitates that Rāmānuja affirm the law of *karma* and confirm that one should *choose* to be devoted to God. He insists that when sins inherited from ages are exhausted, people worship and take shelter under the Lord (*GB* 7-28). It takes many meritorious births before one knows that one is a *śeṣa* to Viṣṇu and that one's acts and existence are dependent on him (*GB* 7-19). A commitment to the importance of *bhakti* would make one assume that nothing can take place, not even the initial impetus to desire faith can come without God's initiation. Rāmānuja accepts both scripture and experience: the importance of *karma* which is proclaimed by scripture and the supreme sovereignty and total unconditioned nature of God's grace which is felt in every moment of devotion. God's justice is affirmed explicitly; he is not merciless, and the inequalities of creation are ascribed to *karma* which is beginningless (*GB* 9-9). Creation is unequal because of the inequality of *karma* among human beings. In a sense, the doctrine of *karma* itself is a limited kind of predestination. If *bhaktiyoga* is the prerogative of the upper three classes, and that is the only way to liberation, those of the lower classes are doomed not to attain liberation in this lifetime.

But this is not, and in fact cannot be, the last word of someone who honored the Tamil poetry of the *āḷvārs*. What we have discussed is just one aspect of Rāmānuja's thought, one side of the twin *vedānta* that is the Śrīvaiṣṇava heritage. In the hymns (*gadyas*) of Rāmānuja, we see a powerful appeal for grace and for service. Here, Rāmānuja claims that he has not performed *bhakti, karma,* or *jñānayoga*—his only hope is the Lord's grace. In the *gadyas,* Rāmānuja surrenders with ardent fervor, confesses that he has no qualifications to reach the Lord, and seeks the goal of eternal loving service to Viṣṇu.

The *Hymn of Surrender* (*Śaraṇāgati gadya*) is different from other hymns in the Śrīvaiṣṇava devotional literature and is a unique piece in its own way. It is apparently a conversation between Rāmānuja and the goddess Śrī, and then, Rāmānuja and the Lord.[15] The work also incorporates verses from Sanskrit epics. The verses thus quoted from the epics or other scripture fit Rāmānuja's mood or are fitted into the Lord's answer. Tradition holds this to be a real conversation, a mystic experience of Rāmānuja, who, overcome by emotion while watching the Lord and Śrī being taken in a procession from the Śrī Raṅgam temple,[16] surrendered himself to them. The first part of the *Śaraṇāgati gadya* describes the Lord's form, his abode, his attendants, and so forth; the second half consists of the Lord's assurances to Rāmānuja. Part of this conversation takes place through scriptural quotations. Rāmānuja surrenders himself through the words of Arjuna (a hero in the epic *Mahābhārata*), asking the Lord to forgive him even as a parent, lover, or friend would forgive those dear to them; in the words of Gāndhari, another character in the epics, he hails the Lord as his father, mother, friend, teacher, wealth, knowledge, as his "all." Through each of these relationships, through the recollections of these myths, the bonds are affirmed, the refuge sanctioned. The Lord assures Rāmānuja of salvation, and the *Śaraṇāgati gadya* records the promises made by the Lord on various occasions.

In the *Śrīraṅga gadya,* Rāmānuja confesses that he does not deserve the goal of loving service (*kaiṁkarya*), because he does not have *bhaktiyoga* or any other good quality. He therefore takes refuge at the lotus feet of Nārāyaṇa (another name for Viṣṇu). The common denominator of all those who surrender (*prapannas*) is expressed here: one comes for protection and throws oneself at the mercy of the Lord because one does not have the strength to adopt a scripturally sanctioned way (*upāya*) which will procure his grace.

Rāmānuja's taking of refuge with the Lord on the basis of his "worthlessness" and his meditation on the Lord as the only refuge, by recalling the myths of redemption and promises made, is important in the Śrīvaiṣṇava tradition. Rāmānuja's faith is seen in the significance that he places on the relationships between the Lord and the human being and on the Lord's promises in the *Bhagavadgīta* and in the *Rāmāyaṇa.*[17] Rāmānuja quotes these in the *Śaraṇāgati gadya* and reminds the Lord of his promise. His devotion and surrender rest on a promise freely made by the Lord and recorded in scripture, a promise of grace and refuge willingly and freely offered in consideration of one's lowliness rather than deserts. Compassion is offered to those who are aware of their weakness, who find no other hope but the Lord's compassion. Salvation is assured to those who surrender themselves, to those who seek refuge with the Lord.

This, then, is the last word of Rāmānuja, a sentiment understood and shared by his disciples and emphasized by them.

KŪRAṬṬĀḶVĀṆ: IN QUEST OF DIVINE COMPASSION

Kūraṭṭāḷvāṉ was a disciple, friend, and scribe of Rāmānuja. He composed five long Sanskrit hymns (*stavas*). They are: the *Sundarabāhu Stava* (*SbSt*), or the *Hymn to the Lord with Handsome Arms;* the *Varadarāja Stava* (*VaradSt*), which is addressed to the Lord at Kāñcipuram; the *Śrī Stava,* in praise of Śrī; the *Vaikuṇṭha* (*VaiSt*); and the *Atimānuṣa Stava* (*AtimānuṣaSt*). Kūraṭṭāḷvāṉ perceives the Lord's compassion (*dayā*) to be general, but his love to be the prerogative of his *bhakta.* When he requests the Lord's compassion, one notices a lingering meditation on his lowliness (*naicyānusandhanam*), and in his celebration of the Lord's accessibility, one senses a playful tone.

In going through Kūraṭṭāḷvāṉ's verses, we see that the requests for the Lord's compassion are on at least three grounds. These points are not stated systematically, but we can glean them easily from the hymns. He claims to be totally devoid of any merit and any good attribute to "deserve" grace and so he takes refuge with the Lord. Second, he believes that the *words of surrender* that he has uttered make him a *"refugee"* or *śaraṇāgata,* and the Lord, because of his earlier promises, has to save him. Finally, we see repeated statements of his connection to Rāmānuja and a plea for compassion based on his spiritual relationship with his preceptor.

The Meditations on His Lowliness

The "meditation on lowliness" (*naicyānusandhanam*) of Kūraṭṭāḷvāṉ is one of the most pronounced in Śrīvaiṣṇava literature. While many of the teachers have expressed feelings of their worthlessness and have reproached themselves for their sins, Kūraṭṭāḷvāṉ's verses are easily the most intense and poignant, and he makes this the very premise for seeking the Lord's compassion.

In several ways, Kūraṭṭāḷvāṉ calls himself a despicable character, who is sinking deeper and deeper into sin and worldly existence:

> Alas, alas! Woe is me! There is no redemption! I am wicked, I fall, I fall. . . . what hope have I to talk of you, what right have I, a worthless, stained person, to even think of you who are full of auspicious qualities! (*VaiSt.* v. 84)
>
> Even after destroying my sins, clarifying my thought (*buddhi*), throwing off the shackles of birth, cultivating good qualities, I still will not be fit for reaching your feet, for I have been sinking in this existence for a long time. . . . (*VaiSt* v. 85)
>
> What is the use of my ranting? I have done every deed which can be called sin—big and small, both consciously and unwittingly. Please forgive me through your grace (*kṛpā*). (*VaiSt* v. 92)

This self-depreciation (*naicyānusandhanam*) does not stop at a confession of his lowliness; Kūraṭṭāḻvāṉ decries his lack of faith and says that he has not even the desire to reach the Lord.[18] He says that his mind is caught in the snares of attachments, that he is prone to the diseases of the body and the mind, but still has not the desire (*abhilāśa*) to reach the Lord (*VaradSt* v. 75). With this intense burden, Kūraṭṭāḻvāṉ feels that it is impossible to reach the Lord on his own.[19]

There is no other way, no other refuge but the Lord's compassion.[20] The faith in the Lord's compassion is overwhelmingly seen in his verses. He hands over the entire burden of the protection of himself, the burden of his future to the Lord:

> O Varada! I have many desires of other [paltry] things; but none towards your twin feet. If I have to develop any desire (*spṛhā*) to your feet, it is your burden (*bhāra*) [to see that it develops]. (*VaradaSt* v. 87)

This desire either to cut one's attachments or to reach the Lord seems to be the minimal requirement that human beings should have. Even this desire, says Kūraṭṭāḻvāṉ, is lacking in him, and he transfers the burden of developing this desire in him to the Lord.[21]

It is the Lord's responsibility to make Kūraṭṭāḻvāṉ's desire grow. Elsewhere, he says that if the Lord feels that he should practice any discipline, *the Lord* should then give the ability to do so to this weak subject:

> O Varada! If you persist in holding that you can only protect those who are fit, you yourself give me the power (*śakti*), the qualification (*adhikāra*), the confidence . . . (*VaiSt,* v. 101)

Kūraṭṭāḻvāṉ also prays to Śrī for *bhakti*:

> Grant me the appropriate words to praise you, a loving (*prema*) mind which ever grows, and *bhakti*. . . . (*Śrī Stava* v.2)

Kūraṭṭāḻvāṉ quite emphatically declares that the Lord has to grant him the qualification to be worthy of salvation.

The Words of Surrender and the Lord's Responsibility

With the taking of refuge in the Lord, Kūraṭṭāḻvāṉ says that he becomes a recipient of the Lord's compassion. He says that "even if I lack the confidence towards you, my ocean of compassion, and have not the faith (*śraddhā*) in the words [of surrender that] I have uttered, please consider this statement which I have said *but once* . . . as having been said often and as meaningful—solely out of your compassion (*dayā*)" (*AtimānuṣaSt* v. 60). In the *Varadarāja Stava* he emphasizes this often:

> O Varada! Even these words of surrender could not have come outside your grace (*prasāda*); therefore, you are gracious (*prasāda*) towards me. Now I live . . . (*VaradSt* v. 88)

These words of surrender, claims Kūraṭṭāḻvāṉ, are his only path and means (*sādhana*):

> O Varada! I have no other way apart from these words of refuge. This is accessible to me. . . . This is the opportune time to show your compassion.
> O Lord! Whoever you are, whatever your manifestations, whatever your work, you are inaccessible to all but your *bhaktas*—and I desire to see you with only my *words of surrender.* (*VaradSt* v. 92)

This is extremely significant, for he proclaims that his words of taking refuge are a means, a *sādhana*, to reach the Lord.[22] Tortured by his alleged sins, having no other refuge and protection but the Lord's compassion, he surrenders to the Lord, and with these words of surrender proclaims himself as a person who has surrendered to the Lord (*śaraṇāgata*). The Lord has to be compassionate to such a "refugee," who has transferred the burden of protection to someone else and has pleaded for refuge. One who has come to the Lord for protection is a *śaraṇāgata*, and this status almost guarantees the Lord's compassion:

> Though I am a sinner, I bear the name "*śaranāgata*" and it is not fit for you who are my Lord to ignore me. When you have wisdom, power, and mercy (*karuṇā*), how can my sins seem prominent? (*AtimānuṣaSt*, v. 61)
>
> Whatever one's caste, whoever the person, whatever his nature, [the Lord] does not make a distinction if he has taken refuge at [His] feet. Such a person, the handsome Lord favors through his motherly affection (*vātsalya*). (*SbSt* v. 30)

The Lord's compassion is the strength of Kūraṭṭāḷvāṉ (*VaradSt* v. 94). In this respect, there is not much difference between himself (one who has surrendered: *prapanna*) and the other aspirants, for nothing can be done outside the Lord's help (*VaiSt* v. 100). The distinction between those who strive through *karma, jñāna,* and *bhaktiyoga* and the one who has surrendered (*prapanna*), whose strength is the Lord's compassion (*dayā*), is collapsed in Kūraṭṭāḷvāṉ's verses.

One sees that Kūraṭṭāḷvāṉ invests an extraordinary faith in the Lord's compassion (*dayā*), which he has declared to be his main support. This *dayā* he seeks through his words of surrender. He is one who has taken refuge (*śaraṇāgata*) and the Lord will protect him through his compassion. These words of surrender are a means (*sādhana*) for him. These words have been uttered by a supposedly insignificant person, and therefore the Lord has scope to show his compassion to the fullest extent. This seems to suggest that the words of surrender are necessary, are words to which the Lord replies with compassion. This, however, cannot be called human "effort," for even the words of taking refuge (*śaraṇāgati*), says Kūraṭṭāḷvāṉ, are spoken through the favor and grace (*prasāda*) of the Lord (*VaradaSt* v. 88). It is in this sense that the Lord himself can be called the way (*hita* or *upāya*). It is his grace (*prasāda*) and compassion (*dayā*) which enable one to reach him.

Can this favor be directed at anyone? Who takes the first step—the Lord or the individual? A clue is seen in Kūraṭṭāḷvāṉ's highlighting of the Lord's "forgiving" quality and his patience. He forgives anyone if they as much as desist from their evil deeds for a moment.[23]

So great is the Lord's patience and forgiving love that the mere *pause* in the process of sinning evokes the Lord's forgiveness. If a mere "negative" act evokes so much of the Lord's forgiveness and love, asks Kūraṭṭāḷvāṉ, is it surprising that he is loving towards his devotee?[24]

Rāmānuja had glorified *bhaktiyoga* but in his hymns had confessed that he was devoid of any merit, incompetent to practice *bhaktiyoga,* and sought refuge with the Lord. Kūraṭṭāḷvāṉ magnifies his sense of worthlessness and seeks refuge with the Lord and his master Rāmānuja. On the basis of his worthlessness, he claims that the Lord *has* to save him, for he has sought refuge with him. There was a strong sense in his hymns that only the Lord can grant salvation out of his grace. This would come even if the human being *stopped* sinning for a while. Kūraṭṭāḷvāṉ's confidence that "surrender" and "coming for refuge" to the Lord will assure one of divine grace was developed by later Śrīvaiṣṇava theologians. In the thirteenth century the community re-evaluates and reformulates its conceptions of *bhaktiyoga* and *prapatti* as ways to end the cycle of life and death. We shall turn to these in the next chapter.

NOTES

[1] Meanings taken from Monier Williams, *A Sanskrit-English Dictionary* (Oxford: Clarendon Press, 1899; reprint, 1960). The scheme of transliteration in this chapter follows the standard forms accepted in Sanskrit and Tamil lexicons.

[2] *Gītābhāṣya* (henceforth *GB*), in *Rāmānujagranthamāla* (*RGM*), edited by P. B. Annangaracariyar (Kāñcīpuram: Granthamālā Office, 1956), introduction to ch. 7., p. 119.

[3] *Śrībhāṣya* trans. Thibaut (in *Vedānta—Sūtras with the Commentary by Rāmānuja,* Sacred Books of the East Series, vol. 4. Oxford: Clarendon Press, 1904), p. 14.

[4] *Ibid.,* p. 17.

[5] "Remainder, residue"; in Śrīvaiṣṇava terminology, an owned one, a vassal. See John B. Carman, *The Theology of Rāmānuja: An Essay in Interreligious Understanding* (New Haven: Yale University Press, 1974), pp. 156–157.

[6] *Vedārtha Saṅgraha* para 243, trans. S.S. Raghavachar (Mysore: Sri Ramakrishna Ashrama, 1956), pp. 186–187.

[7] J.A.B. van Buitenen, *Rāmānuja on the Bhagavadgīta* (Delhi: Motilal Banarsidass, 1st reprint), p. 21.

[8] *GB* 10-2.

[9] "Because you are the Father of all, the most worthy of respect, the preceptor, and greater than all others by virtue of qualities like compassion, therefore, bowing down and prostrating the body, I beg of you, who are the praiseworthy Lord: as a father and a friend show grace to a son who has offended, and as a friend who is entreated with prostration . . . even so bear with me, who am your beloved. . . ." (*Gītābhāṣya* 11-44)

[10] "In order to be a refuge for gods, men, and other creatures, the Supreme Person without at all abandoning his very own nature associates himself with the characteristic form, structure, qualities, and actions of the different classes of beings, and then is born in many ways. . . ." (*Śrībhāṣya sutra* 1-3-1)

In the *Gītābhāṣya* this is also affirmed:
". . . Because of the supreme compassion (*paramakāruṇyat*) and because of love for my devotees (*āśritavātsalya*) and to become a refuge for all I have descended as the son of Vasudeva without leaving my inherent nature. . . ." (*Gītābhāṣya* 7-24)

Kūraṭṭāḷvāṉ, the scribe and associate of Rāmānuja, also emphasizes this point:

"If you had not been born in divine and human wombs . . . we could not have known from any other source that we could take refuge in you." (*Atimānuṣastava* v. 9)

[11] Piḷḷāṉ, a cousin of Rāmānuja, handles the same question:
". . . why is it that everyone does not recognize the Lord who has [such auspicious] qualities and seek him as a refuge (*āśraya*)? It is because he makes those who have no friendship (*sneha*) towards him deluded and so many cannot realize him in his real nature." (*The Six Thousand,* 5-1-3 to 9)

Rāmānuja's emphasis is on the previous *karma* of an individual, and later, on the hatred of the demoniac soul for the Lord. Piḷḷāṉ follows this second emphasis of Rāmānuja in pointing out why some seek the Lord as the refuge and why others do not, but he simplifies it into simple terms of love that one may have towards the Lord.

[12] *Vedārtha Saṅgraha* trans. Prof. S. S. Raghavachar, para 126.

[13] *Gītābhāṣya* 7-17 and 18.

[14] *Gītābhāṣya* 8-14.

[15] Early in the history of Śrīvaiṣṇavism, the question of whether this conversation was a real one seems to have risen. In Periyavāccāṉ Piḷḷai's commentary on the *gadya traya,* the following incident is retold. Empār was a cousin and contemporary of Rāmānuja:
"When Empār asked [Rāmānuja] 'How are we to have confidence that

the Lord Himself has graciously vouchsafed these words', Emperumāṇār (that is, Rāmānuja) graciously replied, 'The Lord has shown His attributes, such as gracious condescension. . . . If He had not willed it, the words could not have sprung through my mouth. Since the Lord has said these words, there is nothing against your having confidence in them. . . .'" (Periyavāccāṇ Piḷḷai, *Gadyatrayabhāṣya,* p. 87.)

[16] Periyavāccāṇ Piḷḷai, *Gadhyatrayabhāṣya,* introduction to *Śaraṇāgatigadya,* p. 3.

[17] Viṣṇu promised protection to all who seek refuge in, or who surrender themselves to, him in verses which later Śrīvaiṣṇavas hold as exceedingly sacred, verses which are believed to remove fear and doubt from the heart of the devotee: "Giving up all dharmas, take refuge in me alone; I shall save you from all sins; do not grieve!" "Anyone who seeks refuge with me saying 'I am yours' is assured of my protection. This I swear." (*Bhagavadgīta* 18-66 and *Rāmāyana Yuddha Kāṇḍa* 18-33)

[18] "I have no faith (*śraddhā*), devotion (*bhakti*), power (*śakti*), or even the desire (*iccā*) to sing your praise or bow before you; nor any regret (*anutāpa*) for not embarking on it . . . Alas! I join the ranks of your enemies. . . ." (*VaiSt* v. 96)

[19] "O Lord who are beyond dualities! O eternally flawless Lord of Hastigiri! I am sinking in this life; I am the ground of all enmity, pride, and avarice; I desire the wrong things; I am greedy and deluded . . . who am I to attain you—you [who] have such great attributes?" (*VaradSt* v. 76)

[20] "O handsome Lord of the forested hills! Having no other way (*agati*), no knowledge, no other refuge (*ananyaśaraṇaḥ*), I keep pleading this again and again, and yet I am guilty, I am of a sinful nature, my mind is disturbed, but I am a vessel for your compassion." (*SbSt* v. 132) "O Varada! Though I have no *bhakti,* no [good] qualities, have done no [good] deed, am not of a comfortable nature and have sins which cannot be expiated, if I attain your feet, your patience (*kṣama*) and compassion (*dayā*) will be crystallized." (*VaradaSt* v. 95)

The verses in which Kūraṭṭāḻvāṇ stresses his spiritual poverty are followed immediately by his taking refuge at the feet of the Lord and saying that he needs his compassion:

"I am guilty of three types of offenses; I am a sinner; I have fallen in darkness. Without any way (*gati*), I who am a vessel for your compassion (*dayā*) seek refuge at your twin feet." (*AtimānuṣaSt* v. 59)

In the *VaradaSt,* Kūraṭṭāḻvāṇ talks of his lowliness in ten verses and takes refuge at the feet of the Lord, hailing him as the Compassionate One:

"I have not done any good deed; I have done all possible evil deeds; I have not a single [good] quality; I am filled with wrong desires, anger, and a thousand other blemishes; O Lord of compassion, O Varada, I take refuge in you."

"O Varada, even these words of surrender (*śaraṇāgati vāk*) did not come from a convinced and full mind (*dhī pūrvika*), but if you have compassion (*dayā*) towards me, I shall live. . . ." (*VaradaSt*, verses 83 and 84)

This is the time, says Kūraṭṭāḷvāṉ, for the Lord to show his compassion (*dayā*). Since he has no qualification to reach the Lord, he feels that he is a fit vessel for his compassion:

"I have not done any good deed, nor have I any knowledge (*vidya*), I have absolutely no *bhakti* to your lotus feet—I am a vessel, my Lord, for your compassion (*dayā*)." (*VaiSt* v. 88)

[21] These words of "transference of his burden" are significant, for, later on, Deśika, following a text called *Lakṣmī Tantra*, calls *prapatti* as *bhāranyāsa* or of the surrender of one's burden, and it is important to note that Kūraṭṭāḷvāṉ's understanding of surrender coincides on this point.

[22] In the thirteenth century, Piḷḷai Lōkācārya holds that *prapatti* is not an *upāya*. *Śrīvacana Bhūṣaṇam sutras.*

[23] "Whatever sin cannot be expiated in a hundred thousand Brahma kalpas, the individual does here in half a second. If this soul who stands guilty in his lifetime but pauses [from his sinning] for just a minute, you forgive him! Is this not wonderful?" (*VaiSt*, v. 61)

[24] ". . . So great is your clemency [that you forgive even those who pause from their sinning for a moment]. And so it is but natural that it should also be directed to those who fold their hands in adoration. When your maternal love (*vātsalya*) is directed to all people without distinction, is it any wonder that you are also clement to those who ardently desire you?" (*VaiSt*, v. 62)

That the Lord's compassion is overwhelming to one who makes a positive gesture is brought out in the verse that immediately follows the one just quoted:

"Through your (mere) will you create, protect, and destroy the worlds—but through your love for your devotee, you ran to Gajendra when he summoned you and even massaged his foot [when you could have just as well have done it by your mere will]!" (*VaiSt*, v. 63)

Bondage and Grace in the Śrīvaiṣṇava Tradition: Piḷḷai Lōkācārya and Vedānta Deśika

Vasudha Narayanan

The beginning of the theological differences which resulted in the social split of the Śrīvaiṣṇava community in the eighteenth century crystallized in the writings of the thirteenth century teachers (Sanskrit: *ācāryas*) Piḷḷai Lōkācārya (A.D. 1264–1369) and Vedānta Deśika (A.D. 1268–1368). The two schools were called the Teṅkalai ("Southern culture") and the Vaṭakalai ("Northern culture"), ostensibly because the former emphasized the Tamil hymns of the twelve mystics (*āḻvārs*) while the latter gave importance to the Sanskrit tradition. The names are misleading; both schools have always followed the "double" (*ubhaya*) Vedānta tradition of the Śrīvaiṣṇavas, honoring both Tamil and Sanskrit scriptures equally.

One of the fundamental differences between the two schools was in the understanding of divine grace which effectively destroyed a human's past *karma* and liberated him or her from the cycle of life and death. This salvific action of Viṣṇu and his consort Śrī, which was absolutely efficacious and which involved no "effort" on the part of the human being, was called *prapatti* or *śaraṇāgati.* As indicated in the previous chapter, the concept, attitude, and sacrament of *prapatti* is central to members of the Śrīvaiṣṇava community. We may recall that Rāmānuja and Kūraṭṭāḻvāṉ accepted *bhaktiyoga* as a way of pleasing the Lord and procuring his grace, but in their hymns had confessed their inability to practice the discipline of *bhaktiyoga* and had sought the grace of the Lord directly, by surrendering themselves to him.

In this chapter, we shall focus on two thirteenth century theologians, Piḷḷai Lōkācārya and Vedānta Deśika. While they differed from each other in their interpretations of scripture and the writings of Rāmānuja, they did not see themselves as starting rival schools of thought. The social split of the Śrīvaiṣṇava community came several centuries later and when it did, the teachers traced different lines of spiritual descent going back to Piḷḷai Lōkācārya and Vedānta Deśika in the thirteenth century.

Let us first consider the views of Pilḷḷai Lōkācārya on the matter of *prapatti/śaraṇāgati* and divine grace and then see how Vedānta Désika differs from him.[1]

PIḶḶAI LŌKĀCĀRYA'S UNDERSTANDING OF *KARMA*, *PRAPATTI*, AND GRACE

In presenting the views of Piḷḷai Lōkācārya, I shall discuss three points which in later years are perceived to be unique to the Teṅkalai sect:

1. The importance of the mediator (Sanskrit: *puruṣakāra*) who ends the human's *and* the Lord's entanglement with *karma* and reconciles them.
2. The understanding of *prapatti* and divine grace (*kṛpā*) which ends a human's *karma* and which entails the unique belief that the Lord enjoys and accepts the faults of his devotees.
3. The basis for divine selection: the role of previous *karma*.

Piḷḷai Lōkācārya addresses the issue of the relationship between the deity and the human being at some length in a book called *The Nine Forms of Relationships*.[2] In all of these, the human being is subservient to the Lord and totally dependent on him. In the *Śrī Vacana Bhūṣanam* (*SVB*), Piḷḷai Lōkācārya emphasizes three relationships: Viṣṇu as the parent (both as a father and as having motherly affection, which is known in Sanskrit as *vātsalya*), as the husband, and as the owner (Sanskrit: *śeṣī*) of the human being who is the truant child; the subservient (and sometimes wayward) wife; and the owned being (Sanskrit: *śeṣa*).

The relationship between the deity and the human being is permanent; it is vital to understand this for, in reading Piḷḷai Lōkācārya, it becomes clear that the eternal nature of this relationship transcends the *karma* that temporarily separates Viṣṇu and the soul. Cognizance of the relationship with the Lord is supposed to free the individual from bondage and make him or her aware of his or her divine heritage, which is service to the Lord.

For Piḷḷai Lōkācārya, the problem of salvation from the human standpoint is simple: human beings are guilty of several offenses and their store of bad *karma* prevents Viṣṇu, the father, who has a strong sense of justice, from saving them. It is in this situation that the importance of mediation is stressed. The two important mediators are Śrī and one's spiritual teacher, the *ācārya.* With regard to the mediation of Śrī, Piḷḷai Lōkācārya writes in his great work, *Śrī Vacana Bhūṣaṇam* (*SVB*):

> When united [with Viṣṇu), Śrī corrects him; when separated, she corrects the human being. She corrects both through advice.
>
> By advice, the Lord's and the human's dependence on *karma* is ended. When [they do not heed her] she corrects the human through her grace (Tamil: *aruḷ*) and the Lord through her beauty. (*SVB, sūtras* 10 to 13)

Maṇavāḷa Māmuṇikaḷ comments on this *sūtra,* saying that Śrī speaks on behalf of the human being and makes the Lord accept him or her. She corrects the human being who has spent several lifetimes ignoring the Lord and makes him or her seek the Lord's protection. She reminds the Lord who counts the human being's faults that we have no other refuge but him by calling to his attention the nature of the eternal relationship that exists between him and the human being.[3]

The tension between the Lord's grace and his sense of justice is portrayed by Piḷḷai Lōkācārya's teacher, Periyavāccāṉ Piḷḷai, in an imaginary conversation between the Lord and Śrī:

> The Lord tells Śrī: "Since beginningless time this human being has been disobeying my laws and has been the object of my anger. If I condone his faults and accept them patiently, instead of punishing him, I will be disregarding the injunction of Scripture." Śrī replies:

> "But if you punish the human being instead of saving him, your quality of grace will not survive."[4]

The Lord is in a quandary: if he does not save the human, his quality of grace will not be displayed; if he does not punish, the injunctions of scripture about ethical behavior will be compromised. Śrī suggests: "Both scripture and grace can be upheld if you show your grace in those *who turn towards you:* the others, you can punish."[5]

Maṇavāḷa Māmuṇikaḷ continues: he says that by Śrī's advice, the dependence of the Lord and the human being on their *karma* will vanish. He describes the human being's "dependence on *karma*" as his entanglement with worldly life; the Lord's *karma* (and surely this word is used in rhetoric to make a point emphatically) is his commitment to his resolution that he will punish all those who sin. Maṇavāḷa Māmuṇikaḷ says that since Śrī is the mother of the human being and the wife of Viṣṇu, she is intimately related to both, and so encourages the human being to turn towards the Lord who is the supreme refuge.[6]

The soul's *karma* has prevented its reconciliation with the Lord, but the greatness of the mediator, says Piḷḷai Lōkācārya, lies in making this very *karma* as the basis for being accepted. Śrī is not the only mediator; an *ācārya* also functions in this capacity and sometimes the Lord himself assumes the role.[7] Piḷḷai Lōkācārya describes the greatness of the mediator saying:

> The greatness of the mediator . . . lies in not merely ignoring the (soul's) defects and lack of good qualities, but in making this very lack of merit as the very reason for accepting [the soul]. (*SVB, sū*tra 15)

This passage forms the crux of the Teṅkalai doctrine of the divine quality known as the tender maternal compassion that the Lord has for the soul (*vātsalya*). *Vātsalya* is described by Maṇavāḷa Māmuṇikaḷ, while commenting on the *sūtra* quoted above:

> The Lord accepts the defect (*doṣa*) and the lack of good qualities joyfully. He does not punish the soul, because he is merciful and patient. He accepts the faults as a 'payment' (for divine grace) because he has *vātsalya.* This is similar to a cow which is normally so fastidious that it refuses to eat the grass that men have walked upon; and yet, it enjoys licking the bodily waste that is found on its calf's body

> immediately after giving birth to it. There is no equal to *vātsalya*. This quality is also seen in the maternal nature of Śrī and makes the Divine mother be one step ahead of the Lord.[8]

The defects and demerits of a soul are no hindrance to the saving action of Viṣṇu. The Lord enjoys them. He chooses to save the human and graciously accepts his or her previous *karma*.

This notion of grace is the base for Piḷḷai Lōkācārya's understanding of *prapatti*. The human being, says Piḷḷai Lōkācārya, should not seek refuge out of his or her own initiative.[9] God chooses of his own accord and we should not try to force his hand by an act of surrender or *prapatti*. Piḷḷai Lōkācārya says that such human acts as *prapatti* which are normally a form of expiation for sins become a sin if one considers them as a demand on the Lord's forgiveness.[10]

To seek refuge, in fact, is appalling; in a show of poetic hyperbole, Piḷḷai Lōkācārya says that a person who does *prapatti* is as reproachable as a wife who has been an adulteress for long, and who now approaches the husband without shame or fear and seeks protection from him! This surely is a radical statement.

Maṇavāḷa Māmuṇikaḷ, commenting on Piḷḷai Lōkācārya's writings, says that the soul which has been wandering through several births, honoring other gods and embracing other values, has no right now to approach the Lord and casually ask for protection like an unfaithful wife. This is the first reason for not seeking refuge. The second reason for *not* actively seeking refuge is implied: the soul, as Piḷḷai Lōkācārya emphasizes, is the *śeṣa*, the owned servant of the Lord and thus cannot take the initiative to approach him on its own. It must wait patiently to be rescued. Since the Lord is the owner and the master, it is his responsibility, his very nature to save, and it would be going against the inherent nature of the human soul to assert itself.[11] It is for this reason that Piḷḷai Lōkācārya rejects *bhaktiyoga* as a way to get Viṣṇu's grace. He asserts that *bhaktiyoga* entails rigorous discipline and effort, and therefore any human who takes this path, by definition, has to have a sense of independence, a certain pride that he is able to embark on this difficult practice. This sense of independence gets in the way of the *śeṣa-śeṣī* relationship that exists between the soul and the deity; and cognizance of this relationship is vital in the scheme of salvation.[12]

What, then, should a human being do? A human being is supposed to have a "knowledge of the soul (*ātmajñāna*), and a prevention of obstruction (to the Lord's salvific action)" (*SVB, sūtra* 60).

"Knowledge of the soul" includes knowledge of one's dependence on the Lord and a knowledge that one is his "owned one" (*śeṣa*). The result of the first, says Piḷḷai Lōkācārya, is the cessation of one's efforts; a knowledge of the second factor will lead to a stopping of activity for one's personal gain (*SVB, sūtra* 71).

While cognizance of one's state of being owned (*śeṣatvam*) is vital, that very cognizance, and in fact any virtue (*puṇya*), stands as a hindrance when a different relationship dominates between the Lord and the soul. When the Lord seeks the soul, even as a man embraces his wife, he does not look for virtue (*puṇya*). Virtue (*puṇya*) stands in the way of the embrace, even as a blouse worn by a woman to adorn herself stands in the way of her husband's embrace (*SVB, sūtra* 161).[13] So any "good" (*puṇya*) or even an excessive feeling of dependence hinders the Lord's embrace (*SVB, sūtra* 163). The Lord seeks the soul with all its defects (*doṣa*); hence trying to expiate oneself of one's defects also stands as an obstruction to the Lord's salvific action. One must not seek to cleanse oneself of one's evil deeds; the Lord will accept one in an "as is" condition. Piḷḷai Lōkācārya illustrates this point with a discussion from the epic *Rāmāyaṇa.*

One of the incidents in the *Rāmāyaṇa* which later theologians are at pains to explain or rationalize concerns the behavior of Rāma after his victory over the wicked "demon" Rāvaṇa. Rāvaṇa has kidnapped Rāma's wife, Sīta, and in the war that ensued Rāvaṇa is ultimately killed. After this victory, Rāma sends word to his wife Sīta, who has been in Rāvaṇa's captivity for ten months, asking her to bathe ceremoniously and then present herself adorned, in front of him. Sīta complies; but Rāma is angered by her appearance. Piḷḷai Lōkācārya says of this: "Remember the words: 'The bath brought on the wrath [of Rāma].' " (*SVB, sūtra* 166). Sīta, he argues, should have appeared with the grime caked on her body, despite Rāma's instructions, understanding intuitively that he wanted to feast his eyes on her and see her in the state that she had been in all these months. Sīta, here, serves as a paradigm for the human soul. Like Sīta, one should wait in bondage, wait for the Lord to rescue one from one's *karma.* But, one should not seek to cleanse oneself of the dirt or the sin that clings to one; the Lord will decide to save the soul and when he does, he will love it, warts and all.

Piḷḷai Lōkācārya asserts: "The soul considers virtue (*puṇya*) to be sin (*pāpa*); the Lord holds the soul's sin to be virtue. . . ." (*SVB*, *sūtra* 280). Maṇavāḷa Māmuṇikaḷ elucidates this cryptic statement. He says that the human being, after reading scripture, may believe that both virtue (*puṇya*) and sin (*pāpa*) are hindrances if one wants liberation. Virtue is desired by people because it leads to a good quality of life *on this earth* but since it keeps them away from the Lord, the devotee considers it to be evil. But if his devotee commits a sin (*pāpa*), the Lord considers it to be a virtue, because of his tender maternal love (*vātsalya*).[14]

Piḷḷai Lōkācārya's interpretation of the term maternal affection (*vātsalya*) follows Periyavāccāṉ Piḷḷai's, who defines the quality as "that which (makes the Lord) accept the defect of the devotee as if it were a good quality." This line of thinking is associated in later years as exclusively Teṅkalai; the Vaṭakalai Śrīvaiṣṇavas hold that *vātsalya* means the "ignoring of the defect." Many of the early Śrīvaiṣṇava teachers had subscribed to the second view, that is, the Lord *ignores* the sins of the devotee. For instance, Kūraṭṭāḻvāṉ, whom we discussed in the previous chapter, says in his hymn to the Lord enshrined in Kāñcipuram (*Varadarāja Stava* v. 20): "O Varada, you do not look at the defects of your devotees." Parāśara Bhaṭṭar, (the son of Kūraṭṭāḻvāṉ) and Piḷḷāṉ (the cousin of Rāmānuja) had also held the same position.[15]

In the thirteenth century, however, Periyavāccāṉ Piḷḷai prefers a different description of "maternal affection": he defines the word as "[that quality] by which [the Lord] through His love, considers the fault of the devotee as a (good) quality."[16] Even the Lord's killing his enemies still comes within the dimensions of *vātsalya:* Periyavāccāṉ Piḷḷai says that it is like a mother who gives her child a stick to play with but, if the child is about to hurt his or her eyes with it, she removes it from his or her hand.[17]

Piḷḷai Lōkācārya and Maṇavāḷa Māmuṇikaḷ follow Periyavāccāṉ Piḷḷai and take it one step further; the faults, the defects of the devotee, are not merely ignored by the Lord, but are accepted and enjoyed. This defect has become the "payment" (Tamil: *paccai*) for grace because of mediation.

Maternal affection and grace are, however, shown only to those whom Viṣṇu chooses. The choice is not random. Viṣṇu chooses—as Śrī advises—those who show "an inclination towards him." In other words, while the Lord enjoys the defects of the human, it is not just any human, but particular ones.

Piḷḷai Lōkācārya, in the fourth (and the last) section of the *SVB* explains how these souls are chosen. In one of the longest *sūtras* of the book, he introduces the importance of *good deeds done unintentionally* in previous births; these form the basis for selection. He says that in heaven, where everyone is happy, the Lord alone is restless, like a sleepless father constantly thinking of a son who is in a distant land. Unable to bear separation from those in the cycle of life and death, he runs to them, grants them bodily organs, the power to act and live, so that he can (eventually) be united with them. Afraid that, if he is seen, the human beings may curse and ask him to leave, he dwells silently within them. He is close to them, without their being aware of it, like a mother who lovingly embraces a sleeping child. He does not leave them because of his relationship with them. He protects, but does not prevent their bad deeds. He grieves and searches for a way to rescue them, but does not come across any deed which even by gross exaggeration can be called a virtue. He seizes upon any excuse: he imagines that there are virtues by telling the souls, "You mentioned my name, you spoke of my residing place, you looked after my devotees, refreshing them with water and giving them shelter." He grafts these virtues on them and imagines these merits even though they are accidental, unintended good deeds and multiplies them tenfold and thus finds cause to save them.[18]

The importance of "unintended good deeds" done even in previous lives is stressed by quoting several illustrative stories. Piḷḷai Lōkācārya alludes to the story of Queen Lalitā, and Maṇavāḷa Māmuṇikaḷ explains this allusion.[19]

What is the basis on which a human being does those unintentional good deeds? Piḷḷai Lōkācārya is true to the *bhakti* tradition: nothing can take place outside the grace of the Lord. It is the compassionate glance (in other words, grace) of the Lord which is the basis for these good deeds done unknowingly; God then uses them as a *pretext* (Tamil: *paṟṟācu*) for saving the human.[20]

This understanding that the unintentional good deed is the reason for the Lord showing his favor is believed to have been held by Rāmānuja himself, according to Piḷḷai Lōkācārya.[21] The question of how these deeds can be called "good" if they are both unintended and not ordained by scripture is then taken up. Piḷḷai Lōkācārya's answer is simple: The Lord calls them "good" even if humans do not; who is to question his grace?[22]

But even these deeds, unintentional though they are, are done by the grace of Viṣṇu for it is he who initially gave bodily organs and the power to act to the human being, hoping that with these he would some day do some good, unintentional though his actions may be.[23] These unintentional good deeds have specific results: the souls who have for long experienced the fruits of sin and virtue done in previous births, later feel disgusted about the endless continuation of life, which is caused by impressions of past *karma.* The souls now begins to wonder: "Who are we? What was our original condition? Where are we headed?"[24] These thoughts turn the human being towards the Lord; the Lord then rescues the human being.

Let us summarize some of the points we have discussed so far: both the Lord and the human being are seen to be attached to *karma* (the Lord's *karma* is defined as his association with his sense of justice), and the mediation of Śrī, the mother of the soul and the wife of the Lord, is seen as necessary to end this "dependence on *karma.*" Piḷḷai Lōkācārya emphasizes the importance of the *śeṣa-śeṣī* relationship between the human being and the Lord, and because the human soul is "owned" by the Lord, it cannot take the initiative of actively seeking the Lord's protection. Consequently, the understanding of *prapatti/śaraṇāgati* is rejected by Piḷḷai Lōkācārya as is the whole discipline of *bhaktiyoga,* because both are seen as unbecoming to the soul's nature of being subservient and totally dependent upon the Lord. However, the human being is encouraged to "turn towards the Lord" and to assent to his salvific action. The Lord accepts the faults of such a person as if they were virtues. Unintentional good deeds done in past lives form the pretext for the Lord's salvific action, but, when really pushed, Piḷḷai Lōkācārya says that even these good deeds come from the grace of the Lord.

VEDĀNTA DEŚIKA'S UNDERSTANDING OF *KARMA, PRAPATTI,* AND GRACE

Karma binds the human to a life without God; the grace of the mediator and the deity ends this *karma.* Vedānta Deśika agrees with these statements, but differs on other issues. He holds that the Lord, out of sheer grace, gives the human a body and the capacity to act, but the human being has to petition for protection.

This asking for God's favor could be through *bhaktiyoga*—as Rāmānuja had suggested—or, if unable to practice it because of one's caste or lack of ability, through a simple prayer for protection that forms the crux of *prapatti*. According to Deśika, differences in *karma* qualify one for either *bhaktiyoga* or *prapatti*. Using this gesture, the act of surrender (*prapatti*), as a pretext (*vyāja*), Viṣṇu saves the human being. Since even this gesture of the human was made possible by the body and the capacity to act that Viṣṇu had so graciously given, *prapatti* was seen as being occasioned by the Lord's initial grace. It was only salvific grace (*prasāda*) that was triggered by the human's confession of humility and asking for refuge. Piḷḷai Lōkācārya, however, considered this "asking" as quite immoral, as is suggested in the simile of the wayward wife. The second major difference is seen in the interpretation of the divine quality of "maternal affection" (*vātsalya*): Piḷḷai Lōkācārya believed that one's defects are enjoyed by Viṣṇu, while Deśika's position was that these defects are ignored by the deity.

Deśika's position on the matter of human bondage and divine grace is summed up in a Sanskrit verse with which he begins a chapter called "The Classification of the Ways to Attain the Goal" in his major work on *prapatti*, the *Rahasya Traya Sāra* (*RTS*).

> The Lord is the way and the goal; this is declared in scripture. His grace is obtained by *bhakti* or *prapatti*. These ways (*gati*) are adopted as a consequence of good deeds done in the past, and the Lord who has the power to create all is responsible for even these deeds.[25]

Deśika believes that *bhaktiyoga* and *prapatti* are the pretexts (*vyāja*) by which the Lord saves the human being from bondage. The difference from Piḷḷai Lōkācārya comes both in his acceptance of *bhaktiyoga* as a viable means of obtaining the Lord's grace and in his calling *prapatti* a way, a means (*upāya*).

The Lord is called the "ever-existing *upāya*" (*sadhyopāya*) and *prapatti* is the "means to be adopted" (*siddhopāya*). The human being petitions the Lord actively through *prapatti*. The Lord cannot show his grace. Unlike Piḷḷai Lōkācārya, who believes that the Lord will save on his own and that no way or means (*upāya*) in the form of *prapatti* is necessary on the part of the human being to attract divine grace, Deśika is emphatic in asserting that although the Lord is omnipotent, he makes human beings adopt some gesture and by that pretext (*vyāja*) protects him. Deśika says that unless the human being supplies some pretext, the Lord can be accused of partiality and arbitrariness.

Deśika anticipates a next question: If the "pretext" (*vyāja*) like *prapatti* is adopted by the Lord's grace, then why did not the Lord make us adopt this "means" earlier? Deśika's answer falls back into the pattern of conservative Hindu traditions, a response seen in Rāmānuja's writings as well. He says that human beings have "beginningless *karma*" and since they have to experience the fruits of their *karma,* the Lord did not make them embark on the act which he could use as a pretext to show grace. The primacy of *karma* and human responsibility is therefore upheld. Deśika adds that this view *has* to be accepted if one is to safeguard the Lord's reputation from accusations of partiality and arbitrariness. Unless the importance of *karma* (and consequently human responsibility) is accepted, says Deśika, no one will be able to answer the question as to why a person adopted a way or means (*upāya*) at a certain time and not earlier. He concludes the discussion, repeating: "It is the common explanation that the [sudden eagerness] for liberation comes because of the differences due to streams of beginningless *karma*. . . . God's omnipotence comes in his determination to protect the human being when he *wants* to do so and when the human being adopts an *upāya* that can be used as a pretext."[26]

Deśika posits two reasons why the soul is bound to the earth and two reasons for its getting liberation. After several chapters of discussion, Deśika says:

> The primary cause for God making the human being the instrument of his sport (*līla*) is his independence and the ancillary cause is that the human being has violated the Lord's commands since beginningless time. The primary reason for making the human being an object of his enjoyment (*bhoga*) in heaven is the Lord's compassion and the *ancillary* cause is the pretext (that is, *bhakti* or *prapatti*) which stops the Lord's punishment which is an obstacle [for liberation].
>
> *Bhakti* and *prapatti* which are the pretexts on which the Lord shows his grace are *themselves the consequence of the Lord's compassion due to special acts of merit* on the part of the human being.[27]

Deśika describes human bondage as the soul being part of the Lord's divine play or sport; liberation is seen as a time when the soul is an object of the Lord's enjoyment. God's omnipotence and his supremacy have caused the human being to be in this world and human *karma* is an ancillary factor. Likewise, divine compassion is the primary cause for liberation, the act of *prapatti* is just an ancillary reason. God's omnipotence keeps us on earth and his compassion liberates us; human *karma* and surrender (*prapatti*) are subsidiary reasons for bondage and liberation. God's omnipotence and compassion are both emphasized by Deśika; he asserts that power without compassion is dangerous to others and that the compassion of one who has no power is useless. But God has both qualities and can help human beings.

What is the nature of *prapatti* according to Deśika? How can human beings allow God to help them? While Deśika accepts that one can practice *bhaktiyoga* or, if incapable of it, is able to surrender to the Lord and seek refuge (*prapatti*), he clearly says that only men of the upper three classes of society can practice *bhaktiyoga,* and even then one seldom finds people capable of it. So *bhaktiyoga* is a "closed" alternative, and *prapatti* seems to be the only way open for the sinful people that we are. *Bhaktiyoga* involves some human endeavor; *prapatti* is total reliance on the Lord's grace. *Bhaktiyoga* was performed by people in times past; the moral climate of the day seems to preclude it in the present. Deśika accepts Rāmānuja's description of *bhaktiyoga,* and we noted the main contours of this topic in the previous chapter. Here, I shall briefly focus on Deśika's concept of *prapatti,* because this is the only viable way "out" of bondage, and because he differs considerably from Piḷḷai Lōkācārya in this matter.

According to the *Lakṣmī Tantra* (twelfth century?), a text held to be sacred by the Śrīvaiṣṇava community, *prapatti* and *śaraṇāgati* are held to be synonymous with several other terms. Vedānta Deśika reflects upon the meanings of *prapatti* and *śaraṇāgati* in some of his works. (A prolific writer, he wrote in Sanskrit, Tamil, and a hybrid language called Maṇipravāḷa, which is a combination of Sanskrit and Tamil.) Here we shall be looking at several of his works, but focusing on his *magnum opus,* the *Rahasya Traya Sāra* or "The Essence of the Three Secrets."[28]

A good starting point to understand *prapatti* is Bharatamuni's (dates unknown) definition which Deśika quotes at several points:

> If one desires something that one cannot obtain, we may ask someone else to accomplish it. The asking of someone to be the sole means is *śaraṇāgati.* That is *prapatti.*[29]

There is an emphasis on three of five elements in this definition. There is a supreme confidence (*mahāviśvāsa*), an actual act of asking, and the total reliance on the person who is asked to accomplish the deed. With this confidence, one relaxes, knowing that someone who has the power and the compassion will do the job that one cannot accomplish oneself. It is in this sense that *prapatti*, which is an act of commitment, becomes at once an act leading to liberation; instead of binding, it becomes emancipating.

It involves a total giving up of the idea of agency and doership, a realization that one is helpless and cannot do something; this is the passive side of the concept. The active part is the asking (with complete, unshakable faith and confidence) of someone else to do the task (*goptṛtva varaṇam*—literally, "asking for protection"). In both aspects, there is a "totality" involved, a total feeling of inadequacy and helplessness (*kārpaṇyam*) and a total faith (*mahāviśvāsa*). The other two elements or factors involved are a resolve and determination to do what is pleasing (*ānukūlya samkalpam*) to the person to whom one is committing or entrusting oneself and a concomitant desire to avoid anything which is displeasing to that person (*prātikūlya varjanam*). These five factors culminate in the total commitment, the total entrusting and "giving over" of the self (*ātma samarpaṇam*).[30]

Deśika finds it easy to discern the several attitudes involved in *prapatti* in Vibhīṣaṇa's seeking of protection and political refuge as found in the *Rāmāyaṇa;* this is the model that one emulates in seeking for spiritual refuge as well. Vibhīṣaṇa's exhortation to Rāvaṇa to give up Sīta is seen as the resolve to do what is pleasing to Rāma. In his banishment and the fact that there is no other direction he can proceed in, nothing else that he can do, one sees Vibhīṣaṇa's "wretchedness" and helplessness (*kārpaṇyam*). In the complete renouncing of his family, wealth, and titles in Laṅka, is seen the abandoning of what would be unfavorable (*prātikūlya varjanam*), and what, in fact, is inconsequential in his new relationship with Rāma. Vibhīṣaṇa's supreme confidence (*mahāviśvāsa*) is evident in his confident declaration of Rāma to be the refuge, the protector of all the worlds, and this is accompanied by a request for protection (*goptṛtva varaṇam*), ending in a total placing and throwing of his self at the feet of Rāma (*ātma samarpaṇam*). What is seen here in Vibhīṣaṇa is a full, unreserved committing and entrusting of himself.

While sacred texts speak of "doing" *prapatti* to reach any goal, the best form of *prapatti* is one which is done with no desire in mind but *mokṣa* or liberation. Whether *prapatti* is a direct way to *mokṣa* or is to lead to further devotion, one gives up oneself completely. Further, those who have undergone *prapatti* (*prapannas*), who long for liberation directly, are to give up completely the burden of protecting themselves and also are to renounce the fruits or consequences which arise from the very action of *prapatti*.[31]

In his "Ten Verses on Abandonment and Entrusting (*nyāsa*)," Vedānta Deśika writes:

> "I do not belong to myself; the burden of protecting myself (that is, salvation) is no longer mine. (I shall not enjoy) the consequences that may result from my actions. They belong to the lord Nārāyaṇa (Viṣṇu)". Saying thus, a man must entrust his soul to the Lord. (*Nyāsa Daśakam* v.1)

The submission of the self, the burden of protection, and the fruits of one's actions are elucidated with several scriptural quotations by Vedānta Deśika. One is to submit oneself, realizing that one's soul does not belong to one, but to God; one should further realize that one is completely dependent on the Lord. Deśika asserts that ideally one should not even ask for liberation, because the *prapanna* should realize that this is certain! This is the best form of renunciation, the highest *prapatti,* and is the closest that Deśika comes to Piḷḷai Lōkācārya's position.[32]

The action of *prapatti* is momentous and profoundly stirring. It heralds in a new tenor of life, and as a sacrament it symbolizes a new birth and beginning. It is important to note that this supreme form of "renunciation" is not a "dropping out" from life. Entrusting oneself to the Lord does not give *prapannas* a license to be free of the regulations and rituals of daily life that are enjoined in the scripture. Vedānta Deśika, a married man, never became a monk but was one who took refuge in Viṣṇu. He maintained the code of behavior enjoined for his caste and his station in life. One had to perform one's duties, but with one difference: no longer are duties performed as a "means" for salvation or to gain temporary pleasures provided by good *karma*—the duties and rituals that are incumbent on one by virtue of one's caste and station in life are to be done for the sole purpose of pleasing the Lord. Vedānta Deśika considers this to be the highest renunciation and the highest commitment for a human being.[33]

The *prapanna* should rest carefree, now that the burden of protecting oneself has been surrendered; one should have no fears or doubts about one's salvation. One rejoices in not having to adopt any other means towards liberation; one is exclusive in one's devotion to Viṣṇu; one is free from depression or anger, knowing all this to pertain to the body; one feels compassion to those who harm one; one realizes that one suffers because of past *karma* which is in force but rejoices that one is working it out speedily.

The attitude of *prapatti* is seen in the verses of a poem called "Sacred Utterance" (*Tiruvāymoḷi*) composed by Nammāḷvār, a saint who lived in the eighth or ninth centuries A.D. The poem has been considered, by the Śrīvaiṣṇavas, to be "revealed" and portrays both the renouncing and committing aspects of surrender:

> Relinquish all;
> having relinquished,
> submit your life
> to him who owns heaven.
>
> Think for a moment:
>
> Your bodies,
> inhabited by your soul,
> last as long as
> a lightning flash.
>
> Pull out by the roots
> thoughts of 'you' and 'yours'.
> Reach God; there is nothing
> more fitting for your life. (*Tiruvāymoḷi* 1-2-3)

The poet speaks in these and several other verses about abandonment, the fleeting nature of the body, relinquishing the notion of "I-ness," and so forth. But the same poet also speaks of his love for the Lord:

> My friend:
> Bigger than this dense earth,
> larger than the seven seas,
> higher than the skies,
> is my love for [Viṣṇu], the one
> who has the color of the ocean. (*Tiruvāymoḷi* 7-3-8)

The kind of renunciation present in the sacrament of *prapatti* has to be seen in perspective against this passionate literature of love which was and which continues to be chanted by the Śrīvaiṣṇavas every day. Against this background, the Śrīvaiṣṇava tradition considers every human being as the "beloved" of the Lord, and Vedānta Deśika draws a formal analogy by comparing the soul who undergoes the sacrament of *prapatti* to a young bride who is given away by her father. The "father" in the sacrament of *prapatti* is the teacher (*ācārya*), who prepares and hands over the soul, which is the bride of the Lord; the bridegroom is the Lord himself ("The Light of *Śaraṇāgati*," v. 30).

We have studied, in this and the preceding chapter, the Śrīvaiṣṇava understanding of human bondage and divine grace. *Karma* binds, the grace of the Lord frees the human being. Rāmānuja in the eleventh century A.D. spoke of *bhaktiyoga* as attracting the grace of the Lord. But he and Kūraṭṭāḻvāṉ also confessed that they could not embark on the long and arduous discipline of *bhaktiyoga*. They surrendered themselves to the will of the Lord. This act was called *prapatti* by the community and recommended for all human beings. In the thirteenth century, Piḷḷai Lōkācārya and Vedānta Deśika differed in their interpretation of *prapatti* but did agree on the primacy of the Lord's compassion and grace in saving a human soul. The paradigmatic acts of protection and the promise of redemption made by the Lord in his incarnations are remembered by the community, and their faith, their total surrender to Viṣṇu, rests on these divine words and promises.

NOTES

[1] Piḷḷai Lōkācārya's differences with earlier *ācāryas* are several; these include his rejection of the validity of *bhaktiyoga* as a way by which the deity's grace is obtained. In many of his positions, he is closest to his father's contemporary, Periyavāccāṉ Piḷḷai (b. 1228), a person best known for his commentaries on the poems of the *āḻvārs*. Piḷḷai Lōkācārya, like Periyavāccāṉ Piḷḷai, wrote primarily in Maṇipravāḷa, a hybrid language of Sanskrit and Tamil, but unlike his predecessor preferred to present his views in the form of brief aphorisms known as *sūtras*. Piḷḷai Lōkācārya wrote about eighteen different works among which the *magnum opus* is the *Śrī Vacana Bhūṣaṇam* (henceforth, *SVB*), a treatise composed of 463 *sūtras*. Maṇavāḷa Māmuṇikaḷ (A.D. 1370–1443),

an *ācārya* whom the Teṅkalais rank as second only to Rāmānuja, wrote lengthy commentaries on Piḷḷai Lōkācārya's *sūtras.* Piḷḷai Lōkācārya's and Maṇavāḷa Māmuṇikaḷ's writings form the core of what is known as the Teṅkalai Śrīvaiṣṇava theology, and I shall quote from both these *ācāryas* drawing primarily from the *SVB,* the *sūtras,* and the commentary.

[2] Piḷḷai Lōkācārya, in his *Navavidha Sambandham,* talks about nine kinds of relationship that exist between the deity and the soul. These include the understanding of Viṣṇu as the Father, the Protector, the Husband, the Owner, the Knower, the Soul (*śarīri*), and the Support; the soul is the child, the protected one, the wife, the owned one (*śeṣa*), the one who is known, the body (*śarīra*), and the supported one.

[3] *SVB,* Maṇavāḷa Māmuṇikaḷ's comment on *sūtras* 9–13.

[4] *SVB,* comment on *sūtras* 9–13.

[5] The word that Piḷḷai Lōkācārya uses is *ābhimukhyam,* which literally means "turning one's face toward" someone. *Sūtras* 9–13.

[6] Maṇavāḷa Māmuṇikaḷ's commentary on *SVB, sūtras* 9–13. *Śrī Vacana Bhūṣaṇam,* in *Śrīmatvaravaramunīntra krantamālai,* ed. P.B. Aṇṇaṅgarācāriyar (Kanci: 1966). This edition is used for all the *SVB* references.

Maṇavāḷa Māmuṇikaḷ continues the discussion on "dependence on *karma*" in a later place. The human being's *karma* comes from his or her being caught in the performing of good and bad deeds which lead to being caught in the cycle of life and death. The Lord's *karma* is his attitude which makes him say: "what can I do if the human being insists on experiencing the consequences of his *karma* . . . ?" Śrī brings about their reconciliation. *SVB* commentary on *sūtra* 155, p. 92.

If the Lord and the human are not amenable to advice, Śrī resorts to other means; she corrects the human through her grace (Tamil: *aruḷ*), the Lord, through her beauty. As Maṇavāḷa Māmuṇikaḷ comments:

> She uses her beauty to entice and enslave (the Lord). She makes eyes at Him, she lets her dress slip down a little. . . . (*SVB* commentary on *sūtra* 13, pp. 23–24)

[7] Viṣṇu is regarded as having the role of a teacher or *ācārya* in the holy *Bhagavad Gīta,* thus showing the way to himself. Since this is a function of Śrī or an earthly teacher who acts as a mediator between the Lord and the human soul, the Lord is whimsically called a mediator unto himself.

[8] Commentary on *SVB, sūtra* 15, pp. 27–28.

[9] He quotes scriptural precedence. In the epic *Rāmāyaṇa,* Bharata surrendered himself to his older brother Rāma who was the incarnation of Viṣṇu, but Bharata's wish was denied. Rāma, however, chose Guha who was "ignorant and of low birth" and showered grace on him. He says that when the human being tries to go to the Lord, *prapatti* will not

work. But when the Lord wants to get us, when he chooses us, our faults will not be barriers. Bharata's virtue (that is, his seeking God on his own initiative) turned out to be harmful; Guha's drawback (in other words, his low social standing) worked to his advantage.

[10] *SVB, sūtras* 142–146.

[11] "With respect to the *upāya*," says Piḷḷai Lōkācārya, "one must emulate Sīta, Draupadī, and Tirukkaṇṇamaṅkaiyāṇṭaṉ" (*SVB, sūtra* 80). He elucidates: "Sīta discarded her strength to save herself, Draupadī dropped her shame, Tirukkaṇṇamaṅkaiyāṇṭāṉ dropped his work." (*SVB, sūtra* 82)

The incidents Piḷḷai Lōkācārya refers to are famous in the Śrīvaiṣṇava community. Sīta, though capable of freeing herself with her power, waited for Rāma to save her. Draupadī, in the process of being stripped of her clothing by a prince in the midst of a royal court, dropped her effort of protecting herself; she stopped trying to cling to her garment, threw up her arms, and sought refuge in Kṛṣṇa who protected her. Tirukkaṇṇamaṅkaiyāṇṭāṉ apparently saw a dog beaten by a servant, at which the owner of the dog took umbrage and killed the one who beat the dog and then killed himself. Tirukkaṇṇamaṅkaiyāṇṭāṉ was struck by the love the master had for a mere dog and wondered how much more love the Lord must have for us. At this point he dropped his work and with utmost faith walked into a temple. In all these instances, there was a supreme confidence that the Lord will save, according to Piḷḷai Lōkācārya. Therefore one can only wait to be saved; if one seeks virtue—by seeking refuge in the Lord as Bharata did—virtue becomes evil, for it is *self-sought* (*SVB, sūtra* 160).

[12] In this context we may mention that Rāmānuja also emphasized the importance of the soul's dependence on the Lord; he said that just as one may mistakenly think of oneself as a lion or as a tiger because of one's *karma,* so too can one think of oneself as independent because of one's previous *karma.* However, the striking difference between Rāmānuja and Piḷḷai Lōkācārya is that the former accepts *bhaktiyoga* and the latter rejects it as unbecoming for the human soul.

[13] This simile is followed by a scriptural quotation. Rāma, an incarnation of Viṣṇu and the hero of the epic *Rāmāyaṇa,* is quoted as saying that even a necklace of pearls which normally adorned his wife Sīta was an obstruction when he embraced her.

[14] Commentary on *SVB, sūtra* 280, p. 158.

[15] Parāśara Bhaṭṭar comments on the divine name "Ignorant One" (*avijñāta*) in his Commentary on the *Thousand Names of Viṣṇu* (*Bhagavadguṇa darpaṇākhyam*), *Śrīviṣṇusahasranāmabhāṣyam,* edited by P.B. Aṇṇaṅgarācāriyar (Kanci: 1964), p. 134.

See also *Tirukkurukai Pirāṉ Piḷḷāṉ Tiruvārāyirappaṭi* (commentary on Nammāḻvār's *Tiruvāymoḻi*), 1-5-10 in *Bhagavad viṣayam,* edited by Sri S. Krishnasvāmi Ayyaṅkar, 10 vols. (Madras: Nobel Press, 1924–1930).

[16] Commentary on Rāmānuja's *Śaraṇāgati gadya* ("Hymn of Surrender"). *Gadyatrayavyākyānankaḷ,* edited by K. Srinivasa Ayyangar (Tirucci: 1976).

[17] *Ibid.,* p. 132.

[18] *SVB, sūtra* 381. Calling the Lord's name and taking care of his devotees are not spoken of as good deeds done knowingly. Rather, as Maṇavāḷa Māmuṇikaḷ comments, if a man, while mentioning the names of his acquaintances, happens to talk of one who bears a name of Viṣṇu, the Lord seizes that act as an excuse to save the speaker. A man irrigating his field may be saved by accident in so far as a passing devotee happens to wash and refresh himself in the flowing water, for the Lord will look upon this as a service done to his devotee.

[19] *SVB, sūtra* 382 and commentary. Lalitā, the queen of Kāśī, was the favorite wife of her husband. Every night she lit a lamp in front of the Lord. When questioned about her good fortune and the reason for lighting a lamp, she, blessed with the memory of her former life, told the other three hundred wives that in times past there was a king called Sauvīra whose minister, Maitreya, built a temple for Viṣṇu on the banks of the River Deli. The brahmin Maitreya lived there and served the Lord by offering flowers, incense and lighted lamps and there, one night in the month of Kārtika, the lamp that he lit in front of the deity flickered and was about to be extinguished. Lalitā says that in that life time, she was a mouse, living in that temple. Desiring to put out the flame, so that she could eat the temple offerings in the dark, she apparently pulled the wick. At that time, she heard a cat mew; trembling out of fright, the mouse died, but its trembling body fanned the flame and the uplifted wick now burnt with its previous brilliance in the temple. Lalitā the mouse died, but was reborn as the fortunate beautiful princess and was endowed with the memory of her last birth.

[20] *SVB, sūtra* 382, pp. 202–204.

[21] *SVB, sūtra* 385.

[22] *SVB, sūtra* 396.

[23] *SVB, sūtra* 387.

[24] *SVB, sūtra* 391.

[25] *Rahasya Traya Sāra* (hereafter *RTS*) of Vedānta Deśika, edited by Śrī Rāmātēcikācāryarsvāmi, vol. 1 (Kumbakonam: Śrī Oppiliyappaṇ Canniti, 2 vols., 1961). This edition will be used in this paper.

[26] *RTS,* p. 238

[27] *RTS,* ch. 23.

[28] Vedānta Deśika, quoting the *Lakṣmī Tantra* 17:75, says that the term *saṁnyāsa* is synonymous with *nyāsa, nikṣepa, tyāga,* and *śaraṇāgati. Saṁnyāsa* is renunciation; *nyāsa* is to abandon, to relinquish, to place or put down, entrust, commit or give over; *nikṣepa* is to entrust, to commit,

to give up one's soul; *tyāga* is to give up, renounce, resign, surrender; and *śaraṇagati* is to come for refuge or protection. For Vedānta Deśika, these meanings are conveyed by the word *namas* which appears in the traditional Indian greeting "*namaste.*"

[29] Bharata muni, *Natya Śāstra* ("The Treatise on Dance"). Deśika quotes this line while commenting on the eleventh century preceptor Yāmuna's poem entitled "The Jewel of Hymns." (*Stotra ratna;* also in *RTS,* chapter 28.)

[30] It is stated in the *Lakṣmī Tantra* that *nyāsa* or *prapatti* has five components, and another text holy to the Śrīvaiṣṇavas, the *Āhirbudhnya Saṁhita,* says that *prapatti* consists of six elements (it includes the submission of the self as the sixth component). Vedānta Deśika quotes these verses often. All these elements are found in every act of *prapatti,* and Vedānta Deśika refers to a paradigmatic incident from the epic *Rāmāyaṇa* to illustrate the points.

The *Rāmāyaṇa* is considered to be the book illustrating *prapatti* according to the Śrīvaiṣṇavas. Rāma, a prince of Ayodhya is in exile, with his wife Sīta and brother Lakṣmaṇa. While living in a forest, Rāvaṇa, the "demon" ruler of Laṅka, abducts Sīta. Rāma finds out where Sīta is and sends a message to Rāvaṇa, asking him to return her. Rāvaṇa refuses, and Rāma prepares for battle. Vibhīṣaṇa, the brother of Rāvaṇa, exhorts him to free Sīta. Rāvaṇa, enraged, banishes Vibhīṣaṇa. Vibhīṣaṇa's roots are cut; he has nowhere to go. Leaving behind his wealth, family, and friends and accompanied by four others who also seek protection, he flees Laṅka and crosses the sea. With full confidence he approaches Rāma's camp and declares:

> Leaving my wife and sons I have come to take refuge with Rāma. Inform the great soul (*mahātma*), Rāghava (Rāma), the protector (refuge: *śaraṇya*) of the worlds, that I, Vibhīṣaṇa, have come [for protection]. (*Rāmāyaṇa, Yuddha Kāṇḍa,* 17: 16–17)

Rāma grants the protection which is sought and the words he says on that occasion have become extremely important in the Śrīvaiṣṇava tradition; this is the Lord's promise of salvation assuring his protection to those who seek it:

> Anyone who surrenders himself (*prapanna*) is assured of my protection. This, I swear. (*Rāmāyana, Yuddha Kāṇḍa,* 18: 33)

[31] These sentiments are voiced both in the *RTS* and in three poems written on the subject of *nyāsa,* a term that is considered to be a synonym of *prapatti.* (*Nyāsa* is "abandonment" and "entrusting.") The word *nyāsa* seems to convey both aspects of the word *prapatti* to Deśika: an abandonment, a sense of renunciation, as well as the entrusting of one's soul to the Lord.

[32] *RTS,* ch. 12.

[33] *RTS,* ch. 13–15.

THE PATH IS NOT *MY* WAY

John Ross Carter

Having seen the impressive manifestation in the Śaiva Siddhānta and Śrīvaiṣṇava heritage of the quality of human awareness to which the English word "grace" refers, we now move to consider the Buddhist testimony as communicated through the centuries by the Theravāda tradition. Although Theravāda Buddhists, particularly in Sri Lanka, have lived alongside Śaiva Siddhāntins and, to some degree, Śrīvaiṣṇavas, there have not been sustained attempts to establish religious colloquia until quite recently. And Christians, Roman Catholics and Protestants alike, have been conversing with Theravāda Buddhists for over a century, with only an occasional breakthrough into profound understanding. Argumentation based on syllogisms that are in turn founded on doctrinal formulations within closed systems is yielding to sustained reflection on the quality of life and consistent testimony shared by Theravāda Buddhists, Christians, and Hindus.

I

In this chapter we will turn our attention to the Theravāda Buddhist tradition. The Theravāda (or "the Way of the Elders") is the form of the Buddhist tradition that developed in India and took on both focus and continuity in Sri Lanka and Southeast Asia. It is enormously difficult for one to try to address the theme of our inquiry, "Of Human Bondage and Divine Grace," as it might pertain to the Theravāda Buddhist case, and this for several reasons. Firstly, this tradition has been on the scene in human history for over twenty-three hundred years and, in its cumulative development in different cultural contexts over the centuries, presents the student of today a massive amount of information and a complex variety of subtle interpretations, as well as lacunae for more investigation. Secondly, the Theravāda is a major religious tradition that has not stressed the centrality of the notion of God in the soteriological process. Thirdly, this tradition, in its classical formative language, does not have a comparable term for the English word "grace." And fourthly, of course, we are limited to only one chapter for our consideration.

We shall attempt to present and then to integrate a cluster of concepts that have been nurtured in the Theravāda tradition in order to suggest a zone of human religious sensitivity that is not foreign to the experience of others who have attempted to communicate their discernment through the concepts of "grace" and "human bondage." This will not be easy, but we will not by that be deterred.

Frank Sinatra has made popular a song that perhaps means a great deal to many today—the song "My Way." The import of the song is that in the final analysis, whatever the case might be, one has no regrets because one can say "I did it my way." With this, as it might relate to living life well, fully, with purpose and meaning in a process of transcending life, Theravāda Buddhists would hardly concur. And a historian is compelled to report the historical fact that no great personality who has significantly contributed to the shaping of the visions held in the hearts of men and women has ever said this, that no great tradition that has brought culture, civilization, and the flourishing of the arts has ever endorsed the sentiment that one is to find both courage and equipoise in reflecting upon one's life to the degree that one can say "I did it my way."

For over two millennia persons have uttered an old and noble refrain, have affirmed the relevance of an inherited tradition for the living of life:

Buddhaṃ saraṇaṃ gacchāmi
Dhammaṃ saraṇaṃ gacchāmi
Sanghaṃ saraṇaṃ gacchāmi

I go to the Buddha as refuge.
I go to Dhamma as refuge.
I go to the Sangha as refuge.[1]

Refuge is taken in the Buddha as examplar and in Salvific Truth (*Dhamma*) that the Buddha rediscovered, the rediscovery of which enabled Gotama to become "the Awakened One," the Buddha.

Refuge is taken in *Dhamma* as both teaching, given by the Buddha without distortion resulting from its having been a part of mental processes or expressed in human speech, and as Salvific Truth, the *raison d'être* of the teaching. *Dhamma* is perhaps the central notion that Theravāda Buddhists have shared for over two millennia in the religious history of humankind. It is a great notion, providing both a centripetal focus in religious living and a centrifugal pervasiveness, through connotation and nuance, into the quality and character of human life as it can be lived at its best. When one becomes engaged with the teaching (*Dhamma*) about Salvific Truth (*Dhamma*) one enters a process that leads through this world, and by leading one through this world well leads one to live unrestricted by the customary limits of this world.

And refuge is taken in the *Sangha*, the order. The term *Sangha* has two levels of meaning in this refuge formula. On one level it refers to the noble ones who have gone before, who have realized the fructification in their lives of the efficacy of the teaching in guiding them to the moment when the penetration of Salvific Truth (*Dhamma*) arises. One is reminded of the metaphor "cloud of witnesses" used by the writer of the Epistle to the Hebrews (12:1) to indicate the continuity of personal faith through the vicissitudes of one's religious heritage. On the second, higher level, one takes refuge in Salvific Truth (*Dhamma*) which enabled those noble ones to realize liberation and continues to offer assurance of such realization to one today.

There is another meaning of *Sangha*, namely, the order of monks, *bhikkhus*, the monastic tradition, in fact the oldest continuing monastic institution in the world today. Obviously, something has been going on in this monastic heritage that has been eminently worthwhile because it has survived the tests of the strain and tension of history. When one goes for refuge in the *Sangha*, it is not for refuge in the monks living in the monastery down the lane, as it were, although one does admire that to which those monks ideally are committed, although they symbolize something that is attractive to one, although one's parents might have bowed down in the presence of these persons. It is not the sociological institution that is a refuge—Buddhists are too smart, manifestly, to endorse this kind of interpretation.

Perhaps beginning with this formula and the subtle notion of refuge might serve the purpose of giving us pause, to keep us from running roughshod over a magnificent testimony on the basis of an inadequately informed projection that the Theravāda tradition is an "atheistic" tradition and, hence, totally incapable of providing insights into the theme of our inquiry. The notion of refuge, occurring in this most visible of Buddhist liturgical acts, suggests that within this tradition that has not endorsed the notion of a Savior God there might be a dimension of human religiousness that is not foreign to a dimension sensed profoundly by persons participating in theistic religious traditions. This dimension is there, I suggest, if we have the wits and perhaps the patience to probe for it.

II

Something happened under the bodhi tree in the sixth century B.C., and a little later a teaching was shared with five mendicants, tradition remembers, in the Deer Park not far from Benares about twenty-five hundred years ago—and the history of Asia, our human religious history, has been marked by the reverberations of those and subsequent events in the lives of men and women who have been Buddhists.

We might not know exactly what the Buddha rediscovered while seated under that bodhi tree—he called it *Dhamma* and also *Nibbāna.* He spent about forty-two years teaching, not in order to explain it clearly but in order to demarcate carefully the *way* (*Dhamma/magga*) leading to it. Two fundamental categories within the Theravāda tradition that will prove helpful in our inquiry are (1) *lokiya,* meaning that which pertains to this world and other worlds, and (2) *lokuttara,* meaning that which transcends this world and the other worlds.

We would quickly be off the mark were we to say that this presents us with a two-tiered universe of sorts, or that the two dimensions are somehow neatly, casually demarcated. If this were the case, there would be a gap of mammoth proportions existing between them and, within the formulations offered by the Theravāda heritage, there would be little hope for a resolution of this soteriological divide. Such is not the case because *lokuttara,* although it transcends the worlds, is, to borrow a phrase shared by Muslims, "closer than the jugular vein." *Lokuttara* is there, here, if only one has the eyes to see it.

One begins with the world in which one finds oneself, a world in which one lives with three root maladies, constituting factors in one's perception of human bondage: (1) passion, intense desire, longing; (2) hatred; and (3) delusion. One begins where one is, in *saṃsāra,* the whirl of continuing lives. In the Theravāda tradition it is stressed that talk about the origin of *saṃsāra* is not immediately relevant for one's understanding of one's present condition in life. When one discerns that things as they are met with are awry, when one finds that one's life is awry, one recognizes authentically the human condition to which the tradition responds.

The world, that is, *saṃsāra,* is analyzed into three important spheres or levels. And these three spheres fall into the *lokiya* dimension. There is another dimension, not bounded by *saṃsāra,* of enormous consequence because it provides the broader and deeper context in which *saṃsāra* is placed, called *lokuttara.*

In all, with the various divisions, there are about thirty levels or planes of existence within three major spheres or realms (*avacara*): (1) the immaterial (*arūpa*) sphere or realm; (2) the fine material (*rūpa*) sphere; and (3) the sphere of sensuality (*kāma*), of the senses, our human sphere and the animal realm, together with several hells.

It is within the *lokiya* that all of this, *saṃsāra,* takes place. Wholesome, freeing action (*kamma*) leads one upward on the scale; detrimental action (*kamma*) leads one downward. But note, although the level of humankind is relatively low on the scale, it has been humans who have made these discernments, who have said these things, have remembered them, have found this way of looking at things to be meaningful. Although, as we will come to see, one can attain final enlightenment in the *arūpa* or *rūpa* spheres, the focus is on the human activity involved on the human level. This is the primary level on which the soteriological process has been focused.

How is *lokiya,* that which pertains to the world, characterized? Is there a discernible pattern? Most generally, *lokiya* is characterized as operating in line with a fundamental principle called "dependent co-production," "dependent origination," or "conditioned co-production," "conditioned co-origination." The principle runs like this:

> When this is, that arises.
> From the arising of this, that arises.
> With the cessation of this, that ceases.

This principle is called in Pali, the canonical language of the Theravāda tradition, *paṭiccasamuppāda*.

The formulation of this principle is an expression of the rediscovery that the Buddha achieved when he attained enlightenment. This principle of causal relations is one of formal concomitance (when this is, that arises) and not a formulation of material causality (when this is, being derived from this in some underlying substantial way through a process of change, that arises).

Taking this principle and applying it to all phenomena and proceses of the world, of *saṃsāra,* of *lokiya,* one finds that there is nothing that escapes it. All is impermanent.

Further, *saṃsāra,* or all that is *lokiya,* is characterized by three signs (*tilakkhaṇa*): (1) all that is within this realm is impermanent (*anicca*); (2) all therein is awry, out of joint, unsatisfactory, suffering (*dukkha*); and (3) all therein is without substantiality, without what might be called a soul (*anattā*).

Given one's intense longing, one's hatred and divisiveness, one's delusion, ignorance shot through with emotively based opinion, one does not discern the real process of the world, of *saṃsāra*—one clings; clinging to what is impermanent (*anicca*) leads to suffering (*dukkha*). And one clings because one craves these things—there is thirst for them (*taṇhā*)—and because one does not know the way things operate, how things have come to be as they are met in human experience.

The Buddha, who is affirmed as having become holistically enlightened, who, it is averred, through a remarkable process of teaching without distortion, of communicating truly through words the realization of that which stands behind words, did not speak of a Saving, Creator God. Gods, of course, there are, but they, too, move in the realm of *lokiya;* they live in *saṃsāra.*

So the stage for our human drama beginning in bondage is set. The witness is shared that we are opinionated people, filled with longing, clinging, "I-ness," "mine-ness," divisiveness, and, too, awryness. We find ourselves suffering; things are out of joint in this world that is characterized as impermanent, awry, and without substantiality.

III

But the testimony of Theravāda Buddhists does not stop with this. Nor, apparently, did the Buddha's rediscovery. There is more, indeed, much more. Right in this world, in this *saṃsāra,* is a *path,* a *way of going,* a mode of life that is present, reliable, authentic, real, right before and behind the eyes if one have the wits to see it.

For centuries, Buddhists have looked upon the human situation and have interpreted that situation in light of four noble truths, the discernment of which enables one to live through this life with noble bearing. We would fail to measure the significance of these truths if we take them to be less than realities—real facts about the human situation—or if we take them to be merely propositions in search of an adequate verification principle, or if we take them to be "truth-claims." The Buddhist movement spread throughout Asia because persons had become engaged with these truths and had found "It is so!", that the human condition and the way to move through it and beyond it are manifested in these truths. The Buddhist movement has hardly spread because Buddhists argued their case, persuaded others that they had formulated propositions more adequately than others, that they had advanced claims about truth that won the day. Buddhists, however, and also, have given testimony, have shared a witness, have said to others, come and see whether "it is so." And others did come to find that it is so, and the oldest continuing missionary movement in human history continues to carry its witness to others today.

The four noble truths or realities that speak to our human condition are, briefly:

1. That life as we find it is suffering, is awry.
2. That craving, literally thirst, is the basis for this suffering—when there is craving, suffering arises.

3. That there is a cessation of suffering: where craving ceases, suffering ceases.
4. And there is a path, a way (*magga*) that leads to the cessation of this suffering.

This path or way is interpreted in two ways, one more descriptive, that is, *path-annunciation,* the other being more suggestive of the experimential dimension of *path-realization.* We will turn to path-realization a little later. It is the description or annunciation of the path that is mentioned regularly in the context of the four noble truths. This path, the fourth of the four noble truths or realities, is eightfold. It is often referred to simply as the eightfold path:

1. proper view
2. proper intention
3. proper speech
4. proper action
5. proper livelihood
6. proper effort
7. proper mindfulness
8. proper concentration or meditative absorption

We are told that proper practice in this path involves, ideally, the mutual interpenetration of all the eight listed dimensions and activities, one with the others. Further, proper practice entails all those human activities that persons consider to be virtuous (*sīla*); that this virtue is at the foundation of concentration or meditative absorption (*samādhi*). But we are also told that there is something more, namely, insight-wisdom (*paññā*). These three categories of virtue, concentration or meditative absorption, and *paññā* are treated very comprehensively in the Buddhist tradition; they comprise the structure of a great work, the *Visuddhimagga,* written by Buddhaghoṣa in about the fifth century A.D.

Living morally, cultivating virtue, is remarkable, is refreshing, we are told, and is the beginning point for a bright future. Yet, this form of practice does not go beyond the *lokiya,* does not lead one beyond the heavens. It prepares one, but does not release one. Good behavior without salvific wisdom remains within the sphere of the conventional; it is noteworthy, even splendid, of course, but it cannot lead to liberation. Buddhists also have made the point that one cannot save oneself.

And concentration, meditative absorption, is not enough. Such is conducive to tranquility, but it pertains mainly to the higher spheres within the *lokiya* realm.

What of insight-wisdom, *paññā*? Insight-wisdom is described as pertaining both to the *lokiya* and to the *lokuttara,* that which transcends the world. In a sense, one might say that *lokiya* wisdom guides a person in the world; *lokuttara* wisdom guides a person through the world.

Upon turning to the experiential interpretation of the path, the path as *path-realization,* one finds that it, too, is considered in an eightfold analysis. This consideration of the path is not too prevalent in books written about the Theravāda tradition for a Western audience. But it is a central formulation within the tradition and represents the way Theravāda Buddhists have chosen to symbolize their discernment of the soteriological process.

The first path, the lowest, is the path of stream attainment.

With this path there is a fruit, a fructification.

The second path is the path of a once returner or once returning.

And this path, too, has its fruit.

The third path is the path of a non-returner or non-returning.

And, also, this path has its associated fruit.

The fourth path is the path of a perfected one, an Arahant.

And this path has its fruit.

There are, then, four paths and four fruits. There is no parallel doctrinal structure between these modes of interpretation, as for example, that the third element of path-annunciation, proper speech in the eightfold path, represents the third element of the experiential interpretation of path-realization, namely, the second path, the path of a once returner. Rather, the four paths and four fruits represent a structure for interpreting modes of deeper and deepening realizations of the four noble truths *in toto.* In considering how this deepening realization might be communicated in words, the tradition has spoken of fetters that fall away with the attainment of the four paths.

The Fetters	**The Paths**
THE LOWER FETTERS	
1. doting on individuality 2. skeptical doubt 3. clinging to mere rules and rituals	When free of these three fetters, one enters the stream; the path of *stream attainment* arises.
4. delight in sensuality 5. ill-will	When one is free from 1–3 and is free of 4–5 in their gross forms, the path of *once returner* arises. When one is quite free from 1–5 completely, the path of *non-returner* arises.
THE HIGHER FETTERS	
6. delight in fine material existence 7. delight in immaterial existence 8. self-estimation 9. restlessness 10. ignorance	When one is free from 1–5 entirely, and totally free from 6–10, one attains the path of an *Arahant*.

The lower fetters are considered to be bonds around the ankles, dragging one downward. The higher fetters are bonds around the neck, pulling one upward. In either case, humankind as it begins its reflection on its condition, finds that it is fettered, bound down, in bondage.

IV

There are two areas in all of this, two zones of inquiry that I would like to highlight as relevant to our understanding of the theme "Of Human Bondage and Divine Grace."

The first is the state of an *Arahant*, who will, upon the passing of this earthly body, attain final and complete *Nibbāna*. The tradition has tried to make it clear that there is not a fundamental eternal self engaged in this *Nibbāna* realization. Further, if final *Nibbāna* is caused, it, too, itself, dependent upon something else for its existence, is subject to passing away. But the tradition avers that the arising of the realization of *Nibbāna* is not fashioned by human thought, is not caused by the mind, arises naturally, is unborn. Here, the tradition makes the point that final liberation, the final attainment of complete *Nibbāna, is not one's doing.* To think otherwise would be not to realize *Nibbāna.*

The second zone of inquiry has to do with the moment of attaining the four paths. The tradition has given considerable attention to the moment of stream-attainment. When this stream is attained, it is said that one will undergo no more than seven rebirths. This stream-attainment occurs when one holistically realizes the four noble truths. When the conditions for the arising of the defilements are present and the first three fetters are absent, then the defiling consequences of mental actions do not arise. The tradition affirms that this is the moment when one gains one's first glimpse of *Nibbāna.* In the gentle words of the *Dhammapada*:

> Better than sole sovereignty over the earth,
> Or the journey to heaven,
> Than lordship over all the worlds,
> Is the Fruit of Stream Attainment.[2]

Intense personal effort is necessary, of course, in the process of discipline, of exercising common sense, of anticipating consequences of one's actions. Yet, as M. Palihawadana, an insightful contemporary commentator, puts it, one becomes aware

> that personal effort is only the 'setting' for the realization of the highest religious truth, that the highest realization can take place only when effort ceases to be, having exhausted its scope and having brought about the knowledge that it too is a barrier to be broken down.[3]

Theravāda Buddhists are not unfamiliar with a mode of discourse central to our theme of "grace". Palihawadana addresses the matter directly. There are

> elements of a common religious conviction: The redeeming change in a person takes place not ultimately by exercising the will, but at its cessation, which is an indispensable factor for contact with supreme reality; it is this contact that truly renews and transforms the person.[4]

From within the Theravāda tradition it is possible for one to say that the path which is available to one right here in the mundane world, one that can be tread in this world, by means of which one can move through the mundane to that which transcends the mundane, was passed down to one by one's tradition. It was given to one through this tradition deriving from the teachings of the Buddha. One is able, consequently, to set out on this path through the exercise of one's will, but at the moment of transition, of personal transformation, when a shift in orientation from the *lokiya* to the *lokuttara* occurs, the will is absent, the mind is infused, the defilements are dropped from the psychic processes, and reality is encountered. One is led to aver, "*I* have not done this, the path is not *my* way."

NOTES

[1] See John Ross Carter, ed. *The Threefold Refuge in the Theravāda Buddhist Tradition* (Chambersburg, Pennsylvania: Anima Books, 1982).

[2] See the recent text, *The Dhammapada: A New English Translation with the Pali Text and the First English Translation of the Commentary's Explanation of the Verses with Notes,* translated from Sinhala sources and critical textual comments by John Ross Carter and Mahinda Palihawadana (New York: Oxford University Press, 1987), verse 178, pp. 43, 239.

[3] Mahinda Palihawadana, "Is There a Theravāda Buddhist Idea of 'Grace'?", in *Christian Faith in a Religiously Plural World,* edited by Donald Dawe and John B. Carman (Maryknoll, New York: Orbis Books, 1978), p. 193.

[4] *Ibid.,* p. 194.

9

EMPTINESS ABOUNDING

John Ross Carter

Within the Theravāda tradition there are differences of perspective, of course, and sectarian developments focusing on monastic institutional structures. With the Mahāyāna tradition, however, a dazzling plethora of alternative formulations awaits the patient inquirer. This rich and multifaceted tradition—which flourished in India, penetrated Central Asia, participated grandly in the complex of human meaning discerned by Chinese men and women, contributed much to Korea, significantly shaped, and simultaneously was informed by, Japanese culture, and provided the scaffolding for much that has formed the experience of men and women in Tibet—is becoming well-known in North America, most popularly in its Japanese and Tibetan forms.

In turning to the Mahāyāna Buddhist tradition in this chapter, one is met with something of a dilemma, which, of course, is not new in a consideration of the Mahāyāna, the "Great Vehicle," or "Great Way," this impressive religious heritage that has contributed significantly to the shaping of Asian history. On the one hand, Mahāyāna is multifacted, much too rich in diversity and history for one to probe into that diversity for the theme of this volume in a single chapter. On the other hand, if one were to be concerned with the points of difference between the Mahāyāna and the Theravāda, especially since this chapter follows immediately one on the Theravāda, one would hardly have time to address our theme. I therefore would like to note distinctive features of the Mahāyāna in broad strokes and to consider zones within this tradition that might complement the contributions made by others to this study.

I suppose it is both accurate and adequate to say that the Buddhist tradition has maintained in consonance both the Theravāda and the Mahāyāna, that liberation, freedom, and salvation are on the side of one who denies oneself. Nothing new here, one might say; perhaps so, but there is probably nothing harder to do or to realize.

Denying oneself could lead to confusion, could represent to some an activity engendering fear, and it is likely that such would be the case were there not a structure of meaning provided for the activity of denying oneself. We have heard, "let him deny (from *aparneonai* = to deny utterly) himself and take up his cross" (Mt. 16:24) and "he who loses (from *apollumi* = to destroy utterly) his life for my sake will find it" (Mt. 10:39, 16:25; cf. Mk. 8:35, Lk. 9:24, 17:33), statements by one great religious teacher, Jesus the Christ. A Zen Buddhist, although applying slightly different interpretations, would not find these statements initially startling.

Let me try to probe a structure of meaning that Mahāyāna Buddhists have bequeathed to posterity, a structure that enables one to let go and be held, to speak poetically.

I want (1) to turn to a notion called "emptiness," then (2) to heed a great Buddhist poet of the eighth century, Śāntideva, who will communicate an interconnection between emptiness, on the one hand, and the orientation of a "being whose purpose is enlightenment (*bodhisattva*)," on the other, in a way that will enable us to understand a sense of self-denial that is simulataneously replete with religious virtues and radical in its pervasiveness. Finally, we will jump several centuries later, as it were, and move to another cultural complex, Japan, (3) to glimpse the Zen strand of the Mahāyāna movement and to reflect on what might be there related to the theme of our study.

I

Emptiness, if not altogether clear to those of us who stand on this side of the breakthrough, is a friendly concept. Not to be associated with the Buddhist sense of "emptiness" are such notions as "great abyss," "nothingness," or "a terror of ultimate annihilation." The Buddha taught that emptiness is the true state of affairs, and his holistic realization of this constituted his Buddhahood.

Let us consider how the tradition has unravelled this meaning of emptiness from the teaching of the Buddha. We have already touched upon the notion of "conditioned co-production" (*paṭiccasamuppāda*) remembered by the Theravāda school. This teaching, more familiar in the West in its Sanskrit designation *pratītyasamutpāda,* is held by Buddhists to be central to all of the Buddha's teachings. Early Buddhist schools, and the Theravāda also, held that this notion of conditioned co-production describes the process of the phenomenal world, called *saṃsāra.* Over against *saṃsāra,* transcending *saṃsāra,* is *Nibbāna* or *Nirvāṇa,* the highest good, perfect and final liberation. All things in *saṃsāra,* it was held, are impermanent because of this process, are contributive to awryness because of this process, are without substantiality, likewise because of this process. But final, complete *Nirvāṇa,* it was held, is unmade, unborn, hence, itself, in its finality, falls outside of the recurrent pattern of this process.

Now there is a great deal of subtlety in this position among the early schools, and among the Theravāda today, and I do not wish to appear to be flipping that subtlety aside in order to move along to a great Indian Buddhist thinker of the second and third century. But for Nāgārjuna, the early schools were not applying the Buddha's teachings faithfully, were not following those teachings boldly, were not taking them far enough. Even concepts are to fall into this category of dependent co-production.

Nāgārjuna thought that if something were to be considered as having being, it must have its own-being, possess own-being. If something has its own-being how can one say of that something that it passes away, loses its own-being? If one were to say that something can do this (that is, can have and then lose its own-being), then one must say that that something does not have its own-being: its being is contingent upon something else. And further, if something has its own-being, how can one say that there was a time when it did not have being, a time before which it did not have its own-being and a time, subsequently, at which it had its own-being? If one were to say that something can do this, then one must say that that something does not have its own-being—there was a time when its own-being was not, its being is contingent upon something else.

Conditioned co-production or dependent origination (*pratītya-samutpāda*) indicates that everything that is dependent upon something else is empty of inherent own-being, is empty. To the extent that *Nirvāṇa* is dependent upon *saṃsāra* for its conceptualization, to that extent *Nirvāṇa* is empty. To the extent that *samsāra* is dependent upon *Nirvāṇa* for its conceptualization, to that extent *saṃsāra* is empty. Nāgārjuna said that on the level of truth in the highest sense, there is not the slightest difference between *Nirvāṇa* and *saṃsāra*,[1] *Nirvāṇa* and *saṃsāra* are one and they are empty. Our objective, then, is to realize, holistically, that all is empty.

Nāgārjuna left us some practical teachings, which reflect much older themes in the Buddhist heritage. Firstly, we live in the realm of two levels of truth. On the conventional level, of course, there is the relative reality of a tree, a Chevrolet, a book, music, a phenomenal ego, a locomotive, and so forth. But on the highest level, in the sphere of the highest truth, there is emptiness. And secondly, Nāgārjuna gave us a warning: emptiness is empty, do not grasp after emptiness, do not try to cling to it as to some kind of substantial absolute.

II

Whereas the early schools taught that one's objective is to become an *Arahant*, to achieve enlightenment having followed the teachings of the Buddha and to attain final *Nirvāṇa* upon death of the physical body, to leave the whirl of *saṃsāra*, with the Mahāyāna the emphasis shifted to one who is a being whose purpose is enlightenment, a *bodhisattva*, to do as the Buddha did, to be as the Buddha was in his former births, to quest for enlightenment, not to enter *Nirvāṇa* but to stay where one is, to stay in *saṃsāra*, even to enter the hells, so to speak, because there was and is nowhere else to which one could actually "go," if *Nirvāṇa* and *saṃsāra* are really on the highest level not differentiated.

And, on the highest level of truth, there is no being that leaves *saṃsāra* for *Nirvāṇa*. The notion of "absence of self" or "non-substantiality" (*anattā/anātman*) was held among the earlier schools and in the Theravāda. In the thought of Nāgārjuna, *anātman* and *pratītyasamutpāda* went hand in hand; the principle of dependent origination and no-soul were interrelated. So in the final analysis, all is emptiness.

And yet the tradition had maintained that the Buddha was the paradigm of compassion, of virtue, of caring. He is called the person of great compassion, *Mahākaruṇāvant*. What is one to make of this?

The person who seeks to cultivate the way of the *bodhisattva*, the way of the Buddha, endorses the fundamental importance of the active virtues, of giving, of caring, of supporting others. It is only in this way that one disciplines oneself for the arising of salvific wisdom in which there is a realization of emptiness. One misses the mark when one raises an ethical dilemma nurtured in the West: how can one have genuine compassion toward another when one and the other are, on the highest level, empty?

The question, rather, might be more productively considered differently. Standing on this side of the breakthrough, one does not know what emptiness is. One is told in the tradition that emptiness transcends being *and* non-being. One is also told, but told indirectly because it has been assumed, that emptiness is such that the active virtues are fundamental in the training leading to its realization, as well as being manifestations of its attainment. This is the zone for our further reflection.

The emptiness realization is the kind of realization that occurs to the mind when the mind is brought into a state or condition of creative passivity or receptive resilience as a result of a process of abandoning ego-centered awareness and a process of caring, supporting, wishing for the welfare of others. Emptiness is more than all of this, yet this way of living is on target, so to speak.

In eighth century northeast India, at Nālanda, an ancient center of learning, the great Buddhist poet Śāntideva wrote in Sanskrit the *Bodhicaryāvatāra*,[2] entitled in one English translation, *Entering the Path of Enlightenment*.[3] This remarkable poet enables one to see how the notion of emptiness does not contradict the active virtues of the Buddhist tradition. Śāntideva wrote:

> Indeed, goodness [*śubha:* glossed by *puṇya*][4] is weak, but the power of evil [*pāpa*] is always great and very dreadful. By what other goodness could evil be conquered if there were not surely the Thought of Enlightenment [*bodhicitta*]? (Matics, pp. 143–44; Skt. I.6, p. 6)
>
> The wretched one who is bound by the fetters of existence instantly is proclaimed a son of the Buddhas. He becomes worthy of being praised in the worlds of men and of immortals when the Thought of Enlightenment has arisen. (Matics, p. 144; Skt. I.9, p. 7)

In his chapter on the "Confession of Sins," Śāntideva begins with a listing of beautiful offerings to offer to the Buddhas and to the *bodhisattvas*—flowers, herbs, mountains of jewels, forests, and so forth—and then writes:

> These I offer mentally to the eminent sages [*muni*] and to their little sons. May the great Compassionate Ones [*mahākṛpa*], worthy of choice gifts, mercifully accept this from me.
>
> I have nothing else for worship [*pūja*]. Therefore, for my sake, let the Lords whose highest object is the mind [*citta*], accept this through my own effort [*ātmaśakti*].
>
> And I give myself to the Conquerors completely, and to their sons. Pre-eminent Beings! Take possession of me! Through devotion [*bhakti*] I go into servitude [*dāsatvam*].
>
> By your taking possession of me I become without fear of existence, I do good [*hita*] to all beings, and I by-pass former sin [*pāpa*], and, moreover, I do no further sin. (Matics, pp. 147–48; Skt. II.6–9, pp. 23–24)

And further:

> Whatever evil, on the endless wheel of rebirth [*saṃsāra*], or simply right here, whatever evil was committed by me, an animal, or caused to be committed, and whatever was enjoyed foolishly, ending in self-destruction, that evil I confess, stricken with remorseful feeling. (Matics, pp. 149; Skt. II.28–29, p. 29)

When moving to his chapter on "Grasping the Thought of Enlightenment," one notes how Śāntideva expresses his dedication to the welfare of others:

> I would be a protector for those without protection, a leader for those who journey, and a boat, a bridge, a passage for those desiring the further shore.
>
> For all creatures, I would be a lantern for those desiring a lantern, I would be a bed for those desiring a bed, I would be a slave for those desiring a slave. (Matics, p. 154; Skt. III.27–28, p. 43)

When speaking of the arising of the Thought of Enlightenment, Śāntideva presents a subtle twin dimension in the consideration.

Insofar as the Thought of Enlightenment is directed toward the welfare of others, it is possible to speak of one's causing it to arise. Secondly, insofar as one refers to one's own competence or self-agency, the source of arising of the Thought of Enlightenment is less clear. Consider the following:

> As the ancient Buddhas [*sugatas*] seized the Thought of Enlightenment, and in like manner they followed regularly on the path of Bodhisattva instructions;
>
> Thus also do I cause the Thought of Enlightenment to arise [*utpādayāmi-eṣa bodhicittaṃ*] for the welfare of the world, and thus shall I practice these instructions in proper order. (Matics, p. 155; Skt. III.22–23, pp. 42–43)

The implication seems to be that it is amiss for one to think that one causes the arising of the Thought of Enlightenment for oneself solely with a focus on oneself. Let us continue with Śāntideva:

> As a blind man may obtain a jewel in a heap of dust, so, somehow, this Thought of Enlightenment has arisen even within me. [*tathā katham cid-api: etad-bodhicittaṃ mama-uditaṃ.*] (Matics, p. 155; Skt. III.27, p. 43)

So we seem to have some imprecision. When the orientation is toward others, one can speak of oneself as causing this thought to arise, as did former Buddhas. But when the reference is to oneself, well, one is less clear. Śāntideva seems to be saying that one hits upon it, *somehow* it happens, *somehow* this Thought of Enlightenment is arisen in one. And this is very important to note.

Śāntideva continues to describe aspects of the *bodhisattva's* commitment to the active virtues leading to the arising of insight-wisdom, wisdom that is salvific. In the closing chapters of his work, he moves to the more rarified stratum of Buddhist thought to share a bit more about what emptiness might entail:

> By holding to the impression of the Void (*śūnya*) [*śūnyatāvāsana*], it is realized that the impression of existence is nothing at all; and, afterwards, by repetition, even this is discarded.
>
> When an existence is not accepted of which it may be said that it does not exist, then, nonexistence is without foundation: How again can it stand before the mind?

> When neither existence [*bhāva*] nor nonexistence [*abhāva*] is presented again to the mind, then, through lack of any other possibility, that which is without support becomes tranquil. (Matics, p. 214; Skt. IX.33–35, pp. 197–98)

But, surely one might say, all of this does not make sense, one talks of beings and then of neither existence or non-existence, of no-beings. Why care? Śāntideva writes:

> It may be thought that because a being cannot be found, there is no one upon whom to bestow compassion; but whatever is done [even] in a state of confusion is because of a purpose.
>
> Yet if there is no being, whose is the purpose? Truly the effort is illusionary; but because it is for the sake of tranquilizing sorrow, the delusion of purpose is not forbidden.
>
> Because of the delusion of self [*ātmamoha*], the concept of one's individuality, the cause of sorrow [*duḥkha-hetur-ahaṃkāra*], is increased. Since it is destroyed in no other way, the concept of nonself is preferred. (Matics, p. 218; Skt. IX.76–78, pp. 228–31)

Now let me attempt to summarize at this stage of our considerations before moving on. We caught a glimpse of the contribution of Nāgārjuna who saw himself as maintaining the centrality of the Buddha's teaching. For Nāgārjuna, one sets out through discipline, self-denial, and meditation to cultivate oneself, to bring oneself to a moment when the realization of emptiness arises—when the realization of emptiness *arises,* mind you. In taking this position, Nāgārjuna, as well as Buddhists of earlier schools, maintained consistency with an old and frequent refrain about the Buddha's bodhi-tree realization. The phrase is that "knowledge and vision arose" (*udapādi*). When the Buddha had done this or that, when he was prepared, knowledge and vision "arose." It happened. Nāgārjuna would, of course, say this is the case with the realization of emptiness, it happens.

With Śāntideva, we have ready agreement about the emptiness-realization moment. He does tend to speak of our agency in causing the arising of the Thought of Enlightenment, an event when one shifts lineage, as it were, and becomes a *bodhisattva,* a child of the Buddhas. But when he speaks of one's agency, he is clear that this is the way the moment is considered as an act for the sake of others.

When he refers more specifically to himself, he introduces the phrase "somehow" (*kathaṃ cid-api*) the Thought of Enlightenment "has arisen in me."

We let the matter stand there for a moment to note in passing that the developing cumulative tradition reflected on the moment of entering the *bodhisattva* career. Some texts speak of a seed, an inherent potentiality for this career that was present, without further elaboration, in the person. Some suggested that this potentiality was inherently in some and not in others, leaving the way open for the inference that some beings were continually to remain in *saṃsāra,* to remain in delusion. Buddhists have considered these ideas too.

But with Nāgārjuna and Śāntideva, we have the notion of emptiness that is tranquil, that is devoid of sorrow and pain, emptiness that is empty, that can be realized in the Enlightenment, which is the same Enlightenment as that of the Buddha, which arises. And the preparation for this moment involves the active virtues in a long process of preparation. But this emptiness is not a principle, it is reality, albeit differently formulated from ways customary to the West, but nonetheless reality.

In the development of the tradition, subtle terms were affixed to this notion of emptiness, terms like "thusness" or "suchness." The overriding concern was to check one from making discursive intellectualizations and positing the fruits of discursive thought as the real. Whatever emptiness or thusness or suchness might be, it cannot be realized through discursive processes within the realm of the customary mental activators or processes (*saṅkhāras*). Whatever it might mean, it cannot be explained through discursive thought.

Certainly we are here alerted to a mode of expressing the non-agency of the person in the Enlightenment realization.

As we would expect, the Buddhist tradition, old and variegated as it is and has been, developed different ways of attempting to communicate the realization of salvific truth, truth on the highest level. In whatever ways the communication was shared, there were recurrent themes:

1. Consistent mitigation of the importance of the phenomenal ego.
2. The enlightenment happens. It is not directly caused by an agent.

3. Virtue is fundamental for the process leading one from where one now is to the arising of the realization.

III

Keeping Nāgārjuna and Śāntideva, our Indian Buddhist guides, in mind, we turn now to consider Zen. But Zen is, in a sense, on the other side of China from India. Already in India, before the Buddhist tradition moved into China, there were positions being taken among Buddhists about an inherent seed or potentiality or Buddhaness (*buddhatā*) or "Buddha-nature" within persons. And the point was then being made by some that this Buddha-nature was in all beings, since it was the reality that was also being suggested by the use of the term emptiness. For Buddha-nature, if it is anything at all, is that which is unsupported by anything, is tranquil and without sorrow, and real. In China, also, there was a weighty and magnificent notion called *tao,* meaning something like "Way," the inexpressible naturalness that is more fundamental than the expressible particularities present in the mind and in the visible world.

We then come to find in the ever enriching and ever deepening, yet surprisingly consistent, Buddhist tradition the presence of a variety of ways to express a fundamental truth: emptiness, suchness, thusness, truth in the absolute sense (*dharmakāya*), true nature, Buddha-nature, *tao,* even one's true self. All of these are poor English attempts to point to a fundamentalness that stands behind notions like being and non-being, true and false, self and no-self, more basic than, and also transcending, conceptualizations like yes and no.

In Zen this is often called True Self, the True Self that is deeper, above, beyond the phenomenal self; the True Self that is free from individuality, that is spontaneous in the here and now (it could, in the Mahāyāna tradition, be nowhere else), the True Self that is emptiness, that is realized, that is a symbol for freedom and liberation.

Zen Buddhists make a great deal about the necessity of one's striving long and diligently for the realization of this True Self. In words, one is told that this realization transcends discursive thought. In actual practice, for some, one is to plunge into the Great

Doubt. These words and this practice represent the understandably human, clearly religious, dimension of the Zen experience, that enlightenment is not one's doing, that it is not caused by one. If one thinks this, one is not in the Great Doubt, and certainly the True Self does not arise.

When I was in Nazenji, in Kyoto, in 1973, visiting with Shibayama Roshi, we spoke through the help of Sumiko Kudo, our interpreter, in some detail about the manner in which enlightenment occurs. I knew that one should not ask what enlightenment is, a frequent question by foreigners. My interest was on how one speaks about the occurrence. "Revelation" did not sit well with Shibayama. "Caused" was abruptly inappropriate. I suggested, one might say "it just happens" and he responded yes, adding that he was comfortable with this way of putting it. Enlightenment arises; it happens.

Zen does not rely upon letters—and perhaps there is no other religious tradition that has written or used letters and words as frequently to stress the inadequacy of words as has Zen. The point is to note that Zen Buddhists are concerned about the likelihood of one's being dependent upon letters, and they really mean it. Realization is the core concern. Not in a vacuum, certainly; that is why Zen monks train for so many years, that is why they study. These are but modes. But the Great Doubt, the complete abandonment of the possession of one's own mind, thoughts, constructs, the total existential anxiety, the doubt of doubt's doubting, is for some Buddhists, the final condition for the happening of enlightenment.

There are at least three major strands of Zen in Japan, another in Taiwan. But the two most popular in the West, two of the major strands in Japan, are Rinzai and Sōtō Zen. Most succinctly phrased, the major difference in these two schools is in the mode of progression, not, as best as I can discern, in the fundamental Zen experience.

Let me share with you observations provided by three outstanding Zen masters. The first two represent the Sōtō tradition.

Shunryu Suzuki Rōshi, in his book *Zen Mind, Beginner's Mind,*[5] draws one's attention to the limitation of one's will, to the inadequacy of one's agency at the moment of salvific insight. He says:

> Strictly speaking, any effort we make is not good for our practice because it creates waves in our mind. It is impossible, however, to

> attain absolute calmness of our mind without any effort. We must make some effort, but we must forget ourselves in the effort we make. In this realm there is no subjectivity or objectivity. Our mind is just calm, without even any awareness. In this unawareness, every effort and every idea and thought will vanish. So it is necessary for us to encourage ourselves and to make an effort up to the last moment, when all effort disappears. (*Zen Mind,* p. 37)

Suzuki Rōshi, like Buddhists before him in South and Southeast Asia, and China and Japan also, indicates that the mental activity of calculating, volitional drives to achieve, lie within the realm of human action (*karma*) and as such are inadequate for the arising of enlightenment. He writes:

> According to the traditional Buddhist understanding, our human nature is without ego. When we have no idea of ego, we have Buddha's view of life. Our egoistic ideas are delusion, covering our Buddha nature. We are always creating and following them, and in repeating this process over and over again, our life becomes completely occupied by ego-centered ideas. This is called karmic life, or karma. The Buddhist life should not be karmic life. The purpose of our practice is to cut off the karmic spinning mind. If you are trying to attain enlightenment, that is a part of karma, you are creating and being driven by karma, and you are wasting your time on your black cushion. (*Zen Mind,* p. 100).

Suzuki Rōshi enables one to see that the notion of emptiness has continued to be instrumental in helping one to understand the way things really are, real but not substantial. This missionary of Zen to the United States stands in the wake of Nāgārjuna and that great Chinese Buddhist thinker Chih-I (538–597). Suzuki Rōshi says:

> In the Prajna Paramita Sutra the most important point, of course, is the idea of emptiness. Before we understand the idea of emptiness, everything seems to exist substantially. But after we realize the emptiness of things, everything becomes real—*not substantial* [my italics]. When we realize that everything we see is a part of emptiness, we can have no attachment to any existence; we realize that everything is just a tentative form and color. Thus we realize the true meaning of each tentative existence. (*Zen Mind,* p. 113)

Kosho Uchiyama Rōshi, attempting in words to communicate a sense of what might be the life of the Universal Self ("True Self," as others have called it, "Big Self," as Suzuki Rōshi puts it), indicates a continuity with Śāntideva's awareness of compassion for others. In his book, *Approach to Zen,*[6] Uchiyama Rōshi says:

> A man who can't find compassion for others within the Self cannot be called a man of zazen who has 'awakened' to the reality of the life of the Self.
>
> Look at the following quotes from the Bible. 'God's will be done.' 'Whether therefore you eat, or drink, or whatever you do, do all to the glory of God.' 'Because God loves us, we know love. We express our love for God by loving others.'
>
> This basic Christian attitude towards life is also the basic Buddhist attitude towards life. (*Approach to Zen,* p. 79)

The other major strand in Zen in Japan is Rinzai, and Zenkei Shibayama Rōshi, one of the great exponents of Rinzai to have lived in our lifetime, has said, in his *Zen Comments on the Mumonkan:*[7]

> One has to cast his ordinary self away and be reborn [note well] as a new Self in a different dimension. In other words, the student must personally have the inner experience called satori, by which he is reborn as the True Self. This fundamental experience of awakening is essential in Zen. (*Zen Comments,* p. 25)

On the inadequacy of the discriminating mind and the necessity that one put this aside, Shibayama Rōshi said:

> To get rid of it [discriminating mind] requires that one's whole being must be the koan. There should be nothing left, and the secret of Zen lies in this really throwing oneself away. One does not have to ask what would be likely to happen after that; whatever happens would naturally and automatically come about [note well] without any seeking for it. What is important here is for him to actually do it himself. (*Zen Comments,* p. 26)

Rinzai Zen Buddhists speak about the Great Doubt, a period through which one pushes oneself with intense, genuine, existential anxiety, to such an extent that the bottom drops out, so to speak. This is the moment, Shibayama Rōshi noted:

> when 'Mu' is awakened to 'Mu,' that is, when he is revived [note well] as the self of no-self. At this mysterious moment, he is like a dumb person who has had a wonderful dream, for he is fully aware of it, but is unable to use words to express it. The Absolute Nothingness ('Mu') is awakened to itself. This is the moment of realization when subject-object opposition is altogether transcended. To describe it we have to use such words as inexpressible or mysterious. (*Zen Comments,* p. 28)

And further:

> Zen calls this experience 'incomparable satori,' or 'to die a Great Death once and to revive from death.' [note well] (*Zen Comments,* p. 28)

About the drive into the Great Doubt, the aspiration to be free of bondage, Shibayama Rōshi shared with us:

> 'Blessed are those who hunger and thirst for righteousness, for they shall be satisfied' (Matthew 5:6) is a Christian saying. The expressions may be different, yet in actually seeking after Truth in any religion, one has to go through the darkness of spiritual struggle.
>
> Young Joshu broke through the barrier and awoke in the great void, [that is, emptiness] vast and boundless. In other words, his spiritual eye was opened for the first time . . . where ordinary mind as it is is Tao. The ordinary mind Zen upholds is not our dualistic ordinary mind, but it has to be the ordinary mind attained by satori. (*Zen Comments,* p. 144.)

IV

We have noted some themes in the Buddhist heritage known as the Mahăyāna. Our theme "Of Human Bondage and Divine Grace" tends not to be immediately translatable into these Buddhists' experiences of the religious life. "Human bondage" is familiar to Buddhists; bondage to passion, hatred, and delusion, bondage, too, to our own mental constructs, bondage to individuality and associated maladies, bondage to misconceptions.

For many Buddhists, "divine grace" does not represent the most adequate view of the situation. But the human sensitivity to the order of the cosmos, the responses made, tends to suggest a familiarity on the part of Buddhists with the deeper religious sensitivities that theists have shared when they have spoken about divine grace.[8]

The true order of reality is a given; that is the way things are, and a person became the Awakened One (Buddha) because he rediscovered this and made this known, and Buddhists seek to emulate the Buddha, aspire to this enlightenment into the true order of reality which is not of one's own making. It is the way things are. And the way things are is given, it is, indeed, a gift, and "gift" is one meaning of our term *charis*, "grace."

Although some Buddhists would tend not to say that this grace is the gift of a Savior, Creator God, they do share with theists, and this in surprisingly refreshing modes and to a significant degree, the apperception that liberation, although one's objective, liberation, the goal of one's discipline, is, in the final analysis, not one's making, is not caused by one, is there, here, and happens.

NOTES

[1] *Mūlamadhyamakakārikā*, ch. XXV, vss. 19–20. See Kenneth K. Inada, *Nāgārjuna: A Translation of His Mūlamadhyamakakārikā with an Introductory Essay* (Tokyo: Hokuseido Press, 1970), p. 158.

[2] *Bodhicaryāvatāra of Śāntideva with the Commentary Pañjikā of Prajñākaramati*, edited by Dr. P. L. Vaidya, *Buddhist Sanskrit Series Number 12* (Darbanga: Mithila Institute of Post-Graduate Studies and Research in Sanskrit Learning, 1960).

[3] *Entering the Path of Enlightenment: The Bodhicaryāvatāra of the Buddhist Poet Santideva*, translation with guide by Marion L. Matics (London: George Allen & Unwin Ltd., 1970). This work also appeared in a paperback edition (New York: Macmillan Company, 1970). The pagination is the same.

[4] The translations, unless otherwise noted, are by Matics, *op. cit.* Sanskrit words in parentheses are in Matics's original. When these words are in brackets, they have been so introduced by me from the Sanskrit original.

[5] Shunryu Suzuki, *Zen Mind, Beginner's Mind*, edited by Trudy Dixon (New York: Weatherhill, 1973 [of the work first published in 1970]).

[6] Kosho Uchiyama Roshi, *Approach To Zen: The Reality of Zazen/Modern Civilization and Zen* (San Francisco: Japan Publications, Inc., 1973).

[7] Zenkei Shibayama, *Zen Comments on the Mumonkan*, translated into English by Sumiko Kudo (New York: Harper & Row, Publishers, 1974).

[8] When visiting with Uchiyama Rōshi in Kyoto in the fall of 1973, along with Miss Sumiko Kudo, who graciously acted as subtle and capable interpreter when the situation demanded, Uchiyama said that on occasion he had noted the similarity of *zazen,* in the deep and broad sense, to what others meant when they used the term "God." He mentioned that his Western students at Antaiji were very disturbed and even argued with their *rōshi,* interesting in itself, that this should not be done, that they, as he put it, would have nothing to do with this interpretation. But Uchiyama maintained that the similarity was the case.

Let me quote some of his published comments:

> *Zazen,* which lets go of all our human concepts, is the primary foundation of our lives; and as such, it watches over us, guides us, and gives strength to our own lives and to society. This is the true picture of Buddhism as a religion. Therefore we can say that *zazen* is to the Buddhist, what God is to the Christian. In Psalm 46:10 it is said, "Be still, and know that I am God," and *zazen* certainly actualizes it. Again, it is said, "The kingdom of God cometh not with observation: Neither shall they say, Lo here! or, Lo there! for, behold, the kingdom of God is within you" (Luke 17:20–21—see also Matthew 12:28; Acts 17:27–28; Romans 14:17; I Corinthians 2:9). In *zazen* we can see directly this 'kingdom of God' within us. (*Approach to Zen,* p. 113.)

10

When broken tiles become gold

Taitetsu Unno

Persons in North America are often surprised to learn that Zen is not the most popular school of Buddhist thought in Japan. Thus far in our study, we have caught a glimpse of the key notion of "emptiness" and some significant contributions by Zen Buddhist teachers. In this chapter, Professor Unno leads us further into interpretations of Zen and then moves to communicate the profound religious insight of the Pure Land Buddhist heritage, the most popular form of Buddhist piety in Japan.

I

The title of this chapter is a saying handed down in Pure Land Buddhism, and it was especially quoted frequently by Shinran, the founder of Jōdo Shinshū, who lived in thirteenth-century Japan. Jōdo Shinshū, or, as it is sometimes referred to in the West, Shin Buddhism, is the culmination of the Pure Land tradition. In Japanese Buddhism there are thirteen principal schools, including Zen, and among these Jōdo Shinshū has the largest number of adherents. Thus, it has been a major spiritual force, and no study of Japanese Buddhism can neglect the contributions made by this school.

Most students in this country have some familiarity with Zen, and on the surface Zen, which stresses self-effort, and Shin Buddhism, which is based on Other Power, appear to be contradictory opposites. But when we penetrate deeply into either one, we see that they are one and the same in the basic understanding of life. And the reason is that they both grow out of the experience of *śūnyatā*, "emptiness" or "voidness," which Professor Carter discussed in the previous chapter. I should like to continue with this notion and begin this chapter by discussing some of the dimensions of *śūnyatā* or emptiness from three perspectives: epistemological, ontological, and ethical, all of which have implications for our everyday life. We want to proceed by asking the following questions: What can we really know (epistemological)? What is truly real (ontological)? And what is real love (ethical)?

Since the basic background information on emptiness has been presented, I shall attempt to discuss it in relation to these three questions that concern all of us at one time or another. In order to do so, I want first to pose the basic problem of human existence in diagram form.

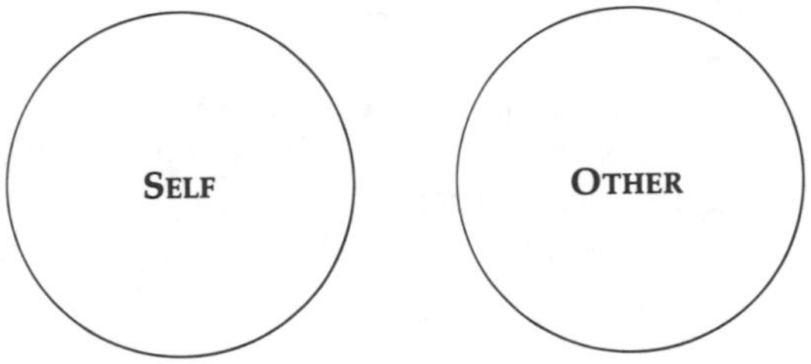

FIGURE 1

Figure 1 delineates conventional thinking and feeling in which there exists the subject or self in contrast to which stands the object or other. Here a seeming distinction is made between the self-enclosed "I," "me," or "my" and the other, whether a person, thing, a living being, or nature. In Buddhist thought this view is called dichotomous or dualistic thinking. The technical term is *vijñāna* or *vijñapti*, which involves not just thinking but also feeling, the two considered as inseparable. It creates the basic division between self and the world and the further division among things and peoples in the world. Since thinking involves language, the words and concepts we use tend to reinforce the divisions, and when they are infused with feelings the divisions become fixed and intractable. If we are unaware of what we are really doing, we create a world of mental constructs and arbitrary conceptions, fixated on the self as the enduring center of the world. Such a view has nothing to do with reality itself in which there are no boundaries; rather, it is a world of delusion, created by our misperception of self and the world. When we continue to perpetuate this ignorance, we are condemned to *saṃsāra,* the infinite finitude of aimless existence.

The world of delusion or *saṃsāra* is compounded by our failure to distinguish between words and reality. Most of us think that every word we use has an objective referent, that it points to something. Thus, when I say table, we can point to the object there. Or when I ask, "What time is it?" we can look at our watches. But when we talk about truth, what is the objective referent? And what about love, what are we referring to? Now Buddhists say that we not only do not know what "truth" or "love" are but that we also do not really know what "table" or "watch" are, as long as we see them from an individual-centered or egocentric viewpoint.

The divisions created by dichotomous thinking, solidified by words and infused with ignorance and greed, create conflict, hatred, prejudice, distrust, and violence, destroying any potential for human kindness and good will. This is the picture of our world today, submerged in *saṃsāra,* and we think that this is the only reality for us. But there is another kind of world, another reality, that is more elemental and basic than the delusionary world created by dichotomous thinking and feeling. And that is the world of *śūnyatā* or emptiness.

FIGURE 2

In Figure 2 we see that both subject and object have been erased, have vanished. Some people think that this is emptiness, that nothing exists, but that is wrong. It is an erroneous emptiness, emptiness wrongly grasped.

Figure 3 gives us the true picture of what we mean by emptiness. It shows the world as it is—things, including the self, as they truly are. Both subject and object exist, but this time devoid of

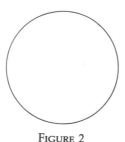

FIGURE 3

any self-enclosure. The result is openness and freedom, beyond the dichotomous framework, but more importantly each reality, whether subject or object, is seen in its non-objective mode of being without any distortion. That is, each reality is seen in its suchness (*tathatā*). Each form of existence is seen from within its own mode of being, rather than from an individual-centered or egocentric position, the self-enclosure that inevitably leads to a distorted vision. This way of seeing is called non-dichotomous or non-dualistic. The technical word is *prajñā*. Sometimes *prajñā* is translated as "wisdom," but it is a knowing and feeling that transcends the dichotomous framework. And that which is seen or realized through *prajñā* is the world of emptiness. Emptiness, the liberation from any form of fixation, is the source of creative love and true compassion, for the separation created by dichotomous thinking has been dissolved, and words and concepts are used to heal and bring together rather than to create divisions and mistrust, as done by the careless use of language by the unenlightened.

When emptiness is understood epistemologically, then, we see things, including the self, as they truly are, rather than as we want to see them from a self-centered perspective. In the separation of subject and object it is clear that what "I" see of "you" is only the periphery, the circumference, and I cannot see what is going on inside of you. How can true seeing or knowing be possible, when the dichotomy prevents me from becoming truly one with you, seeing you from your own standpoint?

There is a famous anecdote about Ikkyū, who lived in fifteenth-century Japan, that illustrates what it means to see a thing as it truly is. One day a governor, known for his wit and humor, of the province in which Ikkyū lived, posted a little sign next to a twisted, gnarled pine tree. Pine trees, especially those growing along the seashore in Japan, are buffeted by strong winds, making them into the crooked shapes that we see. And the sign read, "Anyone who can see this crooked pine tree straight will receive a reward." Many people, walking past the posted sign, stopped and tried to figure out a way to see the crooked tree straight. Some circled the tree, others tried to see it from a distance, a few fell flat on the ground and looked up, and one even brought a ladder to look down on the tree. But no one could see the crooked tree straight, so the prize remained unclaimed, until Ikkyū came along. The moment he read the sign and looked at the tree, he went to the governor's office and said, "I want the prize." Startled, the governor asked, "How did you see the crooked tree straight?" And Ikkyū answered without any hesitation, "It is crooked." A crooked tree is crooked, and to see it as such without changing it is to see it "straight."

When we cling to the notion of "straight" and try applying it to the tree, we go against reality, we try to force it to fit our expectation, and we do not see the tree as it is. To see the tree straight is to let the crooked tree speak to one as a crooked tree, and when one accepts it as such without imposing any subjective notions on it, then one truly sees the tree, one sees it straight. Such an understanding applies to our study of other religions also. When we study Buddhism, for example, we have to be careful about applying our notions of "religion" to it and trying to see it through our conceptual lens. We want to study Buddhism as Buddhism, not as "religion" or "philosophy," both of which have certain Western assumptions not applicable to an Asian tradition.

Perhaps some of you are familiar with the writings of Martin Heidegger, a German philosopher, who died a few years ago. He has two small books, *What is Thinking?* and *Discourse on Thinking,* in which he distinguishes between calculative thinking and meditative thinking. They parallel the distinction between dichotomous (*vijñāna*) thinking and non-dichotomous (*prajñā*) thinking. Calculative thinking centers on the individual, moves towards an object, and deals with things for self-centered advantages. On the other hand, meditative thinking is an openness to the horizon before us, such that each object speaks to persons, revealing itself from its depth. He describes it as the releasement to things and openness to mystery.

In seeing the world non-dichotomously we see things, including the self, as they are. This does not negate conventional thinking nor the use of words and concepts, for as human beings we cannot escape them. But it does free us from being bound to them as ultimate realities. Words as part of the communication network require that we use them precisely and accurately; otherwise, social life would be in chaos. At the same time, however, we must not be confined by them, if we want to see the world as it is.

The way in which we relate to others has multiple implications for life, and the truly human life can be lived only on the basis of non-dichotomous thinking and feeling. In Figure 3 above, we see this kind of life where the subject and object both exist, but neither are bound by the circle of self-enclosure or self-concern. Since no false barriers have been put up, a true understanding can occur between two people which also insures simultaneously a true kind of love. Saint Augustine said something to the effect that when one truly understands another, one loves that person, and when one truly loves another, one understands that person. A similar point is made when Buddhists speak of wisdom and compassion being like the two wings of a bird or the two wheels of a cart.

In wisdom one relates to the world immediately and non-conceptually, and in compassion one enters into the mode of being of another with no separation between self and other. Here we have the manifestation of emptiness, such that each person and being, liberated from self-enclosure, radiates its own light. This is suchness (*tathatā*) or thatness (*tattva*), meaning that each person, thing, or object manifests itself such as it is without any interference from the outside, whether other individuals, society, or God. A thing existing as it is in suchness is the ontological aspect of emptiness.

The world of suchness is expressed poetically and symbolically in the following passage from a Pure Land Scripture, known as the *Smaller Sukhāvatī-vyūha:*

> And in those lotus lakes lotus flowers are blooming,
> Blue, blue-coloured, of blue splendour, blue to behold;
> Yellow, yellow-coloured, of yellow splendour, yellow to behold;
> Red, red-coloured, of red splendour, red to behold;
> White, white-coloured, of white splendour, white to behold;
> Beautiful, beautifully-coloured, of beautiful splendour, beautiful to behold;
> And in circumference as large as the wheel of the chariot.

To relate to another person in suchness means that we accept the other just as he or she is, not as we want the other to be. Our expectations and preconceptions are not forced upon the other. This means that we love another not because the other is beautiful or brilliant or attractive but because the other simply *is.* That is also the way we want to be regarded by others—not for the outer, surface qualities, good or bad, but for just what we are, as we are, and nothing else.

Now, in order for us to relate to the world of suchness, we ourselves must live the life of suchness. We drop all labels placed on both ourselves and others; become free of attachments to our feelings, preconceptions, and expectations; and open ourselves to the world—to others as well as our own self, affirming all beings and things just as they are.

Ontologically, each suchness is "real but not substantial," to use Professor Carter's apt phrase. It is real in the sense that it is tangible, it has shape and form, it resists other objects, it can be touched, and so on, but it is also nonsubstantial, meaning that it is emptiness, in flux, changing, devoid of any immutable, enduring qualities. The Buddhist understanding is that such an entity is a product of dependent co-origination (*pratītyasamutpāda*). Everything in the world—the trees out there, this building, we ourselves, this piece of paper, the stars in heaven, and so forth—is born from various causes and conditions. And when the conditions disperse, they will cease to exist. But while here and now, in this moment, they are real. For example, this chalk which I hold in my hand is real, but before it came into existence in this shape and form, what was it? It was powder. And when it is all used up, does the chalk disappear into nothingness? No, it merely disintegrates into powder. But even now, as it stands before us with this shape and form, what is its content? Powder. The fact that it is basically powder before it became chalk, while it is this chalk, and when it is no longer chalk can be likened to the universal reality of emptiness. The chalk is real but not substantial. It should be added, however, that each speck of powder itself is also emptiness. Not only this chalk, but all things, including human beings, are empty of permanent characteristics, are devoid of substantial being.

When this understanding is extended and deepened, we have the awareness that life is but a vast network of interconnectedness and interdependence. Yet this network should not be grasped abstractly but concretely. A popular Japanese saying makes this point, when it states: "One leaf falling—fall is everywhere." In a single autumn leaf is contained the entire spatial and temporal universe. In the same vein Dōgen, a thirteenth-century Japanese Zen thinker, wrote a famous poem:

In the spring the cherry blossoms
In the summer the cuckoo
In the autumn the moon
In the winter, the snow clear, cold.

When I first read this poem, I thought, "What a simple poem! Even a child could have written it; just an objective picture of the four seasons." But after I began to understand Zen a little, I realized that Dōgen was describing more than mere scenery in a dichotomous subject-object relationship. In this simple poem he manifests the Buddhist world view of interconnectedness and interpenetration. Each concrete reality—cherry blossoms, cuckoo, moon, or snow—not only manifests the particular season of the year but reveals the whole universe. That is, beneath the cherry blossoms of spring awaits the summer to burst forth, the fall to emerge, and the winter to cover the landscape; moreover, the life and death of humanity, of countless sentient beings, are being enacted in the concrete particular here and now. Central to all this is the self, making such an observation, who is an integral and essential part of this dynamic reality.

The working of suchness, as a product of dependent co-origination, may be seen in the evolution of the seed into the sprout, the sprout into a shoot, the shoot into a bud, the bud into a flower, the flower into seed, and so on. Not one of these clings to itself, refusing to open up and grow, as self-centered humankind might. This is what the Japanese call *jinen,* which Keiji Nishitani, a philosopher, defines as "naturalness where there is no technicality, purpose, will, judgment, and discrimination, as a plant grows from within itself without any manipulation."

When we turn to the ethical dimension of emptiness, we may restrict our discussion to its most important quality: love. Love is at the core of any authentic relationship, whether it be with people, things, ideas, or nature. In true love where all self-centeredness has been emptied, where words and concepts are used not to divide but to unite, the self enters into the mode of being of the other and identifies itself completely with the other. In fact, the true self discovers and realizes itself in the other, such that the self becomes the self by virtue of the other, and the other truly becomes itself by virtue of its relationship to the self. Unless this non-dichotomous relationship can be realized, the self will always remain enclosed within its own self-centered concerns.

When you really want to help your friend in distress, there must be complete identification between you and your friend. If there should be even the slightest dichotomy remaining, then the hand that extends its help can be pulled back at any moment, and the concern for the other can easily reveal itself as ultimately another expression for self-concern.

Let me illustrate what I mean about non-dichotomous identification that is essential for the ethical life. This is a true story of a great Zen monk, named Harada Rōshi, who lived in nineteenth-century Japan. He was the abbot of a large monastery, and one day he, together with an attendant monk, had to travel to another monastery. When they came to a river, they discovered that the bridge had been washed away by a recent flood. Like many rivers in Japan, this one was shallow, so people were bundling up their clothes and wading across the water. The men could easily yank up their kimonos, tie them to the belt, carry their belongings, and wade across the knee-deep water. But there was one young woman, dressed in her finest silk kimono, who could not so easily do that, and she stood on the river bank not knowing what to do.

When Harada Rōshi saw the plight of this young women, he offered to carry her across on his back. She climbed on his back, held him tightly, and he carried her across the river. Upon reaching the other shore, he let her down, and they bade farewell and went their separate ways. The young attendant monk was watching all this, fuming to himself, "The master has violated a precept. A monk should not touch a woman. But he has carried a woman!" He could no longer contain himself and voiced his criticism to the master. Whereupon the master looked at the young monk and responded quietly: "I let the woman go way back there, and you are still carrying her!"

To maintain order in society, whether secular or monastic, we must uphold rules and regulations. But, at the same time, they are not absolutes and never should be used to cause unnecessary suffering for others.

The monastic rule of celibacy is crucial to the discipline of a monk, yet it should not be used to condone inhuman treatment of another human being. Harada Rōshi transcended that rule in the spirit of emptiness, extended a helping hand to a young woman, dropped her off, and went on his way. When a person is in distress and in need of help, we do not discriminate between man and woman; it is a human being that needs to be saved. In life characterized by impermanence, the care and concern for another deserve our immediate attention; to postpone any help we can give to others not only reveals ultimate selfishness but ignorance of the fragile nature of human existence. Such is the basic philosophy underlying the art of the tea ceremony.[1]

Intimate is the connection that emptiness has with the truly human life, liberated and free, open and honest. Emptiness nullifies the false boundaries, divisions, and dichotomies which cause conflicts, hatred, bitterness, and violence. It is not a mere concept or philosophical principle; it has a healing and salvific power, a power to move the hearts and minds of people. It is not something cold but warm, not something distant but intimate, not something to be feared but to be revered. Thus, elaborate rituals of worshipping the Buddhas and *bodhisattvas,* the dynamic manifestations of emptiness, are necessary and essential in all schools of Buddhism. Even in Zen, which seems to deemphasize rituals, there are many elaborate worship services centered on the Buddhas and *bodhisattvas.* The monk leads a life of utter simplicity, but he constantly bows with palms together to the Buddha, who sustains and leads him and infuses spirituality in his every act.

II

When the same sense of reverence, celebration, and joy is manifested in a deeply personal way by ordinary people who remain bound to samsaric life and have no opportunities for monastic pursuits, we have the *raison d'être* of the Pure Land movement in the historical evolution of Mahāyāna Buddhism. That is, the salvific power of emptiness is revealed as immeasurable life (*amitāyus*), a true and real life that is not bound by the finite, samsaric life. When one realizes immeasurable life, beyond the subject-object dichotomous mode, then one awakens to immeasurable light (*amitābha*), the form manifesting supreme wisdom. For the vast majority of Buddhists down through the centuries it is the Buddha known as Amida, radiating immeasurable life and light, that is the deeply personal, spiritual reality that makes the realization of emptiness a reality.

In the Pure Land tradition, then, emptiness is basic and fundamental to the religious life. In fact, emptiness that pursues us and pushes us in the direction of religious awakening, utilizing every event in human life as an opening to a deeper appreciation of existence, is known technically as Dharmakāya Buddha. But when this formless, impersonal Buddha is manifested in the dichotomous world, it takes on the form and name of Amida Buddha. Dharmakāya Buddha is emptiness on the level of abstraction; Amida Buddha is emptiness that is real, concrete, and personal. Before proceeding with a discussion of Shin Buddhism, let me briefly compare Zen and Shin, which move in different directions but ultimately lead to the same awakened state.

In both Zen and Shin the basic understanding is that when we are born into human life we are thrust into the world of delusion. Like the egg that is produced by a hen but is not fully realized until it is hatched and the chick appears, so human beings come into the world contained in the ego-shell which must be broken through to be truly born in this world. As long as we remain within our ego-shell, our vision is limited, we cannot see the world as it is, and we do not really experience life. Our task, then, is to break out of the ego-shell and stand under the expansive blue sky, breathe the air of freedom, see the beauty and grandeur of nature, and become truly alive, free of any delusions.

In order to break the ego-shell we can push relentlessly from within until it cracks open—that is the Zen approach. Or we can receive the nurturing warmth of incubation from without until the ego-shell is cracked open—that is the Shin approach. Both liberate a person from the murky darkness of the ego-shell (*saṃsāra*) into the world of freedom (*nirvāṇa*). But what is frequently overlooked is that in Zen there is also appreciation for the incubation from without, the sustaining and protecting powers of the Buddhas without which no religious practice can be fruitful; and in Shin a constant, relentless effort must be exerted in order to truly awaken to Amida's compassion. In sum, the path of Zen requires tremendous self-power, but its ultimate realization is a passivity in activity, and the path of Shin is based on the working of Other Power, but it cannot be realized without activity in passivity.

We will begin to explore the nature of religious life and understanding in Shin Buddhism with a famous *haiku* poem written by Issa, a Shin priest-poet, who lived in the eighteenth century in Japan. The distinctive tradition in Shin Buddhism, ever since the time of its founder, Shinran, is the married clergy. Issa, who lived about a century after the great *haiku* master Bashō, got married very late in life, past the age of fifty. He had a succession of children who all died before the age of one. When he lost his third child, a daughter, he wrote:

The world of dew
Is the world of dew,
And yet, and yet.

As you know, *haiku* is a very short poem, only seventeen syllables in Japanese, but the effect of these pithy poems can evoke many feelings and thoughts from both the conscious and unconscious realms. The expression "the world of dew" is a metaphor for impermanence, flux, change. Summers in Japan are hot and humid, and at dawn dewdrops are found on leaves and flower petals, but as soon as the morning sun appears, they quickly vanish. So, too, is the fragile nature of human life which may disappear in an instant. Thus, when Issa writes, "The world of dew is the world of dew," he is acknowledging the basic teaching of impermanence, that life is short and death is inevitable. But at the same time Issa cannot accept that truth so easily, for when it comes to his own daughter, it is different—"and yet, and yet."

Yes, "the world of dew is the world of dew," but that is an objective statement, a philosophical observation, an abstract truth. It is still reality on the far side. "And yet, and yet" is an existential and spiritual fact, a reality on the near side. What Issa is saying is that I know impermanence as a fact of life, and that is fine, but when it comes to my own daughter, I just cannot accept her death.

Shin Buddhists say that this attachment, this inability to become detached, is the focus of the great compassion of Amida Buddha, enabling Issa to become truly human, to be himself as he is. Having listened to the teaching with his whole being throughout his life,

Issa realized the working of true compassion, the primal Vow of Amida, as being directed to himself, so deeply steeped in karmic bondage. Within the boundless compassion of Amida, Issa could freely cry out, "and yet, and yet." In his own way, Issa manifests emptiness, the freedom to be himself, to be truly human.

Paradoxically, Issa's deep realization of life, through the working of true compassion, enables him to manifest his true samsaric nature. When Mahāyāna Buddhists speak of the truth that the limits of *saṃsāra* is *nirvāṇa,* and the limits of *nirvāṇa* is *saṃsāra,* they are speaking of concrete lived life, an example of which Issa demonstrates in the loss of his daughter. The profound realization of Issa is expressed succinctly by Shinran, when he states in the *Tannishō:*

> When I ponder on the compassionate vow of Amida, established through five *kalpas* of profound thought, it was for myself, Shinran, alone. Because I am a being burdened so heavily with *karma,* I feel even more deeply grateful to the Primal Vow which is decisively made to save me.[2]

It should be noted that there is a universe of difference between grudgingly accepting one's fate, on the one hand, and embracing one's karmic limitations, as did Issa, on the other. While the latter is realized within true compassion that liberates one from past *karma* (*saṃsāra* realized as none other than *nirvāṇa*), the former is infused with ego and is inseparable from bitterness, regret, anger, and fear (*saṃsāra* as the opposite of *nirvāṇa*).

In sum, true compassion enfolds us in non-dichotomous reality, enabling us to express our true human emotions, whether of triumph or loss, joy or pain. It is a liberating affirmation possible only in emptiness. That we can be truly human is because of the activity of the Primal Vow directed solely to those who, by themselves, cannot achieve liberation. The wisdom and compassion of Amida Buddha forsees the delusionary activities of unenlightened beings and has devised a strategy of salvation especially for those in bondage to their past *karma.* Whenever we are lost, confused, uneasy, fearful, or anxious, the Shin person realizes "All this the Buddha already knew" (*Tannishō* IX) and entrusts himself or herself, by virtue of the Primal Vow, to true compassion.

Unlike saints who attain the heights of wisdom and spirituality, Shinran realized the very opposite: his foolish and ignorant nature.

Thus, he asserted that he could never be confused, not because he was wise but because he was foolish and ignorant. This powerful realization sustained Shinran throughout his life, enabling him to enjoy his most creative years in his eighties, writing poetry, letters, essays, commentaries, and revising his major philosophical work, the *Kyō-gyō-shin-shō,* until the very end of his life.

III

What we have been describing fits perfectly into the theme "Of Human Bondage and Divine Grace." In Buddhist understanding human bondage is the product of one's *karma;* no one is responsible for one's life except oneself. Whatever happens to us in life, in the final analysis, is due to past causes originating in our own thoughts and acts. The sufferings we undergo in life may be caused by various external events, but how we cope with them is our sole responsibility. But the ignorance that keeps us in *saṃsāra* is so vast and deep that only divine grace coming from the heart of compassion can deliver us. "Compassion" means the ability to be with another in suffering, and Amida's compassion works in the midst of human suffering, releasing a person from its burden, pain, and sorrow.

The central concern of compassion is inspired by the "other" to whom we can give up our total self; in contrast, sympathy is a concern coming out of the self which may or may not reach the other. Real love is also the movement of care and concern centered on the "other"; in contrast, false love focuses on the needs of the self. One recalls the parable of the mustard seed, the story of Kisagotami, which illustrates true compassion and love based on the awakening to reality.[3]

Traditionally in the Buddhist heritage two motivating factors prompted people to seek the path of enlightenment: one was the awareness of impermanence, most dramatically illustrated by death; and the other was the encounter with karmic evil, the deep-rooted self-enclosure that keeps us submerged in *saṃsāra.* The story of Issa, for example, illustrates the latter, and Kisagotami is a classic example of the former. But both agree that the goal is coming to terms with one's karmic nature and seeing things, including the self, as they truly are.

The ultimate awakening, regardless of path, is the recognition of the unity of *karma* and no-*karma*, of bondage and freedom. In the second case of *The Gateless Gate,* known as "Hyakujō and the Fox," the principal topic is the question of *karma* and no-*karma*. There was once a Zen adept who was asked the question, "Is the enlightened person subject to the law of *karma*?" When he answered "No!" he was immediately turned into a fox. Having heard the Zen presentations of Master Hyakujō, he now understands the true answer and requests the master to ask the same question again. When Hyakujō does so, the fox answers in the affirmative, "The karmic law is never obscured!" He is immediately turned into a human being.

This unity of *karma* and no-*karma* was the *kōan* given to the famous Zen teacher, D. T. Suzuki, just before he came to the United States, in 1897, at the age of twenty seven. The *kōan* was "the elbow does not bend outward." After his arrival in the U.S., Suzuki lived in La Salle, Illinois, working as a publisher's assistant and translator for more than ten years before he returned to Japan.* Suzuki later wrote that he really struggled with that *kōan,* especially because once he left Japan he would not have a master to work with in the United States. "The elbow does not bend outward"—what is the significance of this statement? How does one understand this *kōan* in relation to the question of *karma* and no-*karma,* of bondage and freedom?

When one speaks of freedom, some people may think that it means doing anything one wants to. But freedom does not exist apart from restrictions and responsibilities. One has an elbow; bend it outward. If one should somehow succeed, one will break one's elbow and henceforth will not be able to use it freely. It is only when one fully recognizes that the elbow does *not* bend outward, acknowledging its limitation, that one has the freedom to use it as one wishes. Likewise, the realization of one's ignorance and foolishness, illuminated by Amida's light, and giving up the trust in a powerless self, frees one from suffering the consequences of one's karmic past. In thus becoming reality as it is, one's limited nature, one experiences freedom.[4]

---

* Suzuki worked with Open Court's founding editor Paul Carus. His first book, *Outlines of Mahayana Buddhism,* was published by Open Court in 1908. Suzuki and Carus collaborated on the translations of two Chinese classics, Lao Tze's *Canon of Reason and Virtue* (1913) and his *Treatise on Response and Retribution* (1906), both of which are still in demand.—PUBLISHER'S NOTE.

This relationship between bondage and freedom is also at the core of Shin religious experience. As expressed by Shinran in his metaphor of ice and water in the following verses:

Evil hindrance becomes the substance of virtue,
As in the case of ice and water.
The more the ice, the more the water;
The more the hindrance, the more the virtue.

Having realized the entrusting majestic and expansive
By virtue of Unhindered Light,
The ice of blind passion melts without fail
To instantly become the water of enlightenment.

Our limitations, our bondages, are like ice—frozen, rigid, fixed, the opposite of openness and emptiness. But that very fact constitutes the essence of freedom and liberation to which is likened the life-nourishing water of enlightenment. When touched by the warm compassion of Amida, the ice of evil hindrance, the ice of blind passion, melts instantly to become the water of enlightenment. If we reject ice or reduce it in any way, then we also diminish the amount of water, lessening it and making it non-existent. A parallel idea is found in Christianity, as stated, for example, in Romans 5:20, "Where sin increased, grace abounded all the more."

"Evil hindrance" refers to anything that obstructs the attainment of peace and happiness—anger, hate, jealousy, laziness, complexes, illness, and so on. But it can become the "substance of virtue," virtue here meaning the fulfillment of one's being, the fullness of life. Just as the more the ice, the more the water, so the more the hindrances, the more the virtue. Simply put, it is by living through our sufferings that we can become truly human and come to appreciate life deeply.

The second poem begins with the statement, "Having realized the entrusting majestic and expansive by virtue of Unhindered Light." The entrusting to Amida (*shinjin*) is called "majestic and expansive," because it is not an attitude or act performed by the person but is made possible by a working beyond the human being, the Primal Vow of Amida Buddha. That working which results in true entrusting is "by virtue of Unhindered Light." Unhindered Light is a synonym for Amida Buddha, the light that nothing in this world can hinder or obstruct. It pierces the darkness of ignorance and the stubbornness of egocentricity, melting the ice of blind passion and turning it into the water of enlightenment.

The title of this chapter, "When Broken Tiles Become Gold," is simply another metaphor for the transformation of this foolish and ignorant self into the being of supreme enlightenment. Broken tiles are useless and unwanted, yet when the highest wisdom and compassion sheds its light upon them, they are instantly transformed into a priceless treasure. The lowest becomes the highest, the last becomes the first.

We may summarize the basic teaching of Shin Buddhism by discussing three topics: the working of Other Power, the awakening to karmic evil, and the life of gratitude. In a book called *The Unknown Craftsman* by Sōetsu Yanagi there is a chapter entitled "The Pure Land of Beauty." In this chapter Shōji Hamada, a distinguished Japanese potter, is asked why he prefers working with a large kiln, rather than a small one. He explains:

> If a kiln is small, I might be able to control it completely, that is to say, my own self can become a controller, a master of the kiln. But man's own self is but a small thing after all. When I work at the large kiln, the power of my own self becomes so feeble that it cannot control it adequately. It means that for the large kiln, the power that is beyond me is necessary. Without the mercy of such an invisible power I cannot get good pieces. One of the reasons why I wanted to have a large kiln is because I want to be a potter, if I may, who works more in grace than in his own power. You know nearly all the best old pots were done in huge kilns.

What is called true entrusting (*shinjin*) in Shin Buddhism is not an attitude or an act on the part of the human being. It is life lived within the compassion of Other Power, affirming one's limited karmic nature, yet at the same time assuring our life of boundless freedom. A central teaching of Shin, known as the *Three Minds,* clarifies the way in which we see the working of Other Power. The "Three Minds" refers to sincere mind, joyful entrusting, and aspiration for birth in the Pure Land. Prior to Shinran these there were considered to be religious attitudes to be cultivated by the Pure Land practitioner. Shinran, however, concluded that sincere mind is the mind of Amida Buddha, something impossible for the being of karmic evil, that joyful entrusting arose when the sincere mind of Amida worked in the deluded mind of man, and that the aspiration to be born in the Pure Land was the consequence of sincere mind and joyful faith.

The awakening to karmic evil may be illustrated by a story told about Kichibei, one of countless Shin Buddhists known as *myōkōnin. Myōkōnin,* literally translated as "wonderfully excellent person," refers to a devout Shin practitioner who has plumbed the depth of religious life. Now, Kichibei had a bedridden wife whom he took care of every day for two years. One day a villager said to him, "You must experience fatigue, having to take care of your wife day in and day out." Whereupon Kichibei answered, "Oh no, I don't know what fatigue is, for each day is the first time and the last time." This sounds very much like a model of a detached, enlightened response, but what Kichibei underwent was not that simple.

Undoubtedly, Kichibei took care of his wife as best he could and took an attitude of philosophical resignation. But as the days passed, he surely must have thought: why did this happen to me? Why are the others so lucky not to carry such a burden? Why do I alone have to care for my wife? Why don't her siblings come to help? I wonder if she'll ever get well? When is this going to end? I wish she would die! But as these thoughts, arising from the depths of karmic evil, passed through Kichibei's mind, they were immediately followed by the realization, "All this the Buddha already knew." In that realization he heard Amida's compassionate call, "Come just as you are!" In realizing his ignorant and foolish nature by virtue of true compassion, the burden of caring for his wife and any guilt feeling he might have had were lifted, and he could be grateful for life as a gift. Our world is characterized by change and flux, never still for a moment and filled with unexpected tragedies. When one realizes the gift of life, one cherishes all the more each moment and each day. For Kichibei, who had been awakened to the teachings through constant hearing, each encounter was the first and last time. To live fully each day is to live without regrets or remorse, expressing gratitude to all things, great and small.

The culmination of the life of gratitude is expressed beautifully in the following poem written as the final testament of true entrusting by Mrs. K. Takeuchi, who had several operations and finally died of cancer at the age of forty-seven. She wrote:

In this life
No end to comparing myself to others,
Those above and those below.

Half of my body paralyzed,
Yet I have my right arm,
My ears, my right leg.

Although I have brain tumour,
Yet still there are
Taste, color, sound, voice, words, smell.

They too shall soon be no more,
As my body shall be no more.

But the *nembutsu*, Amida, true compassion,
And Pure Land will always be. . . .
How fortunate and grateful I am!

The religious life of Shin Buddhism does not end here, for in attaining supreme enlightenment at the moment of death, one returns immediately into the ocean of *saṃsāra* to work for the salvation of all beings. This work never ends as long as there exists suffering humanity.

Notes

[1] One of the valued sayings in the art of the tea ceremony is a Buddhist expression, "In one meeting a whole lifetime (*ichigo-ichi'e*)." What is most important in the art of tea is the here and now—past and future are contained in the present moment, and all the countless universes are found in this point-instant. Human life is fragile and passing, each moment never to be repeated in eternity. Thus, one comes to cherish not only this moment of time, but also every person one faces, every utensil used, every word spoken, every fragrance and taste experienced. The extent to which the tea master cherishes all things may be illustrated, for example, by the fact that each small bamboo spoon, used to scoop up the powdered tea, is given its own distinctive name. Such single-minded attention to each particular is possible only in emptiness. Ordinary consciousness is so cluttered with thoughts, words, abstractions, blind passions, and agitations that we cannot truly appreciate the manifestations of life before us. Emptiness is

not only a matter of consciousness, for the total setting of the art of tea itself is emptiness: simple hut, bare walls, openness to nature, a single scroll hanging, a single bud for flower arrangement.

Thus, the host in full awareness of the impermanence of things invests his or her total being into a single cup of tea for each of the guests, respecting their unique individualities and treating everyone as equals in spite of the class distinctions found outside of the tea hut. And each guest, too, receives the cup of tea with his or her total self, sincerity, and appreciation. All this is experienced in the stillness that sharpens and heightens the sense awareness for each moment of life which will never return again. This is the meaning of "In one meeting a whole lifetime."

[2] *Tannisho: A Shin Buddhist Classic,* translated by Taitetsu Unno (Honolulu: Buddhist Study Center Press, 1984), p. 35. In this passage we see the two basic components of Shin religious life—the compassionate vow of Amida (called *hō* in Japanese, meaning "the working of *dharma*") and the being so heavily burdened with karma (called *ki,* meaning "potential (or realized) awakening"). Yet the truth of the matter is that the foolish and ignorant nature of human beings precludes a thorough and complete understanding of either *ki* or *hō*. In the words of Yui-en, the compiler of the *Tannisho,* in a subsequent passage, "How grateful I am that Shinran expressed this in his own person to make us fully realize that we do not know the depth of karmic evil and that we do not know the height of Tathāgata's benevolence, all of which cause us to live in utter confusion."

[3] As a young mother, Kisagotami lost her only child. In deep sorrow and grief she goes to the Buddha, requesting a medicine that would bring her child back to life. Upon hearing the plea of the mother, the Buddha in his wisdom and compassion does not preach about life as suffering. Rather, he immediately instructs her to gather a handful of mustard seeds as a necessary step in obtaining the desired medicine. But there is one condition: the seeds must come from a family that has never known death. Kisagotami, hoping for a miracle, rushes off into the village and asks each household for a handful of mustard seeds. Every family is willing to give her some seeds, but the moment she asks about death in the family, she is denied the mustard seed, for without exception everyone has known the death of a loved one—father, mother, brother, sister, grandparents, grandchildren. Thus, unable to gather any mustard seeds, she returns empty-handed to the Buddha.

But her search was not in vain, for as she makes the rounds of all the households, making the same request and receiving the same answer, Kisagotami undergoes a transformation of consciousness, for she feels deeply the universality of death and her compassion reaches out to all those who must experience the pain of loss. Thus, she is able to give her child the proper funeral rites, and when she returns to the Buddha's presence, she requests permission to enter his order as a nun. She later attains reknown as Kisagotami, the Compassionate One.

[4] This is a difficult matter to understand and perhaps a simpler example may be helpful here. When driving a car, one is free to drive anywhere one wants only insofar as one observes the traffic rules and regulations. These are a kind of bondage, but only by following them can one know the freedom of driving a car to any place one wants. If, however, one disregarded the rules and regulations, one would not be able to drive anywhere freely because of the danger that both our own car and other cars would pose.

11

INTERLUDE: THE WAY OF THE *KAMI*

John Ross Carter

When one thinks of Japan, the aesthetic beauty of the Shinto shrines and the color and robust energy of the numerous festivals come to mind. In very general terms, one might say that Shinto is close to the heart of Japanese culture. At the same time, Shinto is often passed over in colloquia considering the religiousness of humankind, apparently signaling an assumption that scholarly discussions depend upon carefully formulated written documents or scriptures. Persons seeking to understand Shinto, in its multi-leveled expressions, continue to be indebted to the careful work of cultural anthropologists. In this chapter we will attempt, in broad strokes, to focus on religious sensitivities expressed by Japanese men and women within the general frame of reference of "the way of the *kami*," sensitivities which are not foreign to other persons living on this planet.

I use the word "interlude" in the title of this chapter not intending to suggest light entertainment between acts but to suggest a pause, at this point, in the cumulative development of this study. On a superficial level, this chapter is approximately the mid-way point of this study, and hence, perhaps, this chapter might serve as an interlude. Further, we have considered briefly major religious strands related, in one way or another, with seminal thoughts developed from India, and now we turn to a form of religious expression largely indigenous to Japan, before beginning a Western and theistic orientation for the remainder of our study. Moreover, one might take note that the second component of our word "interlude" is derived from Latin *ludere*, "to play," and recall the provocative work of Johan Huizinga, *Homo Ludens, A Study of the*

Play Element in Culture, especially his observations about the relationship of play and ritual in the birth of culture. And central in Shinto is ritual, humankind's response to the presence of *kami.*

Pausing to consider Shinto at this point in our course might be instructive in keeping us aware of the obvious: that although men and women have been religious for a very long time they have also expressed this religiousness in a variety of ways.

In this chapter we are dealing with a multifaceted religious heritage that, in its historical development, is not focused on one historical personage; has no clearly institutionalized, broadly based membership-community; does not yield a sense of voluntary congregational identity (like a church); has not developed creedal formulae; has no notion of a savior; represents no fundamental separation between spirit, the material world, and a creator God; has not addressed the religious setting as humankind being in bondage, seeking divine grace. What is one to do? Pause, marvel, and reflect.

The name given, apparently by Chinese, to the tradition with which we are here concerned is Shinto, the two ideographs (*kanji*) of which are pronounced in Chinese *shen-tao,* and in Japanese as *kami-no michi.* The term "shinto" seems to have come on the scene around the thirteenth century. For centuries, persons in Japan were expressing themselves religiously without naming what they were doing.[1] "Insiders," persons within a heritage or a tradition, seem to go about their activities in an engaged participatory manner, while it is the tendency of the "outsiders," persons standing outside the tradition, to differentiate what they see from their own accustomed norms, to tend to rely on nominal constructs, names.

Kami-no michi, or Shinto as this heritage is better known in the West, has been and is fluid, suggesting an unusual capacity for preserving the new and generating afresh the old. There is no sacred scripture in this tradition and no theology that can be put on a scale with theology in theistic traditions. And Westerners have not quite known what to make of all this. Some have suggested that Shinto is to remain locked in with the Japanese, that it has no universal principles. Some have suggested that the impact of the West, with its strong technological orientation, will hasten the end of Shinto. Shinto, a few have suggested, is a "primitive religion," whatever that might mean, is inseparably bound to an ethnic or racial group, is non-theoretical, and will pass from the scene as the

Japanese become more sophisticated, often meaning, as Japan becomes more like the West.

Some have suggested that Shinto is superstitious, but in the final analysis such observation tells one more about the observer offering such suggestion than about the Shinto heritage. "Superstition" is a peculiarly Western, certainly an outsider's, concept.

Some have said that Shinto has personified nature. In this context "nature" usually has meant "nature" as an outsider understands it, not that discerned by Japanese men and women[2] which the English term "nature" is used to designate. A Japanese might well reply that the West has by and large tended to de-personalize nature, has chosen not to perceive what is and has been there, has read too much out of that to which the word "nature" refers.

In the West, some have argued that religion—a term sufficiently difficult to understand that we might want to be wary of its usage in our study—is not the same as the moral, nor is it the same as the aesthetic, that religion is more than these. But Shinto, *kami-no michi,* is a way, a religious way, and it has continued without this sharp differentiation.

Institutionally, a consideration of Shinto is complex. There was the so-called State Shinto (*kokka shinto*), now largely dismantled, so to speak. There is what is called Shrine Shinto (*jinja shinto,*) the form of worship and related affairs focusing on the shrines. There is Sectarian Shinto (*khyōha shinto*), approximately thirteen sects with leading figures and doctrines. And there are the customary rural practices of old, many still continuing, called by some Folk Shinto. Which is Shinto? Or which is not Shinto? Perhaps both questions are foreign. Rather one might ask, "What is relevant in the way of the *kami*?" Not, mind you, what is the claim of orthodoxy; that just does not fit the case. Rather, what have persons found to be relevant for the living of their lives in the way about which they have known since childhood? For, as you know, Shinto does not do anything or believe anything—people do; it is people who do the doing.

SACRED PRESENCE

And so we turn to Japanese men and women to learn from them what they might have discerned in our world that would be instructive. I should think that the first major category would *not* be a sense of the human predicament, would not refer to bondage, since humankind, being part of a total scheme of things, is fundamentally good and not shackled by sin. The fundamental category, I should think, is Sacred Presence.

I venture now to mention the term *kami,* standing by itself, alone. As a term, *kami* is difficult to understand; its etymological derivation is probably lost, and the suggestions of the fundamental meaning of the term vary. One might hear or read the term in Japanese used variously to refer to that which is also referred to in English as the hair of the head, or as paper, or, as some might word it, as gods. Our concern is to see how the term has been used in the heritage to refer to gods or spirits—better still, to refer to *kami.* Yet even here we cannot understand *kami,* which can be interpreted either as singular or plural. Japanese have not demonstrated a tendency to seek to "understand" *kami.* The key notions rather should be discerning *kami,* perceiving, sensing *kami.*

Our English phrase "Sacred Presence" seems to serve us rather well in communicating the sense of "*kami.*" It is not simply "the sacred," which might entail the ranking of the "sacred" on some theoretical model, or placing the sacred for speculative purposes "out there." Rather it is Sacred Presence, which necessitates the presence of both the Sacred and the person or persons who make the discernment.

Kami can be ancestors, a tree, island, waterfall, noble persons, fox, beaver, wind, rock, mountain, and other dimensions of human experience in the here and now. One might ask, "What are the criteria for judging the presence of *kami*?" Would you recognize that this is a foreign mode of putting the question? Rather, one might ask: what associated dimensions of human awareness form a cluster of discernment when the presence of the Sacred is realized?

First, I should think, would be an ability to see the world, this ordered setting in which our lives are lived, as the arena of hierophany, as a setting fully capable of serving as a mode in which the Sacred is revealed. It seems that this ability is one of discerning a *something more,* more than merely the sum of component parts, more in a waterfall than, say, two parts hydrogen and one part oxygen falling at a determined rate of descent with a velocity yielding potentially such and such in hydro-electric output. More, too, than a lovely waterfall in this or that prefecture, more even than a rainbow. And this discerning is not premeditated, not the kind of thing that one says one will engender or have and subsequently actually will it into existence. One's disposition, one's memory, and the testimony of others will have considerable influence on whether one discerns this something more. If one discerns it in a way that remotely approaches the discernment of Japanese men and women, one will discern it as a presence, as there, and as simultaneously confronting and beckoning one, and as Sacred.

Second, I should think, is the quality of recognizing the unusual as instilling awe, as provoking solemn wonder. Sacred Presence can be gentle, delicate, powerful, mighty, and fearfully profound. And Sacred Presence can be reverently attractive, awesomely alluring. And all of this is found in quality and in attractiveness in differing degrees at different places, and at different times. What is the proper response in this discernment of Sacred Presence?

That response is expected should not go unnoticed. Persons, of course, could choose to do otherwise, could choose not to respond. But part of what Japanese men and women consider to be involved in one's being genuinely human is that one respond. To do less is to be both inattentive and to act inadequately, somehow to be awry.

One then endeavors to respond in purity. The centrality of the notion of purity is in both formal ritual and in personal reflection. And this leads us to our next consideration.

PURITY

Purity is not dissociated from simplicity, sincerity, and honesty. Were it to be so, purity would remain an impersonal concept or exterior condition. Japanese men and women have not only responded personally, publicly, and privately to the Sacred Presence in purity, they have excelled in developing and have chosen to maintain elaborate and highly formal rituals (*matsuri*) for purification and for worship. So elaborate, so sophisticated, are the rituals, conducted with precision, with ancient prayers (*norito*) uttered with carefully structured and preserved intonations, one might miss the notions of simplicity, sincerity, and honesty (*shōjiki*).

Ritual might tend to put some of us off, as it were, might lead some to say that such behavior is merely formal. Apparently, however, Japanese have found that this intricate formal behavior of priests on behalf of the local community in Sacred Presence is the highest form of human behavior in light of which, because of which, the more routine stop-and-go-busy-ness of day-to-day does not slip from order into chaos.

From what are we purified? Works on Shinto do not utilize a great deal of space discussing this question. Apparently, it is thought that the reader will have a fairly good notion of what it is from which one must be cleansed. The ritual act of purification, washing the mouth, washing the hands and forearms, standing while a priest waves a wooden stick with attached paper streamers (*harai-gushi*) before one, are ritual moments designed to represent a transition from the ordinary to the extraordinary, just as gateways and fences, imposing structures and rocks, might represent this in wood and stone—a transition from the ordinary into Sacred Presence; not from the profane, in the sense of what lies outside the presence of the Sacred as fundamentally different from the Sacred, in spite of this dualism frequently being structured elsewhere, because the world is not profane in this sense, not in the Shinto heritage. From what are we purified? It seems to me that most basically one is purified from a will to violation, from that activity that is divisive among persons, that wounds a person, that transgresses the norms of inter-personal relationships, that does not observe the significance of the presence of another, that disturbs harmony, sows discord, that disclaims family, exudes insincerity, warps honesty (*shōjiki*), that violates the "birthing" of the unfolding of life and the world in growth into an optimistic future.

Without texts to go on, or outstanding treatises representing orthodoxy, one is left more or less to infer from whatever written materials are at hand, from one's Japanese friends, from observing rituals, from what Japanese have built, to determine this interpretation of purification from violation. Looking at a shrine, say at Ise or Idzumo, what might an American intend by saying the architectural lines are clean? What might one mean when one says that a beam is true or when one speaks of purity of architectural statement? One notices upon Shinto celebrants cleanly pressed folds of garments (*shōzoku*), sees among them uprightness of posture, fidelity in reproducing *norito* prayers, and faithfulness in impressive remembrance and hospitality, and one begins to discern a complex of values among Japanese men and women in the way of the *kami*, walking and living among the *kami*, in Sacred Presence.

One discerns conformity in human expectations, sincerity in words and deeds, uprightness in behavior, faithfulness, that is, in being true, in friendship. Evil, if we might use this word, is the act of violating this. Evil, violation, is that which strikes at the root of one's personhood.

The *kami,* the perception of Sacred Presence on the part of Japanese men and women, the location of that perception in space and time, in shrine and in ritual, have enabled Japanese men and women to move through a stage of being individuals capable of violation into personhood simultaneously in society and in community.

THE WAY IS GIVEN

In the Shinto heritage, although *kami* bestow blessings (*megumi*), there is little emphasis given to a notion of grace. There is no notion of original sin, nor is there a notion of human bondage. A person can be bad, can commit bad acts, think and act with a will to violation, but one is not saved from violation. If one has committed violation, in the sense we are using it, well, one just has to live with it and attempt to set about afresh to discipline oneself into a bright mind, clear in thought, pure in motive, sincere in execution.

Is there some dimension within this complex, old, changing, flexible tradition and the pattern of human behavior associated with it that we can note as having some similarities with the theme of our study "Of Human Bondage and Divine Grace"? I think not directly. However I think there is a dimension of religiousness that is present that can be recognized as homologous if not analogous.

I have in mind a sense of self-effacement with a simultaneous commitment to the well-being of others that is integral to, and a natural expression of, one's orientation to oneself, one's family, neighbor, to one's community, to the past, in today's world, toward tomorrow, to nature, to the stars, and to more than our eyes can behold.

One's life is fundamentally a gift. Some might say that one has been damned by birth. Not those in the way of the *kami.* Sacred Presence is growth, potential in the process of actualization, is optimistic, open, creative. Life is a gift, and so one respects deeply one's parents, venerates one's ancestors, and their ancestors, eventually the ancestorness of Sacred Presence, which is the ancestor of us all, that is, we who live as Japanese in the way of the *kami.* Life is a gift, whether our life or the life of rice; health is a gift and so also is the harvest.

A good person, like good soil, contributes to the well-being of life.

This world, the world as those of us within the way of the *kami* see it, is a gift. It is not of our making, yet it is there for our shaping, not to mutilate, but to mold, keeping in mind the quality of its being that into which we have been led, that is to say, that to which we have been introduced, keeping in mind that it is a gift.

And Sacred Presence is not fundamentally other than what one basically is, insofar as one participates in life. We have not created *kami.* We have been introduced to *kami,* Sacred Presence.

And note, whether one sees a shrine, or a spot marked by a rope with hanging flax and jaggedly cut paper (*shimenawa*), note well that that marks the spot where persons have responded and continue to respond. The Sacred Presence is prior, is there, and confronts one in its givenness.

Religious response indicates that one recognizes Sacred Presence as being prior to oneself, and hence one bows to that which is prior, and hence, too, one attempts to preserve the heritage, which, also, is prior to oneself. The way of Sacred Presence is a way not of one's making, it is that which leads one into relationships with one's village kinsmen, one's geographical area, one's fellow Japanese, and by extension, with all men and women.

And this relationship, grounded as it is on Sacred Presence, has yielded community in human history, has enabled individuals to become persons, has enabled Japanese men and women to know the sense of being a people as, perhaps, those of us who are Jewish might understand.

The way of the *kami* is not of one's making—yet because one has been introduced to it, one comes to learn that qualities such as simplicity, honesty, clarity, cleanliness, sincerity, loyalty, uprightness of character, evenness in tenor, steadiness in bearing, harmony, propriety in community, yielding to the well-being of others, do not become burdens which one must endure, yield not to legalistic moral codes that bind one, that inhibit one's freedom, but, rather, contribute to a bright and sunny heart.

CONCLUSION

We began this brief chapter by commenting on how this interlude with a consideration of Shinto might give us pause in our reflections. We noted, too, some comments made about this old and fluid tradition. When persons say that Shinto assimilated high culture from China, or assimilated Buddhist practices of representing *kami* in pictoral or sculptured form, or developed or copied Chinese forms of architecture, what is intended is that Japanese in the past assimilated this or that, incorporated or copied this or that and found, thereby, no impairment of their discernment of Sacred Presence.

This tradition has not manifested a need to preserve a form for introducing a person into Sacred Presence through the written word, through rational presentation, analytic clarity or systematic statement. Nor are we met with a tradition that speaks of original sin or human depravity. Conversion, too, is a foreign concept.

And so we pause to reflect. In spite of this significant difference in formal structure between this old and fluid tradition and the traditions which we will have considered in this study, we yet marvel that for many Japanese men and women, a life lived in *kami-no michi*, or Shinto, or in the Way of the *kami*, is a life that is fundamentally not awry, is life abundant, is a life that is genuinely human.

NOTES

[1] See Wilfred Cantwell Smith, *The Meaning and End of Religion* (New York: Macmillan Company, 1963), pp. 70–71.

[2] One should be aware that phrases like "Japanese men and women" and "a Japanese" are used in a very general sense. Some Japanese, particularly urban youth, might not see themselves, initially, as participating in what we are presently considering. Some Japanese have particularly formulated Christian commitments, and others have loyalties to some Buddhist orientations that would preclude self-conscious participation in the religious expressions nurtured and sustained in the Shinto heritage.

12

ANCIENT GREEK RELIGION AND THE GOD OF HUMANITY

John Efstratios Rexine

The testimony left for posterity by the ancient Greeks indicates that they clearly saw the full panorama of human experiences that meets the horizon of human meaning. One finds the affirmation that justice, righteousness, order, and peace are rooted in the divine, that being genuinely human is not merely the consequence of a biological event, not even is it a right, but, rather, it is fundamentally a privilege. Professor Rexine turns our attention to these people of old whose contribution to rational discourse has shaped mightily the intellectual heritage of the West, but whose religious discernments, although generally known, tend rarely to receive adequate consideration.

One of the first things that we should say about the ancient Greek and ancient Roman religions is that they are polytheistic. It is also customary to say that when we are dealing with ancient religions, we are dealing with religions that are primarily cultic. There are a number of things that make these ancient cults different from the traditional Christianity with which we are familiar. There was no such thing in Greek antiquity as an organized church, as we understand it. Another characteristic that differentiates ancient Greek religion from Christianity, Judaism, and Islam, is that there were no Holy Scriptures. Further, since there was no organized priesthood, there were no bishops or archbishops or cardinals or anything of this sort. The kind of things that the priests or the priestesses did was not a full-time job. Also, there was no dogma. There was no creed. There was no "I believe in Zeus, the father; his son Apollo; and Athena, the daughter," a kind of holy trinity of the ancient Greek religion, if there was one. The temples, of which there are so many remains which are of such considerable interest to archaeologists and to contemporary researchers, though they may be thought of in one sense as the houses of gods and goddesses, were not houses of worship. One did not go to a temple in order to worship the god or goddess or whatever the divinity was. The temples were houses, as it were, for the cult statue of the god or goddess. Outside or beyond the temple was an altar. There some form of sacrifice to the god or goddess would take place. Whatever ceremonies did take place were public ceremonies which took place outside the temple and in front of the temple of the god or goddess.[1]

We can see immediately that we are dealing with a different kind of religion, a cultic religion, in which so much of what people believed about a particular divinity, or about divinity in general, could and did vary from region to region. So one would have, and did have, developing all kinds of belief about that particular divinity, and it was not necessary that these beliefs be consistent. In a sense, ancient Greek religion was very democratic.

Certainly most of the ancient divinities were initially viewed as some kind of power over which human beings did not have control, and, therefore, the only way to deal with this power was to appease it, to pray to it, to hope that, at least, it did one no harm. It might not do one any good, initially, but one would hope that it would do good eventually.

It is not unusual to say that belief in divinity began with a notion of the sky, that is, with the heavens, with the God in Heaven, who is such a prominent feature of a great number of the world's great religions, as a weather god. Certainly that has been the traditional view about Zeus, who began as a weather god (and continued to have thunder and lightning associated with him). If one wants the crops to grow, one has to pray to this weather god in order for rain to rain when it should, and not too much rain, either. These beliefs were handed down from generation to generation in an oral tradition that could and did vary. One of the immediate results of such an oral tradition that goes on for over hundreds, if not thousands, of years, is that one does not get consistency.

The first attempt in Greek history, the first attempt in the Western world, for that matter, in the European world, to make some kind of sense out of this vast conglomeration of deities is a work called the *Theogony* by Hesiod, a Greek poet-farmer, who can probably be dated to the seventh century before Christ. Hesiod tries to put into the very brief compass of a poem of a thousand or so lines, that was handed down orally, some kind of organization of the Greek gods and goddesses. It is very important for us, in trying to understand ancient Greek religion and mythology, because Hesiod makes a record of what he thinks are the important stories about the various divinities—not all of them but a great many of them. In some cases, Hesiod will carry on at some length describing the genealogies of the gods and goddesses. That becomes very important because *genea (genos)* in Greek means "a family," and in the *Theogony* one has a series of family trees which try to relate life from the highest point of divinity to human life itself. So one has in this work an attempt to organize knowledge about the gods and goddesses, the first attempt to organize what we might call "theological" or "religious" knowledge of the ancient Greek world.[2]

The ancient Greeks never developed the idea of monotheism—that was the contribution of the Jews. The Greeks, however, did develop a system of henotheism. While monotheism suggests very strongly the belief in one God to the exclusion of all other gods, henotheism is the belief in a supreme deity among other deities. And that is one of the great contributions of Hesiod, in whose work there does exist a supreme ruler who is the father of gods and of humankind. This supreme god is not, however, the creator of the universe. Zeus is the father, literally, of gods and of humankind. He is one (and this is distinctively Hesiodic) who is very much concerned with justice (*dike*) in the world. In fact, justice becomes a goddess, and she is a daughter of the supreme god himself, so that it is a paternalistic religion, if you will.

What Hesiod had initially was a religious system which was based on power, and this led him into genealogy. He began with at least two generations. Before the time of Zeus (who belonged to what is called the Olympian dynasty, which overthrew the dynasty of the Titans), there were the Titans, who based their whole being on brute force, on physical power. The whole conception behind the Titans was force, violence, and power. The dynasty of Zeus and his cohorts was a new dynasty that was to be based not simply on power but which would also involve justice, intelligence, and even love for humankind. Hesiod then conceived of a henotheistic religion. He was neither a priest nor a theologian, and one cannot view his work as a theological document which everyone had to accept. His work, however, was followed to a great extent by Solon, the great sixth century B.C. politician of Athens, who wrote in poetry, and later Aeschylus (fifth century B.C.) in his *Prometheus Bound.*

We find in Hesiod a kind of organizational chart, containing a census of twelve deities, six gods and six goddesses, presided over by father Zeus. And father Zeus contains, within himself, power. There is no god more powerful than he. That is one of the lessons, as it were, of both the *Theogony* and Hesiod's other important piece, the *Works and Days,* that no other divinity, no other power in the universe, has the power that this supreme god has. But this supreme god is a god who is interested in justice, in *dike,* a god who oversees justice not only among the gods and goddesses but also among men and women. That is to say, for the first time, perhaps, in this whole tradition, we see a divinity who is concerned about human behavior, who is concerned about the way in which men and women act, who is concerned about the way in which they treat one another. This, of course, also brings in the question of knowledge.

Now this is where Prometheus comes into the picture. Prometheus was a Titan. He belonged to the generation that preceded the Olympian dynasty. He belonged to a generation which was based on force and power and violence. He was intelligent enough to know what was coming, however, and he sided with Zeus. The gods were and could be prescient, could see beyond what human beings can see, could see into the future. (That does not mean that they were thought to control the future.) Now someone like Zeus is not omniscient. In fact, at this particular phase of the tradition, he is not even prescient, and Prometheus and Zeus get into a kind of power struggle. We have a divinity, Zeus, who has now assumed sovereignty and is pictured as punishing, for some reason, another divinity, Prometheus, who had initially helped him. The name "prometheus" means "forethought" or, put another way, "intelligence." So the question of the relationship of knowledge to divinity arises, and this is very interesting to us in terms of the whole mystery of Prometheus, because he is viewed as a god of intelligence, a god of knowledge. And if one looks upon him as a god of intelligence, and Zeus as a god of power, then there is the question of the relationship between power and intelligence.

The question is then generally raised for divinity: Can one rule simply on the basis of power or must such rule, such governance, be a result of the intelligent use of power? There is also the question, in the case of Prometheus, of whether intelligence by itself is enough. Intelligence in and of itself, the suggestion is strongly made, is not enough; intelligence has to be joined with power. It is the intelligent use of power, not the arbitrary use of power, that humankind is ultimately looking for. This would certainly seem to be what happened in Greek history as the result of the development of the ideas of democracy and democratic institutions.

When we want to find out about these divinities, we can turn to a number of authors, whether they be epic poets, lyric poets, or dramatic poets, who mention these divinities and for whom these divinities are a living part of their world. In a sense, the Greek dramatists became theologians despite themselves. The way in which they presented divinities gives us some clues about what they thought.[3]

The earliest texts that we have in the case of Prometheus, are those by Hesiod and Aeschylus. What is so fascinating about the figure of Prometheus is that he is, as it were, the most outstanding figure of a suffering god in antiquity. Whether one sees him depicted in art, or whether one sees him depicted in literature, what one sees is the startling picture of a "crucified" or "stapled" god. Needless to say, the comparison was made later with the suffering Christ. With Prometheus, one has a figure of a god who is suffering, who is crucified, who is isolated. Why? Why is he doing this—and this is the fascinating part of the question—why is he suffering for humankind? In fact, in the Aeschylean text, he is mocked, too, as he is crucified. He is mocked by the forces around him who accuse him of being *philanthropos* (of the familiar word "philanthropy"), "Man lover." He is accused of loving humankind and is mocked for it. He is suffering for the human race. Not only is he suffering for the human race, but one discovers that he saved the human race from extinction. So he is literally the savior of humankind. There is no reason given, or stated, why he should love humankind. It is a kind of love for the human race that is freely given to humanity, and Prometheus suffers willingly. He suffers this crucifixion, this stapling; he is impaled for humankind. He is supposed to be transfixed somewhere in the Caucasus, in one of the most desolate places on earth, and there an eagle of Zeus is pecking at his liver. He is immortal and so he cannot die. Nothing is more horrible in the ancient view of divinity than to suffer and not be able to die.

The one thing that all human beings are subject to is death, is mortality, and there was a tremendous concern with the question of why human beings have to die. Especially does this concern arise later on in Greek history in the great age of democracy and optimism, where people felt there was nothing they could not do, no scientific inventions that could not be invented, no knowledge that could not be developed. Why was it that there was this limit, this time limit placed on human beings—death?

One of the main characteristics of ancient divinity was the fact that they could not die. On the other hand, they were born. They all had births. They did not exist from eternity. They were given birth at some point or another. And further, this entire substructure was looked at as one big family, beginning with Zeus and going down to human beings. This commingling of human and divine, which might seem very naughty, had a kind of social purpose. One could claim that one's family was related to a divinity, and this placed one at a much higher level on the social ladder than would be the case of those not having a god or goddess as a relative. There was a pyramid beginning from the top with the highest divinity and going all the way down to the bottom. People did claim that their families went back to some affair between a god and goddess.

When a human being consorts with divinity, or the other way around, then the divinity gets something that was not always the case, and that is suffering. Contact with mortality always produces suffering. Prometheus is a god who loves humankind, who gives of himself for humankind, who is suffering for humankind, for thousands[4] of years. The story about the suffering of Prometheus ratifies for everyone that suffering is an innate part of the human experience. It has been ratified by divine suffering, so that we are not promised a rose garden. We are promised suffering. We are promised death. This is part of the human picture, and coming to grips with this is also a part of being human. It is interesting that it should be a god of knowledge that is associated with the human race because the Greeks saw the human animal, as it were, as the only animal that was rational. Rationality and knowledge, therefore, are associated, and Prometheus is their divinity. Prometheus, a Titan, belonged originally to a generation which based its whole being and purpose on power, and he, through intelligence, as it were, through prescience, saw what was coming and sided with Zeus. He saw in Zeus, in the Olympians, the establishment of a new generation of divinities which would be based on order instead of disorder, on justice rather than injustice, that would, in Hesiod's terms, allow for a relationship to exist between the worshipper and the worshipped. That is to say, the supreme divinity would become someone to whom one, as a worshipper, as an individual, could appeal in matters that did concern one.

In the *Theogony* we read:

> Now Iapetus took to wife the neat-ankled maid Clymene, daughter of Ocean, and went up with her into one bed. And she bare him a stout-hearted son, Atlas: also she bare very glorious Menoetius and clever Prometheus, full of various wiles, and scatter-brained Epimetheus who from the first was a mischief to men who eat bread; for it was he who first took of Zeus the woman, the maiden whom he had formed. But Menoetius was outrageous, and far-seeing Zeus struck him with a lurid thunderbolt and sent him down to Erebus because of his mad presumption and exceeding pride. And Atlas through hard constraint upholds the wide heaven with unwearying head and arms, standing at the borders of the earth before the clear-voiced Hesperides; for this lot wise Zeus assigned to him. And ready-witted Prometheus he bound with inextricable bonds, cruel chains, and drove a shaft through his middle, and set on him a long-winged eagle, which used to eat his immortal liver; but by night the liver grew as much again every way as the long-winged bird devoured in the whole day. That bird Heracles, the valiant son of shapely-ankled Alcmene, slew; and delivered the son of Iapetus from the cruel plague, and released him from his affliction—not without the will of Olympian Zeus who reigns on high, that the glory of Heracles the Theban-born might be yet greater than it was before over the plenteous earth. This, then, he regarded, and honored his famous son; though he was angry, he ceased from the wrath which he had before because Prometheus matched himself in wit with the almighty son of Cronos. For when the gods and mortal men had a dispute at Mecone, even then Prometheus was forward to cut up a great ox and set portions before them, trying to befool the mind of Zeus. Before the rest he set flesh and inner parts thick with fat upon the hide, covering them with an ox paunch; but for Zeus he put the white bones dressed up with cunning art and covered with shining fat. Then the father of men and of gods said to him: "Son of Iapetus, most glorious of all lords, good sir, how unfairly you have divided the portions!"[5]

One cannot fool Zeus, and this is the point in the *Theogony* and in the *Works and Days;* that even though Prometheus is the god of intelligence and knowledge, the supreme god cannot be outwitted. After all, if there is going to be a contest in divinity, there is, in this view, only one god who is going to win, and that is the supreme god:

> So said Zeus whose wisdom is everlasting, rebuking him. But wily Prometheus answered him, smiling softly and not forgetting his cunning trick:
>
> "Zeus, most glorious and greatest of the eternal gods, take which ever of these portions your heart within you bids." So he said, thinking trickery. But Zeus, whose wisdom is everlasting, saw and failed not to perceive the trick, and in his heart he thought mischief against mortal men which also was to be fulfilled. With both hands he took up the white fat and was angry at heart, and wrath came to his spirit when he saw the white ox-bones craftily tricked out: and because of this the tribes of men upon earth burn white bones to the deathless gods upon fragrant altars.[6]

This is a bit of etiology; it explains the practice of the institution of sacrifices as done by the Greeks. Ever since that time, the races of mortal humans have burned the white bones to the immortals on the smokey altars. There is a very funny play by Aristophanes called *The Birds* in which two main characters, getting sick and tired of all the litigiousness of Athens, and wanting to leave Athens, make a deal with the birds, who were the original rulers of the universe. One of the first things that the birds do to take over the universe is to cut off the flow of incense or the flow of the smell of these sacrifices from earth to heaven. And if they can do that, they will stifle the gods and goddesses up above. There is even a scene in that play of Prometheus with his umbrella trying to steal fire. There is, then, this element of deception. Somehow human beings are always trying to get away with something. They think that they can deceive the supreme deity. Not so. He sees everything. But he not only sees everything, he also punishes.

> But Zeus who drives the clouds was greatly vexed and said to him: "Son of Iapetus, clever above all! So, sir, you have not yet forgotten your cunning arts!"[7]

For some reason, we human beings, because Prometheus was our god, were to be punished, and Zeus decided to punish us by withholding fire, the great instrument of technology. Of course, with the introduction of fire there is the introduction of one of the greatest discoveries of technology. There is also the introduction of what had been a divine prerogative. Only the gods had fire. Here is perhaps another view on the part of the ancient Greeks. We all, in our own way as human beings, are not only willing at times to try to cheat the divinity, but we are also jealous of the prerogatives of divinity, and we would like to have what the gods and goddesses have. So our representative, Prometheus, stole the fire, hiding it in a hollow fennel stalk. This bit deep into the feelings of Zeus who thunders on high.[8]

Well, Zeus, of course, is not to be deceived even though he lets this happen. Again, this idea of stealth suggests free will on the part of humanity, that human beings can do these things; but there is a price that is paid. What does Zeus do to punish man for the theft of fire? He creates woman. That is the punishment.[9]

What is the point of all this? One can get into an argument with feminists, but the essential point is that one cannot deceive the supreme god. This is made quite clear. It is not possible to hide from the mind of Zeus nor to escape it. Look at Prometheus! Look at the god of knowledge, of intelligence himself: even he could not deceive the mind of Zeus and even he had to suffer for the attempt to deceive the supreme deity.

In the Greek tradition, the first woman is called Pandora. Pandora means "all gifts." The etymology in the text suggests that all the gods and goddesses had given her gifts, and that is why she is called Pandora. But it is Epimetheus, the brother, who brings her as a gift to humankind, and it is through this other divinity that woman is transferred. The suggestion is made that prior to woman, society was idyllic, but that one of the things that really brought troubles in the world was woman's curiosity. Pandora was very curious. Remember she opened a jar, a vase, and she let out of this jar all the illnesses and diseases and discomforts and so on, except hope. She put the lid down, and we do hope that what that means is that there is still hope and not that there is no hope!

Now this suggests something else that is in the *Prometheus Bound* of Aeschylus, that prior to Prometheus' suffering humankind had no hope, that humans knew ahead of time the day of their death. One of the great gifts of Prometheus to humankind was the gift of hope. And that is, in a sense, a gift that came to us through Pandora. We keep on going because we have hope. Otherwise, if we knew that we were going to die tomorrow or the next day, we would be faced with a kind of determinism, then we would perhaps not go on in the same way.

In the case of the earlier Hesiodic tradition, we are presented with an author who is concerned with showing us a henotheistic deity. It is really the story of Zeus but the emphasis is on the father figure—Zeus as the supreme deity among other deities, over whom he has established his authority. He is a god of justice who is concerned with order among the divinities themselves and also in the human society. There are also descriptions of what constitutes a just and an unjust society. The daughters of Zeus are the characteristics of a just society: *Dike,* justice; *Eunomia,* law and order; and *Eirene,* peace. The presence of these three female divinities denotes the just society, as it were. The lack of their presence is characteristic of an unjust society. As daughters of Zeus, they come from, they draw their authority from, their father who was the supreme god.

Another way of putting it is to say that they are aspects of the supreme deity. So Hesiod is concerned with presenting us with a deity to whom we can turn or to whom the ancient Greeks of his time could turn, in whom they could see not simply a god of power but a god of justice, a god of order, a god of peace, and even a god whom one might be able to love or, at least, a god with whom the worshipper could have some kind of relationship. Prometheus is seen as the protector of humankind, as the one who stands up for humankind, who steals for humankind, and who is punished for his act. He has as his beneficiaries the human race.

In the so-called aphoristic dialogue of Plato, called the *Protagoras,* we catch a glimpse of Prometheus and Epimetheus at the time of creation. There is a view that Prometheus was the creator of the human race. That is why he loved it, but we do not have primary sources to document this view. There is another view too which, if one could document it, would be very fascinating, that Prometheus had this love for human beings because he was himself at one point a human being who became a god and therefore knew what it was like to be human and would suffer for humanity. In the *Protagoras* we have a very tantalizing glimpse of the creation, and this view says that during the creation Zeus gave orders that all living creatures be given various things, so that the various animals were given claws and feet and fur coats, and so on, so that they would have protective devices. It was Prometheus who was in charge of this distribution of attributes to the living creatures, but it was through his brother, Epimetheus, that this was done. Unfortunately, Epimetheus ran out of things; poor human beings were left shivering and naked. They were not given any fur coats or claws or fangs and so on. Epimetheus went back to his brother and said, "I gave it all away. What are we going to do for this poor human race? They do not have anything." When Zeus is questioned about this he says, "You are to give the human race justice." Also listed for the human race in addition to justice, are religion and political organization, but the emphasis is on justice.

It is interesting that Zeus says that the gift is to be given to all: "Do we give this to all or just to a select few?" "No, to every human being." This is a way of saying that the human race, every human being, has the sense of justice. It is also a way of saying that the sense of justice is a freely given gift of divinity. The supreme god himself, at least in the Greek version of creation, gave every human being this sense of justice which forms a kind of link between divinity and humanity. The supreme god, Zeus, is interested in what human beings do because he has given everyone this sense of justice.

The *Prometheus Bound* of Aeschylus was produced in the fifth century B.C. We have only the first play of a series, *Prometheus Bound.* We have fragments of the *Prometheus Unbound,* and then there is *Prometheus the Firebearer,* and a satire play, which also had to do with fire, with the stealing of fire. The order of the plays is disputed. *Prometheus the Firebearer* was an etiological play. It indicates to us that Prometheus was worshipped in a cult for having brought fire to humankind. So there was then a cult of Prometheus related to fire worship.

Now what we get in Aeschylus is somewhat of a different story from what we got in Hesiod. We get a picture of a divinity who is bound to a rock, who is suffering, and who is doing so just at the point when Zeus has achieved sovereignty but when he has not fully established that sovereignty. In other words, he has taken over from the Titans, has assumed authority, has become a very powerful ruler. He is a tyrant. So the picture of Zeus that we have in

Aeschylus is not the devout picture of divinity that we get in Hesiod but the picture of an absolute authority who will brook no criticism, who will tolerate no resistance. There is then presented here a picture of two divinities, one of whom is establishing himself but is hardly loveable, an absolute power, with the other god in chains, as it were, being punished for something which we discover to be his love of humankind or his having done something for humankind; one of whom is punishing, the other of whom is being punished severely, one of whom bases his authority on power, the other of whom bases his authority on knowledge and intelligence, one of whom is concerned, let us say, with the order of society as a whole, the other of whom is concerned with the freedom of the individual.

There is another theme that arises in *Prometheus Bound:* the question of freedom. Prometheus is bound, physically, but his mind is free. He thinks as he wishes, whereas at the end of the play, Hermes, who is the messenger of the gods, is physically free but mentally bound. So the whole question of freedom of thought versus physical slavery is also a question that is raised by Aeschylus and that may or may not have been part of the original story.

When Zeus took over power, one of the things that he wanted to do was to destroy the human race. There are many such stories in the Near East and elsewhere: the human race has reached such a state of degradation and impiety that the deity either wants to burn it out or drown it out of existence. There is the whole business of the flood story, which we also have in Greek and Roman sources where Zeus is so disgusted with human impiety, with human behavior. Both Hesiod and Plato make the point that the two things that really distinguish human beings from all other creatures are that they have a sense of justice and that they believe in divinity. These two distinguishing features do not characterize the animals or any other living creatures. And so part of what it means to be human is to have a religious sense. There is inevitably the feeling that the human race has become impious, therefore unworthy of continued existence, and in one story, Zeus had said, "Burn them, get rid of that whole human race," and the other gods and goddesses had said, "No, no, you burn the earth and things will get too hot, and heaven will get too hot and get burnt, too."

The story of flooding is different from the Biblical story. There is a female and a male, the only two human beings who were pious, who got into their little boat, and the flood took place, and so on, and they ended up on Mount Parnassus.[10] Zeus wanted to destroy the human race because of its impiety. But Prometheus was the only one who opposed the destruction of the human race. Of all the divinities, of all these thousands and thousands of divinities, nobody stood up for the human race, and this is why Prometheus is being punished. In Aeschylus, emphasis is placed on the fact that Prometheus is the god of the arts and sciences. He is the god of all knowledge. If there is a gift that Prometheus has given humanity, it is the gift of knowledge—all kinds of knowledge, practical, scientific, religious.[11]

So it is no wonder, perhaps, that Prometheus was such a favorite of humanity. He is a kind of saint, as it were, of the human race. Not only is he the god who saved the human race, not only is he the god who suffered for the human race, but he is also the god who made human life endurable.

Michael Grant's *Myths of the Greeks and Romans,* towards the end of the chapter on Prometheus, cites a number of instances both in art and literature in which Christians of the medieval period were themselves taken with this figure of a suffering god from antiquity, of a god who was a *philanthropos,* one who loved the human race, who saved the human race from extinction, who provided the human race with that which would make life liveable for it, and who did this, presumably, as a kind of act, a kind of gift of grace, as it were, for no apparent reason that we can definitively discover by going through the sources that we have at our disposal.

Finally, it is Zeus who is the protector of guests, friends, and suppliants. Someone in need, someone in trouble, someone bereft can appeal to Zeus, and the supreme god himself, in that case, is the protector. One does not hurt people who are travelling. One does not hurt orphans and widows and the sacred. There is mercy, in that sense, shown by the supreme god, and there is an appeal that can be made directly to the supreme god by individuals who are suffering from the variety of ills, but the only god who freely took upon himself to suffer for the human race was Prometheus.

NOTES

[1] There have been studies by various scholars on the continuing tradition that went into Christianity from antiquity. For example, many

have noted that the Parthenon itself was a temple to the virgin goddess Athena, who has been equated in Greek Christianity to Mary the Theotokos, and even today one can see some of the iconography within the Parthenon because medieval people used the Parthenon as the cathedral of the Virgin Mary. Needless to say, the tradition continues even further. When Ottoman Turkey took over many of these lands, many of these churches were also continued as mosques. So there is a tremendously long continuity in that respect.

Virtually all medieval churches in the eastern Mediterranean were built upon the foundations of ancient temples. For instance, one can actually trace the temple of Poseidon below the structure of the medieval church to Saint Nicholas because Poseidon was the divinity, the god of the sea, and Saint Nicholas the protector of seamen. Even the Church of the Holy Wisdom in Constantinople was supposed to have been built on the foundations of an ancient Greek temple.

There are also folk traditions that continue from antiquity. The celebration of worship of a particular deity on a particular day is in both the Greek and Roman traditions and continued in the celebration of saint's days.

[2] Although he preceded Hesiod, Homer did not consciously strive to present an organizational chart about the divinities. Hesiod, however, is primarily concerned with deities—he is concerned about divinity and what it reflects, he is concerned about divinity and power. The *Theogony* might be described as a "Book of Genesis" of the ancient Greeks. Hesiod's other important piece, the *Works and Days,* specifically contains a "Book of Proverbs" and is the place where one finds the moral teachings of the nation, of the race, reflected in a highly agricultural society in highly agricultural terms. So with Hesiod one has a complete view of life as seen both from the divine and from the human points of view; and in both cases, the poet is concerned with the development of the idea of a supreme deity.

[3] We also have very prominent representation in art, not simply the architecture but the immense amounts of sculpture and so on that have come down from antiquity.

[4] The interpretations of the texts are in dispute as to whether it is ten thousand or thirty thousand years of suffering that Prometheus has to endure.

[5] Hugh G. Evelyn-White, *Hesiod: The Homeric Hymns and Homerica* (New York: Macmillan Co., 1914), pp. 117, 119.

[6] *Ibid.,* pp. 119, 121.

[7] *Ibid.,* p. 121.

[8] Anthropologists have suggested that one can imagine the cave man discovering fire and bringing it back to the cave, hiding it (in the fennel stalk, in this case, which is still used in Greece for transporting fire), having that sense of guilt that somehow something has been discovered

which properly belongs to a god. And this whole idea of stealth is involved.

[9] "Forthwith he made an evil thing for men as the price of fire; for the very famous Limping God formed of earth the likeness of a shy maiden as the son of Cronos willed. And the goddess bright-eyed Athene girded and clothed her with silvery raiment, and down from her head she spread with her hands a broidered veil, a wonder to see; and she, Pallas Athene, put about her head lovely garlands, flowers of new-grown herbs. Also she put upon her head a crown of gold which the very famous Limping God made himself and worked with his own hands as a favor to Zeus his father. On it was much curious work, wonderful to see; for of the many creatures which the land and sea rear up, he put most upon it, wonderful things, like living beings with voices: and great beauty shone out from it.

"But when he had made the beautiful veil to be the price for the blessing, he brought her out, delighting in the finery which the bright-eyed daughter of a mighty father had given her, to the place where the other gods and men were. And wonder took hold of the deathless gods and mortal men when they saw that which was sheer guile, not to be withstood by men.

"For from her is the race of women and female kind: of her is the deadly race and tribe of women who live amongst mortal men to their great trouble, no helpmeets in hateful poverty, but only in wealth." (Hugh G. Evelyn-White, *Hesiod: The Homeric Hymns and Homerica* [New York: Macmillan Co., 1914], pp. 121, 123)

[10] Of which, the Roman source (Ovid) has a rather telling story about the regeneration of humanity: Only two human beings, Deucalion and Pyrrha, survived the flood. Pyrrha, the woman, insists that they go to the temple first to pay their respects to the deity at Delphi and ask what they should do. And the Oracle replied that they should dig up the bones of their mother and throw them over their shoulders. And the woman says in horror, "The bones of mother! What a terribly sacrilegious thing to do!" And Deucalion says, "No, what the Oracle means by the bones of mother, to dig up mother's bones, is to dig up the bones of the mother of us all. Who is the mother of us all? Mother Earth. And what are the bones of Mother Earth? Stones." So the male flipped the stones over his shoulder and from them males were regenerated. And Pyrrha did the same with her stones and females were regenerated. And Ovid comments wryly that ever since then the hearts of human beings have been stone.

[11] "Do not think that out of pride or stubbornness I hold my peace; my heart is eaten away when I am aware of myself, when I see myself insulted as I am. Who was it but I who in truth dispensed their honors to these new gods? I will say nothing of this, you know it all; but hear what troubles there were among men, how I found them witless and gave them the use of their wits and made them masters of their minds.

I will tell you this, not because I would blame men, but to explain the goodwill of my gift. For men at first had eyes but saw to no purpose; they had ears but did not hear. Like the shapes of dreams they dragged through their long lives and handled all things in bewilderment and confusion. They did not know of building houses with bricks to face the sun; they did not know how to work in wood. They lived like swarming ants in holes in the ground, in the sunless caves of the earth. For them there was no secure token by which to tell winter nor the flowering spring nor the summer with its crops; all their doings were indeed, without intelligent calculation until I showed them the rising of the stars and the settings, hard to observe. And further, I discovered to them numbering, pre-eminent among subtle devices and the combining of letters as a means of remembering all things, the Muses' mother, skilled in craft. It was I who first yoked beasts for them, in the yokes and made of those beasts the slaves of trace chain and pack saddle that they might be man's substitute in the hardest tasks; and I harnessed to the carriage so that they loved the rein, horses the crowning pride of the rich man's luxury. It was I and none other who discovered ships, the sail-driven wagons that the sea buffets. Such were the contrivances that I discovered for man—alas, for me! For I myself, without contrivance to rid myself of my present affliction.

"Hear the rest, and you will marvel even more at the crafts and resources I contrived. Greatest was this: in the former times if a man fell sick he had no defense against the sickness, neither healing food nor drink, nor unguent; but through the lack of drugs men wasted away, until I showed them the blending of mild samples wherewith they drive out all manner of diseases. It was I who arranged all the ways of seercraft, and I first adjudged what things come verily true from dreams; and to men I gave meaning to the ominous cries, hard to interpret. It was I who set in order the omens of the highway and the flight of crooked-taloned birds, which of them were propitious or lucky by nature, and what manner of life each led, and what were their mutual hates, loves and companionships; also I taught of the smoothness of the vitals and what color they should have to pleasure the Gods and the dappled beauty of the gall and lobe. It was I who burned thighs wrapped in fat and the long shank bone and set mortals on the road to this murky craft. It was I who made visible to men's eyes the flaming signs of the sky that were before dim. So much for these. Beneath the earth, man's hidden blessing, copper, iron, silver and gold—will anyone claim to have discovered these before I did? No one I am very sure, who wants to speak truly and to the purpose. One brief word will tell the whole story: all arts that mortals have come from Prometheus." (David Grene and Richmond Lattimore, eds., *The Complete Greek Tragedies: Volume One* [Chicago: University of Chicago Press, 1959], pp. 81–83)

A JEWISH VIEW OF BLESSING

Peter Ochs

Customarily, in a study like ours conducted within an academic setting, one might become entrapped by misleading assumptions about the central role of concepts or the crucial importance of normative definitions in one's initial attempts to understand the testimony of Jewish men and women about gratitude for what God has done. Primary in Jewish experience is behavior and not belief, and characteristic of this behavior is a life of gratitude. Dr. Peter Ochs leads us to consider "blessing" as the dimension in one's awareness of a religious response that is homologous to what others have spoken of as a recognition of divine grace.

I

I begin as a traditional Jew. It is evening. The kids have gone to sleep; they were screaming, and now they have stopped. The wife is putting away the boiled chicken for tomorrow. In the distance you see the lights of the little *shtetl,* the little Jewish ghetto, of which we are a part in Europe. I have my *yamulka* on my head as I do all day. It could be any color. This *yamulka* covers my brain really, the top of my head. It is a sign that I always have with me, every moment of the day, a sense of God's presence, and I seek to say to God, I respect that presence. I cover myself in your presence where it counts. I am tired. It has been a hard day, and I have suffered the way everyone suffers. I have had a stomach ache. I have had a little rash. Business was hard. The child is sick; God willing, he will get better. My wife bothered me. God willing, she will stop. This is the last thing I say during the day:

"Blessed art thou O Lord our God, King of the Universe, who closes my eyes in sleep and my eyelids in slumber." And I say this:

> May it be thy will, Lord, my God, and God of my fathers, to grant that I lie down in peace and then that I rise up again to life. Into thy hands I commit my spirit. O Lord, faithful God, thou savest me for thy salvation, I hope.

Then I go to sleep.

I wake up. My wife is there. The kids are running around, noisy already. The first thing I do—put my *yamulka* back on, yawn a bit, then the first prayer I recite, which is the first word I utter in the morning, is this: "I render thanks to thee, everlasting King, who has mercifully restored my soul within me. Thy faithfulness is great." Then I get washed, and that has a blessing, too. There are blessings all day long. There is even a blessing for excretory faculties, you might say. You recite it in the synagogue every morning, blessing God for the little wonders of the pipes he has put in us because if we did not have them nothing would go in, nothing would come out, and then we would die.

After all that is done, I rush off to synagogue. Synagogue really refers to a *minyan,* or collection of ten men (from tradition, the old tradition). I enter the synagogue, the place where these men have gathered, and I sing *mah tovu*:

> How goodly are thy tents, O Jacob, your habitations, O Israel. By thy abundant grace, I enter thy house. I worship before thy holy shrine with reverence.

Beside me other men are saying the same thing by themselves but at the same time. I reach into this bag called the *tallit* bag. (If you are Jewish and you speak a different dialect of the Europeans, *tallis.*) You take this out and you see inside a shawl, a prayer shawl with fringes—white, because we no longer have the blue dye that came from a special shell they used for them—four of them wool with silk, and written on it is a prayer. But before I read the prayer, I cloak my head. And while I do that I utter this meditation:

> Bless the Lord, O my soul. Lord, my God, thou art very great. Thou art robed in glory and majesty. Thou wrapped thyself in light as in a garment. Thou spreadest the heavens like a curtain. I, too, am enwrapping myself in a fringed garment in order to fulfill the command of my creator as written in the Torah, "they shall make fringes for themselves on the corners of their garments throughout their generations" [from the Book of Numbers]. Even, O Lord, as I cover myself with the *tallit* (prayer shawl) in this world, so may my soul deserve to be covered in a beautiful garment in the world to come in *gan eden* (the Garden of Eden). Amen.

Then I say, putting it on my head again:

> *barukh atah adoshem, elokenu melekh ha-olam*—Blessed art thou, O Lord our God, King of the universe, who has made us holy with his commandments and commanded us to enwrap ourselves in this fringed garment.

Then I go ahead and pray with my brethren prayers of petition and request, but mostly blessings about God's majesty, what he has done for us. After the prayers are over, I take off my *tallit,* and I think of food.

I have not eaten yet, so I scurry home about an hour after daybreak, and I sit down after ritually washing my hands, saying the blessing over washing my hands, and break some bread and recite the *motzi. Motzi* means "bring forth." The prayer goes like this: "Blessed art thou, O Lord our God, King of the universe who brings forth bread from the earth." Then I eat, noisily, and yell at the kids. After the meal is over, I recite another blessing thanking God for the food he has given us. Then I go off, mumbling blessings, to work.

Let me introduce myself. I am not a traditional Jew, though I am one who lives a modern form of traditional Judaism. I have to tell you, define for you, who I am because in Judaism there is no abstract truth that can be communicated to another. There is only the embodiment in my thoughts or in your thoughts, if you are a Jew, of a whole system of thoughts. Whatever I say is particular to my embodiment of those truths. This means it is not *the* truth, but there is no way out of this embodiment. And the same goes for you.

And the same goes for all my people collectively. So, as a famous sage, Hillel, said, "If I am not for myself, who is for me?" I have to speak for myself. "But if I am only for myself, what am I?" There is more than myself or yourself. "And if not now, when?" I have to act as myself representing something greater. So I speak in two ways. This is who I think I am. I am a Jew who tries to imitate a tradition of practice.

This tradition is one kind. It is rabbinic practice. Today, rabbinic means representative of that almost monolithic culture of Jews from around 300 B.C. to around A.D. 800, or, as we say, C.E.—the Common Era, during which time a collection of Jewish scholars, called Talmudists, created the Talmud, or really the teaching, the codification of all Jewish thought, practice, and law. This text was composed over centuries by these men (unfortunately, I must use that term), living in a community with its own internal structure over that period of time. These men composed an interpretation of Torah which established the foundation for what we now call normative Judaism. This means not Judaism as lived by every person who is Jewish but that body of not-totally-defined concepts, beliefs, values, hopes, structures, and dreams, which Jews always refer to as our own life-style. So, when I speak as a Jew who does that, who refers back to that Talmud and that system of belief as my lifestyle, I say this: God revealed himself to Moses on Mount Sinai a long time ago by uttering the Torah. Torah, in that sense, means teaching. This teaching came in a form, first of all, of what we call the Ten Commandments, but it does not mean just those commandments. It means those commandments as lived, which means those commandments plus all the interpretations of them by those who live them. All interpretations, all of them by those who live them. So, as a Jew, I say I acquire my lifestyle from those commandments spoken from God on Mount Sinai, interpreted to generations by my forebears. I would say that I am someone who seeks to live with God; by living with Torah, the teaching, and with the people Israel, never alone. These three concepts, God, Torah, and Israel, are the foundations of traditional Jewish thought.

But I am not just a Jew. Wish I were. It would be a lot easier, a lot better. But I also have the burden of being a modern Western person. I say burden because it is not as happy, not as pleasant, intellectually, though it is much more pleasant physically. I am a philosopher, which is not a Jewish thing to be. I think almost all modern Jews are philosophers, which is not a very Jewish thing to be. Let me define what I mean by a philosopher. I do not mean an academician who spouts Plato. I mean someone who has inherited this tradition of philosophy. The Jew says, "I live within a community, with Jews, the people Israel, and with God, and Torah. We lived with other like-minded folk, a more simple-minded people who had folk gods and lived in one place. But things happened, we got more sophisticated than that. We left that constraining community and went off on our own, as individuals. We knew that any different community—Athens, Sparta, Jerusalem—had a particular cultic system, a particular folk system proper to it. Since it is particular, it is not ultimately true. It could not represent everything. Therefore, it limits us; therefore, it constrains us, so we leave it in search for something which is not so constraining. We leave that particular home for something universal. The trouble is that once we have left it, we have left its thought system and we no longer know how to live. What system will tell us how to live? We do not have it any more. What we do is generate philosophy, or a system of looking for a system, out of nothing. What we have is nothing because we have left home."

Another word for nothing is reason, reason in a particularly post-Socratic sense (really post-Platonic, post-Aristotelian sense); reason, meaning that reflective consciousness, thinking, which just reflects and drives us forward looking for more reflection; reason meaning that reflective consciousness, just something which looks and does nothing but continue looking. Why does it look? Why would it look? What is it looking for? A belief? What would be the function of a belief if reason found it or had a belief? In other words, reason searches for a belief which is some certain knowledge, which will once again tell one how to live as one used to know when one was in one's community.

Whenever philosophy, as I use the term, finds a belief, it says, "uh-oh, particular, not ultimately true. Let's keep looking." What is it looking for? For belief. This is the way I understand philosophy.

What I am presenting is a Jewish philosophic reflection on what I believe corresponds, within the corpus of traditional Jewish thought, to the notion of grace. What precisely that correspondence will be I cannot say concisely or use one word for it. It will be called reflection on the aspect of Jewish prayer called blessing. But be careful. It is not only a rabbinic reflection. It is a rabbinic-philosophic reflection. This is all I can do: which means that there should be some contradiction in my presentation, which you should note and interpret on your own. There is no way out of those contradictions for me.

II

We are going to divide the topic into three parts. One will be that aspect of Jewish prayer called Petition. The technical term is *tefilla,* which is the prayer itself, petition, requesting. The second part will be called the Simple Blessing, *b'rakha,* "blessing," in Hebrew. The topic is recognizing grace, the way one seems to be using the term, God's mercy. And number three, Ritual Blessings. The technical term is *birkhat mitzvah* which means "blessing of commandment;" *mitzvah* is a commandment. A commanded act of grace that is God's speech and Torah.

So, here is how I begin. By looking back on what the traditional Jew did from morning to evening and asking why, what does it mean? How does it reflect Jewish thought, and how does it display the way Judaism is different from what we have read about other systems, like the chapter on the Theravāda and the one on the Mahāyāna? Judaism does not have an abstract system of thought, a metaphysic, a philosophy. It has a collection of embodied concepts that tell one how to live. For that reason there will be no concept which translates directly as "grace," because grace is not, in that sense, an action, a way of living. There will be concepts which reflect the notion of grace by showing how it would be enacted. So we are going to look at the action and reflect on what the concept may be behind it.

A

First, prayer. In the evening after a long day when I begin to say, "O God," I am really saying "protect me; God let me live; let me not die in my sleep"—a form of petition that generally is, "O God, do something for me or for us." A petition—"Help!" in other words. For each of the three forms of activity I will be discussing, we divide things into two halves. Every action, such as prayer, has an occasion or event which it is talking about, and it has a speech or a literary form which is spoken to correspond to that event. So we ask, in the evening when I go to sleep, what is the event? What is the occasion which makes me utter this petition?

One does not have control any more. I think it is often a typical human experience that sleep is like death, and one is passing through death. And the Jewish notion here, which is a folk notion, is that you may not live again after you go to this death, this lack of control, this lack of overt consciousness. So fearing death you say to God "Help! I hope when I wake up I am awake." So fear of some kind of death, something physical, is the occasion for the utterance of this petition. What are the forms of petition?

1. "O"—a very important term. One should not merely slip by it in prayer. "O" means exclamation! Exclamation means pointing out where you are to something else. "O" also suggests "wake up!"—something different is going to happen than is happening.
2. "God." God in this sense is a person, not a concept, not a universal something, but a person, being addressed by one's petition. "Help: You, God, help!"
3. "Do." Please do something for me. Act. I want something to happen down here from you.

And, finally, when and where should the action go? In this case, at night when I am physically afraid, to me, because all I am thinking about is death, my death.

The great Jewish thinker Abraham Heschel has said that whenever we experience anything, it expresses a need. I want to categorize what is going on in petition as the expression of human existence on earth. That is, we have petitions because we have material being; we have physical life, and physical life involves a lack of some kind, a need. Eating, sleeping, drinking: I need to drink, I need to sleep, I need to eat, I need to live. So physical life is characterized by needs. Therefore, the Jewish idea of petition corresponds to the fact that human beings, among them Jews, live in a realm of physical existence. Let us examine that realm briefly and see why living in that realm would cause one to want to say "Help!"

The philosopher says, "There is nature." And, one might continue, nature is the realm of physical existence from out of which one cries "Help!", meaning if all a philosopher is is a reflective mind, nature must be that which is not reflecting but reflected. Nature is what is down there when one looks. One thinks, nature is the object of one's looking. So, obviously, why does one say "Help!" when one knows one is in nature, if one is a philosopher? Because one is looking from outside of it. That is why one knows there is not any nature. One is saying "Help!" because one is not there. One is "up here." "Help!" means I do not want to be in nature. I want to be where my reflective consciousness is; therefore, nature is by definition a burden for the philosopher. It is an obstacle. It is bondage. It is a prison, and what the philosopher wants to do is to escape from it. Therefore, his petition, if he uttered one, which he probably does not, would be "Please, whatever I am talking to, which is myself really, please, myself, bring me into myself in this reflective consciousness, away from nature."

But the Jew does not say that. The Jew never says physical existence is a prison. I should not say "never"—there are some funny Jews; most of them, philosophic Jews. Most Jews, if following the rabbis, do not say nature is a prison, because they do not know the concept nature, not in this sense. For the rabbis, the concept that corresponds to the philosophic concept of nature is creation: in Hebrew, *sidre breshit,* the order of nature. That is what one sees around one—the order created by God. Look—something created by God could not be something which of its nature is something one should want to get away from. So, therefore, there is no intrinsic reason why simply being a part of creation should make one feel that one is suffering and, consequently, want to leave it.

Then why does the Jew keep complaining, Oh, help me? Why? Let us turn to Adam and Eve. What happens? God places humanity, Adam and Eve, in the Garden of Eden where, if one notes the text, they appear to have no reflective consciousness of their suffering. Fancy that. They do not think about their *tzores,* their troubles. They just live, eating apples—birds and bees. What happens then? They do something God tells them not to do, and as punishment, evidently, he casts them out of this delightful state of being into a state where the nature around them becomes something they interpret as a problem. He tells them, "I am going to make you work now and suffer and have pain." What is the meaning, therefore? Creation was not at first, in its nature, something burdensome. It became burdensome for human beings because God made it that way. Therefore, I petition God to relieve me of physical problems, not because the physical world, of its nature, is a problem, but because he has made it so that I experience it as a problem, and only he will take the experience of it as a problem away.

What drove Adam and Eve to sin? Curiosity? How would one characterize curiosity? There is a conflict. Interpreting Adam and Eve, the philosopher might say curiosity or something reflective brought them out of the garden. The rabbi, on the contrary, would say nothing reflective brought them out. Rather, it was that stupid other part of nature that brought them out. But which part was it? The rabbis call it the *yetzer ha-ra,* the evil impulse. Impulse means tendency, and evil just means naughty. There is no Jewish notion of evil itself. Satan himself is just this naughty little thing here, the evil impulse. Naughty, meaning what caused Adam and Eve to sin, was the fact that they belonged to nature, and nature does not seem to go by God's rule all the time, or do what he ultimately wants us to do. We have desires, yearnings, and needs. Contrary to what one might find among Mahāyāna Buddhists, desire, here, is a natural function which is not in itself bad. As a matter of fact, the rabbis say were it not for the evil impulse no good would come about for human beings because all human beings' good comes from the struggle over the evil impulse. Not only that, but those who have no impulse or whose impulse is weak never become very good. They become what they were to begin with, sort of average.

God created the creation. Part of that creation was the evil impulse, this tendency to desire things. He gave human beings the command, and they failed to go along with it because of something else he gave them, which was the evil impulse. And then he punished them for what he gave them in the first place, because they were not living up to something else he gave them, and that made them experience all of nature as something bad. What is going on? He was experimenting. He discovered something, the rabbis say; he discovered something he did not know before.

B

The second action that we saw the Jew do in the morning, God willing, is to wake up. He rubs his eyes and what does he say? "Thank you, I am awake. I cannot believe it." In fact, if just waking up can make one feel happy, one is a pretty happy person. "Thank you, God, I woke up." We are in the realm of simple blessing, a *b'rakha,* the first aspect of which is simply thanksgiving.

When a need is fulfilled, the religious person will interpret it as a gift. If the religious person is Jewish, he or she will say, "Thank you, God." If the gift is something physical which fulfilled my needs, the form is not "O God, do me something," but "Thanks, God, if you want, for what you did." Are human physical needs ever fulfilled, really, finally? They are not ultimately, not finally, fulfilled of themselves. What does it mean? For the Jews, physical needs are experienced as needs, that is, as something for which we have to petition God, not because they are that, but because God has made us experience them as punishment for what we did in the Garden of Eden. Therefore, if we are seeing the situation that way, we are going to thank God when they are fulfilled, because he is the one who controls our knowing whether they are fulfilled or not. There is no natural need. There is a God-imposed need, or awareness of need, therefore, there is a God-controlled awareness of fulfillment or gift. Whenever I utter thanks for something I have been given, I am stating first to myself that I see it as coming not from my agencies, but from God. Why? To see why a Jew sees it this way, let us look at a more complete, or complex, form of simple blessing which is not just expressing thanks but is recognizing *blessing* itself.

Let us consider the Jewish blessing, which is the *motzi.* The Jew sits down to eat and, before eating, says, with the *yamulka* on, "Blessed art thou," and then comes the name of God. God has a proper name, by the way, like "George" or "Sam;" we do not say it, but he has one. It is important. Next comes the proper name, which I will just call "the Name," *Ha-shem.* "Blessed art thou, *Ha-shem,* our God, King of the universe"—and then we will come to what he did for us. It is always a form of simple blessing. Blessed art thou, name, our God, King of the universe, who, and he did something, in this case, "who brings forth bread from the earth." So one fills in the specific thing that he does for one, the specific act of gift-giving.

What is the occasion? Eating some bread. Bread for the Jew is a staff of life, stereotypically a symbol of all food. The first thing one says is "blessed" (*barukh*). What does it mean? Blessing is not prayer or petition. Petition has its source in a felt lack, is generated by the source of that lack and will therefore bear within it a kind of physicalistic reference. Blessing, on the other hand, has its source not in a felt lack but in a fulfillment. Why is that the case? The word, "blessed" comes from the root *barakh* which means "to fall on one's knees." Something blessed is not something wonderful, but, rather, something before which we would bend the knee: something with authority over us, with the power to provide for us and with the capacity to receive and be moved by both our supplication and gratitude. Bending the knee is a physical act symbolizing obedience, subservience, supplication, and gratitude. Before whom then do we bend the knee? The Jew says, before no one on earth, before no king, but before God, alone, the Creator of heaven and earth. God, alone, has authority over us, the power to provide for us, and the capacity to receive and be moved by our supplication and gratitude.

So, one is about to take some bread that this ruler has given one out of his bounty. One says "blessed," meaning "I acknowledge that you are the one who controls me, you are the one who is worthy of having the knee bent before you."

"Blessed art thou." The form of the blessing is an attribution. It is a statement: You are blessed, I am attributing to you blessedness. Who is "thou?" The word "thou," *atah,* indicates someone I am immediately talking to. That is the one who is my absolute ruler, who is nearby: a personal, direct address.

Well, who is "thou?" The proper name of God. It is as though one would say, "You, George, the one who spoke to Abraham, Isaac, Jacob; the one who created us, the one who brought us out of Egypt; the one who will give us bounty in the future; you, the one I'm talking to, you're blessed."

"Who are you for us? You are our God." *This* word, God, is a generic term. It is a different term. That other word for God is a word which is the proper *name* of God. This is a generic *term,* "deity." You are our deity. You are the one to whom we look as our ruler. You, the one with a name, are not *my* deity, by the way, but *our* deity. The Jew always thinks *with.* I am always part of a people, and my God, is *our* God, the God of the people I belong to and in terms of which I define myself.

Our God is King of the universe. Why is that affirmed in every formula, every day, every moment, that one recites a blessing? Because that is what "blessed" is all about; acknowledging the king, the ruler, the one who controls. But whom does he control? I know he controls me; that is easy. I know he controls my people, because he is our God. But he controls the entire universe as well, that is, *all* of creation. The word *olam*, which is the term for "universe" in early Jewish thought, meant the physical universe. It later acquired the meaning of "eternity," or of temporal universality, as in *l'olam vo'ed*, "for ever and ever." Both senses are indicated here: the king of time and space.

C

Now why am I attributing to you all of a sudden, out of the blue, all of these wonderful things, O Lord? Because you did something for me, otherwise I would not give a darn. You came out of your distance and did something for me, therefore I now attribute to you majesty, because you are doing something for me. I am thanking you, because you have come down here, right here to this world, made your beneficence concrete, enacted here your love. If it were not for the fact that you have come, I would not have received this blessing. And what have you given me? You have given me this bread, or this wine, or this day, or this teaching, and so forth.

Let us summarize the meaning of blessing. First, the term *blessed:* it refers directly to something—someone—to whom one is giving homage. Second, a series of terms about *who is blessed:* God, and who he is. And third, a reference back down again to *what he did:* for what and where one is. In traditional Jewish, rabbinic life, persons may utter such blessings three hundred times a day. This means that three hundred times a day the activities of everyday life become occasions for them to know again that they have received a gift, that it is God who gave them this gift, and that the gift is right there in their hands. Three hundred times a day these persons may reconsider these concepts, relive this experience, and re-enter this relationship. In this way the rabbinic Jew may come to experience the world as a blessed creation, every part of which is a gift. He or she may begin to see everything in this world as an expression of something God did for us.

III

Why is that important? The key question is going to be: what does a human being live for? What is the purpose of his or her being? Are we saying that the blessing is important because a human being lives for fulfilling needs, and making a blessing makes one aware of when one's needs are fulfilled? No. To the contrary, blessing expresses the fact that, while burdened by needs, human beings live with the purpose of filling their minds with something other than those needs, filling their minds with certain other ideas and words and concepts.

Finally, think of this. If the blessing is an expression of gratitude to God for giving me something, why did I deserve to get it? If you recall, I inherited Adam's sin and am not worthy of being at peace on earth. Why do I deserve to receive this particular blessing? Further, how did I know to utter the blessing, once I received it? The purpose of existence for the Jews is to do what God said he wanted us to do in the first creation story, to live in his image, and the end of life is simply to imitate God. This does not mean to be identical with God, because God is uncreated, while we live in creation and always will. It means, rather, that we want to act within God's created world just as he acts beyond it. This means we want to govern ourselves and to mold ourselves in the image of one who is not limited to this universe. For example, if God is someone who is responsible for everything I see, then God cannot be limited to everything I see. It all came from him, but he is beyond it. This means that I want to make myself into the image of something beyond everything I see, in the image of something which is *not* anything I see.

For the Jew, God gave commandments on Mount Sinai which are Torah, the teaching of how to live on earth. These are specific orders, at least they are heard as specific orders by the Jew, to do certain things on earth, to brush one's teeth, not to murder, to observe the Sabbath. Brush your teeth because that will be one of the interpretations ultimately of how you become healthy, which is to live, which is to observe God's name. The Jew says all of one's life is governed by commandments from God. For everything one does, there is a commandment appropriate to it: meaning, for everything one does, it is possible to do it exactly as God says, and in doing that, to act like God and not as mere creature. Since God is not of this creation, there is no way for the creature to observe his way and know what he wants—unless God speaks to the creature.

God's experiment was to put human beings on earth and hope that, guided by their natural impulses, they would yet live in his image. "How do they know what my image is? I will tell them what to do, and acting out what I tell them will be living in my image." What happened? Adam failed. Eve failed. Cain failed. They all failed, because, guided merely by creaturely impulses, they lacked the ability to enact words spoken from outside this creation. What then does God say at the time of Noah? "The imaginings of human minds are evil always." If left to their own, human beings will always be guided only by their natural impulses and will lack the means to follow God's words. "Of their nature, they cannot follow me. Burdened now by the heritage of their imaginings, they cannot listen to me. So I will wipe them out and try again. I will bring a flood. Saving one human being unburdened by the heritage of human imaginings, I will let human beings people the earth again. But, this time, I will not leave them to their imaginings, their creaturely nature. I will tell them not only what to do, but also how to retrain their impulses so that they will have the power to do what I command them. I will teach them how to live. By my teaching, I will give them a second nature."

For the rabbinic Jew, this teaching is Torah, God's word understood as commandment. To understand this teaching, to study Torah, is to learn in detail how to acquire the second nature, or holy character, that will enable one to live in God's image, rather than in the image of something created. It is to know, in short, how to live in this world as if it were God's creation and not ours. This is to understand every activity in this world as an occasion for acting in God's image, which is to act according to the guidance of God's teaching rather than according to our own impulses. To know how to act this way is to enjoy the blessing of God's teaching. It is to bend the knee before the divine teacher. To utter a blessing, or *b'rakha,* is to bend the knee in this way. It is the fundamental act of accepting God's will over our creaturely will and, thereby, of placing our creaturely life in the service of our second nature.

Let me summarize. We inhabit creation. We suffer because, with Adam, we fail to live in God's image as God obliges us and, made aware of our failure, we find our creaturely lives burdensome. Our failed relationship with God introduces suffering into our creaturely lives. God brings us our suffering, and only he can remove it. We appeal to God in his mercy to remove our suffering. He appeals to us to receive his words as commandments, thereby to acquire the ability to live in his image and thereby receive our creaturely lives once again as blessings and not as burdens. In this world God created, to enact God's commandments is to do right and, thereby, to live this life with joy. God's commandments are therefore the vehicles of God's grace, because they provide us the means of eliciting his own mercy.

Our Relationship with God, the Merciful

Muhammad Abdul-Rauf[1]

So overwhelmingly pervasive is the fact of God's presence and the form of the imperative that the Divine initiative has taken for men and women who have responded to that imperative and who have submitted to that presence that Muslims might have to imagine the condition which others have spoken of as "human bondage." Conceivably, those among us who are Muslims might speak of one being in bondage to one's obstinacy, in choosing not to acknowledge the reality of God, or to one's arrogance, in refusing to discern that the reality is God. Professor Rauf introduces us to Islam and leads us a step further, to see that the ideal of submission (*islām*) to God's will is on the part of one who submits (*muslim*) in a life of grateful servitude.

In the name of God, the Merciful, the Compassionate.

I

Islam is the name of our religion. It should be pronounced with the emphasis on the second syllable, and with an "s," not a "z," sound. It is a religion which now claims over one billion adherents. It is said that one out of every four persons of the world's population is a Muslim.

Islam was proclaimed in the year A.D. 610 through Prophet Muhammad in his birthplace, Mecca, now a Saudi Arabian city. He was then forty years old. Until then he had spent his entire life within Mecca and its surroundings and had never been away from it except on two occasions when he travelled, at the age of twelve and again at twenty-five, to Syria on business.

The basic foundations of Islam center around the concept of monotheism, the existence of God, his perpetual presence, who is One in every aspect. He is One, therefore he has no partner. He is One, therefore he does not consist of elements or parts. He is One, therefore he is unique. He does not resemble any of or from among his creatures. He is neither a substance nor a spirit, nor does he have an image. Therefore, to say that God created man in his image is impermissible, since God is completely different from all his creations. Muhammad proclaimed this pure monotheistic teaching, in addition to a set of moral principles, in Mecca which, it is important to note, was then the capital of polytheism in Arabia.

Mecca which, in a sense, was founded by Abraham and his son Ishmael, adhered at first to the monotheistic belief taught by these two Messengers of God. Yet the succeeding generations corrupted that monotheistic belief and adopted idol worshipping which spread widely among the tribal society of Arabia. Each tribe or clan had its own idol made in the shape of a human being from wood or stone or mud or even from crushed dates. The date idol was especially convenient when people had to travel away from home. When they needed to eat, they ate it, not seeing the foolishness of their belief! However, the idols which were installed in and around the temple in Mecca, called the *Ka'bah,* built by Abraham and Ishmael, gained wide recognition in the whole of Arabia because Abraham had established the practice of annual pilgrimage to the *Ka'bah.* So the sanctuary attracted many pilgrims each year. After the decline into polytheism, they came to worship these gods and to trade at the same time during the season. This brought wealth, prestige, and cultural leadership to the inhabitants of Mecca.

Mecca also enjoyed a strategic position as it was situated midway on the ancient caravan route between the Yemen in the south and Syria in the north. Goods which were brought from the East, like silk and spices coming from China and India, were carried by caravans overland from the Yemen to the north, and the caravans brought goods from the Middle East, for shipping to the East, passing in both journeys by Mecca which was a convenient halting station. The Meccan society developed into a stratified social structure with a privileged class which treated the lower strata of society poorly. The privileged class was given to drunkenness and immorality. They abused the poor and the weak, especially women. They denied them their rights. They even felt ashamed when they begot female children, some of whom were killed in infancy by being buried alive!

It was in that milieu that Prophet Muhammad proclaimed a religion of monotheism and righteousness, condemning all these evil practices, calling for the worship of the one true God and the abandonment of the idols, and for their destruction. As would be expected, he was opposed vehemently and persecuted very severely, as were the few who dared to accept the new religion. Some of them were even killed. However, the traditionally powerful tribal solidarity saved Muhammad's life, as his clan had to defend him.

After thirteen long years of persecution and struggle, Muhammad's enemies conspired to take away his life in a cunning way that would paralyze his clan. Yet he was able to escape to an oasis 280 miles north of Mecca, called Yathrib (Medina), which was more receptive to his teachings because its Arab inhabitants did not have so much stake in the idol worship. After this historic migration, Muhammad had only ten more years to live. Most of this period he had to spend in military struggle defending his small Muslim community from attacks by the Quraysh, the inhabitants of Mecca, and their allies. After eight years of hard military struggle, Mecca succumbed in a bloodless victory and the whole of Arabia was united, for the first time in its history, under the banner of Islam. Though Muhammad died in the year A.D. 632, Islam had such a tremendous vitality that within decades it encompassed the area between the Atlantic in the west and the confines of China in the east.

The Islamic teachings developed during the life of Prophet Muhammad and through him touching all areas of human life. It is important that one bear in mind the totality and comprehensiveness of Islam. It deals with all aspects of human life. It is not merely a spiritual system in the tight sense. It is both spiritual and "secular"; and, in fact, such dichotomy is unthinkable in Islam. The secular and spiritual are one and the same thing, because God's teaching is there, everywhere: in the ritual life, in economic life, in the social life, and in political life.

These Islamic teachings are enshrined in a book which was revealed, as Muslims believe, to Muhammad, word by word. It is believed to be God's own word, not Muhammad's word. Muhammad was only the mouthpiece. These words, or pieces of the whole book, came down to Muhammad over the period of his mission, that is, over about twenty-two or twenty-three years. This book was conveyed by the Prophet to his followers by word of mouth, not as a written document, since Muslims at that time memorized the text—and they knew where each chapter of the book began and where it ended. So initially it was not carried in their hands as a book within two covers, but preserved in their memory. And yet, it was a book with a beginning and an end. This book is called *The Qur'ān,* "the recited scripture."

The Qur'ānic utterances were written down immediately at the time of their revelation by some scribes. Because writing was not yet an advanced tradition with the Arabs at that time, they wrote on rough materials. They did not have paper as yet. These Qur'ānic utterances, however, were collected after Muhammad's death, copied, and then made into a tangible book. It has remained until today uncorrupted and untampered with. The Qur'ān, the Muslim's sacred book, is a recited scripture. It is not basically a written book. When a Muslim learns a part of the Qur'ān, it must be by the oral method, not merely from written symbols, because there is a prescribed way of oral delivery which cannot be adequately learned merely from the written word. No Muslim, strictly speaking, is permitted to recite the Qur'ān without the authority of a teacher who, in turn, must have taught on the authority of an authorized teacher, and so on until the chain of teachers goes up to Muhammad himself. Until recently, it was the custom that one would get an *ijazah,* a sort of license or certificate from one's teacher, saying that the teacher had taught one such and such chapters, or the whole Qur'ān, and that one was authorized by the teacher to recite or read those chapters, or the whole Qur'ān. The teacher would say: I have taught him or her as I learned from my teacher who taught on the authority of his teacher, so and so, and then would continue to mention the series of teachers until Muhammad. So the purpose of the written book is to help the learner, to remind the reader, and to protect against mistakes.

The Qur'ān is very much revered and venerated, but it is supplemented by the records of the deeds and the words of Muhammad himself. And the Qur'ān commanded, "What Muhammad gives should be respected, what he forbids should be avoided"

(59:7). Most of these prophetic records were not written down for some time, because of the fear about the integrity of the Qur'ān and the concern that it should remain pure and unmixed. Therefore, the reports of the deeds and words of Muhammad and his silent approvals remained in the breasts of persons, transmitted from generation to generation by word of mouth for about ninety years. By then, there was no longer anxiety about the text of the Qur'ān getting mixed up with them. The Qur'ānic text became so well-known and familiar and very distinct due to its repeated recitation. Moreover, Qur'ānic copies were ditributed in multitudes. So there was no reason then to fear anything about the integrity of the Qur'ān. At the same time there was a need to record whatever Muslims had memorized of the records of sayings and actions and approvals of Muhammad before the generations that carried those memorized events could vanish. Hence, scholars began to record them in many, many volumes of which, now, about ten great books are standard reference works. This body of the prophetic words and deeds is known as *Ḥadīth.*

So Islam has been preserved and perpetuated particularly through the perpetuation of the Qur'ān. It was and still is memorized by millions in each generation, and is recited from memory as well as from the book. It is broadcast daily over the radio in each Muslim capital and by multitudes of reciters. The solution of any problem that might araise, and the answer to any question, is sought first in the Qur'ān. If not found, a search would be made in the *Ḥadīth.* And this is how Islam has survived until today and how it remains vital and significant to its adherents.

II

For what purpose do we exist on earth? This question, as we all know, has puzzled thinkers and philosophers throughout centuries; but for Muslims, the problem is easily solved. The answer lies in their belief in God's presence and existence and in his inherent attributes. These attributes are perfect, and their perfection requires that they should be operative because inaction is imperfection. For example, God is described as omnipotent. He has overwhelming power and comprehensive knowledge. He is also benevolent and merciful and compassionate and forgiving. How can we imagine that God is forgiving unless we are endowed with the ability to make choices and therefore have the potential to make mistakes? How can we imagine that God is so all-powerful if he had existed all alone and his power was not manifested in his creations? So we exist as a result of God's own attributes.

Yet the Qur'ān also provides another categorical answer to the question, for what purpose do we exist on earth; so also does the *Ḥadīth.* For example, the Qur'ān reads:

> We have not created the heaven and the earth and what is in between them in vain. This is only the thinking of the unbelievers. (38:37)

And again in another verse it reads:

> I have not created the *jinnis* and mankind except that they should worship me. (51:56)

There is also a beautiful *ḥadīth* (when this term refers to a single *ḥadīth* or to a number of them, the word is transliterated with a lower case "*h*") attributed to the Prophet in which he quotes God himself as saying: "I was a hidden treasure. I created the world. Through me they knew me." So, we exist on earth for a purpose; namely, to acknowledge God, to praise him, and to worship him.

The Arabic term for worship is *'ibādah,* and it is used in the second verse I have just quoted from the Qur'ān (51:56). However, it is a difficult term to translate into another language. "Worship" would be a close translation, perhaps, but *'ibādah* also means that created things, by their existence, acknowledge God, his greatness, his perfection, his omnipotence, and his knowledge. In fact, everything in existence, as declared in the Qur'ān, does worship God: "There is nothing except that it praises and serves God, although you may not be aware of the way they do so." (17:40) The inanimate things, the world of plants and the animal kingdoms, by their mere existence, manifest the will of God; they obey his will.

As for humankind, the way of praising God and worshipping him is seen in two ways. A common way which human beings have in common with other existing things is as noted above. But humankind is privileged with something else, with intellectual power, the ability to perceive things, to remember things, to store knowledge, to invent, to draw conclusions, to anticipate, to evaluate, and to be fully aware of things. So humankind worships God also in a special way; namely, a state of deliberate will, consciousness, and awareness. This state of awareness is very important. It is known as *ma'rifah,* "spiritual enlightenment" or "spiritual experience."

When one considers the term "bondage" in the Islamic context, one notes that human beings in Islam are regarded as servants or slaves of God. The word "slave" in Arabic is *'abd,* and to be "'Abd Allah," the slave of God, is regarded a great honor. One might hear this frequently as part of Muslim names. My family name is 'Abd al-Rauf. (Al-Rauf is "the Compassionate One, God.") The Qur'ān (17:1), in the course of relating the story of a night journey supposed to have been experienced by Prophet Muhammad to Jerusalem, refers to Muhammad as "his slave," that is, God's slave. It did not say Muhammad, or use his title as the Messenger or the Prophet, because it was the more honorific thing to be *'Abd* to God.

The term *'Abd* is derived from the same Arabic root as *'ibādah,* the word which denotes worship. Deriving words from a common root is a feature of the Semitic languages, especially Arabic. So, the *'Abd* of God is he who worships God, acknowledges his favors, performs and conforms with the prescribed duties and obligations. One thereby conveys one's acknowledgment of servitude to the Almighty.

So, this is humankind's bondage to God, the Creator and Sustainer: we are his creatures. We are also dependent upon him and upon his benevolence every moment. We worship God as men and women with awareness, with appreciation. This is the meaning of bondage to God in the context of Islam, if we should ever use this term. We exist to fulfill God's perfection, to manifest his greatness, his benevolence, his compassion, and his mercy. At the same time, we bow to him in gratitude. The Sufis would emphasize the type of worship of thinking, reflecting, and meditating, the intense degree of awareness and *'ibādah.* This is the deliberate effort to intensify one's awareness of God and of his favors, to reflect on the power of the Almighty, on his kindness, and on his amazing creations and the secrets in the universe.

Besides all this, Islam has developed certain other ways of pure worship. Most of us are familiar with the phrase "the five pillars of Islam." These include (1) the pronouncement of the *shahādah,* namely, the affirmation to be made by every Muslim: "There is no God but God, and Muhammad is His Messenger." This is regarded to be a very important statement. It is to be repeated as frequently as possible by the worshipper. In fact, it is the tangible expression of the adoption of the religion of Islam. It is the measure whereby an unbeliever becomes a believer and can be accepted by the Muslim community as a member. One can then claim all the rights and privileges that arise from this bond.

Again, Muslims (2) have to perform prayers five times every day. I use the term "perform" because this special type of prayer seems to have no equivalent in other religions. It consists of certain recitations and postures to be assumed by the worshipper, facing the *Ka'bah* in Mecca wherever the worshipper may happen to be. One has to face toward the *Ka'bah* in each prayer. The prayer duty recurs at dawn, at noon, in the mid-afternoon, at sundown, and at night. The prayer is usually performed in congregation and preferably in the mosque.

Again, Muslims (3) have to fast during the day for one full month, Ramadan, the ninth month of the lunar calendar. They abstain from food, drinks, and from direct sensual practices from dawn to sunset each day. Muslims also (4) have to pay alms amounting to roughly 2.5 percent of one's saving and one-tenth or one-twentieth of the land product (one-tenth applies when the agricultural land is irrigated naturally with no efforts and at no cost). It is to be taken from the rich for the benefit of the poor. We also (5) have to perform pilgrimage to Mecca at least once in a lifetime if we have the necessary funds and are in good health. This pilgrimage is the greatest occasion when Muslims of all nations and all colors meet in the same spot. These days, the annual pilgrimage attracts about two million people at a time.[2]

These five pillars of faith constitute what I call the pure type of worship, because all other types of human behavior are also worship in a general sense in the eyes of Islam, although they have also their tangible social, economic, or political aspects. But the five articles just enumerated are pure worship.

So, we exist in order to perform such duties of worship whereby we express our gratitude to Almighty God. In fact, the sense of gratitude is central in Islam. Everything we do has this element of praising God and acknowledging his favors whether it is in the form of action or verbal acknowledgment or prayers or obedience of a divine command. It can also be in a negative sense like fasting or in the form of endurance of hardship like the journey for pilgrimage. In all this, we seek to earn the pleasure of God.

The aim of all our struggle, as Muslims, is to please God and to satisfy our consciences that we have fulfilled our mission. It is not merely to earn happiness on earth. Happines on earth, or rather satisfaction and contentedness, can be attained as a by-product of that final and ultimate goal, namely, to please God by complying with his will and through obedience to his commands. The divine commands constitute a framework of guidance for a Muslim in his or her struggle to fulfill material and spiritual needs. If a Muslim complies with God's will and his commands, he or she will, hopefully, attain contentedness on earth and be worthy of rewards in the hereafter.

Belief in life after death, which is more important than the ephemeral existence on earth, more significant, more lasting, and more meaningful, is one of the five basic beliefs of Islam, which can be put as believing in God, believing in the apostles, believing in the holy books, believing in the angels, and believing in the day of judgment. Thus, Muslims believe in all the past apostles or prophets, beginning with Adam. This unites Islam with all Near Eastern religions in the past. So, those who employ the commonly used phrase "the Judaeo-Christian tradition" are advised to make it "Judaeo-Christian-Muslim tradition," because Islam is very close to these two religions. It acknowledges Moses and Jesus along with the other prophets of the Old Testament. Jesus is a very beloved and venerated prophet among Muslims, who also believe in his mother, the Virgin Mary, and hold her to be the most righteous and virtuous woman (Qur'ān 3:42). Muslims believe in the Torah, the Psalms, and the Gospel of Jesus, though they believe that the scriptures, although containing much wisdom and truth, have not remained intact over time and do not contain the full and undistorted teachings of their prophets.

III

Turning to the term "mercy," which, as defined in the dictionaries, means "compassion and kindness, especially to those who are under one's authority," the divine mercy is the benevolence of God towards all his creatures, especially humankind. The term indicating God's mercy is numerously repeated in the Qur'ān, which consists of one hundred and fourteen chapters of different length. The first chapter is a text of prayers, consisting of seven short verses. Derivatives from the Arabic root for the term indicating God's mercy occur four times in this short chapter, twice in the initial verse, which also initiates all other chapters but one. It reads: "In the name of God, the Compassionate, the Merciful." Muslims recite and seek the blessings of this particular verse almost all the time, especially when they begin anything: reading, writing, eating, drinking, working, and so on. In the Holy Qur'ān, apart from that initial verse, one may count almost two hundred occurrences of the term "mercy," God's mercy.

The *Ḥadīth* also emphasizes the mercy of God. God himself is quoted in the *Ḥadīth* as saying, "My Mercy overcomes my anger." God is also described in the Qur'ān numerous times as forgiving. He is also the avenger, which means that he punishes the culprits, the unbelievers, the sinners, the evil people who disturb the peace of others and encroach upon their rights; yet God's mercy overwhelms his wrath. In fact, God may forgive all sins except those which involve the rights of other human beings.

Let me note a few instances in which God's mercy is manifested, from the Muslim's point of view, in the moral area. God created humankind with a sense of appreciation, of conceiving of moral evaluation, of distinction between good and bad, right and wrong. Humankind is also endowed with the ability of self-criticism and the sense of estimation, along with a sense of self-esteem. Moreover, God proclaimed the right of every human individual to be treated with dignity. Islam does not tolerate the humiliation of an individual. All people are proclaimed, in the Qur'ān, to be equal, having been created from one male and one female. No one has a right to claim preference or a natural privilege over another except through good deeds and righteousness (49:13). Muhammad emphasized this also in many instances. In a *ḥadīth* he is quoted saying: "People are as equal as the teeth of a comb."

Islam is known to be a religion blind to differences based on color or on ethnic origin or wealth. When Islam appeared it immediately restored human rights to all individuals, particularly to women, and it forthwith stopped the bad practice of ill-treatment of female children and put an end to the practice of female infanticide. Islam prescribed a healthy procedure of marriage, put a limitation to the number of women that may be married by one man (before, there was no such limit), organized also the method of separation when it became necessary, stated the mutual rights and obligations arising from the bond of marriage, and gave the individual (male or female) the right to choose his or her partner. If these teachings and principles of marriage have been abused by succeeding generations, such abuse is not the standard principle or teaching. So what we in modern times call "human rights" is essential in the Islamic teachings, not only as a philosophy but also in practice and application.

Furthermore, and this is a very important point in Islam, every human being is born innocent, free from sins and free from any shade of guilt or pollution. We have no concept of humankind being born in a state of sin which can only be cleansed by a sacrament or sacrifice. Every person is held responsible only for his or her own deeds, not for those of any of his or her offspring or of any of his or her ancestors. "Each soul is a pledge for its own deeds" (74:38).

Adam is stated in the Qur'ān to have violated a divine command by eating from the forbidden fruit, but it was his own responsibility. Adam and his wife Eve were not supposed to eat from that fruit, but both were seduced by Satan, the Qur'ān says. It does not say that Adam was seduced by Eve, but it says both were seduced by the evil forces, and then they both were expelled from Paradise. Yet, they both repented and, the Qur'ān says, God accepted their repentance. So they bequeathed no stain of guilt to their offspring by any means. Otherwise, everyone of us would have borne the burden of the guilt of all the sins of our ancestors up to Adam.

The Prophet Muhammad also said "every child is born innocent," which means pure and clean and free from any taint of guilt. When the child grows he or she becomes a responsible agent after attaining the age of majority. So the relationship of the individual to God, from the Islamic perspective, is the relationship of the Master and Creator to his servant.

God has bestowed his benevolence upon his creatures, having created them and endowed them with unlimited potentialities. He favored humankind with intellect and liberty. So persons are not mechanical beings to be turned on without choice or any sort of responsibility or will of their own. God has given to persons power, awareness of their actions, and the ability to make decisions for themselves. That is the privilege of human beings.

Each individual is endowed with forces that are conducive to good deeds, but there are also forces that would seduce and lead to misconduct. So in the struggle between these two sets of forces, the individual is being tested. The one who succeeds in helping the righteous forces overcome the evil forces, the one who can strike in one's life a course of moderation, is the one who is successful. Physically, God's mercy is manifested in the way God created humankind and shaped it. The Qur'ān reads: "We have created man in the best form" (95:4). If we but reflect a little over the harmony of the shape of the face of the human being, how it appears so agreeable! If we just imagine any cut or a swelling in the face, how it will become rather disagreeable, even repulsive! The human face is not only agreeable but also attractive, inspiring fascination and even love. This is a great thing, indeed. And so it is also if we but examine or reflect on the total structure of the human organism. A scientist will see the manifestations of God's power in the subtle structure of the human body and the harmony between the works and functions of the various parts and its organs. If we move from the physical to the intellectual aspect of the human organism, we become more amazed when we learn of the work of our brains, all of which are again great manifestations of God's mercy. So the divine mercy is manifested in both areas, the moral, intellectual area and the physiological area of the human life.

Moreover, we are created, as physical beings, with certain basic needs inherent in our nature, such as the need for air, for water, for food, the need for shelter, the need for clothing. There are also acquired and derived needs which we develop as we grow, and they become necessities, although originally they were not so. However, according to our religion, we are to satisfy our needs in moderation, and not to deny their call for satisfaction. For us Muslims, struggle for the means to satisfy these needs is also "worship" (*'ibādah*), as it is compliance with the divine injunctions.

We are also created with some spiritual needs, although we do not believe in a dichotomy of spiritualism and materialism. We do not even care much to define the term "spirit." The Prophet Muhammad was once asked about this concept. The Qur'ān told him, "They ask you about the spirit. Tell them it is a matter which belongs to God, and you are given only very little knowledge" (17:85). This is the attitude of Islam.

Moreover, the Holy Qur'ān reminds us frequently of God's mercy and benevolence as manifested in the ecological world. The Qur'ān repeatedly reminds us how God has created all that is in the earth and in the heavens and what is in between them for the benefit of humankind and that he made these things subservient to human beings, but they must be respected, not abused or wasted. Human beings are not to be subservient to anything except God, not even to any member of humanity. The individual is only subservient to Almighty God. He or she is the servant and slave to God, not to any mortal nor to anything else. Humankind is required to use and modify all that exists on earth for its benefit, to examine and to seek to discover the concealed potentials endowed in all the created things for the benefit of humanity. And in this way the individual will be considered as worshipping Almighty God. In pursuing his or her sustenance and in consuming it, he or she should strike a line of moderation, always conscious of the watching eye of God the Almighty. So long as one seeks to comply, in anything that one does, with God's will and commands, one is regarded as being engaged in an act of worship.

An important connotation of the term "Islam" is *submission* to God's will and commands. One has to accept the way one is, not to resent it and to say, for example, "Why am I a man and not a woman?" or vice versa, "Why am I short?", "Why am I white and not black?", "Why am I created?" Moreover, one is to obey God's commands and to comply with his teachings.

We are created with needs, and Islam emphasizes that we should satisfy these needs in moderation. Marriage, for example, is recommended very strongly in Islam. Celibacy is frowned upon. We do not have a religious class of hermits who would run away from life, although in the third and fourth centuries of Islam such tendencies began to grow with some Muslims as a result of certain historical vicissitudes. Disparity and failure caused some to seek solace in retirement in ascetic life. And under Indian influence, these tendencies developed into the way of Sufism in which a degree of deprivation is exercised for the attainment of spiritual elevation. This is not quite the orthodox way of Islam. It was not the practice of the Prophet Muhammad, who is regarded as the model for Muslims.

We have a famous saying: we do not eat until we feel hungry, and when we eat, we do not fill our stomach. The Prophet married. He had children, and he ate in moderation. So we do not see in the proper satisfaction of physical needs any violation of reasonableness. In seeking to satisfy these needs, we acknowledge in gratitude the favors of God in providing us with the means of satisfying these needs. We do not regard this to be in any way a hindrance to the spiritual elevation of the individual. Of course we have fasting, which is a physical deprivation, but it is only a temporary abstention, only during the daytime for one month each year. To us, it is quite a tolerable experience, of social and spiritual benefit. When we are bitten by hunger, it reminds us of the great abundance of the many good things provided by God and makes us aware of the plight of the poor. It is a teaching in self-control.

God's mercy is also manifested in his promise to bless the human soul with mercy and forgiveness on the day of judgment, even to those who have been sinners. The Qur'ān says: "Tell my servants, those who have been extravagant against their own interests, despair not of the mercy of the Almighty God. God, indeed, forgives all sins. He is, indeed, the Merciful and the Forgiving" (39:53). In a beautiful *ḥadīth,* Muhammad speaks on behalf of God, promising forgiveness for those who repent in these words: "If my servant comes to me the length of a span, I would go to him the length of his arm. If he comes walking to me, I will go running to him." Again, the Qur'ān states that while an evil deed would be penalized only by an equal punishment, a good deed will be rewarded tenfold (6:160).

So a Muslim feels protected under the umbrella of God's benevolence and anticipates God's mercy, although he should not take advantage of this and depend upon it. One has to struggle to improve one's soul and to comply with the will of God in one's life.

IV

Now the question arises: how can this concept of God's benevolence, compassion, and mercy be consistent with the misfortunes suffered by many people?

A believing Muslim will agree that in order to appreciate good things, on occasion one has to suffer disagreeable experiences. One cannot appreciate health unless one occasionally suffers illness. There is a famous statement in Arabic which says, "Good health is a crown on the head of those who are healthy, but only those who are sick appreciate it." So we tend to take things for granted. When things are normal, many of us tend to forget God, to be indifferent to his favors and even fail in our duties. Without poverty, one cannot appreciate wealth. Without illness, one cannot appreciate good health. Good health and the availability of the means of the satisfaction of our needs is the normal situation. Suffering, which is meant as a test, serves as a reminder of the value, the great value, of the availability of the bounties of God. On the other hand, as the Qur'ān and the *Ḥadīth* explain, even those closest to God, his noble messengers, including Jesus and Muhammad, are not excepted from these exceptional sufferings. These sufferings are meant as a test of the degree of the faith and of how patient and forbearing the person will be. And this, in fact, will raise the individual in his or her level of relationship with God himself. So sufferings are meaningful. They are not in vain. They are not inconsistent with God's mercy. We cannot really appreciate the divine mercy without these exceptional experiences.[3]

Another point that might arise from the context of the current political situation in the Muslim world is the portrayal of Islam as a harsh, militant religion. How can this be consistent with the concept of God's mercy and his teaching that a believer must also be merciful to his or her fellow human beings, as emphasized particularly in the *Ḥadīth* when it says "God only bestows his mercy upon those who are merciful to others"? Those who are hard on others are not worthy of enjoying the divine mercy. How has it come to be that Islam now seems to be harsh, to be violent, and to be militant? I would like to emphasize that Islam is not militant.

The term "Islam" is derived from an Arabic linguistic root which means "peace," and Islam teaches and promotes peace. It is against violence, but it does not tolerate humiliation. Because Islam regards all human beings as equal, no one is entitled to take away the freedom of others or to humiliate them. Yet Islam does not teach one to turn the other cheek to the person who has already struck one on one cheek. It teaches that if one is attacked, but only when one is attacked, one has the right to defend oneself. It teaches that if one is abused or hurt, one has the right to avenge oneself with an equal hurt, but not more. And then it says it is much better if one should forgive. And forgiveness is a virtue of those who are endowed with a great degree of morality and determination. (See Qur'ān 16:126, 42:40–43.) So Islam is not militant. We have to realize that what is happening today, with the so-called "resurgent Islam," is the result of complex factors which together have caused this sort of formation, the universal reawakening of Muslims to the role that must be played by their religion in the modern age. If there is an element of militancy accompanying this reawakening, it is a reaction to difficult experiences of injustices suffered in the past and still perpetrated in certain areas.[4]

It should be noted that elite groups in each Muslim country were patronized and were assisted in the formation of their own political parties on the European model, in order to protect Western interests, after the independence of the Muslim countries. The masses were ignored. Yet as a result of modernization and widespread education, these masses have become literate, educated, and vocal. Their voice was not heard in the past, but now they can speak for themselves and for the other members of the society. So, if there is an element of militancy perceived in certain groups, it is a reaction to these developments. Otherwise, militancy is not a feature of Islam. Islam is for peace and understanding, while not tolerating humiliation.

Strictly speaking, we do not have religious leaders or nonreligious leaders. We are all the same. This being the case, some of us may be more knowledgeable about religion than others, but we are equally responsible for applying the teachings of the Qur'ān. One of these teachings is that we are to resist injustice and to be courageous enough to confront the unjust ruler and to seek to reform him or her. To do so is regarded to be very meritorious. "There is nothing," Muhammad says, "more meritorious than saying the word of truth in front of a harsh ruler." We also have very inspiring records of early persons of piety who stood firm against ruthless rulers. They suffered, even some were beheaded as a result of their daring criticism. And the Prophet Muhammad says, "Whoever becomes aware of something bad, something evil, he should correct it by hand," that is, using physical means. "If he cannot do so, let him do it by tongue. But if he still cannot do so, he should feel the pain deeply at heart," which means to turn away from the evil-doer and give him the silent sign of disapproval, resisting mentally the evil.

God's relation to humankind is that of a Master, a Creator to his created being, his intellectual servant and worshipper. God is the Master and we are the *'ibād,* namely, the servants and worshippers of God. God loves those who are righteous, as the Qur'ān says. He does not love the unbelievers. Love here is used in the sense of approval and reward. It does not mean a sort of sentimental or emotional feeling because human emotions and the concept of sentiment cannot apply to God. These feelings are transitory, and thus are unbecoming to the Eternal God. God is eternal and His attributes are eternal. So when the Qur'ān uses the term "love," as in the statements "God does not love the unbelievers," "God does not love the aggressors or the unjust," and "God loves the good-doers," it means that He approves, accepts, appreciates, and rewards the acts of righteousness and warns against and punishes the acts of the unjust.[5] In Islam, God is viewed with awe and an absorbing feeling of gratitude.

Islam is involved with a great deal of practicality and concreteness. Islam tells its adherents not only how to pray and how to worship, but also how and what to eat, how to walk, how to talk, how to dress, how to greet each other, how to get married, how to conduct business transactions, and so on and so forth. Hence it is often said that Islam is a practical way of life.

This practical life is based upon the Qur'ān. When one reflects upon God speaking the Qur'ān, there arises the feeling of an overwhelming power, the source of benevolence and mercy, speaking to devoted creatures who adore him and appreciate the guiding light descending upon them. It is also a feeling of gratitude and awe and awareness of self-limitation and weakness in the face of the immense magnitude of deep gratitude due to the Beneficent Creator.

Notes

[1] I feel deeply grateful to Professor Carter for the generous invitation, affording me the opportunity of meeting, enjoying, and learning from the assembled scholars. I am equally grateful to his predecessor, Dr. Kenneth Morgan, who very graciously invited me to Colgate at least twice before. It is always a pleasure to come to this serene and inspiring place, to relax, and to enjoy the company of such understanding, learned people.

[2] For more details, see my article "Pilgrimage to Mecca" in *National Geographic,* Vol. 154, No. 5, November 1978.

[3] A question might arise, however, with regard to some features of Islamic teachings, especially pertaining to the punishment applied upon commission of certain violations. This has been featured often in the Western press. Islam teaches that a murderer should be punished by

death. It teaches also that a thief should have his hand severed. It teaches also that a drunkard should be punished. An adulterer should also receive his or her punishment. Much criticism has been made in the news media of the West about the harshness of these punishments—they have been described as manifestations of barbarism.

Such accusations are only manifestations of lack of knowledge and understanding about the wisdom of the law of Islam pertaining to the concept of punishment. These prescribed punishments are really very few, and represent a tiny part of the total spectrum of the teachings of Islam. We should not just look upon them as the totality of Islam, ignoring its ritual and moral and spiritual guidance. Moreover, administering these punishments is dependent upon the prior fulfilment of certain religiously required conditions which, in most cases, are difficult to be realized.

Life is very valuable. No one can take it away except the One who gave it. A mortal cannot encroach upon the life or the rights of another. Murdering is a very severe violation of the rights of the victim and the victim's dependents. Yet, Islam does not say that a murderer must be automatically killed. While Islam gives the state the right to sentence the murderer to death, the family of the victim has the right to forgive the culprit. If they demand the state to have that sentence applied, it is their right, but if for any reason they are willing to forgive, then the state is not obliged to apply the sentence unless it thinks it is in the best interest of society. The Qur'ān says: "In applying capital punishment, you will spare life" (2:179). When the would-be murderer knows for sure that he or she will be killed as a punishment for his or her violation, he or she is likely to hesitate to carry out the contemplated crime.

This question of capital punishment has been controversial in Western society. There are many people in favor of capital punishment, there are many others against it. Those who are against it magnify the aura of the situation of taking away the life of the criminal, but they tend to forget how much more horrible was the scene of the original murder itself. Unfortunately, these violations take place without the surrounding society being aware of what is happening. They are committed away from the eye of the television camera and from the eyes of the people. If a camera could capture the original scene, it would be found more disgusting and as horrifying. Just imagine the scene of a person raping and murdering a helpless girl in the middle of the night, thus violating her honor, and then taking away her life! The leniency of the law in my opinion has led to a great degree of insecurity and to the increase of street crimes. Therefore, the exaggerated criticism of Islam on the grounds of its law of capital punishment ignores its wisdom and the fact that its application depends upon the demand of the family of the victim. It is thus a social remedy and is meant to compensate the surviving victims. It reduces tension in society and relieves the relatives of the victim from harboring grave ill-feelings against the family of the aggressor, especially in a closed society where each person knows the others. If the person who committed murder is left free in the streets, tension will flare into communal violence.

Removing the hand of a thief is a punishment which is applied only under certain conditions, and it is to be lifted in hard economic conditions. It applies in ordinary circumstances and it serves as a deterrent to encroaching upon the property of others. In Saudi Arabia, where the Islamic law applies, one can leave one's car open with one's briefcase full of cash. No one would dare to touch it, and one does not dream at all that anyone would attempt to enter the car or steal the money. To this day one can walk in the streets of Cairo or of any other Muslim capital in the middle of the night in darkness without any fear. Severing the hand of a thief, as a formal punishment, has been rare as have been the occurrences of theft in the context of the prevailing security. This punishment is, therefore, very rarely applied. For example, in Saudi Arabia, perhaps it occurs only once every four or five years.

Compare this to what is happening in the streets of America. How many souls are murdered insensibly every day? Go to any big city, read the local newspaper, listen to the local news; it is about the same: so many cases of rape, so many cases of murder and mugging. If one really can purchase the security of society, the survival of the countless innocent souls, I think if one pays as a price the cutting off of the hand of one culprit every so many years, in my opinion, it is certainly worth it. This practice is not barbaric. It is more barbaric to tolerate these potential criminals who roam in the streets to frighten innocent people, threatening their lives and encroaching upon their property.

[4] One could quote many cases. Take, for example, the experience suffered in Egypt at the hands of the British occupation forces on the Day of Dinshway. A few British soldiers were shooting birds, and a stray bullet killed a person from Dinshway village. The British group just laughed. They did not care. So the simple villagers were deeply offended. Somehow, they beat one or two of the British group. The British authorities set up a court in the same village. The accused were surrounded, summarily tried, found guilty, and then mercilessly hanged on the spot in front of the other villagers, including their own relatives, their parents, wives, and children! There have been many other cases of crude torture, humiliation, and injustices in all parts under the colonial rule, and later under the rule of stooges loyal to their Western masters. These experiences perhaps inspired an element of militancy in some cases. So, we have to understand that what is happening today is a reaction to these long and many hard experiences.

[5] Again, human love is of different categories. There is sexual love, which is marked by a powerful mutual pull between the parties and

has an element of jealousy and fear; there is parental love, which is mixed with compassion; and there is filial love, which is mixed with awe and veneration and might very well be mixed with fear and resentment. So the word "love" in the English usage does not seem to be in keeping with the great, immeasurable degree of veneration due to Almighty God. Therefore, I cannot honestly use that word "love" in the human sense to indicate the relationship between God and his creature in the context of Islam. When we apply the word to God, it means his approval, his reward, or his mercy. So "God loves me" means "he loves my work, he accepts it, he agrees with it." When he does not like a person, it means that he disagrees with what that person has done, and he might punish that person because of it.

15

Grace in the Greek Orthodox Church

John Efstratios Rexine

An old and highly significant strand of the Christian tradition, a strand not well known by most in North America, is the Greek Orthodox Church. Professor Rexine, speaking from within this tradition, enables one to understand the context in which the testimony of this distinguished witness affirms that humanity becomes fully human in communion with God.

I

In the United States, the Greek Orthodox Church has achieved the status of the third largest Christian body in the country. Even though it is a young church in the United States, it is an old church as far as Christianity is concerned—indeed, it considers itself the Mother Church of Christianity. In this country the Greek Orthodox Church until recently has been an immigrant church in which there were language barriers; that is to say, the liturgy, the services, the sermons, and so on have been, and in some cases still are being, conducted in Greek or in Church Slavonic or in Arabic. Of course, one should probably indicate at the very start that it is the Church of Eastern Christendom, of Eastern Christianity, the largest bloc of which were the Russian Orthodox in the Soviet Union and also those living in a good part of the Balkans in countries like Yugoslavia, Rumania, and Bulgaria. It is also the Church to a great many Arab-speaking Christians in the Near East, for instance, the Coptic Orthodox, the so-called Non-Chalcedonian Orthodox of Egypt, who number in the millions. It also was and is the religion of the Ethiopians; Ethiopia, which had its own Non-Chalcedonian patriarch, had the first African Christian Church, once one of the major churches of Orthodox Christianity. There is even a significant Orthodox presence in India. So, the Orthodox Church, even though it is represented by what one might describe as ethnic manifestations in different areas, whether they be Arabic, Russian, Serbian, Bulgarian, Albanian, Greek, Lebanese, or Egyptian, considers itself to be the Mother Church of Christianity, considers itself to be the Una-Sancta, the Church of Undivided Christendom, the Church of the only synods or councils that it believes were truly ecumenical; that is to say, the Church of the first seven ecumenical councils. It believes that no ecumenical councils, no councils that were truly ecumenical, have been held since that seventh in A.D. 787.

We use these terms "Eastern Orthodox" or "Greek Orthodox" because the origins of Christianity were in the Greek East. One has to go back to the conquests of Alexander the Great. The language of the Eastern world was Greek from the Balkans through the northern and eastern parts of Africa through the Near East to the borders of India and China. The Greek language as it was spoken by non-Greeks became known as the *koine* or the common language. It is the language of the New Testament, and so the Greeks especially have a special concern for the preservation of that language, in some ways as the Arabs do for Arabic in the Qur'ān. But Greek represents more than simply the language in which the New Testament was written. It represents the language of the times of the whole of the Near East. It represents the language of communication, as one can note by the presence of the *Septuagint,* a Greek translation of the Hebrew Bible or the Old Testament, because the Jews of this period knew Greek better than they knew Hebrew or else they did not know Hebrew at all. So there is a whole cultural tradition involved when one thinks of the term "Greek," which refers to the fact that the whole of the Christian faith was expressed, initially, essentially in the Greek language. Certainly this is true of most of the early Church Fathers. It is true even beyond the period of the early Church Fathers, that is, through the period of the Byzantine Empire, or the Medieval Greek Empire, from Constantine the Great in A.D. 325 until the fall of Constantinople to the Turks in 1453.

It is a Byzantine Christian empire that had a longer continuous tradition than any other Christian political entity in the world; so the word "Byzantine," after the original name of Constantinople—Byzantium—reflects something, too, of the center of this Eastern Christianity. Constantinople, which was founded by Constantine the Great, is still viewed by the Orthodox as the center of Eastern Christianity, as it were, even though it is now in an essentially Muslim country, even though it never has had the kind of power of, let us say, the pope in the West. There have been Patriarchs of Constantinople, and there have been other Patriarchs, those of Antioch, of Jerusalem, of Alexandria in the East, and the great Patriarch of the West, still recognized as such by the Eastern Orthodox Church, the pope of Rome.

It was a period, initially, in which the Church was one, in which there was an undivided Christianity, in which there were cultural differences between "East" and "West." The differences with Rome resulted in a separation, conventionally assigned to the year 1054, which, even though at that point merely formal, became almost complete with the passage of time because, in a real sense, Rome faced West culturally and Constantinople faced East. Constantinople and the Byzantine empire also had to deal with an immense historical problem: the various attacks upon its integrity from the East and particularly from the Muslims, who eventually did manage to rule over enormous portions of what had been the Eastern Christian Empire.

Administratively, the Orthodox Church is generally organized along ethnic lines, with the Greek Church of Constantinople, which claims as its founder the Apostle Andrew, the Ecumenical Patriarch of Constantinople as it were, holding the honorary position of *primus inter pares,* first among equals. The ancient patriarchates of Alexandria, Antioch, and Jerusalem were also founded by apostles of Christ. The Church of Cyprus also claimed its founding by an apostle. National churches include: the Church of Russia, established in 988; the Church of Greece, which is fairly recent, dating from about 1850; the Church of Bulgaria, 1872; Yugoslavia, 1920; and Rumania, from 1885. There are strong Orthodox Churches in Finland and in Czechoslovakia and a strong Orthodox contingency in Western Europe, in Africa, the Americas, and Australia. One of the strongest Orthodox presences in Africa, one little known and unheralded, is the Orthodox Church in Uganda, which now has its own native black bishops and hierarchy and is supported by the patriarchate of Alexandria, Egypt, and the Church of Cyprus. Athens has also provided free theological training for these bishops.

So the Church is now ecumenical (*oikoumene:* "throughout the inhabited world," "the entire inhabited world") in the true sense of the word. More recent patriarchates, in the sense that they have their own head and govern themselves, are those with large constituencies of Orthodox such as in Russia (conservative estimates indicate seventy-five million practicing Orthodox Christians there). In Yugoslavia, there is a strong Orthodox Church in Serbia; in fact, a Patriarch of that Church has been one of the presidents of the World Council of Churches. Rumania, despite its Roman name, has a predominantly Orthodox population, and so has Bulgaria.

There are in the Orthodox Church what are known as *autocephalous churches.* This means that they "have their own heads," indicating that the church is not a patriarchate but is entirely independent and self-governing with a right to appoint its own head and to conduct its own relations with other churches. Such autocephalous churches are the Church of Cyprus, the Church of Greece, the Church of Poland (there is an Orthodox Church in Poland), the Church of Georgia (that is, in the Russian Caucasus). There are also *autonomous churches,* the ones in which there is a dependence on a patriarchate even though the church governs itself and conducts its own internal affairs. An example of this is the Greek Orthodox Church of America, which is an autonomous church but is dependent on the Patriarchate of Constantinople. In the autonomous churches, the head of the autonomous church is ordained by the Mother Church. For instance, one of the complaints of the Greek Orthodox Church in America, at least in some quarters, is that it cannot be directly represented in the World Council of Churches. It is represented through the Patriarchate of Constantinople, so that if Constantinople appoints a bishop or layman, that person goes as a representative of the Mother Church, not as the representative of the autonomous church.

There is also a very fascinating autonomous archbishopric on Mount Sinai, whose head happens also to be the Abbott of the Monastery of Saint Catherine. (Mount Sinai, previously in Arabic Muslim hands, is now in Israeli hands.) Saint Catherine's is one of the most magnificent examples of medieval Eastern Orthodox monasteries still in existence. It is interesting, too, because it is the one monastery which apparently escaped the iconoclastic movement in medieval times. There are preserved there, in the desert, not only icons nowhere else preserved but also recently discovered manuscripts of the Bible, found at Saint Catherine's and still being studied. There are other autonomous churches like those of Finland and Czechoslovakia. There is also a category of *exarchate* (like the Archbishop of the Americas who has been declared an exarch) which is dependent on the Patriarchate of Constantinople.

Theologically, the Greek Orthodox Church, the Eastern Orthodox Church, recognizes only one head, and that is Christ. No bishop and no priest is considered infallible. Only the Church met in ecumenical synod and guided by the Holy Spirit is believed to be infallible. In the Orthodox Church all bishops, whether they are called archbishops or patriarchs, are all equal with the Ecumenical Patriarch of Constantinople, considered the first among equals. Throughout the whole history of Christendom, the Orthodox Church presents a spectacle of the most venerable antiquity and often of an impressive continuity of life which is second to none in Christianity: its territory has embraced the land where Christ himself was born, lived, and died; it includes bishoprics in cities the names of which are familiar words in the New Testament; it has, by the way, even preserved the titles of these ancient bishoprics, much to the annoyance of many Muslims (at least in the case of Turkey), because most of these are now in non-Christian hands. The Church believes itself to be the Church of undivided Christianity, and it also believes that an eventual reunion of all churches would take place if all of Christianity would return to the undefiled faith of the undivided church. For practical purposes, this would mean the faith represented by the first seven ecumenical councils.

The seven ecumenical councils (or *synods,* to use the Greek word) were all important in the formative stages of the history of the Christian Church. The first ecumenical council convened at Nicaea, the modern day Isnik, in A.D. 325, with 318 representatives responding to a call by the Emperor Constantine to deal with the challenge of Arius and Arianism. Arius taught that Christ was created by God the Father. This would make Christ the creature of the Father and limit him chronologically and make him inferior to the Father. Athanasius the Great, who belonged to the Alexandrian Church and who was considered the great defender of the Orthodox faith, proclaimed as fact what became the substance of the second article of the Nicene-Constantinopolitan Creed: that Christ is the only-begotten son of God, consubstantial (*homoousios*) with the Father. (All of this, by the way, was written in Greek.) It was this first ecumenical synod that was responsible for formulating the first seven articles of the Nicene Creed.

The second ecumenical council was held at Constantinople and was also summoned by the emperor. In A.D. 381, attempts to change the *homoousios* of the first synod were rejected. Patriarch Macedonius, who taught that the Holy Spirit was a creature of the Son, was condemned, and the council proclaimed that the Holy Spirit proceeds from the Father and is sent by the Son. This is the synod that also wrote the final five articles of the Nicene-Constantinopolitan Creed. It is interesting to note here that a patriarch was condemned; in the Orthodox Church, even a patriarch can make mistakes and hence is not infallible.

The third ecumenical synod was assembled at Ephesus in A.D. 431. The heresies of Apollinarianism and Nestorianism were the chief reasons for this council. Apollinarianism denied human rationality to the Incarnate Logos, while Nestorianism made the error of drawing such a sharp distinction between the two natures of Christ, the human and the divine, that it bestowed the name *Christotokos* to Mary, that is, the "Mother of Christ," the man, and not *Theotokos*, "Mother of God." In the Orthodox circles, the term *Theotokos* is used of the Virgin Mary. Now this council at Ephesus rejected both Apollinarianism and Nestorianism, declaring that Christ is God and man with two natures, divine and human, without distinction and without separation.

The fourth synod was summoned by the Empress Pulcheria at Chalcedon in A.D. 451. It was occasioned by the heresy of Monophysitism. (*Monos* and *physis* are derived from two Greek words meaning, respectively, "one" and "nature.") This was a heresy which tried to argue that the divine nature of Christ so absorbed the human nature that both combined to form essentially one nature—*monophysis.* The fourth synod reconfirmed that Christ has two natures which are united in the person of the Logos without confusion and without change. The Orthodox Churches we are discussing, which are Chalcedonian in faith, are also called Eastern

Orthodox; those that do not accept Chalcedon, that is, the position affirmed at the fourth synod, are frequently referred to as Oriental Orthodox or as non-Chalcedonian.[1]

The fifth ecumenical council was convoked at Constantinople in A.D. 533 by the Emperor Justinian, under whose administration the greatest of the Eastern Orthodox cathedrals, Hagia Sophia, was built. This was the second synod to meet in the capital city of Constantinople, and it reaffirmed the decision of the two preceding synods on the two natures of Christ, thus meeting the criticism and opposition of heretical groups such as the Armenians, the Abyssinians, and the Jacobites. It also condemned the errors of Origen (a third-century theologian) and others.

The sixth ecumenical council was the third to be convoked in Constantinople, this time in A.D. 680. In an attempt to conciliate the Monophysites, there was a formula circulated to the effect that though Christ had two natures, one human and one divine, he had but one will. These people were called *monotheletes* because they believed Christ had one will (*mono theletes*), hence, Monotheletism. This heresy of Monotheletism was rejected and condemned by the sixth ecumenical synod, which stipulated that Christ had divine and human activities and wills that are not in opposition to each other but, of course, the divine will is superior to the human will.

And finally, the Empress Irene convened the seventh ecumenical synod at Nicaea in A.D. 787. This was preceded by a long, complicated history and struggle between the Iconoclasts ("image breakers") and the Iconodules ("image servants"). The icon is one of the characteristic features which one sees in an Orthodox church, no matter where the church is. And it was the seventh ecumenical synod that decided that veneration of Holy Icons is allowed as a token of honor but not of worship. Icons are not worshipped but are accorded respect; worship is only accorded to God, and so the theology of icons, which is a subject in and of itself, became one of the basic characteristics of the Orthodox Church.

So the Orthodox Church looks upon itself as the Church that has preserved, so to speak, and worked out the theology of seven ecumenical councils or synods, together with its development through the so-called Eastern Church Fathers. Westerners often look upon the Orthodox Church as static. The Orthodox do not believe their Church to be static but rather to be conservative of early Christianity. The word "Orthodox" itself means "right-believing." The Orthodox believe that they are the preservers of Christian truth and that the truth remains the same whether the Orthodox be Greeks, Slavs, Arabs, or others. The Orthodox are united by a unity of faith and tradition manifested in the Divine Liturgy and especially in the sacrament of the Eucharist. The Orthodox Church belongs to that group of what many historians simply call the Liturgical Churches. Its theology is just as much revealed in its liturgy as it is in the books that are written about its theology.[2] And the Church views itself as apostolic because it believes in the unity of the Church in its historical continuity.[3]

II

In Byzantine theology human nature is not considered autonomous but as destined to share divine life which has been made accessible in God. In this view, a human being's role in the created world can be fulfilled only when the human being preserves the image of God which was part of his or her humanity from the very beginning. According to most of the Greek Fathers, the terms "image" and "likeness" do not mean exactly the same thing. The expression "according to the image," wrote John of Damascus, "indicates rationality and freedom, while the expression 'according to the likeness' indicates assimilation to God through virtue." The image or, to use the Greek term, "icon" of God signifies the human being's free will, reason, sense of moral responsibility—everything, in short, which marks out a human being from the animal creation and makes that being a person. But the image means more than that. It means that we are God's offspring: "In him we live and move and have our being" (Acts 17:28); we are God's kin. It means that between us and God there is a point of contact, an essential similarity. The gulf between the creature and the Creator is not impassable, but because we are in God's image, we can "know" God and have communion with God.

Now if we make proper use of the faculty for communion with God, then we will become like God, we will acquire the divine likeness. In the words of John of Damascus, "we will be assimilated to God through virtue." To acquire the likeness is to be deified. The relevant Greek term is *theosis,* which is often translated, for lack of a better word, by the words "deification" or "divinization." So to acquire the likeness of God is to be "deified." It is to become a second god, god by grace—"god" with a small "g," and here the Church Fathers use a quotation from Psalms 81:6: "I said you are a god and all of you sons of the most high." Thus, the image denotes the powers with which every human being is endowed by God from the first moment of that being's existence; the likeness is not an endowment, it is not an endowment which one possesses from the start but a goal at which one must aim, something which one can acquire only by degrees. However sinful we may be, we never lose the image of God, but the likeness we may attain to by the grace of God depends on our moral choice, upon our virtue, and so God's likeness in us can be destroyed by sin.

Humankind at its first creation was perfect, not so much in the actual as in the potential sense. Endowed with the image from the start, we were called to acquire the likeness by our own efforts, assisted, of course, by the grace of God. Adam, the first man, began in a state of innocence and simplicity. He was a child not yet having his understanding perfected, wrote Irenaeus (second century). It was necessary, Irenaeus said, that he should grow and so come to his perfection. God set Adam on the right path, but Adam had, in front of him, a long road to traverse in order to reach his final goal. Now by this picture of Adam before the fall, one is reminded of those old colonial textbooks, "In Adam's fall we sinned all." This is not the Greek Orthodox view. According to the Western view, which is generally associated with Saint Augustine, humankind in paradise was endowed from the start with all possible wisdom and knowledge; man and woman were a realized, and in no sense merely a potential, perfection. Irenaeus, representing the Orthodox point of view, clearly fits more easily with modern theories of evolution than does the conception of Augustine. The West has often associated the image of God with the human intellect. While many Orthodox have done the same, many others would say that since the person is a unified whole, the image of God embraces the entire person, body as well as soul. When God is said to have made man according to his image, wrote Saint Gregory Palamas in the fourteenth century, the generic word "man" is meant to signify neither the soul by itself nor the body by itself but the two together. The fact that man has a body, argued Gregory, makes him not lower but higher than the angels. True, the angels are pure spirit, whereas human nature is mixed, material as well as intellectual; but this means that human nature is more complete than angelic nature and is endowed with richer potentialities.

In the Orthodox view, the human being is a microcosm, a bridge and a point of meeting for the whole of God's creation. Orthodox religious thought stresses the image of God in humanity. One is a living theology and because one is God's icon, one can find God by looking within one's own heart, by returning to one's own inner self. "The kingdom of God is within you" (Luke 17:21). "Know yourselves," said a desert monk of the fourth century, Anthony of Egypt. "He who knows himself, knows God." "If you are pure," wrote Saint Isaac the Syrian (late seventh century), "Heaven is within you. Within yourself you will see the angels and the Lord of the angels." Of Saint Pachomius, it was reported that in the purity of his heart he saw the invisible God as in a mirror. Because human beings are icons of God, every member of the human race, according to the Orthodox position, even the most sinful member, is infinitely precious in God's sight. "When you see your brother," said Clement of Alexandria (third century), "you see God." And another Father taught, "After God we must count all men as God himself." And still another Father has said, "The best icon of God is man." This respect for every human being, no matter how sinful, is visibly expressed in the Orthodox worship when the priest, in an Orthodox church, censes not only the icons but the members of the congregation, in this way symbolizing and actually saluting the image of God in each person.

Orthodox Christians have acknowledged that conceptual language is incapable of expressing the whole truth and that the human mind is unable to attain the essence of God. This is what Father John Meyendorff calls "antinomy," "theological antinomy," what we might otherwise call a paradox. God has revealed himself in Christ Jesus, and the knowledge of his truth is essential to salvation. But God is also above human intellect and cannot be fully expressed in human terms. In Eastern Christianity the Eucharistic liturgy is identified with the reality of the Church itself, for it manifests both the humiliation of God in assuming mortal flesh and the mysterious presence among men of the eschatological kingdom.

The liturgy is the powerful expression of unity and faith and sacramental life. Perhaps contrary to the view of the theologian that one might find in the Western tradition, the true theologian sees and experiences the content of theology. This experience is not merely intellectual but spiritual—an experience placing the whole person, intellect, emotions, even senses, in contact with the divine existence. In Jesus Christ is the fullness of truth revealed once and for all. Men and women, in their God-given freedom, can experience this truth in various degrees and forms, but no human language is adequate to express truth itself, nor can words exhaust it. Neither scriptures nor the Church's magesterium nor even the saints become the only sources of theology. God can be experienced through means other than intellectual knowledge because there is an opening of God, of his existence outside of his own nature, of his actions or energies through which he voluntarily reveals himself to men and women, and also because there is a peculiar property of men and women which allows them to reach outside of the created order, beyond the level of the created.

The Byzantine theologian, the Orthodox theologian, talks about the energies (*energeiai*) of God, that is, the way in which God manifests himself. The meeting of God's love and energy and of one's capability of transcending oneself is what makes that kind of encounter possible. It is a contemplation greater than knowledge, to which the Fathers refer as the eyes of faith, the spirit, or eventually deification. Very often the Byzantine Orthodox Church has been described as mystical.

Western Christological thought has been dominated perhaps by the Anselmian idea of redemption through satisfaction. The idea that Jesus offered to the Father a perfect and sufficient sacrifice, propitiatory for the sins of humankind, has been the center of Western Christological speculation. If one keeps in mind the Greek Patristic notion that the true nature of humanity means life in God realized once and for all through the Holy Spirit in the hypostatic union of the man Jesus with the Logos, and made accessible to all human beings through the same Holy Spirit in the humanity of Christ in his body, the Church, Christology acquires a new and universal dimension.

Maximus the Confessor (A.D. 580–662), the real father of Byzantine Orthodox theology, has written a great deal on this. Prior to him, Gregory of Nyssa (fourth century) had expressed the view that human freedom does not consist in autonomous life but in the situation which is truly natural to human communion with God. When one is isolated from God, one finds oneself enslaved to one's passions, to oneself, and ultimately to Satan. For Maximus the

Confessor, when one follows one's natural will, which presupposes life in God, and God's cooperation and communion, one is truly free. But human beings possess also another potential determined not by nature but by each human person (or *hypostasis*), and that is the freedom of choice (*gnome*), involving the freedom to revolt against nature and, therefore, the freedom to destroy oneself. This personal freedom was used by Adam and Eve and, after the Fall, resulted in separation from true knowledge and from all reassurance secured by that natural existence. But in Christ, according to Byzantine Orthodox theology, human nature is united with the hypostasis of the Logos and while remaining fully itself is liberated from sin, the source of which is the "gnomic will," that is, a function of the hypostatic or personal life of the individual.

Because it is enhypostasized in the Logos himself, Christ's humanity is a perfect humanity. In the mysterious process which started his conception in the Virgin's womb, Jesus passed through natural growth, ignorance, suffering, even death, all of them experiences of fallen humanity which he had come to save. And he fulfilled, through the Resurrection, the ultimate human destiny. Christ thus could truly be described as the Savior of humanity because in him there could never be any contradiction between the natural will and the gnomic will. Through hypostatic union, the human will, precisely because it always conforms itself to the divine, also performs the natural movement of human nature.

The doctrine of deification (*theosis*) is, in the Orthodox tradition, what salvation is all about. This doctrine is based upon the fundamental Patristic supposition that communion with God does not diminish or destroy humanity but makes it fully human. In Christ, the hypostatic union implies the *communication of idioms, that is, the characteristics of humanity and divinity express themselves in communion with each other. This notion goes back to the Council of Chalcedon* (A.D. 451). Human actions or energies in Christ are said to have God himself as their personal agent. It also can be said that God was born, that Mary is the Mother of God (*Theotokos*) and that the Logos was crucified; and while birth and death remain purely human realities, it can also be said that Christ rose from the dead and sits at the right hand of the Father, having acquired characteristics which naturally belong to God alone, namely, immortality and glory. Through Christ's humanity, deified according to its hypostatic union with the Logos, all members of the Body of Christ have access to deification through grace or by grace through the operation of the Holy Spirit in Christ's Church.

The Orthodox Church rejects any doctrine of grace which would seem to infringe upon human freedom. To describe the relation between the grace of God and human free will, Orthodoxy uses the word cooperation (*synergia*)—this is the practical term which is based on Saint Paul's words: "For we are all God's fellow workers" or *synergoi* with God (I Corinthians 3:9). If one is to achieve true fellowship with God, one cannot do so without God's help. But a human being must also play the human being's own part. The human being as well as God must make his or her contribution to the common work, although what God does is of immeasurably greater importance than what the human being does. The incorporation of humankind into Christ and its union with God requires the cooperation of two unequal, but necessary, forces: divine grace and human will. The West, since the time of Augustine, has discussed the question of grace and free will in somewhat different terms. Orthodox teaching is straightforward. "Behold, I stand at the door and knock; if anyone hears my voice and opens the door, I will come in to him and eat with him and he with me." (Apocalypse 3:20). God knocks but waits for us to open the door. He does not break it down. The grace of God invites all but compels no one. In the words of Saint John Chrysostom, God never draws anyone to himself by force and violence. He wishes all persons to be saved but forces no one. "It is for God to grant his grace," said Saint Cyril of Jerusalem in the fourth century.

One's task is to accept that grace and to guard it, but it must not be imagined that because one accepts and guards God's grace, one thereby earns merit. God's gifts are always free gifts, and one can never make any claims upon one's maker. But humanity, while it cannot merit salvation, must certainly work for it since "faith by itself, if it has no works, is dead" (James 2:17). The Orthodox do not hold that the fall of humankind deprived humanity entirely of God's grace, though they would say that after the Fall grace acts on humanity from the outside and not from within. Nor do the Orthodox say that after the Fall humanity was utterly depraved and incapable of good desires. The image of God is distorted by sin, but the image of God in human beings is never destroyed. An Orthodox hymn for the laity says, "I am the image of thine inexpressible glory even though I bear the wounds of sin." Adam separated himself from God by disobeying the will of God, and humanity is subject to mortality as a result, but the Orthodox do not believe that we are all guilty or that what we have inherited from this Fall is mortality and corruptibility.

Originally, men and women had been created for a mode of propagation that was deifying, divine, and non-material, but the fall into sin meant that this divine plan was replaced and that men and women would be trapped in a material mode of propagation. For this reason, the Logos of God became human to set men and women free from their passion and to restore them to the condition for which they had been created; and so, with Saint Athanasius at the first ecumenical council, one can say, "God became man in order that man might become God."

Easter Sunday can be seen as either a symbol of the future physical resurrection and incorruptibility or as an image of the future deification by grace. Ultimately, these are identical for the believer, and in the Orthodox Church the Easter service is much more highlighted and much more important than any other service. Christmas is important, but it does not have the primacy of Easter Sunday. The very definition of the Gospel was tied to the definition of salvation. It was an embassy from God, and a summons to humankind through the Incarnate Son, and a reconciliation with the Father, granting a reward as a gift to those who have believed Him through eternal deification. The phrase "granting a reward as a gift" suggests an ambiguity in this idea of *theosis* or deification, for it is possible, as it was for Maximus, to say on the one hand that there is no power inherent in human nature which is able to deify it, and yet on the other hand to say that God becomes human insofar as human nature has deified itself. The Biblical declaration "you are gods" was not to be understood to mean that we have the capacity *by nature* or *by our present condition* to achieve deification. One can achieve it and receive this sublime name only by the adoption and the grace of God. Otherwise, deification would not be the gift of God, but a work of human nature itself. No creature is capable of grasping God (this is Maximus again); deification can only happen by the grace of God. Deification is not a matter of human power but of divine power alone; yet this repeated and unequivocal insistence upon grace as essential to deification is not intended to exclude the free will of human beings from participation in the process. Again, to cite Maximus: "For the spirit does not generate a will that is willing, but the spirit transforms into deification a will that has the desire." Maximus' doctrine of salvation is based on the idea of participation and communion—participation and communion that exclude neither grace nor freedom but presuppose their union and collaboration, which were re-established, once and for all, in the Incarnate Word of the two wills.

Eastern theology emphasizes that divine sonship is both a gift of God and an achievement of human nature, and neither of these occurs without the other. Maximus emphasizes that everything that God is—except for an identity in *ousia,* in being, in essence—one becomes when one is deified by grace. Quoting Maximus, Saint Gregory Palamas, a much later theologian of the fourteenth century, was not so much unwilling to call deification symbolic as he was to refer to it as the light of revelation. Palamas sought to preserve the reality of salvation as deification without implying the absurd and blasphemous idea that those who were deified became God by nature. The reality was preserved by the teaching that the Father through the Son in the Spirit deifies those who are deified. Remaining human, according to nature, we become divine according to grace. The blasphemy is avoided by the teaching that the deifying gift of the spirit is not itself the superessential *ousia* of God but the deifying activity (that is, the "energy") of the superessential *ousia* of God. The basic passage on deification, II Peter 1:4, speaks of participation in the divine nature—reality, but not identity. The word "participation" is very important here. To avoid saying that deification makes a human being God by nature, it is necessary to insist that grace is supernatural, that is, beyond nature. So if deifying grace were according to nature, it would indeed produce an identity of nature, of *ousia* (that is, of substance), between the deifying God and the deified human. But the illumination and the deifying activity of God, which makes its recipients participants in the divine nature, cannot be itself the very nature of God. The nature of God is not absent from this activity for it is omnipresent, but the nature of God cannot be shared and, hence, deification cannot be natural but has to be by a certain divine grace. So powerful a reality is this grace that when it is conferred on those who have a beginning, it can elevate them above all ages and times and places, giving them, by grace though not by nature, participation in the very eternity of God without beginning or end.

Having said this, fundamental for Palamas was the notion that

God's essence is unknown, not primarily because of human finitude but because of divine transcendence. So the participation of man in the divine nature needed to be interpreted in such a way so as to safeguard the unchangeability of God without in any way jeopardizing the reality of the gift of *theosis* or deification. In his divine *ousia* (and one uses the Greek word because it means substance, essence, being—all of them) God remains beyond participation and beyond vision, even for the saints, yet that which they see and in which they participate is not a symbol of God but is God himself—the paradox. The God of Christian devotion is simultaneously absolute and related, incomprehensible in his nature and yet comprehended by the saints who participate in his nature. He is absolute by nature, related by grace. This is the supreme instance of the principle that Orthodoxy consisted in, the observance of both aspects of the dialectical truth.

And another antinomy of which Father John Meyendorff reminds us: one and the same God is both nonparticipatory and participatory—the former, because he is above all essence; and the latter, because he has the power, the activity to create us. Since the *ousia* of God is altogether incomprehensible and incommunicable to all human beings, would we have any other means of knowing God truly, if deifying grace and light were not God himself? The *ousia* of God is incommunicable, but the energies of God, the *energeiai* of God, are communicable. The sending of the Holy Spirit at Pentecost had to be distinguished from his eternal procession from the Father, for the former did not involve the incommunicable *ousia* of the Holy Trinity but the grace, power, and action common to the Father, the Son, and the Holy Spirit which were nevertheless uncreated and eternal. (When the phrase "grace of God" refers to an action of God, it means God himself, eternal and uncreated. When it refers to human virtue or graces, it means something created and temporal.) The actions of God—and grace is one of the actions of God—are divine, having neither beginning nor end; yet they have to be different from the divine *ousia* or, as Saint Basil taught, they are varied while the *ousia* is simple.

Knowledge of God is an experience given to all persons through Baptism and through their continuous participation in the life of the Body of Christ in the Eucharist. This requires the involvement of the whole person in prayer, in service through love for God and neighbor, and then it becomes recognizable, not only as an intellectual experience of the mind but also as a spiritual sense which conveys a perception neither purely intellectual nor purely material. In Christ, God assumes the whole of humanity, soul and body, and humanity is deified. In prayer, in sacraments, in the entire life of the Church as community, human beings are called upon to participate in divine life. This participation in the divine life, Saint Gregory Palamas says, is also true knowledge of God.

Further, God is totally inaccessible in his essence, both in this life and in the life of the world to come. For only the three divine hypostases, that is, the Holy Trinity, are God by essence. Human beings, in deification, can become God only by grace, only by the energy of God. Anything that exists outside of God exists only through his will or energy and can participate in his life only as the result of his will, that is God's will and God's grace. The full force with which Palamas affirms God's inaccessibility and the equally strong affirmation of deification as the original purpose and the goal of human existence give full reality to the Palamite distinction between essence and energy in God. His God is a living God, both transcendent and willingly immanent.

Palamas himself considers his teaching to be a development of the sixth ecumenical council's decisions that Christ has both two natures or essences and also two wills, two natural wills or energies. For Christ's humanity itself was penetrated with divine energy, and our own humanity finds access to God in his energy. The energies of God are never considered emanations: they are divine life itself as given by God to his creatures, and they are God, for in his Son he truly gave himself for human salvation. Thus, a man or woman is truly human when he or she participates in the life of God; he or she is not autonomous, either in relation to God or in relation to the world. In Jesus Christ, God and humanity are one, according to the Byzantine Orthodox tradition. In Christ God becomes accessible, not by superseding or eliminating that which is human but by realizing and manifesting humanity in its purest and most authentic form, conforming that which is human with that which is divine. That which is divine in Christ does not diminish humanity but restores humanity. "Christ restores nature to conformity with itself," says one Russian theologian. "Becoming man, he kept his free will in passionlessness and peace with nature." Participation in God is the very nature of human nature. Deification is described by Maximus as a participation of the whole person in the whole God, in the same way in which the soul and body are united. God should become accessible for this participation both by the soul and by the body in order that the soul might receive an unchanging character and the body immortality. And finally, as Saint Maximus the Confessor says, the whole human being should become God, deified by the grace of God-become-human, becoming wholly human, soul and body, by nature and becoming wholly God, soul and body, by grace.

Saint Gregory Palamas also said, "God in his completeness deifies those who are worthy of this by uniting himself with them, not hypostatically, because that belonged to Christ alone, nor essentially, but through a small part of the uncreated energies and the uncreated divinity while yet being entirely present in each." So it is the Holy Spirit who grants to each person created in the image of God the possibility of fulfilling the likeness. There is, of course, one divinity and one action or energy leading humankind to the one eschatological goal, deification, yet the personal hypostatic functions of the Son and of the Spirit are not identical. Divine grace and divine life are not a single reality but God-as-Trinity, nor are they some impersonal essence into which humanity is called to merge. The Orthodox conception is not that, by means of this process of deification, one is somehow drowned in divinity or merged into divinity. Byzantine Christianity requires the distinction in God among the one unapproachable essence, the three hypostases, and the grace or energy through which God enters into communion with creatures. We can be authentically free only when we have been liberated from the determinism of the created and formed existence and have received power through the Holy Spirit; and liberated from the determinism of created and formal existence, we receive the power to share in God's Lordship over creation. Humankind and God in the Eucharist represent the sign of the true Church, where the whole body of Christ is manifested sacramentally in unity and wholeness.

And finally, men and women, while certainly creatures and as such external to God, are defined in their very nature as being fully themselves only when they are in communion with God. This communion is not a static contemplation of God or of God's essence but an eternal progress into the inexhaustible riches of the divine life. This is precisely why the doctrine of *theosis,* the process through which we recover our original relation to God and grow into God from glory to glory, is the central theme of Byzantine Orthodox theology and of the Eastern Orthodox Christian experience itself.

NOTES

[1] These accept only the first three ecumenical councils. The Orthodox Church, the Chalcedonian Orthodox Churches (namely the Patriarchate of Constantinople and the rest of the Orthodox Churches that it represents), are in discussion with the non-Chalcedonian Orthodox Churches (which are represented by the Copts in Egypt, by the Ethiopians in Ethiopia, by certain elements of what little Persian Christianity remains, and among others in Arabic lands who are non-Chalcedonian; another of the non-Chalcedonian Orthodox Churches is the so called non Chalcedonian Armenian Orthodox Church). Non-Chalcedonians argued that the divine nature of Christ so absorbed the human form to form one nature, and so they are often referred to by the Chalcedonian Orthodox as Monophysites.

[2] The statement that the Greek Orthodox delegation to the Faith and Order Study Conference at Oberlin made in 1957 is still one that is presented by the Orthodox at the World Council of Churches and reads as follows:

> The Orthodox Church, through her historical consciousness, declares that she is maintaining an unbroken continuity with the Church of the Pentecost by preserving the Apostolic faith and policy. She has kept the faith once delivered unto the saints free from distortions and of human innovations. Man-made doctrines have never found their way into the Orthodox Church since she has no necessary association in history with one single father or one single theologian. She owes the fullness and the guarantee of unity and infallibility to the operation of the Holy Spirit and not to the service of one individual. It is for this reason that she has never felt the need for what is known as a return to the purity of the Apostolic faith. She maintains the necessary balance between freedom and authority and thus avoids the extremes of absolutism and individualism, both of which have done violence to Christian unity.

The statement goes on:

> . . . the unity which Orthodoxy represents rests on identity of faith, order, and worship. All three aspects of the life of the Church are ultimately safeguarded by the reality of the unbroken succession of bishops which is the assurance of the Church's uninterrupted continuity with Apostolic origins. This means that the uncompromised fullness of the Church requires the preservation of both its episcopal structure and its sacramental life. Adhering tenaciously to her Apos-

tolic heritage, the Orthodox Church holds that no true unity is possible where episcopacy and sacrament are absent and grieves over the fact that both institutions have either been disregarded or distorted in certain quarters of Christendom. Any agreement on faith rests on the authority of the enactments of the seven Ecumenical Councils which represent the mind of the one undivided Church of antiquity and the subsequent tradition as safeguarded in the life of the Orthodox Church.

[3] In the words of one of its leaders:
Church history states emphatically and demonstrates clearly that the Apostolic tradition came first, that in the times of the first centuries of the church, it was through the Apostolic position that Christianity took deep roots and became stable, and that the books which can constitute the Holy Scriptures and their form and number today were preserved because of the Apostolic tradition. It follows, then, that the Apostolic tradition is very valuable and absolutely useful to the life and existence of the Church. It follows also that those who ignore or hold contempt for the Apostolic tradition, as well as those who enlarge tradition and add to it elements foreign to the fundamental dogmas that have been bequeathed to us, suffer a great loss.

16

GRACE AND SALVATION IN THE PROTESTANT TRADITION

Joyce Irwin

The Protestant tradition has played a major role in the shaping of the religious view of North America, and Dr. Joyce Irwin turns our attention to the period of the Reformers, to look there to see the importance of our subjects of "grace" and "human bondage" for persons whose thinking and responses then initiated currents of thought still moving with many of us today.

I

Thy mercies, Lord, to heaven reach;
Thy faithfulness the clouds do preach;
Thy righteousness as mountains huge;
Thy judgments deep no tongue can teach;
To man and beast thou art refuge.

O God! how great thy mercies be!
The sons of men do trust in thee;
With thee they shall be fully fed.
And thou wilt give them drink full free
Of pleasant rivers largely spread.

The well of life is thine by right.
Thy brightness doth give us our light.
Thy favour, Lord, to such extend
As knowledge thee with heart upright;
Thy righteousness to such men lend.

Psalm 36:5–10
(metrical version by
William Kethe, 1561)

This version of Psalm 36 from the Scottish Psalter of 1561 alerts us to two key theological terms, two attributes of God which both the pre-reformers and the Reformers of the sixteenth century considered central to the discussion of God and to the human relationship with God. God's mercy and God's justice or righteousness are referred to in the lines "Thy mercies, Lord, to Heaven reach" and "Thy righteousness to such men lend." God relates to humans through both his mercy and his righteousness; but how do the two go together? To focus only on God's justice can be terrifying. This is what Martin Luther thought when, in writing his commentary on the Book of Romans in the early sixteenth century, he meditated on the words of the first chapter, "In it the righteousness of God is revealed." He says, "I hated that word 'righteousness of God'." Why did he hate it? He felt that one had to become righteous, that in spite of all that we are told about original sin, about our incapacity to please God, the sinner must, nevertheless, become righteous if God is ever to be pleased. And in the sixteenth century, as in the Middle Ages, people took pleasing God seriously because their eternal salvation was at stake. When God's righteousness or God's justice was emphasized, there lurked the threat of eternal damnation. God damned those who could not please him, which meant all those who were not saved by the grace of God. Grace, therefore, was demanded. God saves only through his mercy, for through his justice, no one would be saved.

How is this to be understood? How can we say we are saved by grace? To use that phrase in itself is to jump ahead to Luther's so-called Reformation discovery. How did people understand it prior to Luther? Certainly they said one is saved through the grace of God, but it was through both grace and works, both justice and mercy. Luther, it could be said, took one side. First he was worried about righteousness, and then he focused on mercy. Those medieval thinkers whom Luther ultimately rejected and reacted against had tried to hold them together. They made the two concepts of mercy and justice, grace and works, into one comprehensive unit such that grace and nature complemented each other. Grace and nature—these are two terms that were treated together in the Middle Ages. Grace is understood to be that which is beyond nature; nature is all of our natural capacities, our natural understanding, our will, in addition to the natural world, that is, that which is created. Grace, then, is God's activity in the world, the way in which the divine enters into the created world. Grace is that which brings us closer to God, closer than we can come through our own power. That in itself is problematic. How close can we come? What can we know of God's existence? Can we know, through our natural understanding, through our own knowledge, our mental capacity, that God exists? Can we know of God's nature? Can we understand his attributes? Can we love God? Can we earn his favor? Can we gain salvation?

All medieval theologians would agree that to say that we can earn salvation is to commit the Pelagian heresy. Pelagius, who opposed Saint Augustine in the fifth century, was accused of heresy for overemphasizing what we can do on our own. He almost implied that we can earn salvation on our own merits, and since this was declared a heresy, no medieval thinker dared to commit that error or to claim overtly to be a Pelagian, by siding with him. So all agreed that it must be through God's grace that salvation is earned.

But exactly how much we can do, how far we can go toward the earning of salvation, was a matter of some disagreement. In general, it can be said of medieval thought that nature and grace supplemented each other. They were not in conflict. There was no large gap between the created world and the divine nor was there any discrepancy in the way that one must think about them. It was, for some, a continuum. Our natural powers of understanding, our natural powers of will, can respond to God's grace because there is a remnant of the divine likeness which remains. We are created in the image of God, and though that image was spoiled by the sin of Adam and Eve, which was transmitted to all generations, nevertheless the remnant of the divine likeness remains. Whether we can make any beginnings in God's direction was debated. If it was agreed there was a certain divine likeness, it was not agreed how strong that likeness was. There were those who were called nominalists who said that we can do what is in us. The Latin phrase was *"Facere quod in se est"*—"do what is in you," which may mean simply to be humble; or perhaps it means to love God, perhaps to love one's neighbor, perhaps it means desiring to come to the sacrament. Whatever it is that one is doing, and this would vary according to the theologians, the nominalists thought that one could take the first step. The initial step could be that of the human.

God would, of course, need to lead the human on beyond that, to help, with the second and third steps; but a human being could initiate the process.

Now this was rejected as semi-Pelagian by a number of thinkers who saw the position bordering on heresy. Steering clear of all hints of Pelagianism, they said we are not able to take the first step. We cannot initiate the process of our salvation. Prevenient grace—the grace which comes before sacramental grace, which is freely given to all by God—allows us to respond, in spite of our sin, to the workings of God. Through prevenient grace one is enabled to come to the actual grace that is given through the sacrament. Thus medieval theologians distinguished among different kinds of grace as, in their scholastic manner, they divided and subdivided virtually every category. Saint Thomas Aquinas, for example, in his *Summa Theologica* (II, q.iii, a. 1–5) asked the following questions concerning the "division of grace":

1. "Whether grace is fittingly divided into sanctifying grace and gratuitous grace?"
2. "Whether grace is fittingly divided into operating and co-operating grace?"
3. "Whether grace is fittingly divided into prevenient and subsequent grace?"
4. "Whether gratuitous grace is rightly divided by the Apostle [Paul]?"
5. "Whether gratuitous grace is nobler than sanctifying grace?"

Now there were some, such as Erasmus, who thought all of this was a bit of nonsense. Erasmus asked whether, in fact, the Apostles knew the difference between gratuitous grace, sanctifying grace, and prevenient grace, implying that what medieval theologians had done was to distort the Gospel by making it much more complex than any of the Apostles had intended or were intellectually prepared to absorb. There is a lot of truth to Erasmus's point. On the other hand, the medieval theologians were honestly trying to deal with a very complex problem. The problem, with which no one has yet satisfactorily dealt, is that of the relationship of human power to divine power. Can we say that humans cooperate with God? Is God working in the world? If so, how does he work in the world? Does he use us? What is the relationship of our will to what is considered the omnipotent will of God? If God is omnipotent, how can we have any control even if we think we have free will?

Medieval theologians tried to make enough distinctions to make it possible to say that we do have free will, even though it is limited by God's omnipotence. It is circumscribed by God's power, which places certain limits on our free will, but our free will is a necessary concept. It is necessary because, in order to take responsibility for our moral actions, we must be considered to have some power to say yes or to say no and, therefore, to cooperate. God leads and we follow, but we follow willingly. We are not forced into following God. So, we cooperate with God. Grace and nature, free will and God's grace, are both necessary in order that we become righteous, thus pleasing God. This leads back to the question of salvation. If we have moral responsibility, if we freely cooperate with God's grace, then we can earn salvation. We do not do it all on our own, of course, because it entails a combination of God's work, or grace, and our work. When we cooperate we take in God's grace; it is infused. It becomes a habit with the soul. As Saint Thomas Aquinas wrote, "Man is helped by God's gratuitous will inasmuch as a habitual gift is infused by God into the soul."

There are several points that can be made about that sentence. First, the word "gratuitous" means that there is nothing on the part of the human who receives this grace which is compelling, nothing which precedes God's will. In other words, God freely decides to give his grace. And yet, the word "habitual," with the phrase "infused by God into the soul," indicates that it does become part of the human being. The grace is fed into the soul and it becomes a habit. Through this habit of grace the human being can become pleasing to God. To be sure, it is in a sense God who is being pleased with his own image which he has infused into the human being; nevertheless, there is also a human being with the habit of grace responding to God and, therefore, pleasing God. And so in the concept of the scholastic theologians, when one lived in this state of grace, and continued therein to the point of death, one could expect to achieve salvation because of one's likeness to God.

One familiar with Aristotle's *Ethics* might recognize here a certain Aristotelian emphasis: one becomes a friend of God by becoming a good person, by becoming virtuous, by developing the habit of grace combined with good works. There is a certain resemblance between the eternal salvation that the Christian earns in the sight of God and the happiness that Aristotle talked about. It is a lasting, joyful, and yet contemplative state, a state in which one has trained one's will and one's mind to do the right thing and has thereby become virtuous. One has achieved both moral and intellectual virtue. This Aristotelian model is the background of most medieval scholastic thought. The virtuous person, who through the grace of God has been trained properly and through a long life has attained this state of virtue, has become a friend of God. Just as friends, according to Aristotle, like each other because they see their own goodness reflected in the friend, so God is pleased by the human being who cultivates the divine image and thus becomes like God.

II

This, then, was the background of Martin Luther when he wondered how in the world he could become a friend of God, when he found himself not fully willing friendship with God. He did not feel that he wanted to be God-like; he was in competition with God. He was rebelling inwardly against what God wanted him to do. He could not accept the idea that, beyond following the commandments and doing outwardly good deeds, one had to will God to be a friend and reflect his image. Eventually, after his struggle with the term "righteousness of God," he came to love the term because he came to understand that the righteousness is the mercy. They are not two different things which combine together, but it is through the righteousness of God that one attains salvation. It is not through our righteousness. He reread the words of Romans, "In it the righteousness of God is revealed, as it is written, 'he who through faith is righteous shall live' " (see also Galatians 3:11). He no longer understood that passage to mean that the sinner must become righteous in order to live, but that the righteousness of God is revealed to the sinner who accepts it through faith. It remains God's righteousness. It does not become human righteousness. The human does not become righteous in order to please God.

One of the implications for this is that it does not make sense to talk about cooperating with God's grace. Why not? Because the natural capacity, the natural will, simply does not cooperate; it is not equal to God, as if God and I together can accomplish this, but rather the will is led by God. The will does not really choose. Thus, the second implication is that there is really no free will. Oh yes, we can use the term "free will," and we certainly talk about free will in our everyday activities. We can freely choose to cross the street, to wash the dishes or not to wash the dishes, but when it comes to talking about God and his grace there is no such thing as freedom except as God frees the will. Since we are in bondage to sin, we are incapable of choosing to do the good, incapable of choosing to love God. Luther said that, left on our own to our natural powers, we can only hate God, we can only sin. All our activities are sin. That is not to say that we cannot treat a neighbor nicely, that we cannot be nice to our children, our husbands, wives, and friends, or that we cannot give to charity. Certainly we can do all these things. But Luther was psychologically fairly astute, and he realized that in all these acts which we call morally good, there is a strong mixture of self-will. We want to be recognized. We want to be good people, and we want people to say that we are good, but it is out of a desire for glory to look good in the eyes of others, for satisfaction of our own desires and needs. It is not out of the love of God. We can only do good out of love of God when God acts on our will. The only way we can please God is by seeking God's glory, not our own. God alone can free us to show his glory, free us from self-will, so that what we do is to be for the glory of God.

When we talk about a lack of free will, lack of choice, or inability to do good, that seems pretty harsh. It seems like we are pawns in the hands of God, and in some contexts Luther talked that way. Luther talked about us being clay in the hands of the potter. God makes us the way he wants to make us, which sounds fine if one is on the receiving end of his grace: one gets the grace, one does the good deed, one pleases God. But if one is not, damnation follows. Luther did not spend a lot of time talking about that. He recognized that there would be those who would be damned, and he did not deny that perhaps God planned their damnation, that somehow in his inscrutable will it all followed that many had to be damned and a few were lucky enough to be saved. Harsh as that may seem, Luther thought in a sense that was comforting. What was comforting about it? That we are freed from earning our salvation: it is all up to God. True, it is not so good if we are among the damned, but we can have certitude of salvation through faith. What does that mean? It sounds as though anyone who decides that he or she will have faith, can have faith and can be saved. But it depends not so much on what one decides about one's faith as on the grace of God which makes faith possible. How is faith made possible? It is made possible through Christ, through Christ's crucifixion and Christ's resurrection. Christ suffered for us, thereby earning our righteousness. Christ is the means by which we come to understand God. God is revealed in Christ. What we know about God is seen in Christ and that is his mercy. Luther distinguished between God preached and God hidden; that is, God in his revelation as seen through Christ and the Bible and God hidden, that is, the speculations upon his omnipotence and his omniscience which allow for a good deal more than one finds in the Bible.

There is then something of a discrepancy between God preached and God hidden. All we know is God preached, and yet there is what he calls the hidden and awful will of God, whereby he ordains by his counsel which and what sort of persons he wills to be recipients and partakers of his preached and offered mercy. Thus, the mercy is that which is preached and offered, but there is the hidden will in which God does will the death of a sinner. Luther says God does not will the death of a sinner according to his word, but he wills it according to that inscrutable will of his. So for our comfort, we should listen to the promises of God. We should pay attention to that mercy which he reveals in his will and not pay any attention to the inscrutable will as indicated in the Psalm paraphrase with which we began, the line "Thy judgments deep no tongue can teach." Some things are beyond human understanding, and yet the last line of that verse states "To man and beast thou art refuge." Whatever we cannot understand is not important. We know that God is a refuge because that is the import of his revealed will.

For Luther, then, Christ was central: the historic Christ who lived, the Christ revealed in the Word, and the Christ who becomes present in the sacraments, the Christ, I should say, who is present when the sacrament is celebrated because he promised that he would be present. It is his promise which gives us hope, and his *promise* that comes as close as anything to what Luther means by grace. Grace is not a habit that is infused into humans. Grace is not something that we come to possess. Grace is a promise—a promise that it will be Christ's deeds, not ours, by which we are accounted righteous.

Luther's emphasis on promise is especially important when thinking about the Protestant Reformation doctrine of justification by faith. It is, of course, central to Luther's thought as well as to that of all the other reformers that one is justified by faith alone without works. But when the Anabaptists tried to set up faith as the standard by which one should judge one's salvation, Luther fought back and said no, it is not by the degree of our faith that we judge ourselves. Faith must be in the promise and must never be separated from the promise. Luther defended infant baptism, for instance, because although faith was required, it is primarily through God's working and God's promise that in this act of baptism our sin is wiped away. Anabaptists, on the other hand, felt that the sacrament was of no avail if faith was the means by which the work was accomplished. For Luther the element of promise takes away the subjective emphasis, redirects it into the more objective, historical work of Christ and the sacramental work of Christ. The outward forms remain important. The outward forms of the liturgy, the sacraments, and preaching are the means by which we can come to understand and arrive at faith, but they point to Christ who, rather than our faith, remains the standard.

III

Now if this seems problematic, so it was. On the one hand, Luther had said we are justified by faith alone. We are justified by grace alone. He had criticized many of the sacraments of the Catholic Church saying they were improperly understood, saying all Christians are priests, as if to say we do not need the outward church or the sacraments. But it turned out that this was not really what he meant. He meant that they had been understood in a way that was not that of grace but was that of works, as he defined it. It was a work to attend a mass, which was understood as a sacrifice, something that we do. So he retained the emphasis on the liturgy, on the sacrament, but understood them in such a way that they were God's work, not ours. And so God's outward work still remained the means by which grace comes.

The Anabaptists and many other reformers, however, wrestled with this. If it is by faith that we are justified, then why do we need the sacraments? Cannot God simply work within us, through our faith, through our internal movements of the heart? During the course of the Reformation there were many disputes over how important the sacraments were, how they were to be understood, how important faith was in the sacraments. There were those who put very little emphasis on the sacraments. Luther put more than any of the other reformers, and some of them thought he was much too close to the Catholicism which he had supposedly rejected. But he held to this middle position of pointing out the importance of the objective, the outward forms, because he realized that once one starts trying to judge one's internal faith, it becomes very difficult to say whether one has enough. Especially when predestination becomes combined with justification by faith alone, it becomes a very difficult doctrine. It causes much internal struggling as it did with the Puritans who felt that they must see the faith within. They needed evidence that God was working through them internally, subjectively, in order that they could be assured of their election. Calvin and Luther had thought that the doctrine of election was an assuring doctrine because it said that we do not have to do anything. God does it for us. And yet if salvation is by faith alone, then we must have faith.

Luther, Calvin, and the Puritan reformers all recognized that God leads us to faith, but how, if we want to know whether we indeed have faith, can we know that there is enough to be assured that God has chosen us, that we are of the elect? For the seventeenth century Puritans, internal meditation, introspection on one's sins and on the movements of grace within, became the focus of religious devotion. In this context talk about conversion became primary. One does not find much emphasis on the doctrine of conversion in the sixteenth century. For Luther and Calvin it was not really one's business to find out whether one belonged to the elect. For the seventeenth century Puritans, on the other hand, this determination was all-important, at least for purposes of church membership. If one had not had a conversion experience, if one could not tell of how God worked within one, how God's grace was operative in one's soul, then there was no evidence that one was of the elect and therefore eligible for church membership. Church membership thus became much more selective, and in seventeenth century America there were very few church members, though everybody had to attend church in order to be there when the minister preached, in order that it be possible that one hear the word and receive grace. But very few, comparatively, could give evidence of the grace within.

Over the course of time this conversion, which for the early Puritans was not a sudden momentary experience but a long process with many doubts and backslidings, became a very sudden infusion of God's grace. One had to be able to point to the time when one was converted. Thus Protestantism, in the course of centuries, became a very subjectively oriented theology. One was always looking inward, rejecting the outward forms in favor of a conversion experience. Now conversion seemed to be the only thing demanded; but as long as the Puritans held the doctrine of predestination in the forefront, that was not the case, because one had to keep looking for signs of election. One could not just say one had been converted at a particular time. That might have been a false start of faith; the whole life of faith must be evidenced in the grace within and the works without. This evidence was necessary to demonstrate that one was of the elect; but as the doctrine of election and predestination became less important, the doctrine of conversion became more important.

This one-time-conversion was the key to one's eternal salvation; if one had that moment of conversion one could say that one was saved and there could be no doubt. It was not the same kind of assurance that Luther and Calvin talked about when there was in effect still some doubt because the assurance rested on Christ and not on one's internal experience. With this later doctrine of conversion there is a greater sense of assurance, producing the whole idea of "once saved, always saved." There can be no doubt at any time in the future that God is intending one for eternal salvation. As the nineteenth century approached there were those who, having rejected the doctrine of election, went so far as to have revivals in which they knew how to convert people, how to produce the largest number of saved people.

So revivalism in the nineteenth century is the crass oversimplification of the doctrine of justification by faith begun in the sixteenth century. It consists of such hymns as I am going to quote to end this chapter—very different from that which we quoted at the beginning of the chapter, no longer based on the Psalms where there is a rich relationship with God and a rich understanding of God and the complexity of God's justice and God's mercy. That justice is not in the scene because there is not the same fear of damnation which the doctrine of election had produced. Now there is the sense that God is merciful and all one has to do is trust him. That is one's action. It is something one can do. It is called faith, and faith is thought to be opposed to works, but one begins to wonder, in the experience of the nineteenth century, perhaps at other times, too, if faith is not something that we can produce. We can say, "I believe. I am going to have enough faith. I am going to believe Him and He will save me." It is not that one looks inside and sees God working, leading one to salvation; rather, one understands that all that is necessary is to have faith and one can do it.

Where Luther had said "by grace and by faith," as if they were two sides of the same coin, one has the sense that in the nineteenth century grace is no longer operative but only faith. We almost compel God through our faith. True, he promised his grace, but we are less dependent on his promise than on our acceptance. Thus, I want to close with a hymn that has been popular in the twentieth century but was written in the nineteenth century and expresses this whole emphasis on salvation for eternity. The Gospel is important solely because it offers eternal salvation. Jesus is the Truth. Only trust Him.

Come, every soul by sin oppressed,
There's mercy with the Lord;
And he will surely give you rest,
By trusting in his word.

Refrain:
Only trust him, only trust him,
Only trust him now;
He will save you, he will save you,
He will save you now.

For Jesus shed his precious blood
Rich blessings to bestow.
Plunge now into the crimson flood
That washes white as snow.

Yes, Jesus is the truth, the way,
That leads you into rest;
Believe in him without delay,
And you are fully blest.

Come then and join this holy band,
And on to glory go,
To dwell in that celestial land,
Where joys immortal flow.

THE SACRAMENTAL LIFE OF CHRIST IN US

Leonard Kotzbauer

We now turn to a major expression of the Christian tradition today in North America, and we read the words of Father Leonard Kotzbauer, a priest who served as chaplain to the Newman Community at Colgate University, speaking from within his experiences and from within his religious heritage. Father Kotzbauer reminds us of the way the Roman Catholic Church has maintained the centrality of God's grace expressed through the sacramental rites of the church and in the sacramental presence of Christ in one's life.

I

Consider the presence of God in our lives in a practical way, in the context of current events. If we think in the context of hostages and, at the same time, we talk about disruption of grace in the world, we need to remember that grace or God's presence nevertheless abides in every single person in this world. Would that mean, for example, that a religious leader of a government considered to be hostile would be full of the presence of the Lord? That is an interesting question for us. I have said to our community at worship that really we should be praying for everyone, including the people in Iran, Iraq, and Lebanon. One might not want to see as part of God's presence in the world, his presence in someone or some group of people that could be so hostile or violent or as disruptive or as full of what one might call lack of humanity as people, anywhere in the world, who would torture or deliberately hurt others. Yet, upon reflection, in a practical way, we readily discern even on a comparatively preliminary level, that many times *we* disrupt and hurt and seriously disorient people. We can talk about things in a very theological way, or we can talk about things in something of a practical way when we talk about both God's presence in our lives as well as the bondage that each of us are put through by the disruption created by men and women around us.

We begin, then, aware of the bondage into which we have placed each other. Bondage seems to involve a sense of disruption. Pascal writes, "Truly it is an evil to be full of faults; but it is a still greater evil to be full of them, and to be unwilling to recognize them, since that is to add the further fault of a voluntary illusion."[1] We cannot know God well without knowing our own wickedness. How often do we look at ourselves, how much do we examine ourselves? How much are we willing to admit that there are things wrong with us? Everyone has some fault that is in need of repair. We in the Catholic Church begin our liturgies each time by saying "God help us," together with a confession of faults internally, personally. We thereby indicate that we are sinners and that we need God's presence not only in this liturgical or worshipping service but throughout our lives. Many of us arise at the beginning of the day and pray to God to help us through that day, carefully considering the faults that are part of our own human nature, seeking to correct those faults little by little during that day.

Saint Augustine led a very immoral life in the beginning before he was converted to God. As a man, around thirty-three years old, who really had nothing to do with the things of God in his younger years, he recognized a weakness in himself and felt that there had to be a healing relationship with God.

In *Grace Abounding to the Chief of Sinners,* John Bunyan talks about the same thing:

> Therefore I still did pray to God, that He would come in with this scripture more fully on my heart; to wit, that He would help me to apply the whole sentence, for as yet I could not: that He gave, I gathered; but farther I could not go, for as yet it only helped me to hope there might be mercy for me, "My grace is sufficient"; and though it came no farther, it answered my former question; to wit, that there was hope; yet, because "for thee" was left out, I was not

> contented, but prayed to God for that also. Wherefore, one day, as I was in a meeting of God's people, full of sadness and terror, for my fears again were strong upon me; and as I was now thinking my soul was never the better; but my case most sad and fearful, these words did, with great power, suddenly break in upon me, "My grace is sufficient for thee, my grace is sufficient for thee, my grace is sufficient for thee," three times together; and, oh! methought that every word was a mighty word unto me; as *my,* and *grace,* and *sufficient,* and *for thee;* they were then, and sometimes are still, far bigger than others be.[2]

This also indicates an awareness of the disruptiveness of humankind, a recognition that it was and is in bondage. God's grace and the awareness of God is necessary for us to break through this bondage. This disruption, this bondage, is not a static situation.

We need to be aware that God uses men and women as instruments. Humankind is not molded clay, nor is it inert. Humankind is going to have a relationship with God, maybe consciously, maybe unconsciously. And humankind will, in some way, need this relationship. Saint Bernard says:

> . . . both our works and His rewards are alike the gift of God, and He Who has made Himself a debtor in respect of the latter, has also made us meritorious in virtue of the former. Nevertheless, He deigns to make use of the services of His creatures in establishing their merits, not on the ground of His standing in need of such services, but on the ground of their being of profit to His creatures.[3]

II

Grace benefits everyone. Grace can never be a thing *possessed* because it is a light unceasingly emanating from and returning to God. All grace is given in the church and for the benefit of the church, benefiting both the person receiving it and the community. When a person receives grace, that does not mean that it becomes operative within him or her. It does not mean that someone who receives this grace within the Catholic Church is, therefore, better than anyone else in the world. Rather, one can say that receiving this grace helps one, hopefully, to live a better life.

God presents himself to us right in the world that we are in—whether it be here, home, walking up and down Madison Avenue, working somewhere from nine to five—and gives us the opportunity to make his presence part of our lives. We can realize this presence in everything that we do as individuals, as members of society, as parts of the larger world. It makes no difference really who we are and what doctrinal formulae we believe. What I am saying, as a member of the Catholic Church, is the fact that the sacraments give us another opportunity to bring God's presence into our lives at times when we possibly may need God's presence: when we are first born, when we need to confirm ourselves in the faith of God, when we are married or arrive at a time for vocational decision in our lives, when we are sick and possibly need God's presence, and also when we have become a disruptive person or as Saint Paul would suggest, "dead, in the presence of Jesus." We may need reconciliation with him or we may need the presence of God in what we call the reception of him directly in the Eucharist.

But again, let me emphasize that this does not mean that those who do not receive the sacraments are going to be any less genuine persons than those who do because it depends on how one receives something and uses it.

Before turning to the sacraments, let us consider briefly the priest who represents the church. First of all, a priest is supposed to be a very sanctified individual, which hopefully, he is—and, hopefully, in the future maybe it will be "she" as well. The priest is supposed to be the example for the community. That does not mean that the priest is the most perfect, most holy person in the community. It is important to note that the Catholic Church has changed a great deal in the last couple of decades with regard to this idea of priest as the example for the community.

When I was young, the priest was put on a pedestal and left in the rectory. About all he did was live in his house, go over to celebrate the liturgy, and, maybe, walk around the community and pontificate at times. There was very little active involvement with the community itself, and many of us have had to learn to be human, to be part of the people to whom the grace that we brought from God should have united us and not have separated us. But this situation is changing. There is a shift from a mentality of avoidance —to avoid people, to avoid active involvement in the affairs of the community because the more one gets involved in material things possibly the more one might be pulled away from the things of God—to a reconsideration of what might be called the things of God. The things of God are prayer and contemplation, of course, but also the people that one should be dealing with. But I think, if one is dealing with people and the things of people, one has to be aware of where people are "coming from." Our training now covers the gamut from social work to psychiatric counseling. The important point to understand is that God's grace is in the people of the world, and therefore when one is talking about the presence of God it is not just a sacramental rite where God's presence may arise, but a process of dealing with the problems that people have and where they are coming from, whether it be a problem in spirituality or whether it be a problem with their marriage or whether it be a problem with their own sense of themselves.

It appears that the grace of God has not reached everyone necessarily in the same level, in the sense of God acting with each of us, which is, of course, part of the grace of God. How does the presence of God come to a person who appears to be a harsh leader? Maybe the grace of God is there but might not be operative. Will it ever be operative? In the case of Iran, say, there are men who understand religion in a certain way, therefore, maybe God's grace is operative. I listened to Dr. Rauf talk about Islam and I kept saying to myself, "There are a lot of things he is saying that I have not heard through the news media about Islam!" There are differences in the way God is working with different people, and there are degrees to which persons, all of us, are letting God work.

III

In the Catholic Church, the presence of God is exhibited through the sacraments that God has left here on the earth for us, to bring his presence into our life. Putting aside a consideration of how they were instituted or the question whether Jesus Christ directly instituted these sacraments, let us consider briefly the meaning of the sacraments for us today.

The idea of the sacrament of *Baptism* is to commit someone to God. In a way, that sounds strange when we are talking about a five week old infant. But what we are doing with this sacrament is committing an infant to an institution of God, making him or her a member of God's institutional church. There is continuing discussion about this sacrament, as with the others. Should a person, for instance, be baptized if the parents are not committed members of the Catholic Church? The traditional teaching of our church has been that baptism removes the stain of original sin, the sin of Adam, in the sense that each man and woman has that reflection of sin within them, contrary, say, to Islamic teaching. This sacrament removes that stain of sin from their lives. But also this sacrament brings them within the institution of the Catholic Church.

When we baptize someone into the Catholic Church, the first question that is asked of the parents is what they are asking of God's church. Their reply might be "baptism," or other words may be used, such as faith, grace of Christ, entrance into the church, or eternal life. The exchange continues, in effect, "You have asked to have your child baptized. In doing so, you are accepting the responsibility of training him or her in the practice of the faith. It will be your duty to bring him or her up to keep God's commandments as Christ taught us by loving God and our neighbor. Do you thoroughly understand what you are undertaking?" Obviously there is a commitment which will be apparent, followed by a profession of faith asked of the parents. Each year this profession of faith[4] is renewed during our liturgies at Easter season so that each person is asked to re-commit himself or herself to God.

When a child is baptized he or she is brought into the church and into the benefit of the grace of the worshipping community, those who believe in the presence of God. Baptism brings with it the obligations of following the rules and regulations of the institution. When we bring someone into the benefits, there is also an obligation and a commitment. It brings the grace of God and commits that person into being a person of God, commits that person into the people of God.

The sacraments are given to people at different times in their lives when the re-strengthening or re-emphasizing of the presence of God takes place. *Confirmation* is such a time of re-strengthening. Confirmation, the idea of bringing a person into an adult commitment, signifies that one is now, on one's own, going to commit oneself as a firm believer of God. We ask the head of our community, the Bishop, the fullness of the priesthood, the successor of the Apostles, to ask this adult commitment of the people of our community. This is done currently, approximately at the beginning of high school. One can recall the time one was entering high school and all the things that followed with regard to one's formation as a man or woman and all the problems that resulted from all of the human relationships that were a part of that time. One could have asked, "Could the presence of God, if I realize it in a more vibrant way, help me through the problems of that age coming up?" And that is what that sacrament is given for. One notes again that a person does not have to be involved in these rituals in order to have the presence of God. There is a beautiful book, Edward Schillebeeckx's *Christ: The Sacrament of Encounter with God,* and his whole idea is that routine things that human beings do can be interpreted as sacraments, that there is a sacramentality involved in the total daily operation of one's living a good life and trying to be a good person. There is a lot in that. Obviously, that is a very simplistic statement about the thesis of the book, but it certainly has had a resounding influence upon many people involved in society.

The third sacrament is the *Sacrament of Penance,* or as we call it now the *Sacrament of Reconciliation,* where one reconciles oneself with God. The church believes that this power to forgive sins was given to the first Apostles, and can therefore, be transferred from the Apostles to the Bishops and to the Priests. Many people would question whether that power can be transferred. Actually, God is forgiving sins. A human being is only the mediator who is dealing psychologically with the reconciliation of another human being. It is a beautiful psychological catharsis if people approach it with the idea that one can come in and talk about oneself and the problems that one is having as a human being, knowing that one can rely on a person's (the priest's) expertise to try to develop oneself in a positive way to transcend a weakness or a fault that one has. This sort of counselling does not have to be done by a priest, but this sort of counselling, within the sacrament, can participate in the grace of God. There are currently two forms for the Sacrament of Reconciliation, though reception of the sacrament seems to be on the decline. One option is to sit or kneel behind a dark curtain where the priest does not know who the person is that is speaking. Some people might think it is quite unusual to speak to somebody from behind a curtain. A lot of people like the anonymity of it. Some prefer to come and sit in my office and they will say "I'd like to receive the sacrament." In other words, they are saying, "I'd like to go to confession." We just simply talk. We might talk for five minutes, or an hour depending on what the person has to say. This is an occasion of bringing one out of the darkness and death of sin into the light of grace and God.

The priest is only a human intermediary. It is God who is doing all of this. When a person tells his or her faults or sins to a priest, he is under the most serious reprehension or sin before God if he ever reveals that to anyone, under any circumstance, even death. This sacrament involves two responses: it can take the form of judgment, involving penance in order to make up for one's sins, or it can be a reconciliation where an attempt is made to bring one back to a loving relationship with God and the people around one. When one has done something wrong, the end result often is guilt, and a person needs to do something about that guilt instead of just having it fester within. Here is the question for humanity again, whether the grace of God is really a part of one's life or whether it is inactive.

Concerning the *Eucharist,* the Catholic Church believes that the bread and wine are the actual body and blood of Jesus Christ, not the symbolic presence or representation. Jesus said, "This is my body," "This is my blood." The whole theology here for us in the Catholic Church is that we receive Jesus, himself, and it can be daily at the liturgy of Mass. That reception of Jesus directly into us, bringing his presence into us, helps us to be better persons, because one cannot receive Jesus without making a personal acclamation that one understands what is going on. Hopefully people do not receive the Eucharist as though they are going down to have a beer and pizza. It is not at all like that. There one is just filling one's stomach. But in the Eucharist, one is receiving the body and blood of Jesus Christ, and that, if one does so consciously, should have an effect upon one's spirituality—the acceptance of God's presence within one—the awareness of God's presence which can create the operative action of grace within one's life. The Eucharist is an affirmation of the presence of Jesus Christ.

There are two more sacraments, *Holy Orders* and *Matrimony,* and these are, in a sense, vocational sacraments. They create an atmosphere within one's life and give one the grace of God, again at a specific time in one's life when one begins to consider a vocation, a calling, whether that be to the priesthood, religious life, whether it be to the married state.

There is, further, the sacrament of *Anointing of the Sick.* We used to call it *Extreme Unction.* It used to be the annointing of those who were going to die, to prepare them to go to our Lord; also included in this was the sacrament of Penance. Now the church uses it to ask our Lord to intervene in a person's illness and if it be the wish of God, to cure that person or to help him or her through the suffering of that illness—if not, to ask that the person, then, enjoy as much peace as he or she can in preparing for death. God can still work miracles. Miracles did not end at the time of Christ. The miracle might be that one finally communicates with that boy or girl one has been trying to reach for the last three years. Although not customarily so defined, that could be a miracle at least in a person's life. A miracle could mean a change that one, directly through the grace of God, brings upon another person.

Finally, although the idea of the seven sacraments is basic to the life of the Catholic Church, and therefore, too, I have presented this as a priest, one need not think a ritual is in every case necessary to bring God's grace. One could become so ritualistic that one is bound by the thought that one has to get the priest to do this or that. Any one of us can bring God's presence into our lives immediately.

NOTES

1 Blaise Pascal, *Thoughts: An Apology for Christianity,* edited and with an introduction by Thomas S. Kepler (New York: World Publishing Company, 1955), pp. 86–87.

2 John Bunyan, *Grace Abounding to the Chief of Sinners,* (Chicago: Alec R. Allenson, Inc.), p. 96. First published 1955 in *A Treasury of Christian Books* by SCM Press Ltd., London.

3 The Treatise of Saint Bernard, Abbot of Clairvaux, *Concerning Grace and Free Will,* addressed to William, Abbot of Saint Thierry, translated with an introduction and synopsis and notes by Watkin W. Williams (London: Society for Promoting Christian Knowledge, 1920), p. 74.

4 Do you reject sin so as to live in the freedom of God's children? Do you reject the glamour of evil by refusing to be mastered by sin? Do you reject Satan, Father of sin and Prince of darkness? Do you believe in God the Father Almighty, Creator of Heaven and earth? Do you believe in Jesus Christ, his only son, our Lord who was born of the Virgin Mary, was crucified, died and was buried, rose from the dead and is now seated at God's right hand? Do you believe in the Holy Spirit, the Holy Catholic Church, the communion of saints, the forgiveness of sin, the resurrection of the body, and life everlasting? This is our faith. This is the faith of the church. We are proud to profess it in Christ Jesus, our Lord.

18

INCARNATION: INTERACTION AS A MEANS OF GRACE

Patricia Dutcher-Walls

The theological bases for the Protestant pastoral ministry are replete with rich metaphors and powerful symbols drawn from the Biblical record of the ministry of Jesus, the Christ. But the task of translating that record into the living context of today demands a talent not readily available to many. Patricia Dutcher-Walls, assistant chaplain at Colgate at the time of this course, demonstrates that talent in showing us how God's grace appears in our relationships of love, in the healing ministry of Christ that enables us to become fully human as we were meant to be.

The task I have set for myself is really twofold. I am going to be discussing bondage and grace, the themes of this study, from the perspectives of modern Protestantism. My work as a Presbyterian minister has certainly informed the chapter that I am here presenting. Do not fear. I am not going to give a sermon but I am going to be writing as a Christian.

In this chapter, I will attempt an exposition of one concept in biblical theology. I will be using New Testament sources or Christian scripture to clarify a particular theological idea that we find there and that is the idea of "Incarnation." Then I will attempt an application of that theological idea to modern life as I have experienced it as a modern Christian, a modern person. I am going to try to take some old, what we might consider sort of dead, ideas and translate them so that they have some meaning for modern people. What I hope to do is to show how in my own ministry, in my own life, some older theological concepts apply today at least for someone who stands within the Christian tradition. And, if nothing else, I hope that one will find that these ideas of bondage and grace and using this theological concept of the Incarnation really do have some relevance for understanding who modern people are and how we understand ourselves as human beings, as religious human beings.

I

I want to tell a story. It is a true story that happened to me when, one summer several years back, I worked as a chaplain intern in a hospital. I was training in chaplaincy and the hospital was in Boise, Idaho. During the course of that summer, four colleagues and I, all juniors or in the middle year in divinity school, were training to be chaplains. During the course of that summer each of us had a special area to work in and I elected, for reasons that are unknown to me, to work entirely with cancer patients so that all of the patients I dealt with that summer (except for when I was on call and dealing with emergency cases) had cancer and were in various stages of illness or treatment. Some were recovering, because cancer is not always a fatal disease; some were on the road to recovery. Others were quite clearly on the road to death.

Towards the end of the summer I had a relationship with an old man named Mr. Mitchell and this is the person I want to tell you about. Mr. Mitchell must have been in his seventies, and he had been admitted to the hospital. He had been battling cancer for a number of years, and this was to be his last battle. He had had cancer of the brain. It had been controlled for a while, but then it spread to his spine and now had spread to his lungs. During the time I saw him (I visited with him for about three weeks, the last three weeks of his life) he learned from the doctors that there was no more that could be done for him. The cancer had spread. It was inoperable. Chemotherapy would no longer do any good, but he could be made fairly comfortable. He was not in pain. He was gradually growing weaker as the cancer in his lungs prevented him from breathing properly and that was eventually what was going to kill him.

He was one of the people that I was to see. I visited with him almost every day for three weeks. Sometimes it would be a short visit if he was not feeling well or was in pain and other times we would sit and talk for an hour.

He was pretty far from home. He had grown up in another town in Idaho and his home was there, but this hospital was the center for treating cancer patients so he had been moved from his home town, which meant that his family was not around. His grown children were all off on their own. His wife was also sick and in a hospital in his home town and so could visit him very rarely, which meant that he was basically alone. He was a nice old man. Sometimes, people, when they are sick, quite understandably, get pretty cranky. He managed to avoid that, and so the nurses, everybody, loved him. But the nurses were too busy to give him the kind of care and attention that he really needed, and so it fell on my shoulders to be his primary support person during the last three weeks of his life.

Mostly what we did was talk, and we talked about everything. We talked about his children and his grandchildren. If people have grandchildren, one hears about it, endlessly, and one sees pictures. We also talked about his life and growing up in Idaho. We talked about his church and how proud he had been to be a member of the church and how he used to help out around the church. He built cabinets in the new church kitchen and he was so proud of those cabinets. We talked about those things, and as time went on we began to talk about his illness and how he was feeling about it, the various courses of the therapy that he had gone through. I was pretty new at this. I mean, it was the end of the summer so I had had eight or ten weeks of this behind me, but I still did not really know what I was doing. I was sort of blundering along, trusting the grace of God, literally, that this would be a helpful relationship to him. I was just going in there and saying "Well, how are you today, Mr. Mitchell?" and we would start talking.

But about two weeks into the relationship, when he learned that he was dying and was obviously getting weaker, one day I got together all my courage—and it is amazing how much courage it takes to ask a simple question—I remembered all my training and thought "Okay Patricia, you can do it!" and I said, "Mr. Mitchell, what do you think about when you think about dying?" And his reaction was amazing. He was past the point of being angry about it. Many people are when they first learn that they have an illness that is terminal. He was past the point of making excuses and bargaining and trying to wheedle one more day and things like that. He just looked at me and tears came to his eyes as he said "I'm so disappointed. I'm so disappointed to have to leave all the things that I've known and loved." And then he began to talk about his family and home and church again.

I thought, what an amazing reaction not to be worrying about all these details but just to be sad, just to be disappointed. And from that point on, our relationship took on a different tone. For one thing, we started talking less. I still visited with him as frequently, an hour or whatever he was comfortable with, and then he would take a nap. But we did not do much talking after that point. We did a lot of just sitting—I would just sit by his bedside. We would chat for a while and then we would fall silent and we would listen to the birds outside. It was summer.

About a week later the doctors decided that there was really no more they could do for him at this hospital, that they would send him to a hospital nearer his home. They knew that his time of death was near and that it would be better for him and his family if he were close to them when he was actually going to die. They decided that they would transfer him to this other hospital by ambulance and keep him comfortable all of the way. I visited him the day before he left and virtually nothing was said the whole time I was with him. I really had this incredibly strong feeling that nothing needed to be said, that everything had already been said, that there was no more inside of him fighting to come out, that he was at peace. Amazingly, he was dying and yet he was at peace. He had no more struggles, no more worries, whatever. Somehow all of that had been resolved, and it was as if he were already beginning to detach himself emotionally. He was still fully with us. He was still very aware but, emotionally, he had already begun to detach himself from the hardship he was going to go through, he had been going through in facing up to his own death. Then we said goodbye and we said goodbye with smiles. I learned that the next day he died as he arrived at the hospital in his home town and his wife was by his side.

I thought back on that experience, the whole summer certainly, but particularly my relationship with Mr. Mitchell. I have thought back on that a lot, and I have come to understand a lot more about bondage and grace, although I might not have used those words then. I have come to understand a lot more about human beings and who we are and how we react because of my relationship with Mr. Mitchell. It has been, and I will say this unapologetically, the strongest experience of God's grace that I have ever witnessed. When I am trying to figure things out, I always refer to that relationship and try to see if emotionally, and intellectually, I can understand what went on then. If I can understand that, I will understand who we are as human beings.

II

As I consider the two terms "bondage" and "grace," thinking about them in the context of this relationship with Mr. Mitchell, I would define bondage—the theological word for it might be sin—as fear, brokenness, and separation. In that relationship I also came to understand grace as trust, wholeness, and reconciliation.

I want to explore a bit of biblical theology to give us a theoretical framework for understanding grace in human life. The concept that I will deal with is Incarnation. Incarnation, basically, is defined as the taking on of human or animal form by a divine being. In the Christian tradition we always speak of the Incarnation, and it is capitalized, because in the Christian tradition the Incarnation refers to God's revelation as a human being in Jesus Christ. It is a specific event, a specific person. Jesus Christ is the revelation of God in human form.

The Gospel of John contains the most fundamental expression of this concept in its first chapter. The quotation is in John 1:14—"And the Word (which is the Gospel's word for Jesus) became flesh and dwelt among us full of grace and truth." This is the most fundamental expression of the Incarnation. The other Gospels contain less explicit references to the Incarnation, or to this idea of Incarnation, and it is assumed a little less explicitly throughout the Christian scriptures, that is, in the writings of Paul, the letters and the pastoral letters, and so on. So it emerges as a basic New Testament concept.

The basic Christian affirmation is that God became human in Jesus Christ and that Jesus Christ was fully human and fully divine. This is the key phrase, that he was fully human and fully divine. Now this fully human/fully divine notion represents a tricky bit of theological acrobatics that the early church had to pull off, but the importance of the fully human/fully divine idea in Christianity cannot be understated. From the first through the fourth centuries or so, arguments about this notion of fully human/fully divine, of Incarnation, led to the fiercest debates among Christian groups in the early church. As the dust began to settle, about the fourth century, a consensus emerged that carefully avoided the extremes in agreeing on this fully human divine and fully human formula.

The consensus that emerged in the church avoided the two extremes. What are those two extremes? One extreme they wanted to avoid was "adoptionism" or the so-called "adoptionist" view. The so-called "adoptionists" said that Jesus was not divine by nature but rather that he had been appointed or adopted as God's special representative at some point during his life. Thus, according to the adoptionists, he was certainly fully human but he was not fully divine. He had been adopted. The other extreme was known as "docetism." This view asserted that Jesus was not really a human being, that it was appalling that God would actually take on a human form, that the Divine would actually be known in all of the earthiness of human beings. And so this group said obviously he was not really a human being. He just took on the form, the semblance. He was sort of a facsimile of the human being but his body was not really real; he was not really a human being. Thus, he was fully divine but not fully human.

The early church eventually reached a consensus about Christ, and the consensus was that Christ had two full natures in one body—a divine nature and a human nature. Once the early church came to a consensus, both adoptionism and docetism were labelled as heresies, and people who held them were labelled as heretics.

However, the doctrinal assurance of the fourth century is less than specifically supported in the Gospels. This doctrinal assurance that Jesus is exactly fully divine and fully human is not really echoed in the Gospels. These books were written in the time before dogma, before doctrine became specific and before it became argumentative. The Gospels used the idea of Incarnation. They were sure that Jesus was God and that he was human but they did not worry about how that happened, and in fact, they differ on their interpretation of how and when the Incarnation happened. The Gospel of Mark, which according to most scholars was written earliest, announces Jesus' very special relationship with God at Jesus' baptism. We have the scene of Jesus going down to the river, being baptized by John, and in the midst of the baptism, a voice comes out of the sky "You are my beloved son with whom I am well pleased." For the Gospel of Mark there is absolutely no speculation about Jesus' birth or who or what he was before this baptism experience, and thus the Gospel of Mark comes closest to an adoptionist kind of viewpoint. That is the type of tradition the early adoptionists used; that is the tradition out of which they came. Jesus had been, in some sense, adopted as a special representative at the baptism. The next Gospels to be written were Matthew and Luke; by the time they were written the traditions about Jesus' life had expanded to include a much fuller incarnational view, the way we would understand it today—that was that Jesus was divine from the moment of his conception. This is the view we are probably most familiar with because the story in Luke, how Mary was anointed and the child born of her was of the Holy Spirit, is always read at Christmas. This is the fullest incarnational view, that from his moment of conception Jesus is both divine and human.

However, when we turn to the Gospel of John, we find that this author wants to go back even beyond Jesus' point of conception. He presents the idea that Jesus, as he puts it, the Word, existed with God at the creation of the world; in the words of the beginning of the Gospel of John, "In the beginning was the Word and the Word was with God and the Word was God." It is not good enough that in Mark's Gospel Jesus was adopted. He is "a special person . . . great!" Luke and Matthew come along and say "No, no, it is more important than that. He was divine from the moment of his conception." And then John says "No, no. He was divine from the moment the world was created. In fact, he was with God at the creation." And one can see a development in Christian thought that is chronologically the way the Gospels were written, a development in Christian thought as this notion of the Incarnation becomes more important, for Christian life, for Christian doctrine, for Christian practice. And one also sees the variations that occur between the

Gospels. They all agree on the Incarnation but there are some variations in how they interpret it.

And in addition to these variations in scripture and doctrine about the Incarnation, there have been plenty of differences in interpretation as to the meaning of the Incarnation. Space allows only a summary, one which I think fairly accurately portrays the biblical texts on this subject. I have summarized the meanings of this Incarnation into three principal meanings which I will discuss briefly.

As the biblical view developed in Christian thought, the Incarnation has come to have three primary or principal meanings. The first one is the *communication of God's love.* This meaning would say, in the biblical notion of it, that the Incarnation represents the fullest communication of God's love and concern for humanity in that God's own son was given for the task of salvation. While there had been other teachers and other prophets, the fulfillment of salvation came through the life of God's own son. So because God sent his own son to be his representative, actually to carry out his work, we see the depth of God's love and concern for humanity. That is the first meaning that is placed on the Incarnation.

The second meaning is the idea of Jesus as the *paradigm or model or example of goodness* in a human being. In Jesus' life and ministry of teaching, healing, and compassion, he demonstrated what life was meant to be when lived as God intended, with healing and compassion and understanding.

And the third meaning that is attached to the Incarnation (and this is the one that I will simply summarize) is that it accomplished the work of salvation. The Incarnation is the *accomplishment of God's saving work among humanity, the atonement or ransom, or salvation*—there are lots of theological words used here. The atonement or salvation of humankind was done by God, in the form of Jesus Christ, by taking on our sin at the Crucifixion. Through the Resurrection, a victory was won over the powers of death and sin. This victory over the powers of death and sin makes available forgiveness and new life for human beings.

Now each of these meanings could be explored at length. I have given just the shortest summary of them. Each of them has an entire history of different perspectives and interpretations that has been placed on them. And indeed, we could discuss these at length, too. Further, to do justice to all of these, there are a lot of definitions which one would also have to discuss. What does atonement mean?

What is ransom? What is Paul's view of victory over death? What is resurrection?

III

I am going to put that all aside to move on to my next task—that of translating this idea of the Incarnation and its biblical meanings into a modern interpretation. At this point I am using the word interpretation to mean a modern view of this. I will be building directly on these three meanings of the Incarnation, but I am moving into interpretive theology which I will call incarnational theology. There is liberation theology, this theology, and that theology; incarnational theology is one of these. I find three important interpretations that we can derive from this notion of incarnational theology and from interpreting it. First, incarnational theology holds that God's love and concern for human beings was seen in God's entering human life. Second, that the prime example of goodness is the human whose ministry was in full interaction with other humans. God's presence mediated through a human in relation to human beings, and here I am really thinking of Jesus walking around talking to people, informs our concept of human life—what it is to be human. In this interpretation, a human being is not like an atomistic particle existing separately and individually nor is human life a series of things, ourselves encased from and bouncing off other things, other people. Rather, the concept of human life in this interpretation consists of relationships, both relationships to ourselves as in consciousness we become aware of ourselves and relationships to other people. Life, therefore, is a dynamic process of interaction whereby each person affects and is affected by others in an interrelational network.

What I am asking is that if these two things are true, if the paradigm of human goodness is a human being in reaction and relation to and interaction with other human beings and if God ordains that, if God sent his own son to be that, then we can come up with an interpretation of what it means to be human, what it means to have a human life. That interpretation is that interaction and relationships between people are constitutive of human life, rather than a view which says that one is an individual and that one has sort of a wall around one and everything out there is an object and one is a subject and all are distinct. This view of human life, this interpretation of human life, is saying that the wall that one has around one as subject with all those objects out there is not really a wall. One is connected with other people and other people affect one and one affects them. What is important about one's life is not a sense of oneself as *individual,* but of oneself in *relationship* to other people. So this is a very different concept of human life. It is actually closer to a Jewish concept of human life with the notion of who one is as a person existing in a community, not one as an individual existing over and against the world. So incarnational theology can inform our concept of human life.

Moreover, incarnational theology holds that the paradigm of goodness was the human/divine Jesus, and that we know God and God's saving power through the human form and mission of Jesus. This provides the basis for modern interpretations of the concept of salvation. What does it mean to be saved following this line of incarnational theology? Salvation is not in this view becoming something radically different from or other than we are. It is not trying to become superhuman or more than human or divine. Rather, in this view, according to this interpretation, salvation is the very redemption and perfection of humanity as humans. Salvation is the perfection, redemption (however one wants to call it) of humanity as humans—the restoration to what we were created to be as humans, as intended by the creator. Thus the saving work of Christ makes us fully human.

If God, in the Incarnation, has communicated his love, if this human being Jesus is the paradigm of goodness, if through this human being salvation is accomplished, salvation must be a human thing. Salvation must be something understandable in human experience, in human terms. It must not be trying to lift us out of the human, to make us something different from what we were, from what we are, but, rather, this interpretation says that the concept of salvation is to make us really human, and here we would return to this notion of creation, to help us live the way we were intended to live by the creator aside from all of this bondage and sin. Salvation has enabled us to live in a fully human way.

Thirdly, incarnational theology provides an interpretation for how grace works. This is my main point although the other two are related. Incarnational theology assumes all three of these meanings. Further, this theology acknowledges that it took the entire life, ministry, death, and resurrection of Jesus Christ to accomplish God's purpose for humankind. And incarnational theology holds that grace was mediated in people's actual relationships with Jesus Christ. Again and again in the Gospels one reads stories where, when someone is in conversation, in relationship with this Jesus, healing is accomplished, a person is made whole. It is in relationship with this Jesus that healing, that salvation comes about. This happens both during his ministry, when he was walking around on earth, and, for the Christian, after his resurrection, in that Christians believe that Jesus is still with us in being resurrected from the dead. That is a Christian belief, or at least a traditional Christian belief that Jesus is somehow still spiritually present to believers; thus we can still have a relationship with him in a healing way.

All of this informs our concept of how grace works. At this point, for this interpretation, grace is not so much an object to be gotten, a thing to be had. It is not a result to be sought: "You know, if I just work hard enough I'll get some grace at the end." All of that goes out the window when one reflects on incarnational theology. Rather, grace becomes a quality of life. Grace becomes a quality known in and through *all* of life, not just at a particular time, not just at the end when one goes to heaven. And grace is a quality that is mediated in human interactions where God is present. In human interactions—that means between ordinary people. For Christians, God is present through Christ's continuing life, through Christ's continuing presence with us, and through the power of the Holy Spirit. And those are both, again, an understanding for Christians —that God can be present through Christ's loving presence, through the power of the Holy Spirit.

And this presence, particularly in the community of the church, means that the activity of grace can be continued in human interactions, in, if you will, our day-to-day interactions with other people but it does not require something special. It does not require something different from what we are. It does not require us to go out and work hard. It requires us to *be* in interaction with each other. The process, then, of working out God's grace in these human interactions thus becomes as important as the results, and, in fact, the process, the interactions where God is present, becomes a means of grace—and hence the title of this chapter. The process, the interactions themselves, between people becomes the means, the way grace can be mediated in human life. It is not something out there. It is not something foreign. It is not something two thousand years old.

We are human and how we know God is not as an abstract Other but in the reality of other people all around us. Now this is not saying that the mystic, the hermit, does not also know God and that there is not a direct revelation of God, say, in prayer. But it is saying that God's presence, God's grace, is also available to us in the interactions that we have with people. You can find God's grace in the midst of life. Grace originates from God because God is both creator and then redeemer and then sustainer. It is God who redeems and sustains, helps, comforts, and nurtures human beings, so that the source of grace is God. But another way of putting this is what I am attempting: taking the God/human relationship off the vertical direction and putting it on the horizontal plane. God also becomes present to us in the horizontal, in the day-to-day, in real reactions, and it is in the interaction, it is between two people, that grace happens, that God enters human experience. Because human beings are also capable of evil, our interactions are capable of hurting each other. Now God is not present in those interactions. God is present in the healing, nurturing relationships. Human beings are responsible for making the decision, in the story of the Garden of Eden, to disobey God, and that disobeying was the source of falling from or losing the way we were intended by the Creator to live, so that we are in bondage and that a lot of our interactions are based on fear and brokenness and separation: "I'm looking out for number one and don't care about you." God does not enter there. When I am being arrogant, selfish, rude, God is not there, because God is not arrogant, selfish, rude, looking out for number one. God is not worried about success. Living without God, living in our own arrogance, trying to go it alone—when we do that, we sin. We fall from the way we were intended because we were intended to be living in communion with God and thus in communion with each other.

IV

With this as a conceptual base, I want to explore the story, related at the beginning of this chapter, to see how such an idea of authentic interaction as a means of grace can actually work out. What happened in my relationship with Mr. Mitchell that allowed grace to happen? First, grace was shared when his fears were replaced by trust. In the relationship, Mr. Mitchell was able to explore his fears and express them openly. Neither of us tried to hide from the facts of his illness, his pain, and his emotional reactions to his illness and approaching death. Because we did not try to hide or pretend that everything was all right, he knew that his fears were acceptable and, thus, he too could acknowledge and accept them. In general, a healing interaction occurs when both people know that no matter what happens, no matter what painful subjects are talked about, the companionship will continue. When people are enabled to stay with each other in emotional support, which may be as simple or as difficult as listening to the real fears of another person, then trust is established between the people and trust between people makes fear bearable because it is shared. It does not necessarily make fear disappear but an acceptance and acknowledgment of fear decreases its power to hurt and cripple a person emotionally and thus a healing takes place when trust decreases the power of fear.

Secondly, in my visits with Mr. Mitchell, grace was shared when wholeness replaced brokenness. Once trust had been established, Mr. Mitchell was able to talk about many aspects of his life, his home and family, his work for the church, as well as the course of his illness. He soon became for me a whole human being, not just a client that I was seeing, not just a patient in a hospital. He knew that my interest in him extended beyond the details of his sickness, and we shared stories and jokes as well as very hard moments of pain and despair. Again, in general, graceful interactions lead to a recognition of both people as whole people. Even when one is seemingly reduced to a sick body full of tubes and attached monitors, there is a whole person there which grace discovers, a recognition of the wholeness of life that is shared when one's needs, shame, pain, and sorrow are as fully accepted as one's joys, health, and strengths.

Thirdly, grace was shared as reconciliation overcame separateness in our relationship. Alone in his illness, Mr. Mitchell had been a very lonely man, facing his death by himself and not even able to be completely at ease with himself because of his fears and brokenness. As our interactions developed, a reconciliation occurred because he was able to see his own fears and pain and thus be at peace with himself. And a healing reconciliation also took place between us because he knew another was with him in his sorrow. To generalize, healing interactions are facilitated when both people are prepared to give and receive strength and comfort from each other. Healing can come to those who must "go it alone," but the process of reconciliation is deepened when it takes place in the context of an on-going relationship.

And finally, to summarize, I have found a great depth of understanding of my relationships, such as that with Mr. Mitchell, as I have explored the meaning of the Incarnation. As a Christian and a minister, I find that the meanings of the biblical idea of God taking human form have been a rich source of insight and theological reflection. The concepts of human life as dynamic and interrelational, of salvation as restoring our full humanity, and of grace as a process of authentic interaction, have shown themselves again and again to have real significance for my ministry. And I have come to realize that experiencing God's presence and healing grace in the interactions between people is no figment of my imagination. When I was visiting with Mr. Mitchell, he was not the only one who found healing, because grace is a gift that respects no definitions of who is client and who is minister. The trust, wholeness, and reconciliation that occurred was shared, just as real for me as for him.

How is it that fear is turned into trust, brokenness into wholeness, separation into reconciliation? It is because someone else is with one in the midst of that fear and brokenness and separateness, and so one can become healed.

19

GRACE IN THE PASTORAL MINISTRY

Vernon H. Ross

It is in the day-to-day routine of life that the unfolding of that divine healing quality, about which one speaks when one uses the word grace, seems to appear. The life of a minister is filled with relationships and with demands, a life in which one is constantly "on call" to respond in moments of trauma and bitter despair. It is hard work, the Reverend Vernon H. Ross tells us. And yet, this pastor emeritus of the First Baptist Church, which sponsored and helped organize the Baptist Education Society of the State of New York in 1817, chartered in 1819, later to become Colgate University, lets us see the ordinary nature of a sense of bondage and leads us to understand, too, that when we are faithful to the finest that we have been enabled to discern, grace seems to arise.

I

"Grace" has not been much in my personal bag of churchly words. The Apostle Paul in one of his letters spoke of "faith, hope, and love," and that they are abiding, enduring realities; and in another letter he spoke of "love, joy, and peace" as fruits of the Holy Spirit; and I like those word triplets very much. Paul certainly used the word "grace" a great deal, too, but there is no mention in the Gospels that Jesus used it at all, and I have tended to focus my thought around the Gospels rather than the Pauline epistles.

In his younger days as a rigid, religious personality, Paul

consented to the death by stoning of a Christian preacher named Stephen, and God's grace in forgiving Paul literally meant everything to him. I myself have seldom used the term until these past few months. While some pastors would pronounce a benediction at the conclusion of a worship service with these words, "The grace of our Lord Jesus Christ be with you all," I would more frequently say, "The peace of our Lord Jesus Christ. . . ." In fact some twenty years ago I spent a few hours one day trying to figure out the meaning of the word grace, and gave up on it.

So you see, I have deeply appreciated this study, not just for the opportunity to learn something about other religious traditions, but also for the opportunity provided to learn something more about Christian thought.

I am delighted to have had the opportunity to be a part of this study. Frankly, I am not a lecturer by trade, nor am I the son of a lecturer, to paraphrase the prophet Amos. I am the pastor of the First Baptist Church of Hamilton, New York, having previously served a suburban church in Roselle, New Jersey, and prior to that, a church in Woonsocket, Rhode Island, a New England mill town. I graduated from the Colgate Rochester Divinity School in 1954. I am as proud to be a Baptist as John Rexine is to be a Greek Orthodox or Pat Dutcher-Walls to be a Presbyterian, but I must confess that there are many kinds of Baptists in this world, and I am not proud of all of them.

I stand in a Baptist tradition that has appreciated education, and perhaps you know that the Baptist Church in Hamilton is the mother church of Colgate University. One should also note that Baptists have contributed to the universal church the great doctrine of freedom of individual conscience, and from this has stemmed the first amendment to the Constitution, namely, the separation of church and state.

II

Because I am a pastor, I can share something out of my pastoral experience in the general area of human bondage and divine grace. We have in the preceding chapter by Patricia Dutcher-Walls a beautifully structured theology of grace, so I will concentrate here on the earthy, everyday experiences of a working pastor with his or her people. Grace, if understood, as Pat put it, in terms of trust, wholeness, and reconciliation in interpersonal relationships, is a pastor's daily experience, although, to be sure, I have not been in the habit of identifying grace every moment when I have discovered it.

Various forms of bondage confront a pastor in his or her work. Every person and family in the parish is unique, and every person and family has major problems sooner or later. The minister is called to be a pastor right within the context of those problems, traumas, and difficult moments. So the ministry is a battle of wits, it is hard work, and it is very rewarding, upon occasion at least.

One element of the bondage that a pastor experiences is his or her own ignorance. After one year in divinity school, I became interim pastor in a Presbyterian Church in the wider Rochester area. I picked up rumors fairly quickly that a man had divorced his wife in hopes of encouraging a women to divorce her husband, to leave her children and live with him. The woman was aware of these rumors going around, and one Friday evening called me at the divinity school and asked that I talk with her. I had never had a course in counselling. She met me at the church on a Saturday morning, told me about the rumors, and then asked me straight out, "What shall I do?"

I had no idea what to say, but felt compelled to say something, something "religious." I stalled for a time but she pressed the point, and finally I blurted out, "Have you tried praying about this?" This may have reinforced some guilt feelings, I am not sure, but she went into a mild form of hysteria. I had not helped her one bit. Instead of grace there was worse emotional confusion than ever. I was in over my head. I excused myself as someone not able to help her, and left, before I did more harm. One of our forms of bondage is ignorance, and because the pastoral ministry covers such a vast area of life and living, this ignorance is similarly vast and sometimes appalling.

Another form of bondage in my case is close to the first, and that is in my not being very articulate or precise in the use of words. In 1968, during a worship service on Easter Sunday, I took a few minutes to attempt to interpret for my congregation some aspects of a seizure of the administration building at Colgate University by the black students on campus and over one hundred sympathetic white students. They were protesting against lingering vestiges of racial discrimination in the fraternities. At the time I had been pastor at the First Baptist Church in Hamilton for three years, and thought I could say some needed words, but while I said the right things, I did not say them in exactly the clearest manner, and the roof fell in on me. There was serious emotional turmoil instead of the healing graces—love, joy, and peace. A pastor has to live and to work within the context of such mistakes.

And also there are comparable mistakes on the part of a pastor's congregation. In a former pastorate, I have known a fiery Frenchman, physically very strong, very proud of his leading role in the life of the church and contemptuous of those who liked a game of golf on a sunny Sunday morning. As chairman of the Board of Trustees, he took action one time without the knowledge or support of the board, and when the sexton told me about it, I put a stop to it until the board could act. It was a nasty piece of business, and the board voted with me against him. He was furious. The following Sunday morning while I was shaking hands in the front vestibule of the church, I saw him back the old sexton into the corner, and I heard angry words, "Squealer! Stooge!" It was not the most graceful moment in the life and history of that church! I excused myself, stepped over and tapped this angry churchman on the shoulder, saying, "You take your spite out on me!" His reaction was to cover up like a boxer, and I wondered why. I looked at my right fist, and it was cocked, ready to hit him if he had made a move to attack me. I looked at that fist, surprised, for I had thought of myself as a pacifist, turned and smiled at him. He ran out of the church, came back in, scolded me till he was red in the face and speechless, and ran back out again. He repeated that three times, and all I could say was "Peace." It was disgraceful.

Sometimes as a preacher I have to stand against the social ills of our time. Once I waxed eloquent in the pulpit condemning our Christmas bombing of Hanoi and Haiphong during the Vietnam War. That was a terrible, dreadful business, carpet bombing those cities with B-52s and even heavily damaging the largest North Vietnamese hospital. That sermon brought a considerable reaction from some of our community's better known citizens. If there is one thing we Baptists cherish, it is our freedom, and the pulpit has to be kept free for the preacher to speak as he or she best feels God leads, whether or not the people in the congregation all agree. But for a pastor to speak against popular concepts of national loyalty and patriotism is very difficult, and unless done with unusual skill and grace often does far more harm than good.

Another form of parish bondage is the class structure of the community. A sociologist will describe the social stratification of the churches. Here in Hamilton there are divisions between town and gown, between rural and village, between rich and poor, and sometimes these dividing walls are strong and tough to break through. Two decades ago I bought five acres on tax sale some seven miles out in the hills, southeast of our village, near the tiny hamlet of South Hamilton. Eighty years ago that hamlet was a thriving rural village with a water-powered grist mill and saw mill, a general store, a cheese factory, a gunsmith's shop, two blacksmith shops, a Baptist church, a school house, post office and saloon, but all those institutions are gone now. The church finally closed a few years ago, and the community is quite poor.

I became acquainted with one of the residents of that area, a ragged old recluse who had been sent to a state mental hospital in 1933 for four years, and who had withdrawn from society because he believed any of the neighbors could file a complaint and send him back. I would visit with him, and on occasion arrange for some Colgate students to join me to do some repairs on his old house. Then several years ago his house caught fire. One of his neighbors, picking up the radio transmission of the fire department with a scanner, called me; I went right out, and found the house a mass of flames. The old fellow was off to one side, talking with a fireman and another acquaintance. His back was towards me, and he had not seen me coming. For all he knew I was still in New York City attending a seminar, but I had returned two days early to conduct a funeral service. As I approached the fireman asked him, "Where will you go now?" And he answered, "I guess I'll go live in Hamilton with my friend Reverend Ross." I knew at that moment that some of the rural-village, poor-rich, educated-uneducated social barriers had been broken through. It was for me a moment of grace. And he did live with my family and me for four months, during which time the young people and I built him a log cabin on the foundation of the old house there on the family farm where he had been born, where his grandfather had settled in 1856, and where he had lived alone since his wife died in 1929, except for those four years in a state mental hospital.

Prejudice is another form of bondage closely allied with class structure. It blinds us to the personhood of another human being. Prejudice is generally considered racial in character, but I have in mind here my own personal prejudice towards those who abuse alcohol. My father and I had wonderful times together hunting and fishing, and working in his basement workshop or the garden. But by the time I was out of college, his drinking became a real problem, especially for my mother. Some years later when I was home on vacation, Dad and one of his friends and I spent a day fishing on Lake Erie. We caught our limit of black bass. The weather was magnificent. Dad and his friend had enjoyed two six packs, not enough to do any harm, and we were all relaxed when we stopped in a small village hotel (this was in Southern Ontario, Canada, where the taverns are all called hotels). The only decoration in the room we entered was a sign saying that occupancy was limited to forty-eight men. Women had to drink in another room, and a man, if accompanied by a woman, would have his drink in that other room.

The waiter went from table to table with his schooners of beer, and with barely a word to anyone, but with a warm, reserved attitude made sure that everyone was taken care of. A few businessmen came in, a few farmers and laborers and us fishermen, and everyone minded his own business. There was polite conversation at every table. The atmosphere was genteel, cordial, masculine. I recall that scene as a time of grace, when my prejudices towards hotels were punctured through. I, with my ginger ale, was accepted there far better than my father was ever accepted in the home church. I have often wished that I had gone to the hotel where Dad spent time with his friends, day by day, and had shared similar moments there.

Rumors can also develop into a form of bondage. When I was a student pastor of a church not far from Hamilton, I would stop by the Methodist parsonage on Saturday afternoons to pick up the town news. One Saturday that pastor gathered up his courage and told me directly, "I hear you hate Methodists. It's all over the village." I was thunderstruck. I had just served for a year in an urban Methodist Church as a youth minister, and had gotten along well with everyone except the pastor, who had fired me—and that was his problem, not mine. "There's not a word of truth to it!" I insisted to my pastoral colleague. "What shall I do?" I asked.

"Nothing," said that wiser, older man. "If there's no truth to those rumors, they'll die of their own weight." And they did.

I found that comforting when more recently rumors spread around the village of Hamilton that I was the person secretly behind the rallies of the Ku Klux Klan that were being held at a neighbor's farm near my out-of-town shack that I have built. If I wanted to, some people reasoned, I could have spoken the word, and my neighbor would have put a stop to those rallies. A local businessman actually challenged me on the street one day on this very point, sharing his disappointment with me; I was grateful for the opportunity to assure him that I had done my best on this point, that my neighbor was reared a Baptist and I had no control whatever over how he thinks and acts. In fact, my neighbor reasoned that since he had accepted me as a friend, he could similarly accept the Klan leader as a friend, since that leader considered himself a pastor also, the leader of a little congregation that met in his own home. The Klan-people with their leader turned out to be working people, at the lower end of the social scale, easily led by a man like him, people, however, whom I found I could visit with and listen to and even relate to, while not holding for a moment to their vicious anti-black, anti-semitic views. They did not hold a rally at my neighbor's farm last year, after three years in a row, and while I do not know the reason for sure, I can guess that they simply did not get the media coverage the year before and could not afford to make the trip to South Hamilton for so little attention.

Another form of bondage that a pastor works with is differing theological views within his or her congregation. And there are other forms of bondage within which a pastor attempts to carry out a healing ministry. Perhaps one could think of a hundred others. Another is that a pastor tends to play favorites with his or her people. Recently the weather was sunny and warm and I called on a little eighty-nine year old lady whom I knew would love to go for a ride in the car just to get out of the house. She was delighted; I love her dearly, and we had a grand time together. It is so easy to spend time with those with whom moments of grace are almost assured rather than with people where there is anger, hatred, conflict, trouble. A pastor cannot please everyone; not even Jesus could do that. Another form of bondage is the limited amount of time that a pastor has to work with, and the need to discipline his or her use of time so carefully, to get the reading, calling, sermon preparation, church administration, and youth work even half-way done.

Another is the burden of piety that a pastor is supposed to carry. In the old folks home one day, a man called me over to his bed to whisper to me in shocked and disapproving tones that his aged roommate was trying to get the young nurses to sleep with him. He wanted me to express shock and disgust, but I simply grinned. I also remember my pastorate in New England. There were several barber shops in town, but one in particular was a great social center. It had three or four chairs and there was always activity there—fun, wild stories, laughing, joking. I would put on some old work clothes before going over for a haircut so that no one would ever guess I was a pastor. The barbers were friendly, and regularly they would ask me what I worked at, and of course, I would never tell them. That went on for six months. Then one day when I walked into the shop, the barber at the chair nearest the door called out "good morning, *Reverend!*" I never heard again the kind of ribald stories that characterized the fellowship of that shop. No matter how much I begged those guys to lay off that "reverend" stuff, they had to show respect for the cloth.

Soon thereafter, a newspaper reporter coming to work on New Year's Day saw that the clock on the Baptist Church steeple had not quite made it into the New Year. It had quit at 10:30 p.m. on New Year's Eve. He called me, wrote his story, including the estimate that the clock needed a thousand dollars worth of repairs, and darned if that barber shop did not start the fund drive! The reporter picked up on that story, and public donations soon exceeded the thousand dollars needed. I did not hear any more ribald stories but there were many more moments of grace, in the form of fellowship, trust, and belonging.

III

Grace cannot be bought, packaged, or sold, although Bonhoeffer spoke about "cheap grace," referring to people who try to buy their way into heaven or into God's favor one way or another. Genuine grace happens when people reach out to one another in love and trust, though not always. An old friend in the nursing home shares his room with three other men. One of them has tried repeatedly to reach out to my friend, to engage him in conversation, to become a friend, but the other fellow is not interested. He simply wishes to read, and to sleep with a nurse. One of his roommates said to me recently, "I tried to talk to him, and he told me to go to hell!"

Sometimes grace simply tumbles out of thin air, gratuitously appearing, perhaps, to resemble simply blind luck. One Friday evening while driving from Rochester to Red Creek through a snowstorm, I had to put the car in a snowbank to keep from hitting another car that had spun out ahead of me and was crosswise of my lane. I walked to that car and as I approached, a woman whom I recognized as the organist in my church got out. She was eight and a half months pregnant, and should never have been out in the storm, but she needed groceries, and her husband was home sick in bed. She fell into my arms exhausted, frightened, relieved. How fortunate it was that I should have come along when I did! With help from other travellers, she was soon safely home.

Last summer I took an old friend from a nursing home out to his log cabin to see the remains of his horsebarn which had blown down in a wind storm. We looked around, with him holding onto my arm to steady himself on the rough ground, and then as we were going into the cabin, I pointed to an old hornets' nest on the underside of the front porch roof and told him that a pair of wrens had built a nest there that summer. And as I raised my hand to point to the nest, I saw a little hatchling clawing desperately to keep from falling out of the hole in the bottom of the hornets' nest that the wrens had used. The baby bird dropped into my open hand and within seconds the other three hatchlings did also. I nailed a box onto a post beside the hornets' nest, broke it off and put it into the box, and a few days later found out that the little birds had fledged out all right. Soon they were grown and had left the nest. There is a lot of blood and death in the natural world, but that was a moment for me of not just blind luck but of grace, too.

Grace comes when we prove faithful to the finest and best that we know. There are great reservoirs of strength and selflessness and courage when we are challenged and stretched.

Sometimes a pastor has to be devious, although one cannot do that very often! Once I felt a man in the church needed to get back to gardening to restore his equilibrium. He had become nervous, unsettled, and needed the exercise and the satisfaction from working with his hands at the end of the day. So in the spring I had a church group organize an old-fashioned fair, with prizes and ribbons to be given out in the fall for the best vegetables and flowers. He went for that in a big way, had a great garden, and I will never forget visiting with him one evening as the sun went down and he, wholesomely tired, could work in his garden no longer. I found him a whole person once again, relaxed, at peace with himself and the world.

Sometimes grace comes from the most unexpected sources. When my dad was dying from lung cancer, and the end approached, he asked my mom to read to him from the Bible. "What shall I read?" she asked. "Oh, you know." So she read the Twenty-third Psalm, and when she was finished Dad said to her with a smile, "There, I knew you would know what to read." The next morning he was gone. He died at home; Mom had nursed him for eight months or so, providing far more pleasant care than he would have ever received in a hospital. But he ministered to her when he asked that she read to him from the Bible.

Grace comes unexpectedly, without warning. I once called on a student wrestler in the hospital who had thrown his opponent, but had his elbow broken when his opponent fell on it. I went in to cheer up that chap, but in my imagination I felt his dreadful pain, and walked into his room with a very long face. He cheered me up! His arm was in a sling, and he was in remarkably good spirits.

Neither pastor nor layperson goes around looking for grace. It simply happens, and life is filled with joy and peace, for a moment at least. Being a pastor is a battle of wits, it is hard work, but it is also deeply, keenly rewarding.

The grace of our Creator God, who made us all for love, joy, and peace, abound in your hearts now and abide with you always.

Of Human Bondage and Divine Grace

M. Holmes Hartshorne

We bring to a close our study "Of Human Bondage and Divine Grace," a theme that is neither original nor foreign, we are coming fully to understand, a theme the probing of which leads one to discern the fullness of our humanity at the point that our estrangement is broken down through the agency of another who receives us. Professor Hartshorne turns our attention to our common, and global, awareness that a human relationship rooted in love is therapeutic, that defensiveness crumbles in the act of trust, that being honest to one's humanity requires simultaneously that one fully ascertain the reality of one's bondage, to recognize the source that ultimately frees one, and to acknowledge it.

The title of my remarks is hardly original: "Of Human Bondage and Divine Grace." I will attempt to illuminate this subject from a psychological perspective.

I guess I will have to start with a question. How many of us have seen the movie *Ordinary People?* Most of us. Well, those of us who have not seen it, ought to see it; it is an extraordinarily fine film, dealing with psychological matters in a profoundly human way. That is not always the case. Some psychology never gets beyond rats. In any case, a sufficient number of us have seen it, so I shall refer to it as we go along. The rest of us will have to make as much as possible out of the illustrations by the vigorous exercise of the imagination.

Human bondage is the situation from which any and all psychotherapeutic works begins. In *Ordinary People,* Conrad was clearly a boy in bondage. One could describe that bondage in a variety of ways. He was in bondage to a profound sense of guilt, guilt for being alive. His brother had drowned when their hold on each other over the upturned boat had broken in the storm, and he felt that he had been the cause of his brother's death. He was in bondage to anger: anger over his mother's rejection of him, anger towards the simple injustice of the situation in which he had become guilty through no intent on his part. He was in bondage also in that he was not able to express that anger, even to himself. One could say, using a more ancient description, that Conrad was possessed by a dumb demon.

Many of us are also possessed by dumb demons. That is, there lies in our hearts something so fearful or so shameful, so ineffable that we simply cannot give expression to it. The anxiety which consciousness of it would engender is too great. I think it is important to realize that there is a variety of ways in which the human condition can be described. One can, of course, say that Conrad was neurotic, perhaps psychotic. That is a perfectly legitimate way of describing him. One could also say that he was possessed by a dumb demon. My point is that the human reality is the same. The latter description suggests a difference of perspective, a dimension which might be described as that of ultimate concern, inasmuch as the demon, the demonic, is opposed to the divine. But since we moderns are uncomfortable with both the demonic and the divine, we prefer more neutralized expressions like "neurosis."

In America there are two traditions in psychotherapy. These two traditions are the Freudian and what is loosely called the interpersonal or existentialist tradition in psychotherapy. I want to say a word about each and how each understands human bondage as well as the way each sees release from that bondage.

First let us speak of Freud. Freud's anthropology, that is, his doctrine of human nature, really describes humankind as fated to be in the grip of forces from which it cannot finally escape. In Freud's view all psychic energy comes from what he called *id.* (I am taking the later Freud now, I have not time to go through the full story of the development of his thought.) *Id,* Latin for "it," is, in his words, a seething cauldron of blind desire. That is a pretty vivid description. Fundamentally we are psycho-biological organisms with certain basic desires, which can be defined as sexual, or at least as pleasure-seeking. Since the id is blind, it cannot cope with the world in which it finds itself, and therefore the id develops around itself the *ego,* or consciousness. Freud describes it as a cortical layer, or bark. The function of the ego is to enable the id, which is to fulfill its desires, to deal with what he calls reality, and by reality he really means the outer world. The ego sees to it that our desires are sufficiently modified so that they can be at least partially realized. For example, suppose I get hungry before the end of this hour and a half. Since I have no sandwich in my pocket, the option of eating it is closed to me. It would be undeniably frustrating for me to start chewing on this pad, because I would derive from it no nourishment and little pleasure. My ego is functioning well enough to tell me that the satisfaction of my hunger must wait until I get home.

In addition, Freud also speaks of the *super-ego.* That is that part of the ego which carries on a quite independent existence and has in the first instance the function of conscience. The super-ego punishes the ego for certain of its desires and at the same time (and this is its other function) holds up to the ego ideals which are always beyond its competence. The way in which that develops (I do not think I need take time to go into it) has to do with the Oedipus complex and that sort of thing and those of us who are acquainted with Freud will know what I am talking about. The rest of you, I feel sure, can follow me without my going further into it. Suffice it to say, that when the id seeks to satisfy a desire, the ego will try to check it if the desire is unrealistic or incompatible with the strictures of the super-ego. If a man has, for example, a desire for companionship and there are no women around, then there will be frustration; but the ego, if it is smart, will try to alter the situation so as to bring the organism into proximity with some charming young lady. However, what the ego desires may be incompatible with what the super-ego says is permissible.

One should also note that the super-ego gets its content from the parents, and so it is the embodiment of the super-egos of the parents, the grandparents; in a sense it represents cultural taboos, cultural norms.

It is abundantly clear that the ego has an unenviable job to perform. In many respects, it is the servant of the id, created by the id for the purpose of enabling the id to express itself without coming into collision with either reality or the super-ego. But Freud points out, the ego really has to serve "three harsh masters": reality, id, and super-ego. If it is unable successfully to mediate between the demands of these harsh masters, it breaks out into anxiety, which can take three forms. They are: *reality anxiety* in the face of the demands of reality; *moral anxiety* in the face of the demands of the super-ego; and *neurotic anxiety* in the face of the demands of the id. The result is that the ego, whose function is to be reasonable about things, ends up rationalizing. It gives good reasons for actions and judgments which cannot really be justified reasonably.

It is very difficult for us to discover when we are reasoning about our situation and when we are rationalizing. Rationalization is seductively easy. For example, take a simple innocuous case. One finds oneself at a party, a cocktail party or something of that sort, in some intense social situation, and in one's nervousness and one's zeal one says something utterly stupid, just plain stupid. And this is unkindly pointed out to one by the amused multitudes. In consequence one finds oneself feeling utterly crushed. So what does one do? One immediately finds some poor, inoffensive ear which one can bend, explaining what one really meant and how one happened to say this dumb thing and how it was all a great mistake, and so on—which is to say, one seeks to justify oneself. Much easier to do that than to say "I was just a damned fool"; because if I was a damned fool, probably I am one, and that is something which we feel uneasy about admitting. We rationalize in order to give the hard-pressed ego some sense of ease.

Freud compares the relation of the id and the ego to that of a horse and a rider in which the rider is compelled to guide the horse in the direction in which the horse wants to go. It is a rather nice description. The ego is compelled to guide the id in the direction in which the id wants to go. But we must not forget that because of its essential blindness the id needs the ego.

There are further complications: the instinctual desires of the id are themselves divided. In studying the phenomena of masochism and sadism, Freud recognized an element of the aggressive, which appears to be intimately bound up with sexuality. He came at length to see that there are two groups of instincts, which he described with the Greek words *eros* and *thanatos*—love and death—in other words, instincts whose aim was the promotion of life and the binding of individuals into groups and then the death instinct, which is primarily directed against the organism itself. The prime function of the latter is to return the organism to its original state of non-being. We are saved from that self-destructive component only by turning this drive outward as aggression, and it is in this form that we ordinarily meet the death instinct. Because aggression is a condition for survival (our sole protection against self-destruction), Freud was persuaded that persons could not avoid hating each other, fighting each other; only so could they escape a worse fate.

We are pretty familiar with that self-destructive, suicidal drive. For example, one finds a student friend of one's who tears around the back roads of Madison County at seventy or seventy-five miles an hour with tires squealing. What is the story? Well, of course, he or she is doing it for the excitement, but as an individual of eighteen, nineteen, or twenty years of age, one knows perfectly well that is a pretty risky excitement. The zest for life is in tension with the desire for death. Sometimes one wins; sometimes the other. The id is powerful, and its drives are persistent.

Now, psychic illness is, for Freud, really the enslavement of the ego by the forces of the id. The ego and the super-ego will repress desires which are incompatible with reality but these desires do not go away. They are simply there, and they manifest themselves in a variety of ways. And when they manifest as free-floating anxiety or as a tick or as migraine headaches or as a duodenal ulcer or even as paralysis or colitis (one could go on and list a considerable number of neurotic symptoms), then the only way in which health can be restored is to bring that original impulse to consciousness and help the ego to give it some kind of safe expression.

Thus for Freud, psychoanalysis is a technique by which, through dream analysis and free association principally, the unconscious wish is brought to consciousness and permitted an expression that is compatible with the reality principle. Therapy includes importantly transference, that is, the projection of the patient's unconscious feelings on the analyst, so that they can be more readily recognized, acknowledged, and worked through. In Freud's view it was a technique that could be justified scientifically. That was very important for him. His mode of thinking was determined by late nineteenth century biological determinism, and he was persuaded that psychoanalysis was a practical science.

But there is an interesting comment Freud makes in the last book that he wrote. Speaking of psychoanalysis he writes:

> Our plan of cure is based on these discoveries [which we have been describing]. The ego is weakened by the internal conflict, and we must go to its help. The position is like that in a civil war which has to be decided by the assistance of an ally from outside. The analytic physician and the patient's weakened ego, basing themselves on the real external world, have to band themselves together into a party against the enemies, that is, against the instinctual demands of the *id* and the conscientious demands of the super-ego.

Now notice the next sentence:

> We form a pact with each other. One might well say a covenant. The sick ego promises us the most complete candor—promises, that is, to put at our disposal all the material which its self-perception yields it; we assure the patient of the strictest discretion and place at his service our experience in interpreting material that has been influenced by the unconscious. Our knowledge is to make up for his ignorance and to give his ego back its mastery over lost provinces of his mental life. This pact constitutes the analytic situation.[1]

This notion of a pact between patient and analyst is something that Freud never really developed. I think it was clearly present in his relationship to his patients from the outset, but he could not break free of the nineteenth century ideal of the disinterested, objective scientist who in the analytic situation sat quietly behind the couch on which the patient reclined, out of view, and spoke, when he did, pretty much *ex cathedra.* It is an element in the therapeutic process that was given centrality by the inter-personal and existential schools of psychotherapy. As is suggested by the name, for these therapists what is basic to the human situation is personal relationships, and neurosis is understood as a distortion, a disturbance of basic human relationships. To put it more simply, mental illness is a consequence of mistrust, with the consequent emergence of suspicion and defensiveness, deep anxiety about one's own worth and acceptability, and therefore a mistrust of others and even of life itself. Let me read to you Karen Horney's description of such basic anxiety, for she puts it succinctly and powerfully:

> To approach the problem genetically we must go back to what I have called basic anxiety, meaning by this the feeling the child has of being isolated and helpless in a potentially hostile world. A wide range of

> adverse factors in the environment can produce this insecurity in a child: direct or indirect domination; indifference; erratic behavior; lack of respect for the child's individual needs; lack of real guidance; disparaging attitudes; too much admiration or the absence of it; lack of reliable warmth; having to take sides in parental arguments; too much or too little responsibility; over-protection; isolation from other children; injustice; discrimination; unkept promises; hostile atmosphere; and so on and so on.
>
> The only factor to which I should like to draw special attention in this context is the child's sense of lurking hypocrisy in the environment: his feeling that the parents' love, their Christian charity, honesty, generosity, and so on, may be only pretense. Part of what the child feels on this score is really hypocrisy; but some of it may be just his reaction to all the contradictions he senses in the parents' behavior.[2]

What Horney is suggesting here is, of course, that a child's original attitude is one of trust. Parenthetically, I think that those of us who have wondered some about Jesus' odd saying, that except you become little children you cannot enter the kingdom of Heaven, might consider that this refers precisely to what characterizes little children: a willingness to trust in spite of endless rebuffs, endless evidence that the trust is not merited. They have the childlike wisdom to know that we cannot live without it. Human relations are characterized essentially by trust, and what bedevils our human situation is the degree to which we mistrust each other, the degree to which we are on the defensive lest we be hurt once again. It is interesting to reflect on the fact that the more intimate the relationship between two people, the more anxious they become, because to put it quite simply, the more one sticks one's neck out, the greater the chance that one's head will end up in the bran basket, guillotined by the person to whom one dared to show love—in the expectation, of course, that the love would be reciprocated. When it is not the hurt is excruciating.

Basic anxiety, then, is anxiety lest our trust and our love be betrayed. The inevitable consequence of such anxiety is a distortion in the ways in which we ordinarily relate to others. According to Horney we relate to others in three basic ways:

1. By moving toward people, that is, by coming into relationships with others.

2. By moving away from people, because solitude is necessary for life. One has nothing to give if one cannot be alone without being lonely.
3. By moving against people, because there are times when we have to take our stand against someone who is hostile or who is wrong, with whom we cannot in good conscience agree.

The problem for the neurotic is that these ways become compulsive and contradictory. In his or her anxiety he or she may, for example, be torn between moving toward and moving away, being submissive and being hostile. He or she is hostile and compliant toward the same persons at the same time. Think of Conrad in *Ordinary People* who withdraws from his friends and yet does so with intense pain, and then in his withdrawal becomes hostile towards them. He cannot control his hostility, which is in part occasioned by his having to withdraw. Conrad's relation to his parents is the same; it has elements of contradiction and elements of compulsiveness. He is, in short, torn by inner conflicts, loving and hating the same person at the same time, fighting and submitting, fearing and hoping, hurt yet numb, cut off from others, cut off from himself, and so cut off from life that he has to quit swimming. He cannot do anything; he is immobilized. He cannot do his academic work, in which he was good and which he enjoyed. There is nothing left but to lie out in the sun, as it were, and curl up with his own misery.

Well, what then is therapy? Hannah Colm observes that Freudian analysis with its cold distance, its scientific objectivity, frustrated many patients. Here is what she writes:

> Patients began to object to the inhumanness and artificiality of this authoritatively, intellectually perceived prescription of the analyst, who stayed uninvolved, not feeling but pretended in a rather controlled way always to accept. Yet the uninvolved therapist was supposed to symbolize the lack of authoritative guidance or influence. To an increasing number of patients it did not make sense that the trouble into which he had gotten through frustration should be cured by more frustration—by lack of response, lack of reaction, and by an acceptance which he could not feel to be genuine because it was a method merely learned by the analyst. How could such a prescribed

therapeutic relationship heal the patient who may already suffer from a lack of trust in genuine relationship to people?

What was needed, in the view of these therapists like Colm, was a situation in which acceptance by the therapist was genuine but at the same time, radically critical. When one thinks of Conrad's therapist, Dr. Berger, one has an unusually fine example of that combination of a critical, in many ways quite disinterested and objective assessment of Conrad, and at the same time, a warm acceptance, which at the crisis gives Conrad the strength to make the transition from sickness to health; it also provides him with the pattern for his acceptance of his father.

As I have already indicated, Freud understood the need for the element of objectivity, and his technique demanded that the analyst be disinterested and detached. The patient lay on a couch, and the analyst sat behind it, out of sight of the patient. They did not sit opposite each other and converse as two friends, as is common with the interpersonal school. But for Freud there was, nonetheless, the pact, though in his therapeutic theory he did not make much of it. He recognized that the relationship of the patient and analyst was not purely objective but implied an element of mutual trust and respect, but I think Freud would have been horrified by the notion that it required an element of love—except as transference. That is in part due, of course, to the fact that the word love is a word that is almost lost to us, because nowadays making love is copulating. By love we mean falling in love, a rather sentimentalized version of the erotic. Love in the sense of the simple acceptance of one human being by another human being, as a human being, is almost gone. And what word do we have for it? I do not have to like someone in order to love him, but to love him I have to accept him as I myself want to be accepted. It is so simple! Yet perhaps unattainable.

I am persuaded that a patient will ordinarily know whether there is genuine love in a therapeutic relationship or whether, on the contrary, love is altogether absent and a technical objectivity dominates the relationship. I want to note one or two more sentences from Colm's article. Healing, she says,

> does not result merely from greater knowledge of oneself but from experiencing oneself (as one is) in mutual acceptance in spite of the humanness one finds in oneself and in one's partner. I am not afraid of

> letting counter-transferences [the real feelings that the therapist has toward the patient] enter into my reactions.

And again:

> Healing communion will grow between patient and therapist when both have been able to communicate about their positive and negative feelings and have been able with each other mutually to accept their humanness and to accept each other. The self-inflicted isolation of the patient will cease; he will be able to be part of the human community. The therapist will also have gained in this relationship, and doors will have opened up for him too. Each successful 'encounter' will make the therapist a wiser therapist and person. Only then when the patient as well as the therapist are on realistic grounds, when both can accept the inner polarity of love and hate in human hearts, can they (patient as well as the therapist) move toward their own lives, ready for new encounters and new unions.

Finally, an excerpt from the letter of a former patient after Hannah Colm's death:

> Riding up in the plane to Washington I kept remembering . . . her willingness to sacrifice psychoanalytic orthodoxy in order to share with me, her patient, her own fears and deep concerns, for she believed that only by a sharing in self-giving, only by love, could any true healing take place. . . . The candle expressed her life—it exhausted itself in giving out warmth and light.[3]

Now, before I address the question of divine grace, I would like to share with you this brief excerpt from a book by Fritz Kunkel, entitled *In Search of Maturity*. Kunkel is a Jungian psychotherapist, who tried to effect some kind of amalgam of Jungian psychology and Protestantism. I do not think he was very successful in this, but the paragraph I want to share is in my judgment extraordinarily fine:

> (Catharsis or clarification) begins with the decision not to fight against our vices, not to run away from them nor to conceal them, but to bring them into the light; and this decision enables us to confess. Nobody can truly and thoroughly confess as long as he judges, condemns, excuses, or praises himself. [This is the first hurdle in all psychotherapy. Without the commitment to honesty, psychotherapy cannot

> proceed. Psychotherapy is not something that the therapist does to the patient. It is something that two people do together, and it takes two to do it. The resolve to be honest may fail again and again, but it can and must be reaffirmed.] In so doing, he will repress or forget the most important part of his past, and therefore never discover the truth. But if his desire to be honest is greater than his desire to be good or bad, then the terrific power of his vices will become manifest [Vice is not to be understood in a moralistic sense but as a symptom of illness. It can include moral failure such as compulsive hostility and anger toward others, or extreme timidity and cowardice, but it may be the need to touch every telephone pole as one walks down the street, or never to step on the cracks between sections of sidewalk. That is the kind of vice he has in mind.], and behind the vice the old forgotten fear will turn up (the fear of being excluded from life), and behind the fear the pain (the pain of not being loved), and behind this pain of loneliness the deepest and most powerful and most hidden of all human desires: the desire to love, to give oneself, and to be part of the living stream that we call brotherhood. And the very moment that love is discovered behind hatred, all hatred disappears. [I think Kunkel is over-optimistic here. Hatred can be overcome, but it is less certain that it simply disappears.] The transmutation of power is brought about by the discovery of truth. But truth cannot be taught in words. It must actually be experienced within our own hearts. Furthermore, it cannot be experienced without confession, and confession needs a confessor who becomes the guide throughout suffering, fear, anxiety, anguish, and pain. Dante could not go through hell without Virgil. Such is the task of the psychologist.[4]

That is a great statement. I used to distribute this to classes in depth psychology and religion and say, "This is your pin-up sheet. Stick it up over your desk."

Well, what has this to do with grace? The first thing we have to keep in mind is that escape from bondage, psychologically speaking, is not a human achievement. As one of Kierkegaard's pseudonyms puts it (and I paraphrase), we forge the chains of our bondage with the strength of our freedom. To put it another way, neurotics enjoy poor health. That is a somewhat cynical way of putting it, but the point I am trying to make is that what characterizes the neurotic situation is resolve, resolution, determination, stubbornness. Anyone who goes to a therapist for help resists the help that is offered. Remember the first visit of Conrad to Dr. Berger? He wanted out. He did not like it. And this came up again and again. He became hostile. But at the same time, deep down he knew that he needed help, deep down he wanted help, and he had the resolve to stick with it.

Freud called this reluctance to accept help *resistance.* Why is there this resistance? It is our defensive posture. Our security lies in the neurotic defenses that we have built up, and if a neurosis is threatened by the possibility of health, our defense is threatened, and we become defensive about the very thing we want to be rid of. Therefore there is a factor of will present in the therapeutic situation—the neurotic's will to protect his or her deep insecurity, his or her vulnerable center. The neurotic finds health—if he or she does—in spite of himself or herself.

Why this defensiveness? Because we are so deeply hurt, all of us. We are all so deeply hurt by life, so hurt by those whom we have trusted, by those we love, that we have to defend ourselves. We cannot endure life without defense. So we long for help and ask for it, yet we fear it, lest in trusting our helper we again be deceived and rejected, and hurt all over again. The neurotic cannot help himself or herself. He or she cannot even help himself or herself to be helped because he or she knows too well the depths of human vulnerability and suffering. He or she knows the depths of human deceit. Remember that Conrad, in a moment of tremendous hostility, attacked Berger by smearing his sexual life and describing him as lustful and uncontrolled. On the surface it was absurd, but he had to lash out. And that because he was on the edge of trusting this man.

Trust—that is risky business. How could Conrad know that he could trust Berger, really trust him with his ultimate loneliness and his fear of being worthless? How can we ever know that someone can be trusted? We certainly know that *we* cannot be trusted. How in the world can anyone else be trusted? And certainly there *is* no one, there is *simply no one* who can be trusted without any reservation whatever. What happens in the therapeutic encounter, when it is authentic, is that two people learn to recognize more profoundly how little they can trust each other and that the heartlessness of others is real. How then does the healing happen? Both in accordance with his or her deepest longing and against his or her most resolute resistance the neurotic may be grasped (and I have to use the word, "grasped") by the power of acceptance, by the power of the trust that develops between two persons who know the limits of their own trustworthiness yet will to overcome it.

Certainly the neurotic does not get healed by virtue of his or her own resources, nor is it finally the therapist who heals him or her. The therapist helps one to understand the dimensions of one's life, of one's own bondage, and of one's right to hope for the fulfillment of one's dreams. But where does help come from? How does one get one's life together? Notice in the movie health does not come to Conrad in a sort of steady improvement—"Every day in every way I'm getting better and better." Life comes together for him at the point of his deepest distress, when he is tempted for a second time to commit suicide and then he rushes into desperation, in unconscious hope, almost literally beside himself, to Berger in the middle of the night to give vent to his utter despair and suffering. *And Berger is there.* He is there. "I am your friend." He does not perform some technical operation. He says what he believes and what is true: "I am your friend." And suddenly the reality of it grips Conrad, and his misery and hope come together in a single moment that has the mark of miracle. What cannot be, is.

It seems to me that it is quite proper to use the word miracle in this connection. Healing is literally a miracle. Kierkegaard makes this beautiful statement: "Whether a man has been helped by a miracle depends essentially upon the degree of intellectual passion he has employed to understand that help was impossible, and next upon how honest he is toward the power that helped him nevertheless." I think that is one of the greatest things Kierkegaard ever wrote, and he wrote many. "Whether a man has been helped by a miracle depends essentially upon the degree of intellectual passion he has employed to understand that help is impossible . . ." and if one wants to know why help is impossible, it is precisely because we do not want to be helped (even as we do). To be helped, is to admit that one cannot hack it alone. That violates something deep in us. The impossibility lies in the fact that we will not be helped and to hell with anybody who tries to help us, however desperately we long to be helped. "And next upon how honest he is toward the power that helped him nevertheless." To acknowledge that it has happened is to confess that I take another stance toward others. Conrad quit fighting Berger, quit fighting his parents, and was able to reach out to his father, as Berger had reached out to him. "Dad, I love you too." A beautiful but dangerous confession. His neck was all the way out, but his dad's arms were around him, and they knew that they were father and son.

Let me just illustrate this by an imaginary example but one which I suspect is close to all of us. We live in a time which suffers in the profoundest way from loneliness—not merely personal loneliness but also cosmic loneliness, because we live in a world in which God is dead (to use the common expression). It is a world that has no concern for what concerns us most deeply: our hopes, our fears, our anxieties, our love, ourselves. In consequence our need of others intensifies; they must take the place of God. And so we try to get others to like us, because what is loneliness but the fate of being cut off from others and from life itself? We are cut off, because we fear that if another person really knew us as we are, he or she could not possibly love us. It is not simply that we are not loved; we are not loveable. This is the deepest anxiety, I think, with respect to loneliness. We know so much about ourselves, whom we do not really like, that the thought that anybody could love me as I am, if he or she knew me as I am, is unsupportable. But the more intensely I feel that, the more I have to go out and try to get others to love me. I have to put on the act, develop a charming personality, "win friends and influence people," make people like me. To some extent, all of us most of the time are involved in that.

Now to my example. Take a lonely person, and then suppose that suddenly that person has a true friend, a friend who knows perfectly well the nature of the act that has been put on in trying to win him or her, who is a friend not because he or she has been inveigled into it as the object of a power struggle, but in spite of the attempts to win him or her as a friend. The lonely person may be very naive and suppose that he or she has succeeded in his or her act, but I am suggesting that one finally recognizes someone as a friend in spite of oneself. One can thank one's lucky stars (which would be proper for the Greeks and the Romans—we still seem to have remnants of Greek and Roman religion in our vocabulary) and call it fortunate. Or we can explain it as one of life's many accidents and coincidences. It was a good break. But notice how that trivializes it. Something that is of absolutely decisive importance for one's life—not only to be loved but being thereby set free to love—can one call that a good break without trivializing it? Well, it is done all the time. My point is that when we trivialize something that is not trivial, then consciously, at least, the scope and implications of such a relationship are narrowed to the point where its true significance is lost.

It is important, therefore, rightly to assess the meaning of relationships that overcome life's loneliness, that open doors of real possibility for us. So it seems to me that the gift of a friend in the midst of my loneliness can only be described as a miracle: the impossible has happened. Kierkegaard says in another place that God is possibility. For God all things are possible. This has to be understood in the dimension of human living. We are not talking about so-called miracles like perpetual motion or water running uphill. The miraculous of which Kierkegaard is speaking is the gift of new life despite our opposition to it—and our longing for it.

In our Judaeo-Christian tradition, grace is the gift of new life. Maybe one does not really need the word new. Quite simply, grace is the gift of life, authentic life, life that does not constantly contradict itself. Paul, in his letters, again and again describes the grace of Christ as deliverance from bondage, and Matthew's Gospel records that John the Baptist sent word to Jesus by his disciples to ask him, "Are you he who is to come [that is, the Messiah] or shall we look for another?" Jesus answered, "Go and tell John what you hear and see: the blind receive their sight and the lame walk, lepers are cleansed and the deaf hear, and the dead are raised up, and the poor have good news preached to them." It is a matter of life versus—and one can call it what one wants—death, but in this context death is a kind of living death, which Kierkegaard describes as a sickness unto death. It is a life whose end is death, a death that can never be realized. But there is deliverance from bondage: the miracle of grace. Our awareness of it depends on two things: the depth and intensity of our understanding that help is impossible, and next upon how honest we are toward the power that helps us in spite of our cynicism or our disbelief. Conrad did not expect that Berger was his friend, did not try to win his friendship, did not scheme for "cheap grace." "I am your friend." That came out of the blue—unsolicited, undeserved, unexpected. Conrad accepted it and was healed.

I will close with a passage from Jung, which is found at the end of his Terry Lectures on psychology and religion; it reads as follows:

> The thing that cures the neurosis must be as convincing as the neurosis; and since the latter is only too real, the helpful experience must be of equal reality. It must be a very real illusion, if you want to put it pessimistically. But what is the difference between a real illusion

and a healing, religious experience? It is merely a difference in words. You can say, for instance, that life is a disease with a very bad prognosis, it lingers on for years to end with death; or that normality is a generally prevailing constitutional defect; or that man is an animal with a fatally overgrown brain. This kind of thinking is the prerogative of habitual grumblers with bad digestion. Nobody can know what the ultimate things are. We must, therefore, take them as we experience them and if such experience helps to make your life healthier, more beautiful, more complete, and more satisfactory to yourself and to those you love, you may safely say, 'This was the grace of God.'[5]

NOTES

[1] Sigmund Freud, *An Outline of Psychoanalysis* (New York: 1949), p. 69.

[2] Karen Horney, *Our Inner Conflicts* (New York: 1945), pp. 41, 42.

[3] Hannah Colm, "The Therapeutic Encounter" *Review of Existential Psychology and Psychiatry,* Vol. II, pp. .

[4] Fritz Kunkel, *In Search of Maturity* (New York: 1944), pp. 8, 9.

[5] C. G. Jung, *Psychology and Religion* (New Haven: 1938), p. 114.

A POSTCRIPT

John Ross Carter

Perhaps it might strike one as novel for one to say at the end of our study and reflections that this is a subject which will continue to exceed our grasp. We have launched a consideration of an old and familiar theme, "Of Human Bondage and Divine Grace," but one yet to be thoroughly considered in the context in which we have attempted to consider it. No one of us, at the outset, could have known what we are thinking now, could have known how we are now reflecting upon the issues, could have known what the issues now might be.

One tends not to move swiftly into a definition of grace, not at the end of a course involving a study like this one. With a sense of bondage we seem familiar—a sense of restriction, inadequacy, an awareness that somehow we are fundamentally less than we know we can be enabled to become.

Some of us living in different centuries, in diverse countries, in distinct cultures, expressing ourselves in various languages, have shared with some of us living today a sense of bondage, an understanding of human bondage. Although the detailed elaborations of how this bondage is to be understood have varied—from the soul's being tainted from primeval beginnings to an awareness of one's being unable to say the right thing in a gracious way at the appropriate time, from an evaluation of the soteriological inefficacy of one's own will or self-agency to a recognition of brokenness and estrangement among persons—a resounding affirmation echoes through global time, that can be called human history: to be genuinely human is to know the limits, to know wherein lies the height, the depth, and the breadth of possibilities of human achievement, and also to know (this tends to arise almost simultaneously) that responding creatively, at the arising of the awareness of those limits, to that which lies beyond those limits, represents not a confession of human weakness but an acclamation of human greatness. Discerning those limits in the mode of creative receptivity is not an experience foreign to a first-rate physicist, a sensitive poet, a reflective seer, a humble saint.

Some of us have spoken of an impurity that has tainted the soul from time immemorial contributing to a present sense of bondage to matter, to time, to place, and also to the consequences of actions. Some of us have focused more steadily on the way one's volition provides structures for acts in thought, word, and deed (*karma*) that have consequences which bind one within the whirl of becoming (*saṃsāra*). Some of us have said that ignorance is the chief cause of human bondage, ignorance to the way things really are, whether ignorance of the evanescence of the world or ignorance even of one's bondage. And some of us have spoken of sin, of one's fundamental inability to do that which is inherently genuinely good. Others of us have said that humankind is not in some sort of primordial bondage, that when servitude to God is affirmed, one discovers true freedom in fullness of life. There are some of us, too, for whom the notion of bondage, although familiar, nevertheless is not a primary category for understanding the key interpretations of human life.

We have had a glimpse of all of this. The views expressed in our study have indicated that self-centeredness represents an enclosed self, a personality entrapped. This form of bondage expresses itself in many ways, our contributors have noted: pride and passion, desire and delusion, prejudice and separation, violation and disruption, anger and guilt. With these experiences human beings, of course, are familiar.

It is striking that human beings also acknowledge that freedom, release, liberation, escape from, the transcending of, a kind of centripetal overloading or short-circuiting of this self-centeredness is not the result of human agency. No one frees oneself; at the moment of liberation, no one liberates oneself. The soteriological initiative does not lie within one's own volition, is not the result of one's own cognition. When release arises, it arises as a consequence of the natural order of reality, some of us have averred. Others of us have affirmed that this freedom of release is God's action among and with us—that this is the result of divine grace. All of us have shared a witness that this release into the fullness of life is not one's doing.

From India into Japan, through West Asia into South and Southeast Asia, the Middle East, Europe and into North America, and elsewhere, of course, relinquishing entirely one's calculation, as some of us have phrased it, surrendering entirely one's will to God, as others of us have put it, have been held from generation to generation as activities that are expressions of that which is most noble in human life, as testimonies to what forms the creative response to the limits of human life might take.

And so, upon reading these chapters, perhaps one might have a glimpse at what some of us on this globe have said about human life; to live with a recognition that life can become authentic human life, genuine life, life lived without recurring contradiction, life lived in abundance, in spontaneity, lived fully. Life lived in wholesomeness is not merely to take a position incapable of being empirically verified, as some might have it, is not simply to argue for a theoretical addendum to be attached to the psychologically given as something extraneous to being normatively human or as some sort of pablum, as others might put it, but to understand what it means to be genuinely human.

Glossary

ABBREVIATIONS:

A. = Arabic **P. = Pāli**
G. = Greek **S. = Sanskrit**
H. = Hebrew **T. = Tamil**
J. = Japanese

'abd: **A.** "slave," as in *'abd-allah,* "slave of God."

ācārya: **S.** a religious teacher who guides an adept in the spiritual life. In Śrīvaiṣṇava thought, an *ācārya* can function in the capacity of a mediator of God's grace.

acit: **S.** "not knowing," "without understanding."

advaita: **S.** literally, "not two" or "non-dual." It is variously interpreted by the impressive strands of Indian intellectual history. Both for Śaiva Siddhānta and Śrīvaiṣṇava, reference is made to the soul's being one with, but not identical to, God.

āgāmya: **S.** "which is yet to come," refers to the consequences of one's current actions (*karma*) that will become manifest some time in the future.

āgantuka: **S.** "which has come or arisen," in the sense of being adventitious, not fundamentally irrevocable, and in Śaiva Siddhānta refers to the first two of the three fetters, that is, to *māyā* and *karma.*

ahaṅkāra: **S.** "I-making," individuality, which, according to Śaiva Siddhānta, is one of the internal organs, a product of matter.

āḻvārs: **T.** South Indian Śrīvaiṣṇava poets writing with powerful devotional force, persons who had become "immersed" in the love of Viṣṇu.

Amida: **J.** the name of the Buddha of the Pure Land. The name is derived from the Sanskrit words *amitābha,* "infinite or immeasurable light," and *amitāyus,* "infinite or immeasurable life."

amitābha: **S.** "infinite or immeasurable light," one of the names of the Buddha of the Pure Land, known in Japan as Amida Buddha.

amitāyus: **S.** "infinite or immeasurable life," one of the names of the Buddha of the Pure Land, known in Japan as Amida Buddha.

ānādi: **S.** "without beginning," "beginningless," used in Śaiva Siddhānta thought as an epithet of God, together with *mukta,* "free," and *cit,* "knowing."

anattā: **P.** (**S.** *anātman*), "that which is without soul," "no soul," "insubstantiality," representing a Buddhist analysis of life.

āṇava: **S.** according to Śaiva Siddhānta, *āṇava* is the third fetter, which accompanies the soul, from the beginning, even from birth to birth up until liberation. The traditional derivation of *āṇava* is from *aṇu,* meaning that which is infinitesimal, and, in Tamil, is used to designate an atom. It is said that *āṇava* "atomizes the capacity that the soul has for knowledge."

anicca: **P.** (**S.** *anītya*) "impermanence," one of the three characteristics of life, as Buddhists have averred.

antaḥkaraṇa: **S.** the "internal (*antar*) organs (*karaṇa*)," which are constituted by matter. These organs are mind or intellect (*manas*), will or ability to discriminate (*buddhi*), individuality or "I-making" (*ahaṅkāra*), and the heart or seat of the emotions (*citta*).

anubhava, anubhūti: **S.** "apprehension, apperception," a transforming experiential realization.

Arahant: **P.** (**S.** *Arhat*) in the Theravāda Buddhist testimony, "a worthy one, a perfected person," one who has realized *Nibbāna* and, upon death, has, or will have, realized complete and final *Nibbāna*.

ardhanārīśvara: **S.** literally, "the half (*ardha*) woman (*nāri*) Lord (*īśvara*)." In Śaiva Siddhānta, the form of God in which the right side is male, the left, female, to demonstrate that God is one with his *śakti*.

aruḷ: **T.** "love," regularly the word in Tamil used for grace, meaning love that is not merited.

arūpa: **S.** "without form, formless." In Śaiva Siddhānta, refers to the transcendence of God, beyond form. In the Buddhist case the term "formless" refers to the immaterial sphere or realm of existence that constitutes one of three realms of existence within *saṃsāra*.

arūpi: **S.** "that which is without form," and, in Śaiva Siddhānta, refers to the essential nature of the soul, which is said to be without form.

asat: S. "that which is without life of its own, lifeless," and, in Śaiva Siddhānta, refers to the fundamental status of matter.

Augustine: (A.D. 354–430) bishop of Hippo, a theologian of great talent and influence in the shaping of Christian thinking, both Catholic and Protestant.

bhakti: **S.** derived from the root *bhaj,* "to be devoted to," meaning loving devotion to God.

bhaktiyoga: **S.** the discipline or path of loving devotion to God.

bhakta: **S.** "lovingly devoted one," a designation of a person who has manifested *bhakti,* loving devotion to God.

bhāvana: **S./P.** literally, "cultivation," meaning "the practice of meditation."

bheda: **S.** "difference." In theological discussions *bheda* is regularly combined with *abheda,* "non-difference," and *bhedābheda* (*bheda* + *abheda*), both "difference and non-difference," describes the soul and God. In Śaiva Siddhānta, all three classifications are involved in the discussion.

bhikkhu: **P.** (**S.** *bhikṣu*) "mendicant," also translated as "monk," primarily used for persons participating in the Buddhist monastic tradition.

Bodhisattva: **S.** (**P.** *Bodhisatta*) a "being for *bodhi,*" a being whose life is for the purpose of attaining enlightenment, a mode of interpreting one's life as a Buddhist, known to the early schools and to the Theravāda but stressed by the Mahāyāna movement.

b'rakha: **H.** "blessing," often involving the expression *barukh,* "blessed."

Buddhaghosa: a leading fifth-century Theravāda Buddhist commentator who compiled, in Sri Lanka, commentaries on many of the canonical texts. His great work is the "Path of Purity," *Visudhimagga*.

buddhi: **S.** "will," the ability to discriminate. In Śaiva Siddhānta considered to be one of the internal organs, a product of matter.

Buddhist: one who is characterized by the qualities of the Buddha, a follower of the Buddha, a term used to describe persons who had, until three centuries or so ago, referred to themselves as male or female lay devotees of the Buddha-dharma and male or female participants in the Buddhist monastic order.

Calvin, John: (A.D. 1509–1564) a French Protestant Reformation theologian who contributed significantly to the shaping of Protestant Reformation thought.

caryā: **S.** "that which is to be practiced or performed, service." In Śaiva Siddhānta the term is used to refer to a mode of worship, such as sweeping, cleaning the temple, gathering flowers.

Christian: one who underwent or was prepared to undergo the passion of Christ, later taking on an extended meaning of follower of Christ, then later designating a member of a religious community or a participant in the Christian tradition.

cit: **S.** "thinking," "thought," "having the potential to know, being capable of knowledge, and of understanding," "knowing," also used in Śaiva Siddhānta as an epithet of

God, together with *mukta*, "free," and *anādi*, "without beginning," "beginningless."

citta: **S.** "the heart, the seat of the emotions." In Śaiva Siddhānta considered to be one of the internal organs, a product of matter.

Dharma: **S.** (**P.** *Dhamma*) one of the most comprehensive terms in the Indian vocabulary. Generally, *dharma* refers to behavior that "is fitting," in the sense that such behavior fits the occasion and helps to hold society together. In the Buddhist case, the term takes on great symbolic significance indicating the fundamental truth of reality which, when known, is liberating, freeing. *Dharma* is that to which the Awakened One (*buddha*) awoke, which constitutes his Buddhahood *and* it is that which he taught.

Dharmakāya: "the body (*kāya*) of absolute reality (*dharma*)," the fundamental truth that is also reality which, when holitically known, constitutes enlightenment for Mahāyāna Buddhists.

dike: **G.** "justice."

Dōgen: (A.D. 1200–1253) a great Japanese Buddhist monk-teacher in the wake of whose life and teaching the Zen movement known as Sōtō arose.

dukkha: **P.** (**S.** *duḥkha*) "misery, pain, suffering, awryness," represents a Buddhist pronouncement on the human situation.

garuda mantra: **S.** a sacred formula that pertains to the garuda bird, an arch foe of poisonous snakes. When one is bitten by a poisonous snake, recitation of the *garuda mantra* brings into one's mind the opposing qualities of the garuda bird and hence a force in opposition to the power of the poison.

guru: **S.** a venerable spiritual preceptor.

Ḥadīth: **A.** a collection of several volumes containing sayings, actions, and decisions of Muhammad. A single saying or particular account is also called *ḥadīth*.

Hindu: from Persian (**S.** *sindhu*) for the Indus river, meaning "people of the land of the Indus," later still to refer to people of India (*bhārat*) who live religiously as the people of India do.

'ibādah: **A.** meaning something akin to "worship," but carries a sense also of acknowledging God as God.

ijaza: **A.** a certificate indicating one's being qualified to recite authoritatively "the recitation," that is, the Qur'ān. The certificate gives the lineage of certified instructors.

incarnation: endowment of a human body, "enfleshed," the taking on of human flesh and nature by Jesus conceived of as the Son of God, the Christ.

islām: **A.** "submission," with a later and extended designation of a religious tradition known today as Islam.

jaḍa: **S.** "that which is motionless," in the sense of being devoid of life, referring to matter.

Jew: from **H.** *yehūdi,* through Greek, Latin, Middle English into contemporary English—a descendent of Judah, a member by birth into the Jewish community or by heart in devotion to God's teaching, *torah*.

jinen: **J.** "of itself, natural, spontaneous;" naturalness.

jivanmukta: **S.** literally, "released while living," or "liberated in life," and refers to a person who realizes salvific knowledge but who remains in embodied existence.

jñāna: **S.** "knowledge," and in Śaiva Siddhānta, one of the modes by means of which one worships God; the soul's realization of the inseparable union with God.

jñānayoga: **S.** the discipline or path of knowledge.

Jōdo Shinshū: **J.** "true (*shin*) teaching (*shū*) regarding the Pure Land (*jōdo*)." Often this is abbreviated to either Shin or Shinshū. The most widespread form of Buddhist piety in contemporary Japan.

ka'bah: **A.** a highly revered cube-like building near the center of the great mosque in Mecca. The corners very nearly represent the directions of the compass. Its origin is associated with Abraham and Ismael, and it came to have great religious significance among Muslims.

kami: **J.** a word whose original etymology appears to be lost, meaning "hair of the head" or "paper." The word has been variously translated: "gods," "spirits," and, in this volume, "Sacred Presence."

Kami-no michi: **J.** the Japanese pronunciation of the Chinese characters pronounced *shen-tao*, which has come into English as *Shinto*. The meaning is the "way" (*michi/tao*) of the "*kami/shen*."

karma: **S.** (**P.** *kamma*) "action," either good or bad, but action that yields consequences. Insofar as *karma* keeps one going in the unliberated states, *karma* is considered to be a bond. In Śaiva Siddhānta, *karma* is a bond or fetter and is considered also to be an impurity. In the Śrivaiṣṇava tradition, *karma* is a form of bondage.

karmayoga: **S.** the discipline or path of proper action without calculating the consequences.

kevala: **S.** in Śaiva Siddhānta, refers to the state of the soul before birth. In this state, the soul is fettered only by the impurity of *āṇava*.

Kierkegaard, Søren: (A.D. 1813–1855) a Danish religious author, philosopher, and theologian, of stellar brilliance and profound subtlety, considered by many the first important existentialist.

kōan: **J.** a pithy story or statement not readily capable of rational explanation, used as an object of meditation contributing to a process leading one to a realization of enlightenment.

kriyā: **S.** "observance of religious ritual or ceremony." In Śaiva Siddhānta, it is a mode of worship of God.

lokiya: **P.** (**S.** *laukika*) "world-like," a basic category in Buddhist thought, having to do with what pertains to ordinary life or existence in the worlds (this world and in the other worlds which are also in *saṃsāra*); what is customary within the sphere of human agency.

lokuttara: **P.** (**S.** *lokottara*) "world-transcending," a basic category in Buddhist thought, having to do with soteriological realization of that which is in the world but not of the world, of salvific truth discovered at the arising of insight-wisdom.

Luther, Martin: (A.D 1483–1546) a German Reformation leader, ordained an Augustine friar in 1507, excommunicated in 1521; translated the New Testament into German and launched a German translation of the Bible. He made the initial breakthrough that led to what became the Protestant Reformation.

magga: **P.** (**S.** *mārga*) "path, way." It refers to both the path that is laid out before one in the Buddha's teachings and also to the soteriological realization that arises in one's life.

Mahābhārata: **S.** a classic epic of India that has profoundly shaped the hearts and minds of Indians for centuries. The *Bhagavadgīta,* featuring the dialogue between Arjuna and Kṛṣṇa (or Krishna), forms a part of this great epic.

Mahāyāna: **S.** "great vehicle," a descriptive term adopted by a major movement within the Buddhist tradition that developed in India, was not unknown in Southeast Asia, and spread through Central Asia into East Asia.

mala: **S.** "impurity, dirt, dust"; in general, a defect, applied also to a condition of the soul, often used synonymously with *pāśa.*

malaparipākan: **S.** "ripeness or maturity of an impurity (that is, a fetter)." In Śaiva Siddhānta the term refers to an impurity or fetter which God, through grace, removes only when it is ready for removal.

manas: **S.** "mind" which, according to Śaiva Siddhānta, is one of the internal organs, a product of matter.

mantra: **S.** a religious incantation or sacred formula.

matsuri: **J.** "festival," "ritual," usually formally observed for purification and for celebratory worship of *kami* in Shinto.

māyā: **S.** "illusion," a comprehensive notion variously interpreted within the Hindu tradition.

In Śaiva Siddhānta, *māyā* refers to primordial matter, the source of the fundamental elements, including also the human being.

monophysitism: from **G.** *monophysis,* "one (*monos*) nature (*physis*)," the doctrine that Christ was of one single nature, a position put aside at a synod at Chalcedon in A.D. 451.

mosque: **A.** "a house or place of prayer."

motzi: **H.** "bring forth," a prayer-blessing pronounced, as well as a recognition of blessing, at the breaking of bread: "Blessed art thou, O Lord our God, King of the universe who brings forth bread from the earth."

mukta: **S.** "free," used in Śaiva Siddhānta as an epithet of God, together with *ānādi,* "without beginning," "beginningless," and *cit,* "knowing."

muslim: **A.** "submitter," originally conceived as a person who submits to the will of God, later carrying an extended meaning designating a person belonging to the religious tradition of Islam.

myōkōnin: **J.** "wonderfully excellent person" or "wonderfully marvelous person," wholly devoted to Amida and immersed in the life of *shinjin.*

Nāgārjuna: (ca. A.D. 150–250) a great Indian philosophical interpreter of the Buddhist heritage whose articulation of the notion of *śūnyatā,* "emptiness," provided a foundation for much subsequent Mahāyāna thought.

nāyanmār: **T.** "precursor" or "leader," a composer of engaging devotional hymns in the Tamil

	language celebrating the grace of Śiva. Tradition has remembered sixty-three of these saintly persons who shaped significantly the Śaiva tradition in South India.
nembutsu:	**J.** "recollection or recitation of the Buddha-name." In its inherited modified Sanskrit form, *Namo Amida Butsu,* "O praise Amida Buddha," with the extended meaning of taking refuge in Amida Buddha. The *nembutsu,* initiated by a human being, can be for some efficaciousness in one's religious life. For Jōdo Shinshū, the *nembutsu,* when uttered with transformative power, only can be the work of Amida, of Other Power (*tariki*).
Other Power:	in **J.**, *tariki,* the power of the other; in the Pure Land tradition, the power of the Buddha Amida to lead one to birth in the Pure Land and to enlightenment.
ousia:	**G.** "substance, essence, being, nature."
Paḷḷai Lōkācārya:	(b. A.D. 1264) a leading Śrīvaiṣṇava theologian and interpreter of the thought of Rāmānuja. He has become associated with the Teṅkalai subsect of the Śrīvaiṣṇava tradition.
Pañcarātra:	**S.** sacred writings that focus on Viṣṇu as Creator and Lord, of great significance for Śrīvaiṣṇava.
paṭiccasamuppāda:	**P.** (**S.** *pratītyasamutpāda*) "dependent origination" or "conditioned co-production," "conditioned genesis," a Buddhist analysis of the causal process.
patijñāna:	**S.** "knowledge of the Lord," that is, in Śaiva Siddhānta, the knowledge of God

which must come through the revelation of God.

pāśajñāna: **S.** "knowledge of the fetters or bonds," and in Śaiva Siddhānta carries an extended meaning of "knowledge of the world" in the sense of "fetter-knowledge."

pāśa: **S.** "fetter, bond, rope" holding the soul. In Śaiva Siddhānta, there are three, which are considered also impurities (*mala*): *āṇava,* or root impurity which obstructs; *māyā,* or primordial matter; and *karma,* or actions of thought, word, and deed, together with their consequences which accompany the soul.

paśujñāna: **S.** literally, "creature-knowledge," that is, in Śaiva Siddhānta, knowledge of the soul as being different from the body and the organs.

Pelagius: (ca. A.D. 355–ca. 425) a monk and theologian who challenged Augustine on the notions of predestination and grace, holding that grace is to be found in the natural dispositions within persons which, through reason and understanding, will lead them to an understanding of the gospel message. His position, today referred to as Pelagianism, was considered heretical at the synod at Ephesus in A.D. 431.

prajñā: **S.** (**P.** *paññā*) salvific "insight-wisdom," "liberating gnosis," the beatific moment in the religious life of Buddhists.

prapanna: **S.** a person who has surrendered to God.

prapatti: **S.** "prostration," resorting to God, seeking refuge, surrendering to God. Such a person, one who has surrendered, is a *prapanna*.

prārabdha: **S.** refers to those consequences of one's action (*karma*) that have placed one in this present existence.

prasāda: **S.** a rich term in India's vocabulary, meaning "tranquility," "serene calmness of mind"; meaning also "kindness, graciousness, favor," "a free gift," a term often translated as "grace."

Purāṇas: **S.** writings "from of old," a large group of ancient writings, eighteen of which are generally held in highest esteem and are of utmost meaning among Hindus, particular *purāṇas* being considered of special significance by this or that sect or sub-movement.

Puritan: a movement, seeking both simplicity in liturgy and comprehensive pervasiveness of religious ideas in all aspects of life, that by 1567 in London was following patterns established by John Calvin in Geneva and which later separated from the Church of England.

Qur'ān: **A.** "recitation," coming to mean "recited text," designating a book. The recitation of God's plan for the living of human life, acknowledged by Muslim men and women.

Rāmānuja: a great South Indian Vaiṣṇava theologian, writer of several major treatises. His traditional dates are A.D. 1017–1137. He is the formative figure for the Śrīvaiṣṇava tradition.

Rāmāyana: **S.** a classic epic of India, the story of Rāma and Sīta, that has profoundly shaped the hearts and minds of Indians for centuries.

rūpa: S. "form." In Śaiva Siddhānta, the term is used to designate any form of God's manifestation, such as *naṭarāja,* "Lord of Dance." In the Buddhist case it refers also to a realm of existence within the whirl of *saṃsāra,* the realm of form, a very fine material sphere of existence.

rūpārūpa: S. "form and formless" (*rūpa* + *arūpa*), representing, in Śaiva Siddhānta, a discernible form yet one remaining abstract; a means of God's manifesting himself, such as the *liṅgam,* an elongated rounded stone column of varying height.

sacrament: a ceremonial or liturgical observance considered, among Christians, to have been instituted by Jesus Christ and understood to be a means of bestowal of God's grace.

sahaja: S. "born with"; in Śaiva Siddhānta the term is used in describing the association of the fetter and impurity *āṇava* with the soul.

Śaiva Siddhānta: a significant religious heritage particularly in South India that focuses on Śiva as loving Lord. Śaiva Siddhānta means generally "the culmination or finality in perfection that pertains to Śiva." The force of the designation is "the ideal, final and well-established culmination of human existence that is pervasively qualified by the agency of Śiva." This tradition celebrates Śiva's loving grace.

sakala S. in Śaiva Siddhānta, the embodied state of the soul. In this state, the soul is fettered by all three impurities (*malas*).

śakti: **S.** "power, might, energy," the creative power of a deity. In Śaiva Siddhānta, *śakti* is personified as a goddess, the wife of Śiva, God's power, bestower of God's grace.

saṃsāra: **S.** the web of fettered existence, the whirl of repeated rebirth and redeath, the sphere of human agency and consequences of action, the "infinite finitude of aimless existence."

sañcita: **S.** refers to consequences which are derived from one's actions (*karma*) and which have not yet reached fruition.

Sangha: **S./P.** the Buddhist monastic order. In the threefold refuge, the term *sangha* refers to persons of the past, and conceivably of the present also, who have realized the arising of insight-wisdom.

śaraṇāgati: **S.** "going for refuge," finding refuge in God. In Śrīvaiṣṇava thought, generally considered to be synonymous with *prapatti*.

sat: **S.** "being, existing," "that which is, which really is," "reality," "that which is real, and true, and good"; in Śaiva Siddhānta refers also to what is spiritual, unchangeable, to Śiva, to God.

śeṣa: **S.** an "owned-one," a person who has become a slave to God.

śeṣī: **S.** "owner," used to refer to God as the one possessing or owning a devotee.

shahādah: **A.** "testimony," "witness," as in the form, "There is no God but God, and Muhammad is the Messenger of God."

Shin: **J.** an abbreviation of the Jōdo Shinshū Buddhist movement in Japan, the "true teaching regarding the Pure Land" school.

shinjin: J. "genuine heart," "sincere mind," a key notion in Jōdo Shinshū, meaning something like "entrusting," but probably better left untranslated into English.

Shinran: (A.D. 1173–1262) the formative focal figure of Jōdo Shinshū in Japan. His great work *Kyōgyōshinshō* is pivotal for Jōdo Shinshū. He also wrote a large number of hymns (*wasan*) in Japanese.

shōjiki: J. "simplicity, sincerity, honesty, right and true, righteousness," a word comfortably at home among persons in Shinto and in the Buddhist tradition.

śivāyanama: in Śaiva Siddhānta, a five-syllabic sacred formula praising the name of Śiva. (The formula is explained on page 38.)

sohambhāvana: S. literally, "meditating on 'God am I'." In Śaiva Siddhānta the compound is explained, "to practice meditation (*bhāvana*) on the thought that he (*so*, that is, God) is one with me and I (*aham*) am one with him, that 'I am He', 'I am God', 'I am one with God'." (See page 38.)

sopānamārga: literally, "way of steps" or "path of stairs." In Śaiva Siddhānta it refers to a way of ascent to God.

śraddhā: S. "faith," literally, "placing the heart on."

Śrī: S. the consort of Viṣṇu, the mediator of God's grace, the source of loving compassion, who, according to the Śrīvaiṣṇava heritage, advises Viṣṇu to show favor on his devotees.

Śrīvaiṣṇava: the most prominent form of the Vaiṣṇava tradition in South India. Vaiṣṇava, dedicated to the worship of Viṣṇu, is popular throughout India. In South India, particularly, the worship of the goddess or the role of the consort Śrī has become so integral that the movement has become called Śrīvaiṣṇava.

śuddha: **S.** "cleansed, clean, pure," in Śaiva Siddhānta, the state of the soul after liberation. In this state, the soul is rid of all the impurities (*malas*).

śūnyatā: **S.** "emptiness," a Buddhist affirmation of the underlying condition of things.

svatantra: **S.** "self-dependent, independent," and in reference to God, not being dependent upon anything.

tallit: **H.** a white prayer shawl (often with blue stripes) with four fringes of wool and silk.

Talmud: **H.** "instruction," "what one is to learn," and refers to the collection of writings pertaining to the procedures by which Jewish men and women are to live.

tathatā: **S.** literally, "such (*tatha*)-ness (*tā*)," or "thusness," the true order of reality.

tattva: **S.** a fundamental "element" that helps constitute the make-up of the world, that has evolved from primordial matter (*māyā*). In Śaiva Siddhānta there are thirty-six of these elements. (See note 9 to Chapter 1.)

Teṅkalai (Teṅgalai): **T.** "Southern Culture," the branch of the Śrīvaiṣṇava tradition which, although respecting both the Sanskrit and the Tamil scriptures, tended to revere the Tamil writings. This school is known as the "cat-hold school," suggesting a view of the soteriological process: one, like a kitten, is picked up and carried away by one's mother. Contrast with *Vaḍakalai* (*Veḍagalai*).

Theogony: **G.** the name of a work by the Greek poet-farmer Hesiod, dated probably to the seventh century B.C., in which there is an attempt to provide an organizational scheme for the gods and goddesses.

theosis: **G.** "deification" or "divinization," the affirmation that persons can become deified by God's grace, a testimony stressed in the tradition of the Orthodox Church.

Theravāda: **P.** literally, "the position (*vāda*) of the elders (*thera*)," or "the Way of the Elders." The form of the Buddhist tradition that developed in India and took on both focus and continuity in Sri Lanka and Southeast Asia.

Thomas Aquinas: (A.D. 1225–1274) a Dominican Italian philosopher-theologian, a professor of theology in Paris, and an intellectual of the Church, maintaining the indivisibility of truth, of great influence on the shaping of Christian thought.

tilakkhaṇa: **P.** (**S.** *trilakṣaṇa*) a Buddhist analysis of the "three characteristics" of ordinary life: impermanence, awryness, insubstantiality.

Torah: **H.** "teaching," sometimes translated "law," which is given to humankind by God and the following of which is the privilege of persons who are Jewish.

Vaṭakalai (Vaḍagalai): **T.** "Northern Culture," the branch of the Śrīvaiṣṇava tradition which, although respecting both the Sanskrit and the Tamil scriptures, tended to place more stress on Sanskrit writings. The school is known as the "monkey hold school," suggesting a view of the soteriological process: one, like a baby monkey, holds tightly to one's mother in order to be carried away. Contrast with *Teṅkalai* (*Teṅgalai*).

vātsalya: **S.** tender maternal compassion. In Śrīvaiṣṇava thought, God is noted as having this *vātsalya* for the human soul.

Vedānta Deśika: (A.D. 1268–1368) a leading Śrīvaiṣṇava theologian and interpreter of the thought of Rāmānuja. He has become associated with the Vaṭakalai subsect of the Śrīvaiṣṇava tradition.

Veda: **S.** "knowledge," refers to any one of a group of ancient scriptures of the Hindu tradition considered to be revealed.

vyāpi: **S.** "pervasive," referring to the essential nature of the soul as discerned in Śaiva Siddhānta.

yamulka: **H.** a small cap worn to symbolize one's humility in the presence of God.

yoga: **S.** literally, "yoking, joining," a method of religious discipline and sustained spiritual undertaking, and a practice of abstract meditation. In Śaiva Siddhānta, *yoga* is a mode of worship of God.

Zen: a Japanese pronunciation of a Chinese character pronounced *ch'an,* which represented to the Chinese the sound of the Sanskrit term *dhyāna,* meaning, originally, "meditation" or "rapt musing," but coming to represent an important distinct Buddhist movement, for which meditation is the central practice, with subsects in East Asia.

Index

A

'abd, 193
abhāva, 114
abheda, 41
abhilāśa, 67
ābhimukhyam, 91 n5
Abraham, 181, 188
absence of self, 110
Absolute Nothingness, 120
Abyssinians, 213
ācārya, 75, 77–78, 90
acit, 12
action, 6–7, 15–16, 31, 40, 83, 118; salvific, 80, 83. *See also karma*
acts: of charity, 33; liturgical, 98; meritorious, 51
Adam, 178–79, 184, 195, 197, 215, 218, 229, 246
adhikāra, 67
adoptionism, 256
advaita, 41–42
aeon, 6–7
Aeschylus, 158–59, 163, 165, 167
Africa, 208–9
āgāmya, 18
āgantuka, 23
aham, 38
ahankara, 4–5, 14
Alcmene, 161
Alexander the Great, 208
Alexandria, 209–10, 212
āḻvārs, 58, 64, 75
America, 205 n4, 209
Amida Buddha, 133–35, 138–39
amitābha, 133
amitāyus, 132
Amos, 266
Anabaptists, 235–36
ānādi, 19
ananya, 41
ananyaśaraṇaḥ, 72 n20
anattā, 100, 110
āṇava, 18, 20, 21, 23–29, 34–35, 37–40, 47–48, 49, 54
Andrew, Apostle, 209
angels, 215
anger, 196, 254, 271, 276, 285, 292
anicca, 100
annointing the sick, sacrament of (sacrament of extreme unction), 248
aṇpu, 48
antaḥkaraṇa, 4, 30
Anthony of Egypt, 216
Antioch, 209
aṇu, 24
ānukūlya samkalpam, 87
anubhava, 43
anubhūti, 43
anutāpa, 72 n18
anxiety, 276, 278–81, 285, 288; as moral, 278; as neurotic, 278; as reality, 278
aparneonai, 108
Apocalypse, 219
Apollinarianism, 212
Apollo, 156
apollumi, 108
Apostles, 195, 230, 246–47
Apparswami, 43–44
Approach to Zen, 119
Arabia, 188, 189

Arabic, 192, 196, 200, 207
Arabs, 208, 214
Arahant, 104, 110
ardhanārīśvara, 50
Arianism, 211
Aristophanes, 162
Aristotle, 232
Arius, 211
Arjuna, 61, 65
Armenians, 213
aruḷ, 48, 77
arūpa, 29, 99
arūpi, 3, 47
asat, 4, 12, 20 n8, 25
āśraya, 62, 71 n11
āśritavātsalya, 63
atah, 181
Athanasius, 212, 220
Athena, 156, 168 n1
Athene, 169 n9
Athens, 158, 162, 175
Atimānuṣa Stava, 66, 68, 72 n20
Atlas, 161
ātma samarpaṇam, 87
ātmajñāna, 79
ātmamoha, 114
ātmaśakti, 112
Augustine, 215, 229, 242
Australia, 209
autocephalous churches, 210
autonomous churches, 210
avacara, 99
avesa, 36 n27
Awakened One, 97, 121
awareness, 148, 180
awe, 149, 203

B

Balkans, 207–8
baptism, 235, 245–46, 257
Baptist, 266, 269, 271–72
Baptists, 268
barukh atah adoshem, elokenu melekh ha-olam, 173
barakh, 181
Bashō, 134
benevolence, 198, 200
Bernard of Clairvaux, Saint, 243
Bhagavadgīta, 61, 63, 65
bhaktas, 50, 66
bhakti, 58–59, 64, 68, 72 n18, 85, 82
bhaktiyoga, 59–63, 65, 69, 70, 75–76, 79, 83–84, 86, 90
bhāra, 67
bhāva, 114
bhāvana, 38
bheda, 41
bhedābheda, 41
bhikkhus, 97
bhoga, 21 n9, 85
bhuvana 21 n9
Bible, 119, 211, 234, 274
birkhat mitzvah, 176
births, 15, 23, 27–28, 30, 33, 40, 43, 51, 64
bishops, 211
blessings, 151, 171–73, 176, 180
blindness, 20, 24, 34
Bodhicaryāvatāra, 111, 121 n2
bodhicitta, 111
bodhisattva, 108, 110–12, 113–15, 132
bodhi-tree, 114
bondage, xiii, 1–3, 5–6, 11, 13, 16, 18, 23, 25–29, 31, 33, 38, 48, 52, 59, 77, 80, 84–86, 95–96, 99–100, 104, 120, 135–38, 143 n4, 146, 148, 151, 187, 193, 242–43, 252, 255, 260, 262, 266–69, 270–71, 275–76, 285, 289, 291–92
Bonhoeffer, Dietrich, 272
b'rakha, 176, 180, 184
Brahma, 11, 29, 36 n16, 50
Brahman, 61–62
Brahma Sūtra, 64
brokenness, 255, 263–64, 291
Buddha, 97, 100, 106, 108–11, 115, 116, 121, 135, 140, 142 n3
Buddhaghosa, 102
Buddhas, 112–13, 132
buddhatā, 116
buddhi, 4–5, 14, 35 n2, 67
Buddhism, 16, 127, 132; Mahāyāna, 132; Pure Land, 123;

Shin, 133–34, 139, 141
Buddhist, 98, 103, 114, 118–19, 125, 128–30, 133, 153 n2; Indian, 109; Mahāyāna, 108, 135, 179; Shin, 140; Theravāda, 101, 105; Zen, 108, 117
Bulgaria, 207, 209–10
Bunyan, John, 242
Byzantine: Christianity, 222; Orthodox Church, 217
Byzantium, 209

C

Cain, 184
Cairo, 205 n3
Calvin, John, 236–37
caryā, 33, 51, 54 n15
caste, 69, 84
catharsis, 247, 284
Catholic Church, 242–46, 248–49
Caucasus, 159; Russian, 210
celibacy, 131, 199
Central Asia, 107
Chalcedon, 212, 218
charis, 121
"cheap grace," 272, 289
Chih-i, 118
China, 116, 118, 146, 153, 189, 208
Christ, 157, 159, 209, 211–13, 216–17, 219, 223–24, 237, 241, 245–46, 248–49, 249 n4, 255–56, 260–61, 266, 289; natures of, 256
Christian, 95, 119, 122 n7, 207, 252, 257, 286
Christianity, 138, 155, 167 n1, 213, 256; Eastern, 216; Greek, 168 n1
Christian tradition, 253, 255
Christotokos, 212
church, 155, 210–11, 237, 249 n4, 253–54, 256, 263, 266–69, 272–73; membership, 237; of undivided Christendom, 208
Church of the Holy Wisdom, 168 n1
Church Fathers, 208, 215
Church Slavonic, 207
cit, 5, 12, 19
citta, 5, 14, 112
Clement of Alexandria, 216
Clymene, 161
Colm, Hannah, 282–84
commandment, 176, 183–84
communion, 214, 221, 224, 262
community, 151–52, 175, 244, 246, 260; class structure in, 269
compassion, 62, 65–69, 73 n24, 85–87, 90, 111, 114, 119, 128, 133, 135–36, 138–40, 195, 206 n5, 258, 142 n3
confession, 242, 248, 285, 287, 291
Confirmation, 246–47
Constantinople, 168 n1, 208–9
conversion, 236–37
Coptic Orthodox, 207
Copts, 255 n1
Corinthians, 219
council, ecumenical, 208, 225 n1
courage, 253, 273
creation, 2, 6–7, 11–12, 23, 28–29, 164, 178
Creator, 11, 20, 181, 193, 202
Cronos, 161, 169 n9
crucifixion, 258
cycle, life and death, 58, 70. *See also saṃsāra*
Cyprus, 209–10
Cyril of Jerusalem, 219
Czechoslovakia, 209

D

damnation, 51, 233, 238
Dante, 285
dāsatvam, 112
Day of Dinshway, 205 n4
dayā, 66, 68–69, 72 n20
death, 3, 82, 134, 136, 142 n3, 160, 164, 177, 195, 248, 254, 259, 261, 263, 276, 278–79, 289
deification/divinization, 214, 218, 220. *See also theosis*
deity, 79, 83, 157, 164, 181
delusion, 20, 24–25, 27, 34, 39, 99–100, 120, 125
democracy, 159–60

demon, 13, 80, 276
desire, 14, 276–78, 285
destiny, 24, 218
determinism, 164, 224
Devasenapathi, V. A., xiv–xv, xvii n1, 46 n30
devotees, 32, 39
devotion, 20, 58, 222, 236
Dhamma, 97–98
Dhammapada, 105
dharma, 57, 63, 142 n2
dharmakāya, 116, 133
dharmaśāstras, 55 n15
dhyāna, 60
dike, 157–58, 164
discrimination, 4, 14, 267, 281
diseases, 27, 163
dissolution, 7, 23, 28–29
divinities, 159, 161, 164
divinity, 156, 158–60, 161–62, 165–66, 168 n2
docetism, 256
Dogen, 130
doṣa, 78, 80
duḥkha, 100
duḥkha-hetur-ahaṃkāra, 114
dvaita, 41
dying, 253–54

E

Easter, 220, 246, 267
Eastern Orthodox, 208, 213, 225
Ecumenical Patriarch, 209
Eden, Garden of, 173, 178, 180, 262
ego, 4, 115, 118, 135, 277–80
egoism, 20, 34
Egypt, 181, 205 n4, 208, 210
Eirene, 164
eros, 278
election, 237–38
elements, 7, 16, 26, 30
emptiness, 108, 110–11, 113–16, 118, 123–26, 129–30, 132, 135, 138
energeiai, 217, 222
enjoyment, 13, 19; plane of, 30
enlightenment, 15, 25, 29, 50–51, 99–100, 115, 117, 136, 138–139, 193
Ephesus, 212
Epimetheus, 161, 163–65
Erasmus, 230–31
Erebus, 161
estrangement, 275, 291
eternity, 3–4, 23–24, 41, 47, 182
Ethics (Aristotle), 231
Ethiopians, 208
Eucharist, 214, 216, 222, 248
Eunomia, 164
Eve, 178–79, 184, 197, 218, 229
evil, 136, 139–40, 151, 184
evolution, 3–4, 11, 27–28, 49
exarchate, 211
existence, 1–3, 7, 16–19, 23–24, 37, 113–14, 124, 126, 149, 166, 177, 183, 215, 217
Extreme Unction, sacrament of, (sacrament of annointing the sick), 248

F

faith, 62, 64, 97, 214, 225 n2, 234–38, 244, 246
faithfulness, 151, 172
fear, 255, 263–64, 285, 288
fetters, 5, 13–16, 20, 23, 27, 38–40, 47, 103, 111
Finland, 209, 211
five pillars of Islam, 193
form, 3, 6–7
freedom, 1–2, 35, 39, 108, 133, 135, 137–38, 166, 292
Freud, Sigmund, 276–80, 283, 286
Freudian analysis, 282

G

gadyas, 64, 65
gadya traya, 71 n15
Gāndhari, 65
garuda-bird, 38
garuda mantra, 38
Gateless Gate, 137
gati, 72 n20, 83

Genesis, Book of, 168 n2
Georgia, Church of, 210
gift, 47, 152, 164, 182
Gītābhāṣya, 59–61, 70 n2
God, 2, 4, 5, 7, 11–20, 24–35, 37–42, 47–48, 50, 52–53, 58, 83, 88, 96, 100, 119, 121, 122 n7, 128, 146, 156–57, 159–60, 165, 167, 171, 173–74, 178–79, 181–85, 188–89, 191–96, 198–210, 203, 211–12, 214–16, 218, 220–21, 223–24, 228, 230–38, 241–49, 249 n4, 253, 255–62, 268, 272, 274, 289–90, 292
goddess, 156, 160; Greek, 157
gods, 157, 170 n11,
goptṛtva varaṇam, 87
Gospel(s), 230, 238, 256–58, 261, 265; of Jesus, 195; of John, 255, 257; of Luke, 257; of Mark, 257; of Matthew, 257, 289
Gotama, 97
grace, xiii, 1–2, 27–29, 32–33, 35, 39–40, 48, 52, 54, 57–59, 63, 65–66, 70, 75–78, 81–85, 90, 95–96, 104–5, 120, 136, 138, 146, 151, 167, 175–76, 219, 221–22, 228, 230, 233, 235–38, 241–43, 245–46, 248–49, 252–53, 255, 260–67, 270–75, 284–85, 289–92
Grant, Michael, 167
gratitude, 139, 181, 203
Great Doubt, 117, 119
Great Vehicle, 107
Greece, Church of, 210
Greek Orthodox, 207, 208, 210, 215, 266
Gregory of Nyssa, 216
guilt, 248, 267, 276, 292
guru, 32–33, 35, 37–38, 40–42, 49–51

H

ḥadīth, 191–92, 196, 200–201
Hagia Sophia, 213
haiku, 134
Harada Roshi, 131–32
harai-gushi, 150
harmony, 41, 152
Ha-shem, 180
hatred, 99, 125, 132, 271, 285
healing, 261, 263–64, 286
health, 201, 279, 284
heart, 4, 40, 42
heaven, 82, 173, 192
Hebrew, 176, 208; Bible, 208
Heidegger, Martin, 127
hell, 17, 20, 51
henotheism, 157
Heracles, 161
Hermes, 166
Heschel, Abraham, 177
Hesiod, 157, 159, 161, 164, 168 nn2, 8
Hesperides, 161
hierophany, 148
Hillel, 174
Hindu, 11, 24, 57, 60, 95
hita, 112
Holy Orders, sacrament of, 248
Holy Spirit, 211–12, 216, 219, 224, 225 n2, 249 n4, 257, 261, 265
Holy Trinity, 223
Homer, 168 n2
homoousios, 212
honesty, 149, 152, 284
hope, 164, 234, 265
Horney, Karen, 280–81
Huizinga, Johan, 145
humanity, 164–65, 199, 219
humankind, 2, 157, 159, 166
humility, confession of, 84
"Hyakujō and the Fox," 137
Hymn of Surrender, 64
hymns, 1, 52, 66, 70, 75
hypostasis, 218

I

Iapetus, 161–62
'ibād, 202
'ibadah, 192–93, 198
ichigo-ichie, 141 n1
icon, 213–14, 216

id, 276–80
idioms, communication of, 218
idol, 188–89
Idzumo, 150
ignorance, 23–24, 34, 100, 125, 137, 139, 267, 292
ijazah, 190
Ikkyu, 126–27
illness, 163, 249, 253–54, 263, 279
image, 214, 232
impiety, 166–67
impurities, 4, 11, 13, 18–20, 25
Incarnate Word, 221
incarnation, 252, 255, 257–60, 264; as accomplishment of God's saving work, 258; as communication of God's love, 258; as example of goodness, 258
incense, 162
India, 95, 107, 111, 116, 145, 208
I-ness, 89, 101
injustice, 161, 281
insight, salvific, 117
insight-wisdom, 113
instincts, 278, 279
intelligence, 6, 42, 157–58, 162–63, 166
Iran, 241
Iraq, 241
Irenaeus, 215
Irene, Empress, 213
Isaac, 181
Isaac the Syrian, 216
Ishmael, 188
Ise, 150
Islam, 155, 187, 189, 191, 193–95, 199, 201, 204 n3, 245
Isnik, 211
Israel, 172, 174
Issa, 134, 136

J

Jacob, 172, 181
Jacobites, 213
jaḍa, 4, 25, 30
Jainism, 16
Japan, 108, 117–19, 123, 131, 137, 145–47
Jerusalem, 175, 193
Jesus, 108, 201, 238–39, 244–45, 248, 249 n4, 255–61, 265–66, 271, 281, 289
jewel, 112–13
Jew(s), 157, 171, 174, 176, 180, 184, 208
jinen, 130
jinja shinto, 147
jinnis, 192
jivan, 37
jivanmukta, 37–40, 49
jñāna, 31, 34, 51, 55 n15, 69
jñānayoga, 61, 63
Jōdo Shinshū, 123
John the Baptist, 257, 289
John of Damascus, 214
joy, 43, 60, 132, 268, 274
Judaeo-Christian, 195, 289
Judaism, 155, 176; normative, 174; traditional, 173
judgment, 195, 248
Jung, Carl, 289
Jungian psychology, 284
justice, 157–58, 165, 228, 238
Justinian, Emperor, 213

K

Ka'bah, 188, 194
kāma, 99
kami, 145, 146–48, 150–53
kami-no michi, 146–47, 153
kamma, 99
Kāñcipuram, 66, 81
kanji, 146
kalpas, 135
karaṇa, 21 n9
karma, 16–18, 20, 23, 25–28, 30–31, 37–40, 47–51, 54, 58–59, 62–64, 69, 71 n11, 75–80, 83–84, 85–86, 88–90, 118, 135–36, 292. *See also* action
karmayoga, 61
kārpaṇyam, 87
karuṇā, 69

Kāśī, 93 n19
katham cid-api, 115
kevala, 18–19, 21 n19, 25
khyōha shinto, 147
Kichibei, 140
Kierkegaard, Søren, 285, 287, 289
Kingdom of Heaven, 281
Kisagotami, 136, 142 n3
knowledge, 2, 4–7, 11–12, 16, 19, 24, 26, 30–34, 37, 39–40, 43, 47, 60, 158, 160, 162, 166–67, 191–92, 198, 217
kōan, 137
koine, 208
kokka shinto, 147
Korea, 107
kriyā, 34, 51, 54 n15
kṛpā, 76
Kudo, Sumiko, 117
Kunkel, Fritz, 284–85
Kūraṭṭāḷvāṉ, 66–70, 75, 81
Kyō-gyō-shin-shō, 136
Kyoto, 117, 122 n7

L

Lakṣmī Tantra, 73 n21, 86
Lalitā, 82, 93 n19
Lanka, 87
Latin, 145, 230
Lebanese, 208
Lebanon, 241
liberation, 2, 16, 18, 23, 26, 28–31, 33–34, 39–43, 47–52, 54, 63, 81, 87, 89, 97, 103, 105, 108–9, 121, 126, 135, 292; theology, xiii
life, 118, 128, 132–33, 135, 140, 150–51, 167; ethical, 130; Jewish rabbinic, 182
līlā, 53, 85
liturgy, 214, 235
Logos, 212, 217–18
lokiya, 98–100, 102–3, 106
lokuttara, 98–99, 103, 106
l'olam vo'ed, 182
love, 20, 32, 39, 48, 50–51, 59–60, 70, 81, 90, 125, 130, 136, 158–59, 203, 205 nn2, 5, 206 n5, 230, 233, 260, 268, 272, 274, 278, 281, 283, 285, 288
ludere, 145
Luther, Martin, 228–29, 232–37

M

Macedonius, 212
magga, 102
mah tovu, 172
Mahābhārata, 57, 65
Mahākaruṇāvant, 111
mahākṛpā, 112
mahāviśvāsa, 87
Mahāyāna, 107, 110, 176
Maheśvara, 29, 50
mala, 4, 13, 19, 25–26, 39, 54
malaparipākan, 34
manas, 4–5, 14
Maṇavāḷa Māmuṇikaḷ, 77–79, 81
Maṇikkavaçakar, 21 n16, 44, 50, 52–53
Maṇipravāḷa, 86
mantra, 32; five-syllabic, 39
ma'rifah, 193
Mass, 248
Matrimony, sacrament of, 248
matsuri, 149
matter, 2–4, 6–7, 12–14, 16, 26; primordial, 11, 27
Maximus the Confessor, 217, 220–21, 223–24
māyā, 3–4, 6–7, 11–12, 14–16, 20, 23, 27, 30, 36–38, 47, 49; pure/pure-impure, 16
Mecca, 187–89, 194
Mecone, 161
meditation, 33, 38, 58, 60, 173; on lowliness, 66
megumi, 151
Menoetius, 161
mercy, 176, 195, 198, 228, 238
merit, 78, 219
Messenger, 188, 193
Messiah, 289
Methodists, 270
Meyendorff, Father John, 216, 222

Middle Ages, 228–29
Middle East, 188
mine-ness, 101
mind, 4, 14–15; discriminating, 119
minister, 237, 252, 264, 270; as pastor, 267
ministry, 252, 261, 267
minyan, 172
miracle, 249, 287, 289
mokṣa, 88
Monastery of Saint Catherine, 210, 211
monks, 97, 117
monophysites, 213
Monophysitism, 212
monotheism, 157, 188–89
monotheletes, 213
Monotheletism, 213
morality, 201
Morgan, Kenneth W., xv, xvii n2, 203 n1
Moses, 174
mosques, 168 n1
Mother of God, 212. *See Theotokos.*
motzi, 173, 180
Mount Parnassus, 167
mu, 120
Muhammad, 187–91, 193, 197–99, 201–2
mukta, 19, 37
mūla, 25
Mūlamadhyamakakārikā, 121 n1
muni, 112
muses, 170 n11
Muslims, 99, 187, 190–91, 193–96, 202, 205 n3, 209, 211
myōkōnin, 140
Myths of the Greeks and Romans, 167

N

Nāda, 35 n16
Nāgārjuna, 109, 114, 116, 118, 120
naicyānusandhanam, 66–67
Nalanda, 111
namaśivāya, 38
Nammāḻvār, 89
Nārāyaṇa (Viṣṇu), 65
nature, 3, 6–7, 13–15, 24, 27, 30, 178, 212; angelic, 216; karmic, 136; samsaric, 135; soul's, 83
Navavidha Sambandham, 91 n2
nāyaṉmārs, 1, 58
Nazenji, 117
Near East, 166
Nestorianism, 212
neurosis, 276, 286, 289
neurotic, 276, 282, 285–87
New Testament, 208, 252, 256
Nibbāna, 98, 104–5, 109
Nicaea, 213
Nicene-Constantinopolitan Creed, 212
Nicholas, Saint, 168 n1
nidhānam, 62
nikṣepa, 93 n28
The Nine Forms of Relationships, 76
Nirvāṇa, 109–10, 133, 135
Nishitani, Keiji, 130
Noah, 184
non-Chalcedonian, 208, 213
norito, 149
North India, 58
no-soul, 110
nyāsa, 88, 93 n28

O

obscuration, 28–29
Oedipus complex, 277
oikoumene, 210
olam, 182
Old Testament, 195
Olympians, 157, 161
omnipotence, 61, 85–86
oneness, 38, 42
openness, 125, 127, 138
Ordinary People, 275, 282
organs, 4–5, 7, 14–15, 19, 29, 31, 42, 47, 83
Oriental Orthodox, 213
Origen, 213
Orthodox, 214, 220, 213; Church, 219
other, 124, 136
Other Power, 123, 134, 139
Ottoman Turkey, 168 n1
ousia, 221–22

P

paccai, 81
Pachomius, Saint, 216
pain, 5, 15–16, 49, 252, 263, 274, 282, 285
Palamite, 223
Pali, 100
Palihawadana, M., 105
Palamas, Saint Gregory, 215, 221
pañcākṣara-mantra, 39
Pāñcarātra, 57
Pandora, 163
paññā, 102–3,
pāpa, 81, 112
Parāśara Bhaṭṭar, 81
Paradise, 197
paṟṟācu, 82
Parthenon, 168 n1
pāśa, 13, 15, 20, 31, 34
pāśajñāna, 31
Pascal, Blaise, 242
passion, 99, 138, 220
pastor, 266–68, 270, 272–74; experience, 266; ministry, 267
paśu, 6, 34
paśujñāna, 31
paśu-puṇya, 55 n15
path, 79, 105; -annunciation, 102; eightfold, 102; -realization, 103
paths, 103; four, 103, 105
pati, 31, 34
paṭiccasamuppāda, 100, 109. *See also pratītyasamutpāda*
patijñāna, 31–32, 37, 39, 49, 51
Paul, Apostle, 219, 244, 255, 259, 265, 289
peace, 164, 171, 183, 196, 201, 254, 264, 266, 268, 274
Pelagianism, 230
Pelagius, 229
penance, 33, 63, 248, 249; sacrament of (sacrament of reconciliation), 247
Pentecost, 222
Periyavāccaṉ Piḷḷai, 90 n1
Persian Christianity, 225 n1
Peter, Apostle, 221
petition, 175, 177
philanthropos, 159, 167
philosopher, 174, 178
philosophy, 2, 127, 176, 197
Pilgrimage to Mecca, 203 n2
Piḷḷai Lōkācārya, 58–59, 75–84
Plato, 164, 175
pleasure, 5, 14–15, 49
Poland, Church of, 210
polytheism, 188
polytheistic, 155
Poseidon, 168 n1
power, 16, 27–28, 49, 61, 87, 132, 156–59, 166, 168 n2, 191, 197
prajñā, 126–27
Prajna Paramita Sutra, 118
paramakāruṇyat, 71 n10
prapanna, 65, 69
prapatti, 62, 70, 73 n21, 75–76, 79, 84–86, 88–90; as *śaraṇagati,* 76, 83
prārabdha, 18
prasāda, 62, 68–69, 84
prātikūlya varjanam, 87
pratītyasamutpāda, 109–10, 129. *See also paṭiccasamuppāda*
pratyakṣata, 60
prayer, 149, 172, 175–76, 245, 262; *norito,* 150
preacher, 266, 268
predestination, 236, 237
prejudice, 125, 270, 292
prema, 68
Presbyterian, 152, 266
presence, sacred, 148–50, 152–53
preservation, 28–29
priest, 216, 241, 244, 247–49, 235
Prometheus, 158–59, 160–67
Prometheus Bound, 158, 163, 165–66
Prometheus the Firebearer, 165
prophet, 192, 195
Protagoras, 164
Protestant Reformation, 235
Protestantism, 237, 252, 284
Proverbs, Book of, 168 n2
Psalms, 195, 238

psychotherapy, 280, 284; two traditions of, 276
pūja, 112
Pulcheria, Empress, 212
punishment, 30, 31, 163
puṇya, 80–81
Purāṇas, 57
Pure Land, 132, 139
purification, 51, 150
Puritans, 236–37
purity, 38, 40
puruṣakāra, 76
Pyrrha, 169 n10

Q

Qur'ān, 190–93, 195–98, 200–3, 208
Quraysh, 189

R

rabbinic, 174, 182
Rahasya Traya Sāra, 84, 86, 93 n25
Rāma, 80, 87
Ramadan, 194
Rāmānuja, 57, 58–66, 70, 75, 82, 90, 91 n1
Rāmānujagranthamāla, 70 n2
Rāmāyaṇa, 57, 65, 80, 87, 94 n30
ransom, 258–59
Rāvaṇa, 80, 87
reality, 12, 106, 125, 127, 130, 136, 277
rebirths, 39, 105
reconciliation, 244, 255, 263–64, 267; sacrament of (sacrament of penance), 247
redemption, 90, 260
Reformation, 228, 236
refuge, 61–62, 65, 67, 69, 70, 77–79, 84, 86, 97–98
relationship(s), 79, 83, 242–43, 247, 253–55, 257, 259–63, 267, 275, 280–81, 283–84, 288–89; *advaita*, 41; non-dichotomous, 131; the nine, 91 n2
religion, 127, 147, 157; ancient Greek, 155, 288; henotheistic, 158; paternalistic, 157, Roman, 155, 288
Resurrection, 249 n4, 258, 261
revelation, 37–38, 117, 255, 262
reward, 5, 18, 30–31
righteousness, 189, 196, 232
Rinsai Zen, 117, 119
ritual, 146, 149; blessings, 176
Roman religion, 168 n1, 288
Romans, Book of, 228, 232
rōshi, 122 n8; Harada, 131–32; Kosho Ushiyama, 121 n6; Shunryu Suzuki, 117–21; Zenkei Shibayama, 117, 119–20, 121 n7
Rudra, 11, 29, 35 n16, 50
Rumania, 207, 209
rūpa, 99
rūpa-arūpa, 29
Russia, 210; Church of, 209
Russian Orthodox, 207

S

Sabbath, 183
sacrament, 230, 235–36, 245–48
sacred, 148–49; presence, 148–50, 152–53
sacrifice, 33, 156, 162
Sadāśiva, 29, 50
sādhana, 68
sadhyopāya, 84
sahaja, 23
saint(s), 21 n19, 46 n30, 53, 128, 135, 167, 168 n1; days of, 168 n1; Śaiva, 43, 52, 54
Śaiva Siddhānta, xiv, 1–5, 6, 11, 13, 21 n19, 25–26, 28–29, 33, 37, 51, 57, 95
Śaiva Siddhantins, 27, 41–42, 48
sakala, 18–19, 25
sākṣātkāra, 60
śakti, 27–29, 33, 35 n16, 36 n18, 38–39, 45 n6, 50, 67, 72 n18
salvation, 58–59, 77, 79, 88–89, 108, 135, 141, 172, 219, 221, 229, 234, 236–38, 258, 260, 264
samādhi, 102
saṃnyāsa, 93 n28

saṃsāra, 99–101, 109–10, 112, 115, 125, 133, 136, 141, 292
sañcita, 18
Sangha, 97
sankhāras, 115
Sanskrit, 59, 75, 86, 109, 111
Śāntideva, 108, 111–14, 116, 119, 121 n3
śaraṇagata, 66, 68–69
śaraṇagati, 62, 69, 75, 93 n28
Śaraṇagati gadya, 60, 64–65,
śaraṇagati vak, 72 n20
śaraṇam, 62
śarīra, 91–2
sat, 12, 20 n8, 25, 27
Satan, 179, 197, 217, 249 n4
sat-asat, 12, 20 n8
satori, 120
Saudi Arabia, 187, 205 n3
savior, 63, 98, 121, 146
Schillebeeckx, Edward, 247
Scottish Psalter, 228
scripture, 32, 57, 60, 76–77, 81, 88, 146, 252, 255; interpretation of, 59
self, 4, 60, 114, 116, 119, 124; -centeredness, 292; -conceit, 39; -effort, 51; -elevation, 24; -evaluation, 39; fixation, 124; -forgetfulness, 43, 47; -surrender, 47
senses, 2, 5, 12–14, 32
separation, 255; of church and state, 266
Septuagint, 208
Serbia, 210
śeṣa, 60–61, 77, 79–80, 91 n2
śeṣa-śeṣi relationship, 79, 83
śeṣatvam, 80
śeṣi, 61, 62, 76
shahādah, 193
shen-tao, 146
Shibayama, Zenkei, 117, 119–120, 121 n7
shimenawa, 152
Shin, 123, 133, 135, 138
shinjin, 138–39
Shinran, 123, 134–35, 139
Shinto, 146–47, 150, 153; Folk, 147; Sectarian, 147; Shrine, 147; State, 147
Shoji Hamada, 139
shōjiki, 149–50
shōzoku, 150
shrine, 145, 172
shtetl, 171
Siddhānta, 36 n27
siddhopāya, 84
sidre breshit, 178
sīla, 102
sin, 38, 50, 79, 83, 148, 183, 200, 215, 233, 246–49, 249 n4, 255, 258, 260, 262
Sinai, Mount, 174, 183, 210
Sita, 80, 87
Śiva, 1, 11, 20, 27, 29, 32–33, 35 n2, n16, 38–39, 50, 53, 58
Śivajñāna, 32–33
Śivajñānapādiyam, 55 n15
Śiva-puṇya, 55 n15
śivāyanama, 38
Slavs, 214
Smaller Sukhāvtī-vyūha, 128
sneha, 71 n11
society, 151; just and unjust, 164
Soetsu Yanagi, 139
sohambhāvana, 38
Solon, 158
sopānamārga, 34, 51
sorrow, 114, 263
soteriological initiative, 292
Soto Zen, 117
soul, 3–7, 11–16, 18–20, 23–34, 37–41, 43, 47–52, 59, 78–80, 82–83, 88, 90, 173, 215, 224, 231, 291
South Asia, 118
Southeast Asia, 95, 118
South India, 57–58
sovereignty, 158, 165
Sparta, 175
spirit, 4–6, 14, 25, 27, 47, 146, 198, 221
spirituality, 132, 135

spṛhā, 67
Śraddhā, 68, 72 n18
Śrī, 57, 64, 75, 78, 83
Śrībhāṣya, 59–60
Sri Lanka, 95
Śrīmatvaravaramunīntra krantamālai, 91 n6
Śrī Raṅgam temple, 65
Śrī Stava, 66, 68
Śrī Vacana Bhūṣaṇam, 73 n2, 76
Śrīranga gadya, 60, 65
Śrīvaiṣṇava, 57–59, 64–65, 70, 75–76, 86, 89–90
Stephen (Saint), 266
stream-attainment, 105; fruit of, 105
śubha, 111
suchness, 115, 128–30
śuddha, 18, 25–26
śudras, 60
suffering, 29, 160, 184, 249
Sufis, 193
sugatas, 113
suicide, 287
Summa Theologica, 230
Sundarabāhu Stava, 66
Sundaramūrti Swāmi, Saint, 53
śūnya, 113
śūnyatā, 124
śūnyatāvāsana, 113
super-ego, 277–80
surrender, 69, 79; *Hymn of Surrender*, 64; words of, 66, 68
Suzuki, D. T., 137, 137 fn
Suzuki, Shunryu, 121 n5
svatantra, 7
synagogue, 172
synergia, 219
synods, 208, 211, 213
Syria, 188

T

taboos, 277
Taiwan, 117
Takeuchi, Mrs. K., 140
tallit, 172–73
Talmud, 174
Talmudists, 174
Tamil, 1, 24, 47–48, 58, 75, 86, 91 n6
taṇhā, 100
Tannishō, 135, 142 n2
tanu, 21 n9
tao, 116
tatalai, 47
Tathāgata, 142 n2
tathatā, 126, 128
tattva, 128
tattvas, 3–4, 16, 26, 30, 36 n16
tea ceremony, 132
tefilla, 176
temples, 48, 156, 168 n1
temptations, 28, 38
Ten Commandments, 174
Teṅkalai, 58–59, 75–76, 78, 81, 91 n1
thatness, 128
theists, 120
Theogony, 157–58, 161–62, 168 n2
theologian: Byzantine, 217; Hindu, 59; medieval, 231; Orthodox, 217
theology, 213, 217; biblical, 252, 255; Byzantine, 214; Byzantine Orthodox, 225; incarnational, 259–61; liberation, xiii, 259; living, 216
theosis, 214, 218, 220, 222, 224
Theotokos, 168 n1, 212, 218. *See also* Virgin Mary
therapist, 284–85
therapy, 253, 279
Theravāda, 95–96, 98, 176
thinking, calculative, 127; conventional, 127; dichotomous, 124–25; meditative, 127; non-dichotomous, 128
Thomas Aquinas, Saint, 230–31
Thought of Enlightenment, 114
Thousand Names of Viṣṇu, 92 n15
Three Minds, 139
thusness, 115
Tibet, 107
tilakkhaṇa, 100
time, 3, 26
Tiruvāçgam, 21 n16, 50
Tiruvāmoḷi, 89
Titan, 157–58, 160

Torah, 173–74, 176, 184, 195
tradition, 108, 146, 151, 153, 156, 214; Asian, 127; atheistic, 98; Buddhist, 107, 115; Hesiodic, 164; Hindu, 85; Mahāyāna Buddhist, 107, 116; monastic, 97; Pure Land, 133; religious, 96; theistic, 146, Theravāda, 103, 107
Trinity, 156, 222
True Self, 116–17, 119
trust, 238, 255, 263–64, 272, 281, 283, 286
truth(s), 15, 24, 41, 110, 238–39, 285; four noble, 101–2, 105; salvific, 97, 115
Turkey, 211
Turks, 208
Twenty third Psalm, 274
tyāga, 93 n28

U

ubhaya, 75
ubhayavedāntācārya, 58
udapādi, 114
Uganda, 209
Una-Sancta, 208
Unhindered Light, 138
union, 39, 41–42, 47
United States, 118
Universal Self, 119
universe, 173, 182; two-tiered, 98; King of, 172
The Unknown Craftsman, 139
upāsana, 60
upāya, 65, 73 n22
utpādayāmi-eṣa bodhicittaṃ, 113

V

vaikuṇṭha, 59, 66
Vaikuṇṭha gadya, 60
Varadarāja Stava, 66, 68–69, 72 nn19, 20
vātsalya, 69, 73 n24, 76, 78–79, 81, 84
Vaṭakalai. 58–59, 75, 81
vedānta, 64
Vedānta Deśika, 58–59, 75–76, 83–88, 90, 93 n28, 94 nn30, 31
Vedartha Saṃgraha, 59, 62, 70 n6
Vedas, 57–58, 60
Vibhīṣṇa, 87
vidya, 73 n20
Vietnam War, 268
vijñāna, 124, 127
vijñāpti, 124
violence, 125, 157
Virgil, 285
Virgin Mary, 168 n1, 195, 249 n4. *See also Theotokos*
virtue, 80, 82–83, 111, 116, 138, 214, 232
virtues, 50, 108, 115
Viṣṇu, 11, 29, 50, 57–59, 64, 72 n17, 75–77, 79, 83, 88
Visuddhimagga, 102
Vow, Primal, 135, 138
vyāja, 84–85
vyāpi, 3, 47

W

way, the, 98, 116, 153; Lord as, 84; of the Elders, 95
will, 2, 4–5, 14, 105, 213, 219, 229; divine, 213; free, 163, 219, 231, 233; gnomic, 218
wisdom, 103, 126, 128, 135; *bhakta's*, 63; salvific, 102, 111, 113
Works and Days, 158, 162, 168 n2
world, 7, 11, 13–15, 17, 19, 23, 26, 30, 39; European, 156; Western, 256
World Council of Churches, 210
worship, 33–34, 194, 198, 213

Y

yamulka, 171–72, 180
Yathrib (Medina), 189
Yemen, 188
yetzer ha-ra, 179
yoga, 32, 34, 51, 54 n15
Yugoslavia, 207, 209–10

Z

zazen, 119, 122 n7

Zen, 108, 116–17, 118–20, 123, 130–33, 137
Zen Comments on the Mumonkan, 119
Zen Mind, Beginner's Mind, 117
Zeus, 155–57, 159, 161–65, 167, 169 n9